GENERAL WILLIAM S. HARNEY

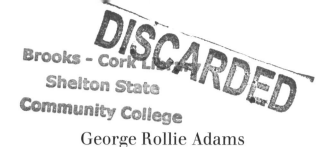
George Rollie Adams

GENERAL WILLIAM S. HARNEY

PRINCE OF DRAGOONS

University of Nebraska Press ✳ Lincoln & London

University of Nebraska Press

Lincoln and London

© 2001 by the University of Nebraska Press

Manufactured in the United States of America

Library of Congress Cataloging-in-Publication Data

   General William S. Harney : prince of dragoons / George Rollie Adams.

     p. cm.

   Includes bibliographical references and index.

   ISBN 0-8032-1058-2 (cl : alk. paper)

   1. Harney, William Selby, 1800–1889. 2. Generals–United States–
Biography. 3. United States. Army–Biography. 4. United States–History,
Military–19th century. 5. Indians of North America–Wars. I. Title.

E181.H28 A33 2001

355'.0092–dc21

[B]   00-044737

For Diana, Sara, and Amy

CONTENTS

List of Illustrations   ix

List of Maps   xi

Preface   xiii

1   Son of Tennessee Pioneers   1

2   A Time for Learning   8

3   Boatman, Woodsman, Indian Fighter   23

4   "That Infernal Pay Department"   43

5   "War to the Rope" in Florida   55

6   The Road to Mexico City   80

7   "Prince of Dragoons" in Texas   105

8   "Great White Chief" on the Plains   120

9   Return to Riverine Warfare in Florida   146

10   Civil Unrest in Kansas and Utah   159

11   The Pacific Northwest, "No Ordinary Sphere"   182

12   "Loyal Soldier" in Missouri   215

13   "Our Old Friend" as Peace Commissioner   242

14   A Time for Reflection   274

Notes   287

Selected Bibliography   349

Index   365

ILLUSTRATIONS

following p. 158

1. William S. Harney, 1850s
2. *Col. Harney Storming the Citadel on the Summit of Cerro Gordo*
3. Brig. Gen. William S. Harney, late 1850s
4. Little Thunder
5. Spotted Tail
6. Father Pierre-Jean DeSmet
7. Lt. Gen. Winfield Scott
8. Indian Peace Commissioners, 1868
9. Indian Peace Commissioners at Ft. Laramie
10. Railroad delegation at Fort Sanders

MAPS

1. Upper Mississippi Valley, 1828–32 / 33

2. Florida in the Seminole Wars, 1837–42, 1856–57 / 61

3. Texas and Northern Mexico, 1847 / 89

4. Scott's Road to Mexico City, 1847 / 99

5. Eighth Military Department, 1854 / 109

6. Platte River Country, 1855 / 123

7. Battle of Ash Hollow, 1855 / 130

8. Department of Oregon, 1859 / 185

9. San Juan Islands, 1859 / 196

10. The West of the Indian Peace Commission,
    1867–68 / 248–49

 # PREFACE

HISTORIANS HAVE WRITTEN extensively about the United States Army and its role in frontier America during the nineteenth century. Most scholars have focused on military conflicts and peacekeeping responsibilities, particularly on the Indian wars and the army as a constabulary. Other investigators have examined the army's contributions to western exploration, map making, road building, and other internal improvements. Most recently, historians have described the army's impact on economic and community development and its emergence as a professional organization and one of America's first bureaucracies. These latter works, especially when read alongside earlier studies of staff departments, provide a broader picture of how the army understood and performed its duties.

Over the years a significant amount of the historical literature about the army has been biographical. Studies of the lives and careers of army officers abound. However, proportionally fewer such works have appeared during the last twenty or so years, for at least three reasons. First, scholars have already studied and restudied most of the army's leading figures, as well as many of lesser significance. Second, historians have been using other approaches to develop a more comprehensive overview of the army's multifaceted activities. And third, researchers have become increasingly interested in military families, other noncombatants, Indian perspectives, and other previously neglected stories that add balance to overall knowledge. These shifts of method and attention correspond to a larger trend in western history that emphasizes the twentieth century and topics of more immediate interest, such as race, ethnicity, culture, gender, and the environment.

Why, then, investigate yet another nineteenth-century military career as the nation enters a new millennium? Because examining individual lives still provides a popular and effective means to explore and communicate connections and relationships between people and events over time. Attaching human faces to historical issues can expose moral complexities more subtly and help make cultural clashes more apprehensible. Thus it seems useful to consider a heretofore incompletely examined military career within the context of recent scholarship about the army in general.

A number of factors make William S. Harney worthy of such attention. Although he is little known today except among military historians, he enjoyed a national reputation during his lifetime. Only eighteen regular officers held an unbreveted brigadier general's rank or above between the army's reduction in strength in 1821 and the start of the Civil War in 1861. Five of those eighteen entered the army as Mexican War volunteers and served relatively briefly. Among the other thirteen, only four served longer than Harney's forty-five years. His career reveals much about the army's role in major national events. It highlights the limitations of the army's resources compared with the immensity of its responsibilities. It illustrates the army's function in implementing federal Indian policies. It demonstrates the futility of the army's European-based fighting methods against Indian warriors using guerrilla tactics. It exemplifies the army's role in enforcing federal law. And it illuminates key aspects of the army's organizational structure, how its officers behaved, and some ways in which military service affected personal lives.

Harney entered the army in 1818, only three years before Congress reduced its size by more than half and Secretary of War John C. Calhoun advanced the idea of an expansible army to accommodate future growth. Although Congress never approved this concept formally, the government practiced it, and Harney benefited from it in each of the next three decades as the army expanded in response to domestic and foreign developments.

During his early years of service, Harney participated in a keelboat expedition to make treaties with Indians on the upper Missouri River. He took part in routine garrison duty, frontier fort building, and other activities that collectively occupied most of the army's time and resources. For a while he also performed administrative duties as a staff officer in the Pay Department. In the 1830s, he fought in the Black Hawk and Second Seminole Wars, helping facilitate one of the most lamentable chapters in American history, the removal of eastern Indians west of the Mississippi River.

In his middle years, Harney took part in the nation's first war on foreign soil and won acclaim for charging up Cerro Gordo to clear Winfield Scott's way to Mexico City. Afterward he commanded troops assigned to keep peace between settlers and Indians in Texas, prevent Mexican smugglers and revolutionaries from entering the United States, and ensure peaceful elections in pre–Civil War Kansas. Twice, officials in Washington selected him to lead major military expeditions across the Great Plains, once in 1855 to punish Sioux Indians for interfering with the flow of white settlers along the Oregon Trail and again in 1857–58 to enforce federal authority in Brigham Young's Utah.

During the concluding phase of his career, Harney commanded the Department of Oregon and almost started a war with Great Britain over the boundary between the United States and Canada. Later, as commander of the Department of the West, he failed to act decisively during the Missouri secession crisis, and President Abraham Lincoln removed him from command amid false accusations that he was a Southern sympathizer. Following retirement and the Civil War, Harney served on three commissions appointed to establish peace with Indians between the Mississippi River and the Rocky Mountains. In the last of those assignments he helped establish the policy of concentrating all plains Indians on reservations, and he closed his public life in 1869 as administrator of the Sioux reservation district in Dakota Territory.

Like many other officers of his time, Harney had no formal military education, and like all of them, including West Point graduates, he had no training in fighting Indians. Yet his contemporaries, military and civilian alike, admired his skill and ingenuity as a combat leader. In Florida, he advocated unorthodox tactics and pioneered riverine warfare. In his campaign against the Sioux in the mid-1850s, he demonstrated that the army could and would use large columns of troops to wage total war against particular groups of Indians in summer or winter.

Also like many other officers, Harney exhibited ambivalent feelings toward native people. He considered them culturally inferior, yet he developed a personal familiarity with many of them and sympathized with their plight. On some occasions he treated them with contempt and on others with courtesy. Almost always he respected their military ability, and he punished them severely for both real and perceived transgressions against whites. In his later years he championed fair and just treatment of them under existing law.

Harney also shared with many other officers an acute desire for promotion and a contentious and quarrelsome nature. He was bold, courageous, ambitious, opportunistic, occasionally innovative, and sometimes insightful, even smart. But he was also impulsive and obstinate. He used political influence to advance his career and quickly took offense at perceived slights, both professional and personal. On occasion he could be generous, yet often he was callous, arrogant, boisterous, and peevish. Far more than most officers, he was quick-tempered and vindictive, and he possessed a well-earned reputation for colorful profanity and fits of violence. Not uncommonly he abused enlisted men, and in 1834, he beat a household servant to death.

As with other officers, military service shaped Harney's social and family relationships. Around 1830, while stationed on the Wisconsin frontier, he fathered a child with a mixed-blood Winnebago woman. Later he married the daughter of a wealthy St. Louis businessman, but unlike many army wives, she always remained at home in Missouri and never lived with him during his frontier assignments. They quarreled over money and his career and eventually became estranged.

Historians who recall Harney recognize that he deserves his reputation as an effective Indian fighter. But most historical works containing anything beyond references to his Indian service portray him only as colorful, high-strung, mean, administratively inept, or some combination of those. His life and personality merit a fuller treatment, one that considers him in the context of both his origins and his evolving surroundings and associations. His career deserves an examination that judges his behavior and actions more acutely and assesses his impact more completely. Those who may be interested in him and his times deserve a better basis upon which to decide to what extent he merits their condemnation, admiration, or some evaluation in between.

Harney has been the subject of only one original full-length biographical study, an uncritical, mostly undocumented, and occasionally erroneous treatment published in 1878 by Logan Uriah Reavis, a professional journalist, prolific author, and St. Louis booster. Although there is no direct evidence that he interviewed Harney for the book, the two men knew each other, and Reavis implies that they at least discussed the project. Because they lived in close proximity prior to publication, it would have made sense for Reavis to request Harney's input. And given Harney's intense desire to have his role in the Missouri secession crisis understood, as well as his concern for appearances, as reflected in most photographs of him, it would have been logical for him to cooperate in providing information. Further, the book contains anecdotes for which there are no other known sources. It also contains testimonials that Reavis solicited from many of Harney's contemporaries, along with a few letters and reports reprinted from published government documents. The work that follows draws impressions and anecdotes from the testimonials and on rare occasion cites one of the documents, but otherwise it relies upon Reavis only when there is other supporting evidence or when he describes behavior or attitudes that Harney also exhibited in instances documented from other sources.[1]

Harney left only a small collection of personal papers, and unlike numerous other army officers, he kept no journal and wrote no memoirs. A fair amount of personal material survives, though, particularly in the collections of his wife's relatives. Those papers and his own, when combined with published and unpublished military records, other public documents, newspaper accounts, writings and recollections of people who knew him, and histories of the surroundings and times in which he grew up and operated, enable a clear portrait of the man and his career. When quoting these writings, I have preserved the spellings, capitalization, and punctuation of the originals.

Harney's story as told here owes much to many people, none of whom are responsible for the accuracy of its factual or interpretive content. Several historians who never read a word of it influenced it significantly. Chief among these are Edward M. Coffman, Francis Paul Prucha, William B. Skelton, and Robert M. Utley. Because the historical literature is so vast, space considerations permit only a stringently selected bibliography and require notes dedicated almost entirely to primary sources. But I am grateful to all the many scholars, listed and unlisted, whose findings and perspectives provided background and context.

Roger L. Nichols of the University of Arizona suggested this study and provided continuing guidance and encouragement that ensured its completion. Both he and Gerald W. George, former executive director of the American Association for State and Local History, taught me much about clear and concise exposition. Strong Museum board chairs Betsy W. Harrison, Alan Illig, and Fred W. Smith, together with their fellow trustees, generously provided the professional leave necessary to finish the writing. Scott G. Eberle, Nicole Ladewig, Roger L. Nichols, Charles Phillips, and Vernon L. Volpe read and commented insightfully on the entire manuscript, and James A. Crutchfield provided helpful suggestions regarding Harney's early life. Gayle Adams, Karen Banker, Rose Platania, and Bonni Rheinwald rendered important clerical assistance at various stages of the work, Don Strand helped with illustrations, and Elaine Durham Otto executed expert copyediting.

Staff at numerous historical societies, libraries, and archives answered inquiries, arranged for interlibrary loans, provided copies of source materials, opened their collections for examination, offered invaluable research leads, and helped track down illustrations. Their work, together with that of others like them, is indispensable to historical scholarship and the collective memory of our country. Those whose assistance proved especially critical include Lutie Higley and other staff of the University of Arizona Library; Frances Stadler and other staff of the Missouri Historical Society; Ellen Whitney of the Illinois State Historical Library; George Chalou, Elaine Everly, Dale Floyd, Robert Kvasnicka, Richard Maxwell, and other staff of the National Archives; and Susan Drexler, Jeri Laskowski, and Carol Sandler of the Strong Museum. In addition, John M. Harney, great-grandson of William S. Harney, provided genealogical data, and Linda Harney MacDonald and Brian Weigand provided other family-related information. I am indebted to them all.

Finally, I am particularly grateful to my wife, Diana Adams, and to our children, Sara Ann Adams and Amy Kristina Hee Sook Adams, for their love, understanding, and support during this undertaking. To them it is dedicated.

CHAPTER 1

Son of Tennessee Pioneers

YEWITNESSES disagree about who fired first, but when shots rang out near the entrance of City Hotel, one shattered Andrew Jackson's upper left arm and lodged against the bone. The future president of the United States bled profusely while his former business partner, John Coffee, and Stockley Hays, one of Rachel Jackson's nephews, scuffled with Jesse Benton and his older brother, future United States senator Thomas Hart Benton. Bystanders rushed in, broke up the melee, and carried Jackson to a room at the Nashville Inn, the town's other hostelry. Doctors worked feverishly and considered amputation, as blood soaked through two mattresses.

The fight, which occurred on September 4, 1813, had been brewing since June, when Jackson acted as second for William Carroll in a duel with Jesse Benton. The Benton brothers and Carroll had served under Jackson the previous winter following an American declaration of war against Great Britain. Appointed major general of United States volunteers. Jackson had organized more than two thousand Tennesseans and, as huge crowds watched, led them ceremoniously out of Nashville, intent upon expelling Britain's Spanish allies from East Florida. Carroll and the Bentons remained with Jackson three months later when the troops trudged back into town sick, weary, and disappointed that the War Department had recalled them. The duel grew out of disagreements on the homeward trek, and Jackson sided with Carroll. When the disputants took their positions and received the order to fire, Jesse Benton contorted himself to present a smaller target, got off the first shot, and hit Carroll in the hand. Carroll fired, too, and sent a bullet searing across Benton's buttocks. Both the wound and his performance humiliated Jesse Benton, and when Thomas Benton, who had gone to Washington on military errands for Jackson, returned home and heard what had happened, he became incensed. In no time at all, public gossiping incited the shootout.

The doctors saved Jackson's arm, but they could not remove the bullet, and he remained in bed three weeks. He had not fully recovered when word arrived that on August 30, one thousand Creek Indians had struck Fort Mims, a traders' stockade about forty miles north of Mobile, and killed more than five hundred men, women, and children. The victims included friendly Indians, mixed-bloods, and black slaves, as well as white settlers. Although the attacking Red Sticks represented only one of several Creek factions, news of the killings terrorized the entire region. Even as far north as Tennessee, people feared that Creeks might fall upon them at any moment. The state legislature, then meeting in Nashville, authorized five thousand volunteers, and Governor Willie Blount ordered Jackson to organize twenty-five hundred of them immediately, enter the portion of Mississippi Territory that is now Alabama, and prevent an invasion of Tennessee. Throughout the state, men responded to the call, and on October 7, Jackson, his arm still in a sling, took command of his army in Fayetteville, about seventy-five miles to the south.[1]

Few among the two thousand or so people living in and near Nashville could have avoided being caught up in this excitement. Thirteen-year-old William Selby Harney resided in Haysborough, a small settlement six miles north, down the Cumberland River. His father, Thomas Harney, had helped establish the community in 1799, along with Robert Hays, Rachel Jackson's brother-in-law. Over the years Thomas had earned a living variously as a farmer, merchant, and surveyor, and he came in contact with many people, including Jackson, whose plantation lay east a few miles upriver. More than passing acquaintances, the two men shared an interest in horses and Freemasonry.[2] Young William could not have viewed the second war for independence from Great Britain from the same perspective as his father or Jackson. However, the boy's age and family connections positioned him for more than a casual interest in the violent public altercations, Indian scare, and gathering of two huge frontier armies within less than a year. These dramatic events created impressions for a lifetime, and later as an army officer William participated in similar scenes. He also demonstrated personal characteristics reminiscent of some of the leading players, including a quick temper and a strong inclination for violence.

William's eventual pursuit of a military career dovetailed with both his childhood environment and his family background. His ancestors had a history of frontier migration and military service. Like many families in the trans-Appalachian West, the Harneys traced their lineage to England and Ireland. At least one Harney had come to America by the mid-1600s and settled in Maryland. His descendants included William's grandfather, Thomas Harney, who lived with his wife, Hannah Mills, on a farm in Sussex County, Delaware, near the Maryland border.

When the American colonies declared their independence from Great Britain, at least two of Thomas's sons, Selby and Thomas Jr., fought in the Revolutionary War. Both distinguished themselves in battle, with Thomas rising to the rank of major and Selby to colonel. For their services, North Carolina granted each of them land in what eventually became Tennessee. Thomas received 640 acres on the right bank of the Cumberland.

After the war, Thomas Harney married Margaret Hudson, also from Sussex County and of Irish ancestry, and by 1791 the couple had three sons. In that year Thomas took advantage of the new opportunity afforded by the land grant and moved his family from Delaware to the rolling hills of middle Tennessee. There, during the next nine years, Margaret Harney bore two daughters and three more sons. William was the youngest of these, born August 22, 1800.[3]

Thomas and Margaret Harney's experience resembled that of friends, neighbors, and tens of thousands of other pioneers. During the last quarter of the eighteenth century, Americans left their eastern homes in unprecedented numbers to occupy the vast frontier between the Appalachian Mountains and the Mississippi River. Drawn by accessible land, speculative fever, and the prospect of fulfilled dreams and ambitions, they moved along rivers and wagon roads into western New York, the Lake Plains, the Ohio River Valley, and the Cumberland Plateau. Transmontane population grew so rapidly that two frontier territories soon became states, Kentucky in 1792 and Tennessee in 1796. This westward migration assumed even greater proportions in the nineteenth century, as the United States purchased Louisiana from France in 1803 and extended the nation's western boundary eventually to the Pacific Ocean. William S. Harney was a product of this era of frontier development and territorial expansion.

By frontier standards the Harney family lived comfortably. Although Haysborough consisted of only a few families, by the time William was old enough to read, Nashville enjoyed a growing reputation as a bustling center of commerce. It boasted a post office, a newspaper, several mercantile houses, a tannery, a cotton gin, and numerous shops in which tinsmiths, coppersmiths, blacksmiths, cabinetmakers, shoemakers, tailors, saddlers, and others crafted and sold their wares. Flatboats laden with pork, tobacco, and other products departed the Nashville waterfront regularly bound for New Orleans. There Tennessee traders sold both goods and vessels and returned home overland on the Natchez Trace. In 1806 two entrepreneurs maneuvered a Louisiana keelboat to Nashville, and within a few years, regular upriver traffic brought Tennesseans sugar, coffee, and other previously difficult-to-obtain items.[4] Thomas Harney did not live to see much further development in the area. One day in July 1813, while he stood in his yard talking to a neighbor, one of the servants struck the family dog, and it bounded out of the kitchen toward its master. When Thomas reached out to pet the animal, it bit him. He gave little thought to the incident at the time, but eventually he fell ill with rabies. After a lengthy period of suffering, during which a Nashville band traveled to Haysborough one day especially to play his favorite tunes, Thomas Harney died on October 24, 1813.

With the Indian scare still on and Jackson's army maneuvering through present northern Alabama, one of William's older brothers, James Harney, joined his mother in providing parental guidance. Ten years William's senior, James had returned to Haysborough from Kentucky sometime after 1811, and his presence lent stability to the family. He operated a mercantile business until 1817, when he went back to Warren County, Kentucky, to become a justice of the peace.

William's two oldest brothers, Benjamin Franklin Harney and John Milton Harney, studied medicine at the University of Pennsylvania during these years. When they finished, Benjamin entered the army, and John established residence in Kentucky. Except for one brief period in late 1815 and early 1816, Benjamin remained a military surgeon until his death in 1858. John pursued several careers. Deeply depressed because his wife died a few days after the birth of their only child, he left Kentucky in 1815 and traveled east. Over the next decade he worked as a newspaper reporter in New York City, toured Europe, founded the *Savannah Georgian* newspaper, returned to Kentucky, converted to Catholicism, and became a priest. John's experience provides the sole revelation about the Harney family's early religious preferences and suggests only that they were Protestants.[5]

Despite the divergent paths Benjamin and John took after medical school, their educational and career achievements provided examples for William. In those days most children received early instruction at home from parents and elder brothers and sisters. When old enough, William entered Cumberland College. Founded in 1786 by Thomas B. Craighead, a Presbyterian minister and Harney family neighbor, the school turned out a number of successful students, many of whom traveled daily back and forth from Nashville by ferry. While attending college between 1814 and 1816, William formed a lasting friendship with Edward George Washington Butler, a ward of Andrew Jackson. Others enrolled at the school during those years included future United States senator and Constitutional Union presidential candidate John Bell and future Tennessee congressman and Louisiana governor Edward Douglass White.[6]

In the antebellum South, most adolescent males learned hunting, fighting, swearing, and drinking from their fathers, older brothers, or peers. And boys fortunate enough to attend college found a curriculum that emphasized personal honor and built self-esteem. William's adult life indicates that his youth fit both of these patterns. While he and his friends pursued their boyhood interests and studies, the War of 1812 continued on several fronts. As it had from the outset, fighting occurred along the eastern Great Lakes and back and forth across the New York and New England borders with Canada. In March 1814, Jackson, aided by such future luminaries as Davy Crockett and Sam Houston, crushed the Creeks at Horseshoe Bend in present central Alabama. From there Jackson moved south, repulsed a British attack at Mobile, invaded Spanish East Florida without authorization, and temporarily occupied Pensacola. In January 1815, some two weeks after British and American commissioners had agreed to peace terms in Belgium, he defeated British forces at New Orleans in the most celebrated battle of the war.

When news of the victory reached Nashville sometime later, townspeople marked the triumph with lighted candles in their windows. And when Jackson returned home on May 15, jubilant Nashvillians turned out en masse. Cheering, they escorted him to the county courthouse, where former congressman and nationally known War Hawk Felix Grundy hailed him with a long recitation of his military successes. The students of Cumberland College recited an ode to the conquering hero, and a week later Tennessee's leading citizens gave a grand banquet in his honor. Shortly afterward his aide, John Reid, began working on a Jackson biography. Reid died before completing the volume, but John Henry Eaton, later United States senator from Tennessee and secretary of war during Jackson's presidency, took up the task and finished it the following year. Book, subject, and author received national attention when it appeared.[7] As a Jackson neighbor and friend of one of his wards, William had particular cause to read and absorb the publication.

Sometime after Jackson's return to Nashville, Cumberland College closed temporarily due to lack of funds. This ended William's formal education and forced him to think about his future course. His friend, Edward Butler, entered the United States Military Academy at West Point in September 1816, and Jackson's nephew, Andrew Jackson Donelson, and fellow Tennesseans David M. Porter and John J. Abercrombie gained admission the following summer. New West Point classes averaged less than thirty cadets then, and acceptance of another Tennessean that same year would have been extraordinary. Most officers still entered military service directly from civilian life. Even though Congress had sharply reduced the size of America's wartime army and along with it the number of officer appointments, West Point could not turn out enough men to fill all the vacancies. Academy graduates almost always went to engineer, artillery, and ordnance units, and so mounted rifle and infantry regiments offered civilians the best alternative route to a commission. In late 1817, William went to visit his brother Benjamin, then stationed in Baton Rouge, Louisiana, headquarters of the U.S. Army's First Infantry Regiment. Baton Rouge Barracks housed more than three hundred soldiers, and William spent several weeks among them.[8] He impressed the officers, and either upon his request, Benjamin's insistence, or their own initiative, several of them recommended William for an appointment as a second lieutenant.

Capt. Alexander Gray, a fellow Tennessean, endorsed Harney first. Writing to the secretary of war in January 1818, Gray claimed "an intimate acquaintance" with him and stated that he "possesses the qualities and the respectability that fits him for such a station." Gray noted further that Harney's appointment would be "highly agreeable" to the other officers in the regiment. A few weeks later Maj. Richard Whartenby, Capt. William Christian, Lt. Robert L. Coomb, and eleven other officers, all men with whom Harney would serve, proclaimed him qualified "to discharge the duties of an officer with benefit to the service and credit to himself." Consequently, Harney received a second lieutenant's commission dated February 13, 1818. When he accepted it, he followed in the footsteps of his father, his Uncle Selby, his brother Benjamin, and Andrew Jackson, the man who had loomed largest in the public scenes of his youth and had only begun to affect his future.[9]

CHAPTER 2

A Time for Learning

AS LOUISIANA governor Jacques Villeré approached the Baton Rouge Barracks parade ground, soldiers of the First Infantry Regiment fired fifteen guns in salute. When he reached it, they marched in line for his review. Seventeen-year-old William S. Harney had accepted his commission as a second lieutenant in the regiment just two days earlier, and he had attributes that would make him stand out in a military ceremony, even though he knew little about an officer's role. At six feet three plus inches, he towered conspicuously over most men of his day and possessed a fair complexion, square face, piercing blue eyes, dark auburn hair, broad chest, and gaunt waist. Throughout his life people took note of his appearance and straight carriage. Jefferson Davis, who first met him ten years later, described him as "physically, the finest specimen of a man I ever saw."[1]

As Harney soon discovered, his new responsibilities usually involved far less pomp than the activities on this June morning in 1818. The War of 1812 had been over for three and a half years, and although agreements either made or in negotiation promised demilitarization of the Great Lakes and resolution of Canadian boundary disputes, a number of territorial and security issues remained unsettled in the Gulf region. Andrew Jackson had invaded Spanish East Florida again, this time ostensibly to suppress Seminole Indians along the Georgia border but in effect to seize the entire panhandle and peninsula for the United States. At this same time, Secretary of State John Quincy Adams carried on negotiations to secure Florida permanently and fix boundaries between the Louisiana Purchase and Spanish territory in the West. Finally, all along the coast, but especially off Louisiana, remnants of Jean Lafitte's pirates harassed shipping and smuggled contraband.[2] During the next six years, Harney engaged in activities related to all these issues and more.

Except for West Point, established in 1802 and still focused almost solely on military engineering, the army had no formal program for training new officers. They learned by doing, or as Davis later noted, through "practical sense which tests all theory by actual observation." The War Department had only recently begun to develop uniform administrative procedures, and its tactics manuals consisted of little more than translations of European systems developed by Frederick the Great and Napoleon. The most recent, prepared by Brig. Gen. Winfield Scott in 1815, served as a guide for drill and maneuvers. Harney used it and subsequent editions between 1818 and 1824, as he served in Louisiana, Massachusetts, Maine, Florida, and Missouri. During these times he functioned as an acting company commander, assistant adjutant, assistant commissary, recruiting officer, and member of court-martial boards. He became particularly acquainted with the latter while being court-martialed twice himself. Through these diverse experiences Harney found out that the army operated mostly as a frontier constabulary, helping enforce federal laws and maintain order.[3] He learned how the army managed many of its administrative affairs and how it recruited enlisted men. He discovered that officers quarreled frequently over petty matters, and he demonstrated his own considerable capacity for contentious behavior. In addition he felt the loneliness and boredom of frontier garrison life and the debilitating effects of unhealthy southern climates. And he had an opportunity to serve briefly with Andrew Jackson in a symbolic act of American expansionism. Some of these experiences he enjoyed. At least one he loathed. From most he learned. In all he began laying the foundation for a career that, counting his post–Civil War Indian service, spanned more than fifty years.

Harney's first assignment placed him in Capt. Ferdinand K. Amelung's company, and less than two weeks after the governor's visit, Maj. Richard Whartenby ordered the unit southwest to New Iberia to help customs officials suppress smuggling in that vicinity. After a temporary hiatus to assist Jackson against the British at New Orleans, Jean Lafitte had reemerged in 1817 as the leader of this illegal trade and increased it sharply. Operating from a stronghold on Galveston Island, some two hundred miles west of their previous base in Louisiana's Barataria Bay, the freebooters displayed Mexican and Venezuelan flags and preyed upon ships of all nations. They seized such taxable and easily marketable goods as jewelry, lace, silk, linen, glass, leather, and nails, and then slipped the captured items through coastal waterways and overland by pack mules into New Orleans and other towns for sale free from import duties. In addition to taking the items from their rightful owners, Lafitte and the others deprived the federal government of important revenue. They also sneaked slaves into Louisiana and sold them to planters in violation of federal anti–slave trade laws.[4]

U.S. naval vessels tried to stop these clandestine activities, but they lacked navigation charts for Louisiana rivers and could not press pursuit. The numerous inlets in Atchafalaya and Vermilion Bays afforded the outlaws excellent hiding places and easy inland access. Eventually custom collector Beverly Chew appealed to Brig. Gen. Eleazer W. Ripley, commander of the Eighth Military Department, for troops to help enforce the civil laws.[5]

Consequently, Captain Amelung moved some sixty men from Baton Rouge during the last week of June 1818. Soon after his company reached New Iberia and began establishing a camp, Amelung selected a sergeant and sixteen men to search for smugglers. Taking supplies for eight days, he left Harney in command of the remaining force with orders to finish flooring the tents and "pay particular attention to the discipline and good order of the camp and see that no depredations are committed on the citizens–and their property." When Amelung returned, he found that despite his instructions "considerable disorder and misconduct" had occurred, and he promptly reduced a sergeant and a corporal to the rank of private for their part in the disturbances.[6] Despite being the officer in charge, Harney escaped reprimand. Clearly, though, the boy lieutenant's first responsible assignment ended unsatisfactorily. Amelung's company remained at New Iberia at least through August, and during that time Harney helped patrol the smugglers' potential land routes on foot and their inland waterways in boats. He participated in the capture of some contraband goods, but although these efforts gave him his first taste of constabulary duty, they had no lasting impact on Lafitte's gang. Piracy and illegal trade continued in Louisiana and elsewhere on the Gulf Coast for several more years before authorities brought it under control.

By early November, Amelung and his men had returned to Baton Rouge, and in December Harney got his first opportunity to act as temporary commander of an entire company. Claiming illness, Amelung secured a furlough of indefinite length, but before he left he turned over "all public property and papers belonging to his Company to Lieut. Harney, taking his Receipts for the same." A few weeks later Amelung resigned his commission to become sheriff of Baton Rouge Parish, and Robert L. Coomb received promotion to captain and Harney to first lieutenant. Officers often left the army for desirable civilian jobs, but in this instance Harney benefited more than Amelung, who was killed in a duel the following year. Advancement for line officers depended upon seniority and attrition rates in their regiments, and ordinarily promotions did not come this quickly. For example, West Point graduates in the classes of 1821–23 needed a median of six years for their first promotion. Circumstances handed Harney his in less than one.[7]

Harney's advancement coincided with orders sending his company and two others to Fort Claiborne, about 125 miles up the Red River at Natchitoches, for other constabulary duties. Both Indian-white and international relations necessitated military presence in northwestern Louisiana. For years unprincipled whites in the region had traded with Caddo and other Indians illegally, sold them whiskey, stolen their livestock, turned them against federal agents, and incited intertribal warfare. Naturally, Indian attacks on white settlers ensued. Americans who disputed Spain's claim to Texas caused additional problems. Even as Secretary of State Adams worked at concluding a treaty in which Spain renounced all claims to West Florida, ceded East Florida to the United States, and accepted a western boundary that ran along the Sabine, Red, and Arkansas Rivers and then westward to the Pacific Ocean, some persons wanted to invade Texas and grab it, too. Thus, troops at Natchitoches had the twofold task of curbing illicit trade and preventing mischief-making border crossings by both Texas Indians and unscrupulous and ambitious Americans.[8]

Under command of Capt. William Christian, the detachment of reinforcements traveled by boat up the Mississippi and Red Rivers, pausing only on December 29 at Alexandria, where they unloaded their supplies, dragged their empty transports over rapids, and then reloaded before proceeding on to Natchitoches. After arriving at Fort Claiborne, the troops spent most of their time on routine duties required to operate and sustain the post. Like soldiers in dozens of other garrisons across America, they drilled, cultivated a vegetable garden, cleaned the water well, and whitewashed quarters. Harney served regularly as officer of the day and on court-martial boards. These disciplinary bodies met frequently to hear charges involving violations of military regulations. Procedure called for three officers to hear enlisted men's cases and from five to eleven to hear those of officers. Most trials convened for petty offenses, and the drudgery of garrison life accounted for most of those. Whiskey led to many of the rest. Before 1830, the army provided liquor as part of the daily ration. Not surprisingly, drunkenness and "conduct unbecoming and disgraceful to a non-Commissioned officer and soldier" became frequent charges at post tribunals, and in one instance in February, a Fort Claiborne court-martial stripped three sergeants of their rank during a single session. Two belonged to Harney's company.[9]

The young Tennessean did not like his new situation. Northwestern Louisiana seemed "a fine country" but isolated. Scarcely a month after arriving in Natchitoches, Harney wrote his brother James complaining that "there is not three full blooded whites living in the town." He had made one military foray into the countryside, and now about to go on another, he predicted forlornly, "This is my second expedition and I am sure it will be the last, if I ever return." Still only eighteen and saddened by news that his sister Eliza had died, he missed Benjamin, who remained in Baton Rouge with the rest of the First Infantry, and he longed for his family. "O I would give the world to see you all only one day," he declared.

Homesickness did not keep Harney from meeting "a great many families going across the Sabine to settle." Nor did it prevent him from getting into a brawl with the parish sheriff while attending a family fishing party. During horseplay the sheriff, described as "robust" and "powerful," dunked an older man in the water, and the victim's daughter urged Harney to the rescue. Without hesitating he plunged into the fracas in full uniform and ended up soaked and in a bear hug. After he worked himself free, spectators had to restrain him from drowning the sheriff.[10] This kind of impulsive, hotheaded behavior occurred commonly in frontier settings, but unfortunately it characterized Harney's entire life.

Despite disliking Natchitoches, the irascible lieutenant had to endure it for several more months, during which he served in various capacities. He remained a company commander until mid-April, then became acting adjutant in charge of post clerical chores. For a time he performed that job while commanding yet another company, and on May 22, General Ripley appointed him acting commissary in charge of post provisions. Known as detached service, this practice of assigning line officers from infantry, artillery, or mounted rifle service temporarily to staff positions occurred at all levels of command. It helped the army meet communications, logistical, and other support requirements across the country, and for Harney and other young officers like him, it also provided useful experience in military administration.[11]

During the summer of 1819, Harney and another First Infantry lieutenant drew assignment to regimental recruiting duty in Boston, and after they departed for New England, the troops in Natchitoches moved to a new post, Fort Selden, nearby.[12] From there and later from Fort Jesup closer to the Sabine, U.S. soldiers continued to guard the Louisiana border until after the annexation of Texas in 1845.

The recruiting assignment exposed Harney to yet another important aspect of military operations. In 1819, the army had an authorized strength of less than twelve thousand troops, but even so, it could not keep its ranks filled. American soldiers generally earned less money than most laborers, and enlisted military life offered no comforts. Few men wanted to try it, and of those who did, one in five deserted before completing his service.

Most recruiting efforts focused on northern cities, which had the largest and most concentrated populations of free laborers, semiskilled workers, artisans, and newly arrived immigrants. Generally the army required only that recruits be white, English-speaking, twenty-one to thirty-five years in age, able-bodied, and free of disease. Recruiting officers witnessed simple physical examinations of potential enlistees, recorded brief personal information about those that passed, and sent them before a magistrate to swear an oath of allegiance.[13]

Harney executed this monotonous but essential duty less than a year. In June 1820, he rejoined his regiment in Baton Rouge. There, as the soldiers labored to enlarge the barracks, he carried out many of the same garrison duties he had performed previously in Louisiana. After only a few months, though, he became ill, and on February 24, 1821, he received a furlough of four months "for the recovery" of his "health." Troops serving in regions with heavy rainfall and swampy terrain endured a variety of illnesses, including malaria, diarrhea, dysentery, spinal meningitis, and occasionally yellow fever. Between 1819 and 1824, Baton Rouge Barracks had the unfortunate distinction of being the most sickly post in the army. It continued to house about three hundred soldiers, and each year more than 20 percent of them died of natural causes. Benjamin Harney, who had become medical director for the entire Eighth Military Department, including all Louisiana and Mississippi Territory, attributed most of the maladies to hardships arising from constructing the barracks. Cutting and hauling logs from a cypress swamp fifteen miles distant pushed the men beyond their physical limits.[14]

Whatever illness Lieutenant Harney suffered, he went home to Tennessee, and soon after arriving in Nashville, he found Andrew Jackson preparing to leave for Pensacola. In February, the Senate had ratified the treaty in which Spain ceded East Florida to the United States. President James Monroe had appointed Jackson territorial governor, and shortly the man who had coveted East Florida for years and twice seized control of it would formally receive it on behalf of the American government. Because he needed an additional aide, Jackson asked Harney to accompany him to Pensacola for the transfer ceremony. Having had a few weeks to visit his family and regain his health, he seized this chance to serve under the nation's most popular military hero.

Going to Pensacola with Jackson resembled detached service. However, this instance differed in one important respect. Although Jackson continued to issue orders regarding military aspects of the transfer, he no longer served in the army. He had resigned his commission in order to take the governorship. Several factors influenced his decision, and one of them held significant future consequences for Harney, as well as for the army itself. Earlier in the year Congress, now concerned with internal issues and seeing no immediate foreign threats, had passed legislation reducing the authorized strength of the army from 11,709 to 5,586 enlisted men and from 680 to 540 officers. Without providing specific approval, this law allowed for an expansible army. George Washington and Alexander Hamilton had originated the idea in the 1780s. Articulated now by Secretary of War John C. Calhoun, this concept assumed that if the army maintained a skeletal structure of fighting units with a high percentage of officers to enlisted men, it could fill out its ranks with recruits during times of crisis. With the plan came also a conviction that the restructured army had two primary missions: a constabulary role to maintain coastal fortifications and keep peace in frontier regions and a preparedness role to stay ready for another war with a European power. Emphasis on the latter led to disproportionate attention to European tactics, which usually proved ineffective against American Indians. This inappropriate approach frustrated Harney, along with many other officers, numerous times in future years. More immediately, restructuring the army meant that it had too many generals, and appointing Jackson to the Florida post provided an easy means of eliminating one.[15]

In mid-April 1821, the Jackson entourage, including Rachel Jackson and Harney, set out from Nashville to Cantonment Montpelier about twenty miles above Mobile. Jackson planned to wait there while final arrangements for Florida's transfer reached completion in Pensacola some forty miles southeast. The party traveled by way of New Orleans, where they arrived on April 26 and enjoyed a warm welcome. The public reception continued for four days and provided many memorable moments for all, including Harney, who at age twenty remained highly impressionable. After continuing their journey by ship on Lake Pontchartrain and the Gulf, the travelers reached Montpelier only to encounter several weeks of annoying delay before dawdling Spanish officials in Havana released documents essential to the transfer. In mid-June, Jackson crossed into Florida with occupation troops and camped fifteen miles north of Pensacola. Disagreement with Col. José Callava about details of the Spaniards' withdrawal led to further delays, but Jackson proceeded with plans for the ceremony and selected Harney to command the American guard detail. Although his original leave had expired by that time, he had received a four-week extension.[16]

Finally, Jackson and Callava concluded the arrangements. At seven o'clock on the morning of July 17, 1821, U.S. troops marched into Pensacola. As their band filled the Gulf air with martial music, they paraded through spectator-lined streets to the Governor's Palace. There two guard details, twenty Americans and twenty Spaniards, moved into formation facing each other. Between them stood a flagpole from which Spanish colors waved over the city. The Americans attached their standard to the same halyard, so that when they lowered the Spanish banner, they raised the United States colors simultaneously. The soldiers halted the two flags at half-mast while Spanish troops fired a twenty-one gun salute. Then the guards hoisted the American banner to the top of the pole, official representatives signed appropriate papers, and the Spanish detail withdrew. A twenty-five-gun salute by the Americans concluded the observance. Although it moved some Spanish Floridians to tears of regret, this precisely executed international ceremony excited the Americans and confirmed another step in what they regarded as their country's destiny to expand. Equally important to Harney, during the four months preceding the transfer, he had developed a closer association with Jackson, whose influence on his career did not end here.[17]

His duties in Pensacola finished and his furlough over, Harney returned to Baton Rouge and his regiment in August 1821. When he arrived, he found more than half the garrison ill and his brother so busy that a civilian physician had been hired to assist him. Harney had no desire to remain there if he could avoid it, and upon learning from a fellow officer that Lt. Robert C. Brent of the First Artillery Regiment wanted to move from Fort Sullivan, Maine, to a southern station, Harney proposed that they trade assignments. Perhaps unaware of conditions at Baton Rouge, Brent readily agreed and appealed to the adjutant general of the army to allow the exchange.[18] The War Department approved his request in November, but Harney became ill again and remained in Louisiana until the following spring. When Benjamin Harney requested another medical furlough for his brother, Brig. Gen. Edmund Pendleton Gaines, commander of the Western Department, denied it, but he granted the young officer permission to spend a month in Tennessee while en route to New England. After visiting with his family, Harney reported to Fort Sullivan in June 1822 and remained there on routine duty until the adjutant general ordered him and Brent to rejoin their original regiments.

Harney returned to Louisiana early in the spring of 1823.[19] He did not have to spend another summer and fall in the unfavorable climate, though. A series of events then unfolding on the upper Missouri River soon prompted the transfer of several First Infantry companies to the vicinity of St. Louis. Ever since the end of the War of 1812, the government had been trying to stabilize the nation's northern and western frontiers by securing peace agreements and establishing a permanent military presence among Great Britain's former Indian allies along the western Great Lakes and in the upper Mississippi Valley. The treaty efforts had produced only ceremonial effect, and erecting army posts had achieved only mixed success. At about the same time that Harney commenced his fourth stint of duty in Louisiana, frontier entrepreneur William H. Ashley and a large party of trappers led a major fur-gathering expedition into Indian country on the upper Missouri River. The Arikaras, traditional middlemen in the fur trade with Rocky Mountain tribes, resented the intruders and attacked them on June 2, 1823, near the present border between North and South Dakota. After killing fourteen whites and seizing a portion of their furs, the Arikaras drove the remaining trappers down the river. When Col. Henry Leavenworth, commander of Fort Atkinson on the Missouri River at Council Bluffs, learned of the attack, he decided to punish the Indians. Eventually he led 230 soldiers, 60 fur company men, 43 boatmen, and a party of Sioux Indians, traditional enemies of the Arikaras, up the river toward the latter's villages. Meanwhile, Blackfeet Indians ambushed another group of Missouri Fur Company traders near the Yellowstone River, killed seven, and took a store of furs valued at $15,000.[20]

General Gaines had responsibility for all territory west of a diagonal line from the southern tip of Florida to the western edge of Lake Superior. Alarmed by the Indian attacks, he feared that the upper Missouri tribes would form an alliance against all whites. On July 26, 1823, he ordered Brig. Gen. Henry Atkinson, commander of the department's Right Wing, to go up the Missouri, support Leavenworth's forces, and "give a timely check to the hostile spirit which has recently manifested itself among the Indians" there. To reinforce the troops already at Atkinson's disposal, Gaines directed Col. Talbot Chambers to transport six companies of the First Infantry from Baton Rouge to St. Louis "to be held in readiness" should Atkinson need them.

The detachment chosen for this task included Harney's company, and sometime in August, he and the other reinforcements embarked from Baton Rouge on steamboats. After pushing up the Mississippi River in the summer heat, the troops reached St. Louis during the first week in September and then proceeded to Fort Belle Fontaine, a few miles north of the city on the Missouri River. Harney exercised temporary command of one of the companies while the detachment awaited further orders.[21]

President Monroe and Secretary of War Calhoun had approved the plans Gaines made, but Calhoun ordered him not to move the First Infantry group, or similar reserve companies of the Seventh Infantry, from Fort Belle Fontaine unless Leavenworth miscarried in his expedition against the Arikaras. Well before the First Infantry companies had landed at St. Louis, Leavenworth's allied force had reached Arikara territory. They had failed to recover the stolen furs, but the Missouri Fur Company men had burned the Indian villages.[22] Atkinson reported on September 13 that the Arikaras had been "severely punished," and accordingly he retained the reserve companies at Fort Belle Fontaine in compliance with War Department instructions. He believed, however, that the Indians would renew hostilities at the first opportunity and "that the Missouri will be shut against us" north of the Arikara villages "if an imposing military force does not visit that country the next season." Thus, while Atkinson formulated plans that would ultimately send many of them up the Missouri, Harney and most other men of the First Infantry detachment settled in for the winter.

In January 1824, Atkinson sent two of the First Infantry companies to New Orleans, but the others, including Harney's, remained in Missouri.[25] He liked his new station, for despite continuing as a temporary company commander for several months, he had time for horseback riding and occasional social visits to St. Louis. He also had an opportunity to become better acquainted with two other young officers with notable military careers ahead of them, Capt. David E. Twiggs and Maj. Stephen Watts Kearny. Harney enjoyed amicable relations with both men for a time, but late in the spring he had the first of two heated disputes with Kearny. In both instances, Harney behaved obstinately and had to face court-martial.

Both cases grew in part out of boredom associated with routine garrison duty. The first episode occurred on May 29 but stemmed from a series of lesser confrontations. While dining with Kearny in his quarters, Harney and Lt. Thomas P. Gwynne began discussing the cost of having uniforms altered. When Gwynne observed that a council of administration should set the prices that military tailors charged enlisted men, Harney asserted that the council should also set prices for officers. Kearny, a man of formal manners and strict discipline, reminded him that army regulations required officers to make individual agreements with tailors. According to Gwynne, Harney proclaimed that he would "never make contract with a Taylor [*sic*] to do work" for him. Kearny, at that time Harney's commanding officer and himself strong-willed and quick to anger, replied that if Harney repeated the statement he would be arrested. Peeved by Kearny's rebuke, Harney responded imprudently that he would not repeat his sentiments but would act according to them. Although Gwynne testified later that junior officers generally expressed themselves candidly at dinner, Kearny then accused Harney of having "been for some time too free in his remarks." To this Harney exclaimed, "If I have, then arrest me." Kearny obliged.

On June 7, before a general court-martial, Harney pleaded not guilty to the charge of "Mutinous and Insubordinate Conduct." During three days of proceedings, he maintained that "subordination is the grand basis of our profession" and "my standing motto." But the court found him guilty nevertheless and sentenced him to official reprimand in departmental orders. Clearly the strong personalities of both men helped transform an otherwise unimportant off-duty conversation into an issue of military discipline, but this was not unusual. Petty quarreling occurred often among army officers at all levels. The officer corps was a relatively small, distinct group, and army regulations and policies remained in an evolutionary state. Officers jealously guarded their careers and took umbrage at the slightest offenses, real or perceived.[24]

Following their initial clash, the major and his stubborn lieutenant continued at odds, and soon their mutual animosity, combined with further poor judgment by Harney, brought about a second, more serious trial that should have taught him a lesson in obedience and responsibility. This time the trouble occurred after Harney received command of a company again and coincidentally contracted gonorrhea. Eventually he began missing roll call, and for nine consecutive days he failed to take charge of his company at morning drill. He claimed his illness prevented his doing so, but in apparent contradiction he performed his afternoon duties as usual. On the ninth day, August 22, Kearny sent Asst. Surgeon Richard M. Coleman to examine him. The doctor found Harney sitting on his veranda partially dressed and complaining of diarrhea and headache but showing no external sign of illness. Kearny informed him that if he did not drill his company he would be arrested. Certain that his illness justified his actions, Harney refused to obey and again insisted that he was sick. Kearny then had Coleman make a second examination, and this time Harney had a slight fever. The physician believed this stemmed solely from agitation, though, as now Harney had become angry. A short time later he skipped morning inspection, and Kearny found him still sitting on the porch of the officers' quarters, placed him under arrest, and charged him with "Unofficerlike & Ungentlemanlike Conduct," specifically disobeying orders and using a "feigned pretense of being sick" to avoid duty.

When the five-day trial began on August 26, Harney pleaded not guilty to all charges. He stated that his medicine caused him to get up frequently during the night, lose sleep, and feel weak. Coleman said the medicine he had given Harney for gonorrhea should not have that effect. The surgeon had no sympathy for him in part because army doctors considered venereal disease much less common and less threatening than most other diseases they saw regularly, and generally they paid it little regard. In addition to Coleman's testimony, the prosecution sought to prove Harney's fitness by pointing out that he, his roommate, and several other junior officers had chased a bat around Harney's room for thirty minutes after tattoo on the night of the twenty-first. Defense witnesses testified that Harney had frequently expressed concern about his illness, that he had indeed been up often at night, and that between August 14 and August 22 he had avoided his favorite exercises, horseback riding and "jumping" with other officers. Lieutenant Gwynne related that Harney had ridden three miles to attend church earlier in the month but had regretted making the trip because the ride had increased his discomfort. Gwynne noted also that Harney had often indicated his fondness for drill and his disappointment that he could not participate in it.

After hearing all the witnesses, the tribunal found Harney not guilty of pretending to be ill, but guilty of failing to perform his duties. The board felt that he had been well enough to drill his company, and accordingly, on September 1 they sentenced him to suspension from command for three months. On that same day, however, General Atkinson remitted the sentence and returned Harney to duty because the First Infantry detachment had orders to move to Fort Atkinson.[25] The trial made no lasting impression on Harney, except to confirm that he could defy authority and get away with it. Although no one ever again formally accused him of neglecting his duty, he charged unrestrained through the rest of his career, disregarding regulations and orders on several future occasions with more at stake than daily protocol and practice.

Harney had been in the army six years now, and they had been a time for learning. He had overcome his early dejection about army life, served in several instructive capacities, and become familiar with military routines and procedures even though he had not always followed them. He had observed and taken part in some of the ways the army performed its job as a frontier constabulary, and he had advanced to the rank of first lieutenant. He had also participated with Andrew Jackson in an elaborate and memorable acknowledgment of the latter's role in expanding America's territorial boundaries. In spite of his ill-considered behavior at Fort Belle Fontaine, the boy officer had grown to manhood and made important professional progress. Now he stood poised to assume more responsible duties and to take advantage of even more challenging opportunities for growth in his chosen profession.

CHAPTER 3

Boatman, Woodsman, Indian Fighter

O N T H E morning of September 17, 1824, four First Infantry companies under the command of Maj. Stephen Watts Kearny boarded the keelboats *Muskrat, Mink, Raccoon,* and *Beaver* at St. Louis. Each company commander had charge of a boat, and assuming that Kearny listed the craft and their commanders respectively in his meticulously detailed journal, 1st Lt. William S. Harney commanded the *Muskrat.* Curious onlookers lined the riverbanks as the boats, laden with soldiers' baggage and supplies, got under way. Until recently, none in the crowd had seen craft like these. General Atkinson had been experimenting for a year on new ways to propel keelboats, and finally he had settled on a device that allowed men sitting along the sides of a boat to push a slide apparatus that turned a series of gears and a paddlewheel. Troops had tested the machinery and boats on trial runs between Fort Belle Fontaine and St. Louis during the summer. Now Atkinson planned to use these and other similarly equipped vessels in efforts to resolve the problems with Indian relations and fur trade on the upper Missouri. He accompanied the boats to Fort Belle Fontaine, where they arrived on the nineteenth and took on sixty recruits for the Sixth Infantry at Fort Atkinson. With the additional men assigned equally among the four craft, the flotilla made ready to continue upriver toward Council Bluffs.[1]

This represented the first step in the expedition that Atkinson had proposed after Henry Leavenworth's operations against the Arikaras in 1823. Atkinson had wanted to send a larger force up the Missouri, build an army post near the mouth of the Yellowstone, and ensure that hostilities did not reoccur. While Harney and the other First Infantrymen had passed the winter at Fort Belle Fontaine, Atkinson had completed plans to carry out those tasks. At the same time, uneasy westerners, fearing that further disturbances would prevent Americans from competing with British companies for the rich Rocky Mountain fur business, had urged Congress to approve a commission to negotiate treaties that would ensure peace and regulate trade with the tribes. Former Tennessean Thomas Hart Benton, now representing Missouri in the Senate, introduced such a measure, and President Monroe signed it on May 25, 1824. The legislation authorized a commission and appropriated money for it and a military escort. Monroe selected Atkinson and Benjamin O'Fallon, Indian agent for the upper Missouri, to represent the government. When Atkinson learned about his assignment in July, too little time remained to gather the necessary trade goods, supplies, and boats and travel upriver before winter, and so he postponed the expedition until 1825. However, by sending Kearny and the four First Infantry companies ahead to Council Bluffs, he could provide a stiffer test for the boats.[2]

This first leg of the expedition also launched a new phase in Harney's career, one that illustrates the army's ongoing efforts as frontier peacekeeper and its willingness to deal brutally with Indians when peace seemed impossible. From 1824 to 1832, the strapping Tennessean served almost exclusively in the upper Midwest and carried out increasingly responsible assignments. Through his experiences on the waters and in the Indian villages of the upper Missouri and on the streams and in the forests of Wisconsin and Illinois, he became familiar with native people, observed how the government conducted treaty councils with them, and fought them in the Black Hawk War. He also developed outstanding wilderness expertise and earned a lasting reputation for physical prowess, impulsive and stubborn behavior, and a quick temper. Along the way he remained under the influence of Andrew Jackson, formed friendships with Jefferson Davis and Abraham Lincoln, served briefly under Zachary Taylor, and made Winfield Scott a lifelong enemy.

Kearny's boats set out from near Fort Belle Fontaine at 5:30 A.M. on September 20, 1824, and plied up the Missouri for six weeks despite a series of mishaps. The machinery broke down frequently, and wind, rain, snags, and sandbars impeded progress. On September 24, the *Muskrat* and the *Mink* struck a sandbar, and their crews worked all night to pry them loose. Often the men caused additional delays. Several deserted, and Kearny sent patrols ashore to search for them. One unhappy soldier slit his own throat in mid-October, and another fell overboard from Harney's boat and drowned. Generally he and the other commanders maintained discipline, though, and the crews sometimes amused themselves by racing their vessels.[3]

The keelboats reached Council Bluffs on November 2, three weeks ahead of several private craft that had left St. Louis about the same time, and the soldiers disembarked in good health. This demonstrated clearly that Atkinson's paddlewheel vessels were faster than conventional keelboats propelled only by oars, poles, sails, or towlines, and so he began preparing additional craft for the spring expedition. With enthusiastic support from the War Department, the troops at Fort Atkinson worked through the winter of 1824–25 equipping eight boats. Atkinson assigned the *Beaver, Otter,* and *Muskrat* to Kearny's First Infantry detachment and allotted five others to elements of the Sixth Infantry under Colonel Leavenworth. Depending on their individual capacity, each boat would carry forty-eight to sixty men.[4]

While these preparations went forward, Harney and two second lieutenants, James W. Kingsbury and Rueben Holmes, became so excited about the approaching expedition that they dreamed of launching an even more extensive venture the following year. In complete disregard for regular channels of military communication, Harney wrote boldly in January 1825 to his old family friend Andrew Jackson, who by then had been elected to the Senate. Undoubtedly believing that Jackson, an ardent expansionist, would look favorably on his idea and help him make it a reality, Harney proposed to lead a party from Council

Bluffs in the spring of 1826, "pop up the River Platte" to its headwaters, cross the mountains to the Pacific Ocean, survey the coast northward to Russian territory, and return via the upper tributaries of the Missouri. "A wish to serve is our stimulus," he wrote Jackson, and "I feel confident we will do our country some service and ourselves a little honour." Obviously hoping for Sam Houston's help, too, Harney closed by asking Jackson to extend regards to that fellow Tennessean, who now represented Nashville in the other house of Congress.[5]

Obviously the prospect of adventure and personal recognition motivated all three would-be explorers, but Harney had the additional inspiration of having observed Jackson's military glory in Tennessee and Florida. As the trio waited on the threshold of territory traversed by Meriwether Lewis and William Clark twenty years earlier and by Stephen H. Long more recently, their ambitions soared. Although they hardly needed it, Kearny served as a constant reminder of what they might achieve. He had accompanied Long on his scientific expedition in 1819 and now, following a practice he had begun then, Kearny wrote his daily journal in the same leather-bound pocket book he had carried on that occasion. The three partners' planning proved futile, though, for Jackson did not respond, and they had to content themselves with the immediately unfolding enterprise.

At 7:00 A.M. on May 16, 1825, 435 men left Council Bluffs aboard eight keelboats and headed up the Missouri. Forty horsemen under Capt. William Armstrong followed on shore to serve as scouts and hunters. Harney remained in command of a company and presumably the *Muskrat.* During the first two days, the troops established their daily routine. After progressing twelve miles on May 17, they stopped for the night, pulled their craft within ten to thirty feet of each other at the water's edge, and pitched their camps by companies on the shore parallel to the river and facing the boats. One company at each end of the line set its tents in a row perpendicular to the river and facing outward so they could keep watch. The next morning a bugler awakened the men before dawn. Knowing that a long and arduous day lay before them, Harney and his comrades arose in the darkness and dew, dismantled and packed their camp equipment, boarded the transports without pausing for breakfast, and got under way at 4:30. For four hours they pushed against the current, and after traveling about six miles, they stopped to eat. Refreshed, they set out again at 10:00 A.M. and made another six miles or so before halting at one o'clock for their midday meal. Once more they rested an hour and a half and then continued upriver until the approach of darkness. Except when bad weather or trouble with the boats forced changes, they adhered to this schedule throughout their journey.[6]

As the flotilla moved northward, boat crews encountered problems similar to those the First Infantry troops had faced during their trip from St. Louis to Council Bluffs the preceding autumn. Mechanical failures and minor accidents involving snags, sandbars, and strong currents forced them to stop from time to time and make repairs. Occasionally strong headwinds slowed their progress. Rainsqualls occurred often, soaking the men and their equipment, and on June 3 a nighttime thunderstorm pelted them with hail. Nevertheless, with the additional assistance of oars, tow lines on occasion, and sails whenever the wind blew favorably, the paddlewheel keelboats proceeded against the current up the winding river.[7]

On June 8, the commissioners and their escort reached a village of more than nine hundred Poncas at the mouth of White Paint Creek in present northeastern Nebraska, more than three hundred miles above Council Bluffs. Having found little game to hunt, Armstrong's mounted force had arrived two weeks earlier, and the Indians had been waiting for the boats. The proceedings over the next three days set a pattern for subsequent meetings with other tribes farther upriver. Soon after disembarking, the troops cleared ground for a camp, and in the afternoon Atkinson and O'Fallon met the Ponca leaders and explained the reason for the visit. Meanwhile, the soldiers unloaded and cleaned the boats, restowed the cargoes, and welcomed a mounted express that arrived from Council Bluffs with letters and papers.[8]

After breakfast on June 9, Atkinson ordered the troops to assemble in dress uniforms on a grassy plain near the village. There in the summer heat Harney and the other company commanders drilled the soldiers for an hour, as Atkinson, O'Fallon, and the Ponca men, women, and children watched. Following this effort to impress the Indians with white men's military skill, the commissioners met the chiefs and headmen in council. Having already prepared the text of a treaty, the commissioners explained its provisions, stated the whites' desire for peace, and discussed O'Fallon's role as Indian agent. The Poncas did little more than listen before agreeing to sign the document.

All the treaties that Atkinson and O'Fallon made during the expedition contained the same basic stipulations. The Indians recognized U.S. sovereignty over them, promised to respect Americans authorized to travel in their territory, and pledged to trade only with men licensed by the government. They also agreed not to provide military assistance to enemies of the United States. The government promised in turn to protect the Indians from unjust injury, send them licensed traders, and maintain peaceful relations. After the chiefs and other leaders had signed the treaty, the commissioners gave them four guns, knives, tobacco, blankets, coarse woolen cloth, and various trinkets. The whites paid a small price, indeed, for what they hoped would be a guaranteed opportunity to tap the rich fur resources of Indian country unmolested. The entire proceeding mirrored in format most other white-Indian treaty councils from the Lewis and Clark expedition forward. Whites and sometimes Indians went through diplomatic rituals, the two sides stated demands and requests often without understanding each other, and then the whites distributed presents. As Harney's career unfolded, he experienced many such scenes, often as a major actor.[9]

While the dignitaries participated in the ceremonies, boat crews repaired machinery and readied their craft for continued ascent of the river. Harney helped supervise this activity and did not observe much of this first council. The next morning, the Indians entertained the soldiers with tribal dances, and shortly after noon the boats pulled away from the village.[10]

Enjoying wild gooseberries picked along the banks and fresh buffalo and antelope meat furnished by the hunters, the troops reached Fort Kiowa, an American Fur Company trading post about five hundred miles above Council Bluffs, on June 17. There they paused six days while Atkinson and O'Fallon conferred with the Teton, Yankton, and Yantonnai Sioux. When they finished, Harney signed his name for the first time as witness to an Indian treaty.[11]

On the last day of June, the flotilla reached the mouth of the Teton

River near present Pierre, South Dakota. There the commissioners awaited several nearby tribes and then met them in council. On July 4, the men received an extra ration of liquor to celebrate Independence Day, and the Oglala Sioux treated the commissioners and most officers to "the flesh of 13 dogs boiled in plain water in 7 kettles, much done." Afterward, the diners drank river water and smoked Indian ceremonial pipes. Later, aboard one of the transports, Atkinson and O'Fallon served wine and fruit to the officers. After concluding treaties with the Cheyennes and the Saone and Oglala bands of Sioux, the whites continued upriver to the Arikara village. There, the soldiers demonstrated their artillery, and the commissioners signed pacts with both the Arikaras and the Hunkpapa Sioux.[12]

On July 18, the expedition headed for a cluster of five Mandan villages on the Knife River immediately north of present Bismarck, North Dakota, where they arrived on the twenty-sixth. During this stretch of the journey, howling wolves and swarms of mosquitoes kept the men awake at night. At the earthen Mandan towns, the troops camped ten days as Atkinson and O'Fallon concluded treaties with Minitarees, Mandans, and Crows. Talks with the latter tribe almost ended disastrously when O'Fallon, enraged with the Indians' impatient demands for presents, struck at least three Crow chiefs on the head with his pistol. As a precaution, Atkinson ordered the troops to prepare for battle, but he succeeded in calming the disturbed Indians.[13]

Despite this incident, the atmosphere at the treaty grounds remained amicable enough that Harney could engage in two races with a Crow warrior. The contests gave both men an opportunity to show off. In the first race across eight hundred yards of grassy prairie, souvenir-laden pockets slowed the long-limbed officer, and the Indian defeated him decisively. Confident that he could prevail if properly attired, Harney dumped his load and called for a second contest. Now a crowd of Indians and soldiers gathered to watch and bet buffalo robes, twists of tobacco, ponies, coffee, and sugar on their favorite. At the start, the warrior leaped ahead of Harney by fifteen feet. Then with the troops shouting encouragement, Harney narrowed the gap and crossed the finish line first by a step. Atkinson congratulated him, and he became known among the upper Missouri tribes as "the fastest runner" on the northern plains. Both Indians and whites still talked about the race forty years later. Most army officers regarded native people as culturally inferior and an impediment to white settlement, and given his boyhood experiences and acquaintance with Jackson, Harney could not have thought differently. However, he had now dined and sported with Indians, and in doing so he had gained a measure of familiarity that helped shape future associations with them.[14]

From the Mandan villages the expedition continued up the Missouri toward the Yellowstone, where the commissioners hoped to meet Assiniboines and Blackfeet. Arriving on August 17, the whites found no Indians but paused anyway, as the level prairie abounded in wild game. William Ashley and a small fur trading party happened by two days later with beaver pelts from the Rocky Mountains, and Atkinson offered them transportation and escort home. The trappers accepted, but they had to wait several days while Atkinson and most of his command, including Harney, searched for the Assiniboines and Blackfeet farther upstream. Leaving the other troops behind to hunt buffalo for the return trip to Council Bluffs, Atkinson's detachment proceeded to Two Thousand Mile Creek but encountered only a rapidly narrowing waterway. Unable to continue, they dismantled their paddlewheels and prepared happily to descend the river. When they returned to their base camp on August 26, they immediately loaded Ashley's furs, the scouts' horses, and fresh meat, and the next morning the entire party headed down the Missouri.[15]

The boats traveled up to sixty-five miles a day in the favorable current, and with one exception, only minor mishaps slowed them. In mid-September, a submerged snag tore three holes in the hull of the *Muskrat,* which carried half of Ashley's furs. Three feet of water filled the craft, and the crew towed the disabled boat onto a sandbar and worked through the night patching the holes. Drying the soaked pelts required another day of labor.[16]

The flotilla arrived back at Council Bluffs on September 19, having traveled more than two thousand miles since mid-May. With winter approaching, the Sixth Infantry moved into the old Fort Atkinson barracks, while the First built temporary quarters and storehouses from hand-sawed planks. The commissioners completed their business by holding talks with the Otoes, Pawnees, and Omahas in October. Within five months, Atkinson and O'Fallon had concluded twelve treaties with sixteen tribes. Although neither those documents nor the long river voyage ensured protection for whites in the upper Missouri valley, the expedition had demonstrated that a sizable military force could travel safely through the region and conduct peaceful and friendly councils with the Indians. Harney had contributed to that success. He had also received an introduction to plains Indian tribes and acquired useful experience in river transportation. Fittingly, he now learned that he had been promoted to the rank of captain in a commission dated May 14, 1825.[17]

Most of Kearny's detachment of First Infantry remained at Cantonment Barbour, their new Council Bluffs quarters, until the spring of 1826. In May they transferred to Fort Belle Fontaine, and in July they began constructing Jefferson Barracks, a new post on the west bank of the Mississippi River a few miles south of St. Louis. In the meantime, Harney drew garrison duty in New Orleans and enjoyed that cosmopolitan city's colorful social life for more than a year. In April 1827, he rejoined the First Infantry detachment at Jefferson Barracks, there reunited for a time with his brother Benjamin.[18]

When Harney returned, the upper Mississippi region seemed ready to erupt in war. For more than a decade, contradictory treaties, conflicting tribal land claims, and encroaching lead miners had strained Indian-white relations in northern Illinois and present southern Wisconsin. The Sac and Foxes and the Chippewas had ceded land and mineral rights to the federal government. But the Winnebagos had continued to roam the area, and by 1826 two developments led them to think they could expel the white intruders. False rumors suggested that the United States and Great Britain might go to war again. And the army, believing it no longer needed two of its frontier posts, had withdrawn from Fort Crawford at Prairie du Chien near the mouth of the Wisconsin River and from Fort Dearborn at Chicago. Suddenly whites seemed less formidable.[19]

After Prairie la Cross Winnebagos committed several acts of violence in early summer 1827, John Marsh, Indian subagent at Prairie du Chien, believed they would stop only if "the most severe measures are resorted to" or when "they are exterminated." Although harsh, these words echoed the sentiments of many frontier whites throughout the century. With alarm spreading and miners fleeing the lead district, General Atkinson, Michigan territorial governor Lewis Cass, and Indian superintendent William Clark met in St. Louis in July and devised plans to stem the crisis. Cass would confer with the Sioux, Sac and Foxes, Menominees, and peaceful Winnebagos and try to keep them calm. In the meantime, Atkinson would proceed up the Mississippi with a force of infantrymen, reoccupy Fort Crawford, and if necessary go on up the Wisconsin River and coerce the Winnebagos into submission.[20]

Initially Harney's role in that mission amounted to little more than spectator, for the troops encountered no resistance. However, he got his first glimpse of the country where he would spend most of the next five years. On July 15, almost six hundred soldiers, including Harney's First Infantry company, boarded steamboats at Jefferson Barracks and headed up the Mississippi to Fort Crawford. Eventually Atkinson sent Harney's unit and most of the other troops about eighty miles up the Wisconsin River, while Maj. William Whistler led a smaller force up the Fox River from Fort Howard near Green Bay. These diagonal movements through present lower Wisconsin frightened the Indians, and in a council with Atkinson they promised not to disturb whites there. In return, he pledged that the government would try to settle conflicting Indian-white land claims in the mining district. Prematurely, government officials applauded these steps as a peaceful conclusion to the Winnebago difficulties.[21]

Late in September 1827, the Jefferson Barracks troops returned to that post, and shortly afterward Harney left on an eight-week furlough in Washington, where he spent the Christmas season and managed to antagonize Brig. Gen. Winfield Scott. Harney's offense stemmed from sheer bull-headedness. Having enjoyed his first sojourn in the national capital, he applied on Christmas Day to Maj. Gen. Jacob Brown, commanding general of the army, for a two-month extension of leave. Harney explained that General Gaines, commander of the Western Department, had issued the original furlough and told him that he could apply directly to Brown for additional time. However, since then Scott,

1. Upper Mississippi Valley, 1828–32

a stickler for administrative detail, had replaced Gaines temporarily and informed Harney that he must submit any extension request through regular channels. Miffed by what he regarded as Scott's interference, he requested the extension from Brown's office anyway. This obstinate display succeeded only in making Scott a lifelong adversary, and Harney returned to Jefferson Barracks in January 1828.[22]

Although Atkinson had prevented war in the upper Mississippi valley in 1827, the potential for violence still existed. The events that unfolded next involved Harney more directly and influenced his future conduct in Indian affairs. Reports circulated that the Winnebagos had withdrawn to the southern tip of Green Bay and begun killing deer and drying the meat in preparation for some future campaign. Meanwhile, whites continued to intrude upon mineral lands claimed by the Indians. In an attempt to protect both whites and native people, the War Department decided to establish a new military post in the heart of Winnebago country at the portage of the Fox and Wisconsin Rivers, about thirty miles north of present Madison. In August 1828, Maj. Gen. Alexander Macomb, the new commanding general of the army, directed Maj. David E. Twiggs of the First Infantry to select the site for the new fort and assign three companies to erect it. Harney commanded one of the designated units.[23]

Twiggs reached the portage with his command on October 7 and chose a location for the new post, which he named Fort Winnebago, on the right bank of the Fox River. With winter at hand and supplies scarce, Harney and his compatriots faced a difficult task. Despite a shortage of tools, the soldiers went promptly to work. Laboring without blueprints, they followed the traditional pattern for frontier forts, and by early November they had built two blockhouses, erected log huts for temporary quarters, and started a 120-foot-square palisade. They then set to work on permanent facilities and toiled through the winter cutting flooring, weather boarding, and other planking. Twiggs expected to finish the fort by November 1829, but interruptions to prevent whites from trespassing on Indian land delayed completion until late in 1830.[24]

During much of this time Harney commanded a detachment of woodcutters in the pine forests north of the construction site. They selected trees, felled them with whipsaws, and floated the logs down the Wisconsin River in rafts. Although he had hated the wilds of northwestern Louisiana a decade earlier, Harney thrived on the rugged life in the Wisconsin woods and acquired outdoor skills that proved invaluable during subsequent service in the Florida Everglades. Satterlee Clark, a sutler at the fort, recalled later, "I think it is conceded that for frontier service Captain Harney had no superior anywhere." When they completed the logging, he and his men returned to the fort, where he remained until June 1831.[25]

Despite the relative isolation of Fort Winnebago, Harney and his fellow officers found opportunities for social and recreational activities. In the fall of 1830, Indian agent John H. Kinzie arranged for his bride to join him at the post, and Harney took a detail to meet her in Green Bay and convey her and her household goods back to the fort by boat. He greeted her with news that Major Twiggs's wife had been "the only white lady" at Fort Winnebago "since the past spring" and "impatiently" awaited "a companion and friend." Instead of accompanying Mrs. Kinzie back to the post, though, Harney decided to "remain a few days longer" in Green Bay, and he sent her ahead with only the boat crew. This bothered her not at all, and she grew fond enough of him to bake a mince pie for him and then chuckle when, unaware that she had made it, he exclaimed in the presence of her husband that it tasted unfit to eat.[26]

Juliette Kinzie wrote later about those and numerous other aspects of life at Green Bay and Fort Winnebago, but like most observers of the time, she never mentioned anything about officers' relationships with native and mixed-blood women. However, both Harney and Twiggs apparently had at least one sexual encounter with them. Two mixed-blood Winnebago women had children who carried the officers' names and whom area residents regarded as their offspring. According to sworn affidavits collected by federal Indian claims commissioners, Julia Grignou bore a son named David Twiggs about 1829, and Ke-sho-ko bore a daughter named Mary Caroline Harney sometime that same year or the next. Intimate relationships between officers and Indian women occurred with some frequency in frontier regions throughout the century, and a number of officers kept Indian mistresses. Not surprisingly, the men and their families recorded little information about these liaisons, either officially or privately. Neither Harney nor Twiggs maintained long-term contact with the mothers or the children, but in 1832 Harney witnessed a treaty that provided land to Mary Caroline and three other Winnebago mixed-bloods.[27] Nothing about his relationship with Ke-sho-ko and Mary Caroline prevented

Harney from accepting prevailing negative white attitudes about native culture or moderated his future willingness to deal brutally with Indians. But it increased his familiarity with native people and indicated an ambivalent attitude toward them.

For recreation and to help the troops get fresh meat for their mess, Harney, like many other officers in frontier posts, kept a pack of hunting dogs at Fort Winnebago. Also, like most company commanders, he supervised the cultivation of a vegetable garden to furnish variety in the soldiers' diet and guard against scurvy. In at least one instance, keeping dogs and raising foodstuff proved incompatible and provoked Harney to a fit of anger. He watched over his company's garden plot with particular care, and one day he saw a half-grown hound trotting across newly prepared seedbeds. When he rushed toward the dog shouting profanities, the frightened animal bounded across the remaining rows, scrambled over the garden fence, and raced for safety. Giving no thought to his own destructive path through the beds, the enraged captain dashed after him, leaped over the fence, overtook the hapless creature, and beat him.[28]

Unfortunately, Harney also became irrational when provoked by humans, and he displayed his violent temper often at Fort Winnebago. On one occasion, he caught a miner selling whiskey to soldiers illegally, tied him to a flagpole, and flogged him unmercifully. For enlisted men violating military regulations, officers frequently bypassed proscribed punishments and devised methods of their own. Satterlee Clark recalled one incident when a "very large" soldier, said to be the post's "champion pugilist," remarked to Harney, "If you were an enlisted man, or I was a Captain, you could not treat me in that way." Harney escorted him to the rear of the barracks, "told him to consider himself a Captain, and do his best." After Harney knocked him to the ground "about a dozen times," the man said, "Captain, I have been a Captain long enough" and "I would now like to be reduced to the ranks."

Harney did not always come out on top during these episodes. An incident during the winter of 1829–30 made him a laughing-stock. It evolved when he set out to flog an Indian for a minor breach of garrison rules and thought first to have some fun at the man's expense. Believing since his race with the Crow in 1825 that he could outrun any tribesman, Harney arranged a contest with his prisoner on the frozen Fox River. If the warrior won, he would escape punishment. If not, Harney would thrash him. At the appointed time, the two men stripped to the waist and Harney donned moccasins. Given a head start, the Indian sped across the ice with the heavier captain pursuing closely waving a strip of rawhide. Suddenly the intended victim darted over a patch of thin ice, and Harney plunged into freezing water. As the fortunate Indian escaped, the surprised officer clambered out of the river and stormed shivering and cursing to his quarters.[29]

Stories about Harney's escapades and temper followed him throughout his career, and those who knew him shared them inside the army and out, verbally and in print. Jefferson Davis, who served as a second lieutenant at Fort Winnebago during part of Harney's sojourn there, formed a lifelong friendship with him, and in later years the two visited from time to time and recalled bygone days in Wisconsin. Some things, however, Harney did not want told. In 1879, when he accepted an invitation to dine and reminisce at Davis's home in Mississippi, he admonished his host not to "say anything" in front of the other guests "about the Butchers Sister in law" at Fort Winnebago.[30]

While the troops at Fort Winnebago busied themselves with general garrison chores, the army shifted its principal attention on the upper Mississippi to the Sac and Foxes. Historians have labeled the ensuing sad affair the Black Hawk War. Caused generally by federal efforts to move Indians off homelands desired by whites, the conflict took shape through a series of misunderstandings and miscalculations by both sides and featured killings and reprisals by both. It demonstrated the complexity and frequent impossibility of the army's peacekeeping role, and it ended in a single major military engagement, during which hundreds of Indian men, women, and children lost their lives.

When the Sac and Foxes had given up their land and mineral rights in 1804, the government had told them they could remain on ceded territory east of the Mississippi River until officials decided to sell it. By the time that occurred, most Sac and Foxes had already moved to the western side. However, some, under the leadership of the Sac warrior Black Hawk, returned each spring to their old villages along the Rock

River in northern Illinois to plant crops. They caused no harm, but whites objected anyway. In June 1831, General Gaines assembled a combined force of Illinois militia and federal troops, including Harney's First Infantry company, at Fort Armstrong near the mouth of the Rock and forced Black Hawk and his followers back across the Mississippi. Gaines believed that British-Canadian traders had encouraged the Indians' recalcitrance, and so with assistance from a friendly Sac chief, Keokuk, he persuaded Black Hawk to sign a capitulatory treaty in which he agreed not to visit the British again and not to recross the river without permission from American authorities.[31]

This agreement did little to reduce tensions. No clear tribal boundaries existed west of the Mississippi, and the Sioux resented Sac and Fox hunting parties in territory the former claimed. Following several clashes with Sioux and Menominee warriors, in July 1831 some eighty to one hundred Sac and Foxes ambushed and killed twenty-five Menominees near Fort Crawford.[32] In September, federal authorities assembled Sac and Fox leaders at Fort Armstrong and demanded that they hand over the persons responsible. Keokuk said the attackers would have to surrender, but they had no intention of doing that and turned to Black Hawk for understanding and advice. Coincidentally, the Sac chief, Neapope, returned from Canada about this same time and reported that British agents had said the Sac and Foxes still owned their Illinois land and the British would help them hold onto it. Neapope said also that Prophet, a Winnebago leader, would assist them against the whites. Buoyed by this news from the north and a growing number of new followers from various disaffected tribes, Black Hawk vowed to return to Illinois in the spring of 1832.[33]

When spring came, the army, ignorant about intertribal relationships and patterns of leadership within tribes, mistakenly worried more about the likelihood of warfare among Indians than about Black Hawk. In March, Macomb received reports that the Menominees planned to retaliate against the Sac and Foxes, and he instructed Atkinson to demand again that the Indians who led the attack in July surrender. Macomb hoped this would calm the Menominees and their allies, the Sioux. Unfortunately, he did not anticipate Black Hawk's actions. Early in April, Black Hawk crossed into Illinois south of Fort

Armstrong with less than five hundred warriors and perhaps as many as fifteen hundred women and children. They skirted the post and headed up the Rock River, confident that Prophet's Winnebagos and possibly a few Potawatomis and Kickapoos would help them fend off any white assault. At this juncture, neither the army nor the Indians knew the other's intentions.[34]

Although usually adept at dealing with native people, Atkinson blundered badly with Black Hawk. Instead of seeking a council with him, the general conferred only with friendly Sac and Fox chiefs, trying once more unsuccessfully to secure surrender of the warriors who had attacked the Menominees. He dispatched messengers to Black Hawk, but they brought back contradictory reports about his plans.[35] In the meantime, Black Hawk's anticipated Potawatomi and Winnebago allies decided not to join him and even refused to give his people provisions. Disillusioned, he now resolved that "if the White Beaver [Atkinson] came after us, we would go back" across the Mississippi. Unaware of Black Hawk's conclusion, Atkinson decided late in April that "the whole frontier" would "be in a flame" if he did not "at once take the field."[36] As a witness to these crucial developments, Harney learned the value of talking directly with potentially hostile native leaders.

The Indians had now moved to a position about twenty miles above Dixon's Ferry on Rock River, and Atkinson prepared to overtake them there and force them back toward the Mississippi. On May 8, he mustered about 1,700 Illinois militiamen into U.S. service and sent 1,500 of them overland under Gen. Samuel Whiteside toward Dixon's Ferry. The others and some 340 regular troops, including Harney's company, followed by boat under the command of Col. Zachary Taylor. In efforts reminiscent of Harney's experiences on the Missouri, they moved laboriously up the Rock River, pushing their craft with poles and pulling them from on shore with tow lines.[37]

Meanwhile, the inexperienced volunteers, accompanied by Illinois governor John Reynolds, reached Dixon's Ferry first. Whiteside halted most of them there, but Reynolds persuaded him to send Maj. Isaiah Stillman ahead with 275 men to search for the Indians' camp. When Black Hawk sent messengers under a white flag to make arrangements for his people to return unmolested down the river, the volunteers panicked, shot one of the flag bearers, and pursued the remaining warriors on horseback, killing several. The survivors warned Black Hawk about the onrushing whites, and thinking that their overtures for peace had been rejected, he and some forty men ambushed Stillman's advancing rabble. Surprised again, the militiamen fled, leaving behind eleven slain comrades.[38]

If previous misunderstandings and errors of judgment had made peaceful resolution of the Sac and Fox dilemma unlikely, these events made it impossible. While Black Hawk and his people headed slowly toward southern Wisconsin, exaggerated versions of Stillman's defeat spread swiftly. After a white farmer beat a Potawatomi and forty tribesmen responded by killing fifteen settlers on May 20, fear paralyzed the region. Neither Atkinson nor Black Hawk believed now that the difficulties could be settled peacefully. And in Washington, Andrew Jackson, now president, ordered the army to demand that Black Hawk and his lieutenants surrender and, if they refused, to attack and disperse them.[39]

Atkinson spent the next two months trying to keep the militiamen in service, find Black Hawk's camp, and gather supplies for a campaign against him. During the last two weeks of May, Whiteside's volunteers searched unsuccessfully for the Sac and Foxes above Dixon's Ferry and in the Sycamore Creek country north of the Rock River. Regular troops under Taylor and Harney joined in the latter effort. The soldiers found only a deserted village and signs showing that the Indians continued to move northeast, but Harney gained valuable experience in wilderness pursuit.[40] Before the month ended, the militiamen grew impatient to return to their homes, and Atkinson discharged them. He then called on Reynolds for three thousand new volunteers, and those who enlisted proved as unruly as the first bunch. When they assembled at Ottawa in June, one experienced officer described them as like "a swarming hive . . . galloping about, 'cussing and discussing' the war, and the rumors thereof."[41] Their ranks contained men who had reenlisted for a second thirty-day term, and those included twenty-three-year-old Abraham Lincoln, with whom Harney often swapped yarns. Because of his and Lincoln's jocular storytelling and their similar heights, some men called them "the two ponies."[42]

While the volunteers gathered, Atkinson had more clothing and provisions transported up the Rock River to Dixon's Ferry. Harney led at least one of these supply details in June and experienced difficulty getting his loaded boats over the upper rapids. In the meantime, Black Hawk's starving followers, finding little game and fish, resorted to eating roots and bark, and he decided to descend the Wisconsin River and "remove my women and children across the Mississippi, that they might return to the Sac nation again."[43]

Oblivious to Black Hawk's plan, Atkinson finally got his forces ready to move, and on June 15 he wrote Macomb that he would "never cease" pursuing the Indians "till they are annihilated or fully and severally punished and subdued." With four hundred regulars and almost three thousand volunteers divided into three detachments, Atkinson started up the Rock River. In the mixed terrain of prairie, woodland, and swamp the troops tired quickly, and although scouts found numerous signs of the Indians, Atkinson's slow-moving columns gained little ground on them.[44] Throughout the exhausting search Harney remained active, "a bold, dashing officer, and indefatigable in duty," as one young West Pointer recalled later. On July 11, Atkinson sent the tireless captain with an advance party of eighty men to track the Indians through a swamp near the White River. After following the trail for twenty miles, Harney concluded that the Indians remained several days ahead of the main body of pursuers. Although dismayed, Atkinson kept his troops moving northward toward the Wisconsin River. On July 21, near Blue Mounds, volunteers found Black Hawk's band preparing to cross the river. The militiamen attacked the fleeing Indians and killed eighty or more, while the rest escaped in canoes and on makeshift rafts.[45]

As soon as he learned of this encounter, Atkinson rushed his force to the Wisconsin. On July 26, he selected thirteen hundred men, including Harney's company and the other regulars, to continue the pursuit. They took two days to build rafts, but once across the river, they quickly found the distressed Indians' trail. In their haste and panic, the weary people discarded kettles, blankets, and other camp equipment and abandoned their sick and wounded as they fled through the dense forest toward the Mississippi. Starving, they slaughtered their pack horses for food and left the stripped carcasses lying where they fell.[46]

On July 31, the pursuing army emerged from the thick timber and underbrush onto a sunny prairie near the Kickapoo River, and through a series of forced marches they approached within a few miles of the Indians late on August 1. By this time Black Hawk had left the defenseless band, and some of its members had managed to get across the Mississippi. Others worked feverishly building rafts. After resting only a few hours, the soldiers arose to the bugler's call at 2:00 A.M. on August 2, and in an early morning mist, they struck the Indians near the junction of the Bad Axe and Mississippi Rivers. In fierce and close fighting, Harney charged forward with his company, and the soldiers chased the Indians across several sloughs and through dense undergrowth and high grass. While suffering only 11 fatalities, the aggressors killed at least 150 and perhaps as many as 300 Sac and Foxes and captured about 50 others. The dead and wounded included many women and children who fled for their lives before the onslaught. The army often found it difficult to keep from killing noncombatants when fighting native people, and sometimes, as here, it did not try to avoid doing so, especially when the idea of punishment permeated officers' thinking. Exposure to these views and participation in the Battle of Bad Axe significantly influenced Harney's subsequent dealings with Indians in Florida and on the Great Plains.

Within a few days after the battle, Atkinson released the volunteers and moved the regulars down to Fort Crawford. A short time later, friendly Winnebagos captured Black Hawk, and the army imprisoned him at Jefferson Barracks.[47] This concluded the Black Hawk War, Harney's first major Indian campaign, and his service as an infantry officer. During his years in the upper Missouri and Mississippi valleys he had formed ambivalent attitudes toward native people, engaging them both individually through face-to-face encounters and collectively through brutal combat. He had seen some ways in which cultural complexities and the army's relatively small size inhibited its role as peacekeeper. And he had gained skills, made acquaintances, and demonstrated behavior that combined with his attitudes and observations to shape his future performance as an officer. Harney had become an able boatman, accomplished woodsman, and experienced Indian fighter.

CHAPTER 4

"That Infernal Pay Department"

THE DATE was January 27, 1833, the place St. Louis, and the ceremony Catholic. The bride was a thirty-year-old Missouri socialite, and the groom was a thirty-two-year-old army officer whose plans to go home had given way to romance. In the years following the Black Hawk War, Capt. William S. Harney's life and career took several unanticipated turns, some pleasant, some not. Initially this seemed a happy one.

In September 1832, having had no significant leave in five years and "anxious to visit friends in Tennessee & elsewhere," Harney asked for a two-month furlough with permission to apply for an extension of up to one year. Inasmuch as the army commonly granted officers leaves of several months, Col. Zachary Taylor, commander of the First Infantry Regiment, gave Harney an initial furlough of sixty days, and subsequent orders from the War Department extended it to ten months. In October 1832, he stopped in the growing frontier metropolis of St. Louis, where he intended to remain only a few days before continuing on to other destinations.[1]

Situated near the confluence of the Missouri and Mississippi Rivers, St. Louis boasted a population of more than five thousand and served as a major crossroads for merchandise and people moving in and out of the western half of the nation. River men, teamsters, laborers, lawyers, well-to-do businessmen, and others mingled on the city's crowded streets and rude waterfront by day and retired in the evening to neighborhoods ranging from ramshackle to refined. High crime and a shortage of fire-fighting services plagued everyone, an active press reported important events, and libraries, schools, theaters, artists, and others provided emerging social, cultural, and educational amenities.[2]

After arriving in St. Louis, Harney spent considerable time with Mary Mullanphy, fifth daughter of wealthy Missouri entrepreneur John Mullanphy. Two of Mary's older sisters had already exchanged marriage vows with soldiers—Catherine with Maj. Richard Graham and Ann with Maj. Thomas Biddle—and Harney's appearance, outgoing manner, and uniform created appeal. He, on the other hand, recognized the potential benefits of Mary's social and economic status, as army officers often married into wealth.

Aside from their family connections with military service, the couple had little in common. Harney was handsome and self-assured, while Mary was plain and shy. He came from a pioneer Protestant family and had been educated at a frontier college. She came from a well-to-do Catholic family and had been schooled at convents in New Orleans and Europe. He accommodated her heritage in part by converting to Catholicism.[3]

Insofar as is known, Harney never told his bride about Ke-sho-ko and Mary Caroline, but whatever happiness the couple shared early in their marriage did not last. Their divergent backgrounds may have accounted for some of their marital difficulties, but over time financial matters, Harney's fiery temper, and his lengthy absences on military assignment caused most of their problems.

Trouble began almost immediately and seemed incessant during the next three and a half years. In that brief span, Harney sought, received, and bungled a staff position as an army paymaster. During a fit of rage, he committed a murder, and although he evaded legal punishment, he and his family feared for a time that he would not. He also coveted Mary's family wealth and eventually had to rely on a portion of it to escape heavy debt. Harney emerged from all this with two promotions, thanks to political connections and the concept of an expansible army. His experiences illustrate the administrative apparatus required to pay army personnel, how officers could beat the seniority system, and how military service often adversely affected families.

By the time of his wedding, almost eight years had passed since Harney's last promotion, yet among seventy infantry captains he ranked only forty-second in seniority. Realizing that his next regular advancement could be years away, he sought a commission as a lieutenant colonel in the army's only mounted regiment. The War Department had launched this unit the previous year to help with Indian problems and now wanted to reorganize it as the First Dragoons. Congress seemed certain to approve the change, and Harney believed he might get the commission because appointments to new regiments did not depend on seniority. However, the job went to Stephen Watts Kearny. It then occurred to Harney that Andrew Jackson, who had just begun his second term in the White House, might help him find some other alternative. The ambitious captain traveled to Washington in April, called on Jackson, and came away with an appointment as one of fourteen army paymasters. Although this was a staff position that required him to relinquish his place in the regular line of promotion, it carried a major's commission. On average, graduates of the West Point classes of 1821–23 were fifty years old when they made major. Harney had made it nearly twenty years sooner. Equally important, paymasters operated and lived much like civilians, and because the officer he replaced had been stationed in Memphis, Harney thought he might be allowed to reside in St. Louis. That would please Mary and her family.[4]

The new paymaster soon discovered that his position made him a military accountant. He had no qualifications for the work and did not like it. The army had become one of the nation's first major bureaucracies, and the paymasters' branch, like all staff departments, required a high degree of specialization. Assigned to districts, paymasters traversed them with a military escort, paying the troops in cash approximately every two months. Harney's region included Jefferson Barracks, Fort Smith in northwestern Arkansas, and Forts Gibson and Coffee in present eastern Oklahoma. For him, as for most paymasters, traveling proved easier than bookkeeping. With responsibility for up to $100,000 annually, paymasters had to know all army regulations governing the remuneration of both regulars and volunteers of every rank and had to keep balanced accounts of all payments for salaries and all allowances for clothing, subsistence, forage, transportation, and servants. For these efforts, paymasters received an annual salary of about $500. Allowances increased Harney's total compensation to approximately $1,700.[5]

The job went badly from the beginning. Harney received no training and had to post a $20,000 bond before he could take charge of government funds. In July, Paymaster General Nathan Towson sent him copies of military laws, a table of post offices and distances, pay schedules for all personnel grades, the army register for 1833, and a pamphlet on accounting. The paymaster general also sent $70,000 and orders to go at once to Fort Leavenworth on the Missouri River and help Maj. Asher Phillips pay troops there. In addition, Towson informed Harney that when he returned, he would be stationed in Memphis. Disappointed, Harney traveled to Fort Leavenworth with a small guard detail to protect the payroll, a clerk to help with the bookkeeping, and two slaves, Albert and Peter, to perform menial chores. A similar entourage accompanied him on most subsequent pay journeys. After completing the payments at Fort Leavenworth, he returned to St. Louis, paid troops at Jefferson Barracks, and in November forwarded his first accounts to Towson. "I very much fear you will find something wrong in them although I can not," Harney wrote without his usual self-assurance. He also asked Towson to change his assignment from Memphis to St. Louis. The paymaster general denied that request but subsequently transferred him to nearby Jefferson Barracks.[6]

Harney had several weeks with Mary before making his first trip to Forts Smith and Gibson late in December 1833. Unhappily, while he worked those posts, his mother died in Tennessee, and he did not learn about it for several weeks. At Fort Gibson, Harney "had some difference with the officers" about muster rolls and travel allowances for dishonorably discharged soldiers, but he insisted that he understood the pay regulations and made his payments accordingly. Irritated because troop commanders had questioned his decisions, he requested a ruling from the paymaster general on the disputed points. Towson confirmed that he had acted correctly.[7]

Spring brought new problems. In March, two of the men who had signed Harney's bond wanted to end the arrangement, and he had to find new financial backers. That same month, Towson informed him that Paymaster Phillips had erred two years earlier while paying Illinois militiamen for federal service during the Black Hawk War. Instead of compensating the volunteers from the time that they had rendezvoused, Phillips had paid them only for the period between actual enrollment and discharge. Towson ordered Harney to make the additional payment as soon as possible. It proved an aggravating chore. The government owed only about $6,000, but to distribute it, Harney had to visit at least eight Illinois counties. Advertising his itinerary in advance, he had to go to each county seat and check each volunteer's claim against muster rolls and militia officers' sworn statements about which men had been present during the rendezvous. He also had to certify the claims of widows and other survivors of deceased militiamen. And finally, he had to keep all those records separate from his regular army accounts. Harney began disbursing the payments in May, but before he could complete them, malarial "ague and fever" forced him to return home and leave his clerk to finish the task.[8]

In April, Mary's sister Ann had asked the Harneys to stay in her house while she traveled to France. They consented, and in early June, after returning from Illinois and obtaining Towson's permission to move from Jefferson Barracks, Harney joined his wife at the Biddle residence. The couple soon regretted the move, however, for on June 26, Harney brought shame to himself and the entire household. After growing irate with one of the female servants, a slave named Hannah, he seized a piece of rawhide and beat her repeatedly upon her "head, stomach, sides, back, arms, and legs," leaving her severely bruised and bleeding. She died the following day, and a coroner's jury ruled that she "came to her death by wounds inflicted by William S. Harney."[9]

Displaying no remorse about his reprehensible act, he worried only about his own safety. To escape arrest, he fled to the countryside and then proceeded to Washington to seek a transfer from Missouri. Meanwhile, Mary and her family became frightened and embarrassed. Although the press paid little attention to the killing, Mary's brother-in-law, James Clemens Jr., thought the whole community seethed with rage. He wrote Harney on the fourth of July that "if you had remained [in St. Louis] one day longer I feel confident they would not have given you the benefit of a trial." On July 28, 1834, a county grand jury indicted Harney for murder, and Clemens warned him, "Do not come back to this place–depend on it if you were here now it would go hard with you."[10]

Despite the horror of Hannah's death, many people in Harney's day felt little or no anguish for slave and servant victims of such violence. The intense interest that Clemens perceived in the case seemed unusual to him. "Accidents similar to yours," he wrote Harney, "have happened to others here of which no notice was taken either by the people or any of the courts." Clemens "strongly suspect[ed]" that "the excitement" stemmed "principally" from an earlier episode in which Harney threatened to thrash a St. Louis auctioneer "relative to the burning [of] General Jackson's picture." Prior to that event, Clemens wrote, "I am confident" that "if the citizens here were not you[r] friends . . . they were not your enemies."

Accounts of the incident differ, but it occurred after Jackson's 1832 veto of a bill to recharter the Bank of the United States, an institution popular with the St. Louis mercantile community. One day Harney passed in front of an auction house and heard the auctioneer and a crowd of patrons deriding the president and proclaiming that a picture of "the Hero of New Orleans" must be "worth a cent, surely." "One hundred dollars," shouted Harney breaking through the packed room. Astonished, the auctioneer asked him if he were serious. This proved a mistake. Harney handed over his money and his address, then seized the man by the collar, dragged him to the floor, cursed his "damnable impertinence," and threatened to do additional harm if he said anything more. No one ventured to interfere, and Jackson's robust defender released his victim, strode out the door, and continued up the street.[11]

While Harney tarried in the national capital, his problems grew worse. Clemens informed him that the public scandal had so upset Mary that she had become physically ill. In addition, Harney's clerk had trouble completing the Illinois militia accounts. When those pay reports finally reached Washington late and without Harney's signature, the assistant paymaster general complained that "the army and government are greatly prejudiced by . . . delays caused by . . . your private affairs." Before he had fled, Harney had also been soliciting signers for his new bond, and completion of that task fell now to Mary. After the grand jury returned its verdict, however, no one outside the Mullanphy family seemed willing to assist her husband. Fortunately, Clemens suggested that he, three of Mary's sisters, her brother Bryan, and another of her brothers-in-law sign the document, which they did in August.[12]

In the meantime, Towson could not allow Harney to sit idle in Washington waiting for St. Louisians to forget his crime, and so the paymaster general sent him temporarily to Camp Armistead, about fifty miles south of Knoxville, Tennessee, to replace a paymaster who had fallen ill. After completing that assignment and receiving "a great many letters" from Missouri friends claiming that "the excitement is very much abated," Harney decided to return home and try to extricate himself from the legal proceedings. En route he stopped in Nashville and discussed his problem with Jackson. The president "talked to me as he would have done to a son," Harney recorded without elaboration.[13]

Encouraged, he resumed his journey, but on his way up the Mississippi River early in September, he stopped in Kaskaskia, Illinois, at the home of Senator Elias K. Kane, a former Nashville attorney and friend of Ann Biddle. Believing it unsafe for Harney to appear in the city before the circuit court convened in November, Kane and others persuaded him to lay over in Illinois. Mary, still unwell, joined him at Kane's place. From there Harney informed Towson of his lingering predicament and complained that "there is a mistery in this affair which I cannot unravel!" Recalling the auction house incident, he blamed "the lower orders [who are] governed by politicks and religion." They "*hate* the President," he asserted, and "will persecute *any* officer of Government . . . on the slightest pretext." Determined to frustrate his perceived antagonists, Harney asked Towson to leave him assigned to St. Louis "at least sufficiently long to show them that I cannot be frightened out of the country." Having already appointed Paymaster Thomas Wright to Harney's district for the rest of the year, Towson sent the troubled major orders allowing him to remain in St. Louis only until "you have got through your present difficulty." Afterward he must move to Memphis.[14]

Before Towson's letter reached Harney, the circuit court opened in St. Louis. Anxious to present his case before a jury but fearing the judgment of St. Louis residents, Harney entered the city early in November, submitted to arrest, and petitioned for a change of venue "to some county in which a fair trial may be had." On November 5, Circuit Judge L. E. Lawless shifted the case to Franklin County. A few days later, Harney walked the streets of St. Louis for the first time in months, and to his surprise he encountered only "smiles, warm pressures of the hand, and hearty welcomes!!!" While probably never as great as he and his friends imagined, public interest in his case had subsided, but still he had to stand trial. Judge Lawless scheduled the proceeding for November 25, 1834, in Union, a small town about fifty miles to the west. Several subpoenaed witnesses for both the prosecution and the defense failed to appear, though, and the judge postponed the case until the spring term of court.[15]

If those developments calmed Harney, he did not remain that way long. When he received Towson's letter reassigning him to Memphis, he felt "much surprised and mortified" because he had forgotten about requesting a transfer. Angry about Harney's irresolution, the paymaster general informed him that the department could not conduct its affairs "to suit the vacillating wishes of one of its officers." The strain of the year's events showed clearly in Harney's reply. "My mind has been very much harassed in consequence of my private difficulties," he wrote. Thinking only about how Towson viewed his lapse of memory and not about Hannah or Mary, he added, "How foolishly I have acted, how simple." Insisting that "an inactive life" did not agree with him, he asked Towson to return him to duty as soon as possible.[16]

While Harney fretted about his reputation and contemplated his trial, bookkeeping errors continued to plague him. In October, federal auditors had found that during his first year as a paymaster he had disbursed incorrect sums in at least seventeen instances. Although aggravating, those did not constitute serious errors. Most paymasters made similar mistakes just as frequently, and usually the differences could be corrected in the next payment to the soldiers involved. However, in November Harney again could not account for several hundred dollars, and he had to borrow money to reimburse the government.[17]

Meanwhile, the days dragged slowly by as the Harneys waited for the circuit court to open in Union. It finally convened on March 23, 1835. The presiding judge, Charles H. "Horse" Allen, had a reputation in which Harney could take comfort. A loyal Democrat, the robust jurist traveled his circuit with a brace of pistols and delighted in watching street fights. Harney appeared before him and pleaded not guilty. The prosecution and the defense each took a day to present their arguments, calling between them fifteen witnesses, none of whose testimony the court recorded. On March 25, the jury returned a favorable verdict. Although clearly responsible for Hannah's death, Harney stood legally acquitted. White society in the 1830s cared little about the death of a slave, and the murderer proceeded with his life and military career.[18]

As soon as Paymaster General Towson learned the outcome of the trial, he forwarded $42,500 to Harney and sent him to Fort Gibson to pay Col. Matthew Arbuckle's command. Harney hired a new clerk and left St. Louis on May 4. He and his entourage traveled by boat down the Mississippi and then up the Arkansas to Little Rock. From there they continued on horseback through driving rainstorms in the Ozark foothills. After swimming half a dozen swollen streams, they reached Fort Gibson on May 30 only to find that Arbuckle had moved several companies to Fort Towson about 125 miles south. Harney paid the soldiers who remained, and suffering again from malarial chills and fever, he sent his clerk to pay the detached force. However, before the man reached Fort Towson, many of the troops left for field service, and so he returned to Fort Gibson and thence to St. Louis. Arbuckle became "quite displeased," and Harney thought him "unreasonable."[19]

At home, difficulties continued to mount. In July, Harney lost his temper again and challenged an acquaintance to a duel. Although the War Department had prohibited dueling more than twenty years earlier, enforcement had been erratic, and army officers had continued the practice. At least thirteen died in duels between 1815 and 1826. Officers fought few duels after 1827, but the combatants included Mary Harney's brother-in-law, Thomas Biddle. He and Missouri congressman Spencer D. Pettis killed each other in 1831 after arguing over the Bank of the United States, which Biddle's brother, Nicholas, headed. Given Harney's recent difficulties, the experiences of his youth, and the more recent Biddle example, it is not surprising that he stood ready to resolve a dispute in such fashion. Fortunately for both parties, the challenge came to naught.[20]

The summer also brought more financial problems. Harney had made several overpayments at Fort Gibson in June, and now Towson informed him that during three months of the preceding summer he had drawn his salary twice, once from his own allotment and once from another paymaster. "Such mistakes," Towson warned him, "show a negligence in keeping your accounts which, if not corrected, will subject you to serious losses and require unpleasant explanations." Apologetically, in August Harney promised to reimburse the department $500. "Everything which has occur'd" within the past year "appears to me now, like a dream," he wrote, and "even my health has been seriously affected, without my knowledge."[21]

Harney expected to repay his salary overdrafts with money from Mary's inheritance. John Mullanphy had died in 1833, and although litigation had delayed settlement of the estate, Harney believed the remaining problems would be resolved soon. Earlier he had written Towson, "I have, as you know, a handsome fortune almost within grasp." Now he reminded the paymaster general that when "my Father in Laws estate is divided" it "will oblige me greatly." Clearly he considered access to wealth a major benefit of his marriage.[22]

Although his work seemed more and more formidable, Harney traveled to Fort Gibson again in August to disburse $30,000. This time he remained there until all the soldiers had come in from the field. In December, he made a similar jaunt and did not get back to St. Louis until early in February 1836.[23] Shortly afterward, Mary bore their first child, a girl whom they named Ann Biddle in honor of Mary's sister. Coincidentally, Harney sought now to extricate himself from "that infernal pay department." Writing to the secretary of war in April, he explained that three years experience as a paymaster "has taught me that it does not suit me well as the *line*," and he requested a transfer back to regular duty.[24]

With Congress thinking about authorizing a second regiment of dragoons to bolster frontier defenses, Harney persuaded Missouri senator Lewis F. Linn to recommend him as the unit's commander. The position required a colonel's rank, though, and when the bill passed in May, David E. Twiggs got the nomination and the attending promotion from lieutenant colonel.[25] Fortunately, however, the lieutenant-colonelcy of the new regiment went to Arkansan Wharton Rector, who preferred a paymaster's job, and Harney's duties soon enabled him to take advantage of that. In July, Towson ordered Harney to Tennessee to pay volunteers. While en route he got together with Rector, and they agreed to ask Jackson to switch their commissions. On August 15, 1836, they visited the president in Nashville and he granted their request.[26]

Elated by his promotion and the prospect of serving in a mounted unit, Harney returned at once to St. Louis to close his paymaster records. To his dismay he found a deficit of almost $15,000. Appalled by the size of the imbalance and certain that "there is a mistake which I cannot see," he informed Towson of his discovery and asked him not to "make this matter known to more than you can *possibly* help." Harney promised to refund the money as soon as Mary received her patrimony. Meanwhile, he kept perusing his records and located about $4,000 deposited at various disbursement points. He forwarded the money to Washington immediately and pledged to send "as much more as I can *rake* and *scrape*."[27] Harney could not determine how he had mislaid the remaining amount, though, and the Treasury Department began withholding money from his pay. Because he owed more than twenty times his annual salary, stoppage continued until the settlement of John Mullanphy's estate sometime after 1841.[28]

The Treasury directive concluded Harney's frustrating experience as a staff officer. This period had begun well enough with his marriage and promotion to the rank of major. But his violent temper had cost Hannah her life and caused Harney and his wife considerable anguish. Through ineptitude and carelessness, he had performed poorly as an army paymaster, and that, too, had caused family disruption. He had done one thing effectively, though. He had capitalized on political connections and the army's bureaucracy and expansion to promote his career. Many officers took or attempted these routes to advancement, but he used them with extraordinary success. Had he remained in the infantry in 1833 instead of accepting the paymaster's post, he still would have ranked only twenty-first on the infantry captains' seniority list. Now, at age thirty-six, he held the rank of lieutenant colonel.[29] Of equal significance, having escaped jail or worse, identified his wife's money as the solution to his financial problems, and used political influence to advance his career, he had no reason to doubt that he could continue to defy authority and bully people who offended him.

CHAPTER 5

"War to the Rope" in Florida

A FEW MINUTES before daybreak on February 8, 1837, war whoops awakened 250 largely untrained dragoons sleeping behind a hastily constructed log breastwork on the southern shore of Lake Monroe in east central Florida. Springing to arms in early morning fog, they met a hail of bullets from four hundred Seminole warriors under the leadership of Emathla (Philip to whites). One ball slammed into the chest of Capt. Charles Mellon, killing him instantly. Another ploughed into Midshipman John T. McLaughlin, who only a week earlier had helped move the troops by steamboat up the St. John's River from Volusia. Unable to see their attackers clearly in the mist, the inexperienced soldiers fired wildly, hitting little and wasting ammunition. Exasperated officers, including Lt. Col. William S. Harney, exhorted their men to remain calm and choose their targets. Lt. Col. Alexander C. W. Fanning, a small, fiery, one-armed veteran of the War of 1812 and commander of the army detachment, called for fire from a small cannon aboard one of the steamboats, and for three hours soldiers and Indians fought fiercely in the growing dawn.

Emathla had planned to strike the troops a devastating blow and drive them from his country for good, and unaware of his

55

enemy's preparation, he and his warriors had moved quietly into position during the night. Even though he surprised the soldiers, he and his attackers could not penetrate the breastwork and push them back. As the fog lifted, the Indians withdrew with their dead and wounded. When the troops emerged from cover, they found only bloody belts and straps, a pouch of bullets, some knives, and trails made by survivors dragging fallen comrades into the surrounding wilderness of palmetto palms and live oaks. The breastwork had saved the command. Harney had suggested it after helping scout the area, discovering Seminoles nearby, and recognizing the dragoons' exposed position. Fanning reported later that during the fighting Harney had "displayed . . . the greatest boldness & vigor, & inspired his newly enlisted men with great confidence" as they repulsed one of the largest Indian war parties yet assembled in Florida.[1]

Scarcely a month after closing his paymaster books, Harney now performed the type of service for which temperament and experience prepared him best. The country had greater need for him in this role, too. During the mid-1830s the army grew more professional and incurred new challenges. The percentage of West Pointers in the officer corps increased, careers grew longer, officers looked increasingly to Europe for military models, and several newly established, though short-lived, military journals provided service-related news and information. In addition, egalitarian impulses in national society stimulated strong antimilitaristic sentiment that heightened officers' group identity. At this same time, filibustering along the Canadian border and Indian affairs in the Southeast required new vigilance and activity. Florida presented a particularly difficult problem because fighting Indians did not fit easily into some officers' professional self-image. Many sympathized with the Seminoles, and few wanted to serve in a humid, swamp-ridden area they understandably viewed as a death trap. Over the course of the Second Seminole War, 1,466 army regulars, including 215 officers, succumbed in Florida, but only one-fourth of those died in action. Disease claimed most. The combination of all these concerns, along with increasing economic opportunities in civilian life, produced a higher officer resignation rate than at any other time between the end of the War of 1812 and the start of the Civil War.[2]

Whatever others thought, Harney had been more than ready to trade bookkeeping for malarial swamps and Indian fighting. While he completed his accounting chores during the autumn of 1836, other recently appointed officers of the new Second Dragoons Regiment had spread throughout the nation recruiting men for ten companies. By December, more than three hundred had joined the regiment, and the War Department had sent them to Florida to help force the Seminoles to move to Arkansas Territory. Four companies had sailed from New York City on Christmas Day and picked up another en route at Charleston, South Carolina.[3]

Meanwhile, Harney had traveled from St. Louis to Washington in late December and departed there for St. Augustine on the last day of the year. In that stately old Spanish city, where handling military supplies had become a mainstay of the local economy, he had met Brig. Gen. Thomas S. Jesup, commander of all U.S. troops in Florida. Jesup had ordered Harney to take four of the new companies, rendezvous with Fanning and two companies of the Fourth Artillery in Volusia, and then proceed up the St. John's River searching for Emathla, his son, Coacoochee (Wild Cat), and their followers.[4]

This marked the beginning of four long years of notable and often hazardous service for the new dragoon officer. He had arrived just in time to help Jesup pursue a goal—remove the Seminoles—that had eluded three previous commanders for fourteen months. Eventually Jesup failed, too, and the struggle with the Seminoles became the longest, most expensive, and most exhausting of all federal efforts to move eastern Indians to the West.

The conflict lasted from 1835 to 1842, cost the government an estimated $35 to $40 million, and took the lives of an indeterminable number of militiamen, civilians, and Indians in addition to the 1,466 regulars.[5] Frequent changes of command, repeated negotiation, generally undistinguished military activity, and atrocities by both sides characterized the war, but Harney emerged from it as one of the army's most skilled and best known Indian fighters. He also became one of the most brutal and vindictive. Deploring his superiors' continual insistence on using traditional tactics against an enemy proficient in guerilla warfare, he ultimately devised his own riverine methods, and both the army and the navy used them to help bring the war to a close. He also contributed significantly to exploration of the upper St. John's River. Collectively, his experiences illustrated the government's persistent dedication to Indian removal, the ineffectiveness of the army's European-based techniques against unconventional tactics, and its slowness to embrace new methodologies in the face of overwhelming need. His service also exemplified the toll of Florida's climate and topography on military personnel and the ongoing ambivalent attitudes of officers toward native people.

White Americans and Florida Indians had been at odds with each other since before Harney was born. Those early collisions and the Seminole War of 1818 had left a legacy of ill will, and when the United States took possession of East Florida from Spain in 1821, whites already regarded the Seminoles as nuisances. Encroachment upon Indian land exacerbated Indian-white relations but figured less importantly in Florida than in most other eastern regions because whites found much of the peninsula unsuitable for settlement. Slavery also contributed to Indian-white antagonism. In addition to owning slaves and according them greater independence and acceptance than white masters, the Seminoles also harbored runaways. Thus whites viewed the Indians as both an economic and a social menace. Naturally, when war came most Florida blacks fought alongside the Seminoles.[6]

The legality of the government's removal efforts rested upon three treaties and one congressional act. In 1823 thirty-two chiefs, representing only a portion of the territory's native population, signed the Treaty of Moultrie Creek, relinquishing their claims to most of Florida. For this and their promise to help capture and return runaway slaves, they received 4 million acres in the center of the peninsula, $6,000 worth of livestock and agricultural implements, and an annual annuity of $5,000 for twenty years. Despite the treaty, whites in search of fugitive slaves harassed the Indians, and because much of the reservation land proved worthless for cultivation and stock raising, Seminoles preyed on whites for beef cattle and other provisions. In 1830, in response to this and other Indian-white conflicts in the eastern United States, especially the South, Congress passed the Indian Removal Act, requiring all Indians to move west of the Mississippi River.[7] Two years later, fifteen

Seminole leaders signed the Treaty of Payne's Landing, consenting in exchange for food and clothing to go to present Oklahoma and live among the Creeks. Because the chiefs insisted on inspecting that country before moving, the agreement allowed seven to go see it. They made the journey early in 1833 and then put their marks on the Treaty of Fort Gibson, binding their people to emigration.[8]

When the government tried to enforce that compact in 1834, the Indians balked. They did not want to leave their homes or unite with the Creeks. Nevertheless, public insistence on Seminole relocation grew daily, and in October, President Andrew Jackson, the country's leading proponent of removal, directed that "a sufficient military force . . . protect our citizens and remove . . . the Indians" according to "the Stipulations of the Treaty." The army had too few troops in Florida to coerce its native population, though, and so officials conducted new talks in 1835. Those meetings achieved little. Most Seminoles still refused to emigrate, and some resorted to violence. On December 18, about eighty under Osceola (Powell) attacked a baggage train and killed six militiamen in north central Florida. Ten days later, in concerted actions, those and other Seminoles murdered Indian agent Wiley Thompson in that same vicinity and killed all but 3 members of a 108-man artillery detachment under Maj. Francis K. Dade near the Withlacoochee River.[9]

These attacks dashed all hope for peaceful removal. After two hundred regulars and four hundred Florida militiamen under Bvt. Brig. Gen. Duncan L. Clinch clashed with Osceola's men farther down the Withlacoochee on December 21, federal and local authorities prepared for war. Early in 1836 Congress appropriated $600,000 for the undertaking, and volunteers streamed into Florida from all over the South. To conduct the campaign, the War Department first chose Brig. Gen. Winfield Scott, but his clumsy, slow-moving, European-based tactics failed within five months. In a rare move, federal authorities next placed Florida governor Richard K. Call in command. He also failed to defeat the Indians, and so in November 1836 President Jackson and Secretary of War Lewis Cass gave General Jesup the task of trying to dislodge and remove the estimated five thousand Seminole men, women, and children. To do this he had approximately two thousand regular soldiers, some six thousand volunteers, and orders to attack Indian strongholds along the Withlacoochee, occupy the territory between there and Tampa Bay, and erect a line of military posts across the peninsula, from the mouth of the Withlacoochee to Volusia.[10]

In January 1837, Jesup marched one thousand men into the Withlacoochee country, divided them into several detachments, and began a war of attrition. Fanning's thrust up the St. John's with Harney formed part of this campaign. By the end of the month, several detachments had skirmished successfully with Seminoles, and on February 3, Chiefs Otee-Ematular (Jumper), Micanopy, and Abraham, a free black man, agreed to a fifteen-day truce and a council, which Jesup scheduled for February 18 at Fort Dade on the upper Withlacoochee. Although the band that attacked Fanning and Harney at Lake Monroe did not participate in the agreement, Jesup ordered Fanning to pull back to Volusia anyway. Fanning delayed the movement for several days so Emathla would not think he had forced it.[11]

In the meantime, Jesup began to doubt that Otee-Ematular and the others would attend the council. He wondered if the army had pressed them hard enough. "If I were as well acquainted with the country as the hostile Chiefs are," Jesup wrote the secretary of war, "I would undertake to defend it with five hundred men against as many thousands." His concern seemed well founded when only Abraham and two lesser chiefs showed up on the eighteenth. Disappointed, Jesup decided to give the Indians more time, and finally on March 6, Otee-Ematular, Holartochee (Davy), and Yaholoochee, representing Micanopy, appeared. They signed a capitulatory treaty in which they agreed to cease fighting immediately and assemble their people for emigration by April 10. In return, Jesup told them they could take their slaves with them, a concession authorities had previously refused to grant. On March 18, Micanopy came in and signed the agreement, and Jesup declared, "I now for the first time have allowed myself to believe the War at an end."[12]

To ensure that all Seminoles, including Emathla, accepted the Fort Dade agreement, Jesup decided to send Harney back to the Lake Monroe breastworks, now renamed Fort Mellon. If any Indians surrendered there, he was to receive them politely and help them get across the peninsula to the emigration depot at Fort Brooke near Tampa Bay.

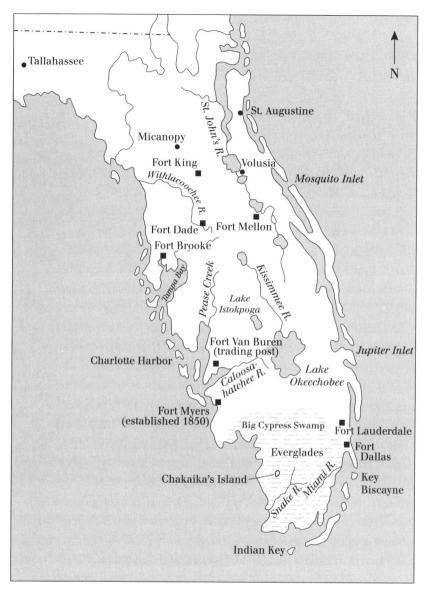

2. Florida in the Seminole Wars, 1837–42, 1856–57

Because another campaign would be necessary if some Indians still refused to leave, he also had orders to build storehouses and gather supplies at Fort Mellon. Preferring an assignment closer to the primary surrender point, Harney requested permission to join Jesup at Fort Dade. He denied the petition and assured his eager subordinate that Fort Mellon would be "important in its bearing upon the Indians." Thus, with his command enlarged by two companies of South Carolina volunteers and a group of friendly Creek Indians under Chief Paddy Carr, Harney moved up the St. John's and reoccupied the Lake Monroe position late in March.[13]

In April he received additional instructions. Now worried about the slowness with which the Indians were coming in, Jesup wanted to force them to go to Tampa Bay for provisions. Accordingly, he ordered troops in central Florida to round up Seminole cattle and drive them to St. Augustine for shipment west. He instructed Harney, in addition, not to give the Indians corn or allow them to purchase anything from the post sutler. Jesup also directed Harney to explore the St. John's River above Lake Monroe, determine whether it could accommodate a steamboat, and report on the region's topography. Such information would prove invaluable if fighting resumed, for as Jesup noted, the army had "as little knowledge of the interior of Florida, as of the interior of China."[14]

In time Harney learned that Jesup had been right about the strategic value of Fort Mellon. More and more Seminoles congregated around the post. Late in April, some Indians sent their cattle to the fort, and during the first week of May, six leaders, including Osceola, Arpiucki (Sam Jones), Coacoochee, and Coi Hadjo, came in with a "great many of their warriors and children." Harney "had a private talk" with them and shared his tent with Osceola, who, along with Coi Hadjo, promised that all would go to Tampa Bay within a few days. Meanwhile, finding many of the native people "literally naked," Harney disobeyed Jesup's instructions and allowed them to purchase shirts from the sutler.[15] These friendly gestures toward the Seminoles provide further evidence that Harney felt both comfortable with Indians and ambivalent about them. He sympathized with their needs but remained committed to removing them. Now, as before and in the future, he did not question repressive federal Indian policies, because he accepted the prevailing white notion that native people stood in the way of progress. When he met Indians in military campaigns, he fought hard and often ruthlessly. At other times, like these, he treated them humanely.

While Jesup waited for the Indians to arrive at Tampa Bay, Harney explored the upper St. John's and found that steamboats could navigate it for fifty miles above Fort Mellon. He also discovered another lake, which now bears his name. By May 8, Micanopy, Otee-Ematular, and a few other chiefs had gone to Fort Brooke, but most of those who had talked to Harney remained near Fort Mellon. Jesup spent the entire month contemplating a renewal of war. On the twenty-fifth, he asked Harney if the troops "might by a rapid and unexpected movement capture the greater part of their women and children." Harney considered such action unnecessary and impossible. He both trusted the chiefs with whom he had talked and doubted that sudden action could succeed. They have "not less than *twenty-five hundred red warriors, good warriors*" in this vicinity, he told Jesup.[16]

Both officers had erred in thinking that the Indians would emigrate peacefully. On the night of June 2, 1837, Osceola and Coacoochee entered the detention camp at Tampa Bay with two hundred warriors and freed approximately seven hundred of their people. That and ensuing public criticism of his leadership almost caused Jesup to resign. He had discovered, as had Atkinson with Black Hawk in 1832, that Indian patterns of authority and leadership did not conform to white conventions and perceptions. "We have laboured under a delusion in regard to the authority of the chiefs," he concluded. "No engagement made" by them "has any binding force unless approved by the heads of families. All the treaties . . . are therefore utterly worthless." Dejectedly he declared, "Emigration I consider impracticable. The Indians, generally, would prefer death to removal from the country, and nothing short of extermination will free us from them." Accordingly he suggested giving them a permanent reservation in Florida. Secretary of War Joel R. Poinsett maintained, however, that if the government did not continue the war, it "would betray great weakness . . . tarnish the honor of our arms . . . [and] violate the sacred obligations . . . of the United States to protect the persons and property of the citizens of Florida." Jesup disagreed, but nevertheless he prepared an extensive fall and winter campaign to drive the Indians from the territory. Florida's wet summer climate would subvert any earlier effort.[17]

While Jesup planned, Harney enjoyed a brief respite. Assigned temporarily to replace ailing Bvt. Brig. Gen. Walker K. Armistead as commander in northeastern Florida, he spent several weeks in St. Augustine, where cool sea breezes, botanical gardens, and coquina-stone houses provided a refreshing change from the upper St. John's wilderness. Harney liked the old city's active social life, and during his stay there he gave a "grand ball" at which "beautiful Minorcan girls" and their partners waltzed to the music of violins and tambourines.[18] Following a brief return to the backcountry in August, he received leave to visit his wife and daughter in St. Louis. He remained there until October, when the adjutant general ordered him back to Florida to join the last of the new Second Dragoon companies, which tramped overland twelve hundred miles from Jefferson Barracks, Missouri.[19]

Before Harney returned, the army captured Emathla, Coacoochee, Coi Hadjo, and Osceola near St. Augustine. They agreed to talk under the protection of white flags, and Jesup, having decided to take the chiefs by any means, violated the truce banners and seized them. Despite the hatred that many whites felt for Indians, this treachery earned Jesup widespread criticism outside Florida and made a martyr of Osceola, who died in prison a few months later. Nevertheless, the desperate general used the same tactic later to grab Micanopy and several other chiefs. Accusations of trickery mattered little. Results counted more.[20]

By October, Jesup had nearly nine thousand men in Florida, including almost half the regular army and about four thousand volunteers from other states. Orchestrating a massive sweep through the heart of the peninsula, he sent Col. Zachary Taylor with the First Infantry Regiment, several additional companies, and a group of Missouri volunteers to the Kissimmee River with orders to push south to Lake Okeechobee. Smaller detachments would join them there after moving inland from each coast just above the Everglades. Jesup split his main force into four columns and ordered them to scour the country on both sides and south of the St. John's River. Bvt. Brig. Gen. Abraham Eustis commanded the principal column of approximately two thousand men, who moved up the river in boats. Harney preceded them with a small party early in November, built a wharf on Lake Monroe, and reoccupied Fort Mellon for use as a supply depot. Clearly happy being active again, he rode "through the neighborhood" searching for signs of Indians. This characteristically bold but unnecessary risk, which he could have delegated, turned up only the trail of two or three men whom he concluded were "spies no doubt."[21]

Supplying Jesup's large command proved a massive undertaking. The army had to move rations, forage, ammunition, horseshoes, blacksmith's tools, axes, scythes, grinding stones, rope, tents, oil stoves, and myriad other supplies into the swampy wilderness, and in December Jesup assigned this chore to the Second Dragoons. He put Colonel Twiggs and most of the dragoons to work building a wagon road south from Fort Mellon and ordered Harney to take one company of regulars and two militia units and push the supply boats as far up the St. John's as possible. Recognizing that Harney would prefer to forge ahead untethered and pursue Indians, Jesup assured him, "I consider this duty of infinitely more importance to the success of the Army than any you could perform in the field." The work occupied Harney constantly for several weeks as the Indians retreated steadily before Jesup's advancing columns.[22]

Meanwhile, Taylor moved inland from Tampa Bay with 1,000 men. They marched down the west bank of the Kissimmee River, reached the northeast shore of Lake Okeechobee, and there encountered 500 Seminole warriors. On December 25, 1837, the soldiers engaged the Indians in one of the biggest and most heated battles of the war, and although the troops suffered 26 dead and 112 wounded, by the twenty-eighth they had captured 180 Indians, 600 head of cattle, and 100 horses. Less than three weeks later, Taylor's forces rendezvoused with Jesup's on the eastern side of the lake, and together they continued to pursue the Seminoles.[23]

On January 24, 1838, Jesup's consolidated command discovered an estimated two to three hundred Indians hiding in the dense vegetation of a hammock on the Lockahatchee River, a small stream flowing into the ocean at Jupiter Inlet. He ordered an immediate attack, and this time Harney got a chance to fight. While artillerymen blasted the thicket with grapeshot and hissing Congreve rockets, Harney's dragoons and a group of Tennessee volunteers charged the Indians on foot through the black water of a cypress swamp. When the Tennesseans on his left drew most of the enemy fire, Harney decided to take "a portion of the dragoons," swim across a creek on his right, and strike the Indians' rear. His fifty or so men labored through the water, lost half their ammunition, and exhausted themselves before they reached the opposite shore. Only seventeen had enough stamina left to rush the Seminoles, but Harney dashed forward anyway. This surprise assault, combined with the fire that the volunteers poured against the Indians' front, forced them out of the hammock, but they eluded capture by fleeing into the Everglades.[24]

Following this Battle of Lockahatchee, Eustis, Twiggs, Harney, and several other senior officers went to Jesup and suggested that he end the war by allowing the Seminoles to remain in southern Florida. Removing them seemed an impossible task not worth the effort required to accomplish it. Although the secretary of war had vetoed this idea once already, Jesup agreed to think about presenting it again. On February 8, 1838, he conferred with Chiefs Halleck Hadjo and Tuskegee, and when they told him they wanted peace and would welcome any part of the territory, "however small," Jesup recommended that Poinsett abandon "*immediate* emigration." If you do not, the veteran officer contended, "the war will continue for years to come." He suggested that the government restrict the Indians to southwestern Florida and build a trading post for them at Charlotte Harbor on the Gulf Coast. Strong garrisons there and at Tampa Bay could easily prevent depredations, he thought. As before, Poinsett declared that removal "is the law of the land" and refused to accept Jesup's counsel.[25]

By the end of March, Jesup had captured nearly twenty-four hundred Seminoles since assuming command and had driven as many more into the extreme southern part of the territory. Some of these had moved back to the middle of the peninsula, however, and resumed hostilities. Weary of what now seemed a useless struggle, Jesup asked to be relieved, and in April the War Department replaced him with Taylor, who had been breveted a brigadier general after the Battle of

Okeechobee. Used frequently either to recognize meritorious service or bypass the seniority system, or both, brevets were honorary promotions, and sometimes they caused jealously and bickering, but not in this instance.[26]

Before Jesup relinquished command, he ordered Harney to take two hundred men to Fort Lauderdale, relieve Col. James Bankhead, slip into the Everglades via the New River, and pursue Arpiucki's band. This assignment gave Harney an opportunity to test Samuel Colt's new multichambered revolving rifles. Like most officers, he took a keen interest in new military equipment, and with his usual persistence, he had pestered Jesup and Poinsett until they agreed to purchase fifty of the new weapons and let him experiment with them. Anxious to secure approval for their universal use, Colt delivered the rifles personally in March.[27]

On the thirtieth of that month, Harney and his newly armed detachment set out from Jupiter Inlet and traveled three days under a scorching sun through sticky, drying marshes. Having found little drinkable water, the soldiers arrived at Fort Lauderdale on April 2 with their throats dry and their commander in a foul temper. Unwittingly, Bankhead had captured several Indians and scared off others whom Harney had hoped to use as scouts, and he feared that volunteers at the fort would hinder him further. "I have no faith in them," he told Jesup, and "I have force enough without them." Harney had now observed volunteers in two Indian wars, and like most other regular officers, he viewed them as undisciplined and undependable. Never mind that in theory they helped make the army expansible in accordance with need. Their popularity among civilians despite generally poor performance offended the regulars' sense of professionalism.[28]

Harney expected to pursue Arpiucki in boats, but the glades near the fort proved too dry. A collaborating chief told him, however, that he could reach the Indians' hideaway from south of the Miami River. Consequently, on April 15, anxious now to complete his mission and "leave this infernal country," Harney sent his Colt-armed dragoons by steamer to Fort Dallas near the Miami's mouth. The rest of the command proceeded overland, scouting as they went. At Fort Dallas, Harney found only fifteen assorted sailboats and other craft, barely enough to transport one hundred men, but he remained determined to go after the Indians. Jesup had speculated earlier that they would try to avoid him by retreating deeper into the glades, but undaunted, Harney believed that if the Indians could cross them, "I can do it also, and will."[29]

On the night of April 22, Harney, fifty artillerymen, and the dragoons sailed twenty miles down the coast and spent the next day searching unsuccessfully for Indian trails along the shore and in a tangled mangrove swamp. On the twenty-fourth, they found fresh tracks leading southwest and followed them on foot for several hours across boot-piercing coral rock and rugged saw grass swamps. About noon they discovered seventy-five Seminole men camped with their families in the edge of a pine barren. Upon spotting the soldiers, the Indians abandoned hunting bows, cooking utensils, blankets, and other gear and ran for their lives. Harney divided his force into three squads, sent two of them around the Indians' flanks to prevent their escape, and charged straight ahead with the other group. For two and a half hours, the soldiers scrambled after the Indians, pausing only occasionally to exchange shots with them from behind pine trees. Harney raced along with his men, firing his own Colt rifle. The morning's trek inland had already exhausted the troops, however, and eventually the Indians outran them and vanished into the wilderness. Although the soldiers captured a woman who confirmed this was Arpiucki's band, Harney correctly evaluated the clash as "like most other Indian fights in Florida ... little harm was done on either side." His only satisfaction lay in having demonstrated that he could find Indian camps in the Everglades.[30]

Recognizing that he could do no more now, Harney gave his men two days' rest, then trudged back to the coast and proceeded to Key Largo at the southeastern tip of the peninsula. He thought he could find an inland water route there and continue the chase, but the effort proved futile. Thus, on April 29 he returned to Fort Dallas, where, unable to procure more boats and much-needed shoes for his troops, he abandoned the search. He refused to concede defeat, though, for now he knew the type of tactics required for successful pursuit into the Everglades. Unaware that two years would pass before he entered that morass again, he told Jesup, "I have no doubt but I can catch these Indians if I can get Boats and a good guide and Pilot."[31]

When General Taylor assumed command in Florida in May 1838, the War Department reassigned some of his forces to the Canadian border and the West. Colonel Twiggs and six companies of the Second Dragoons went to Oklahoma, but Harney remained behind with the other four. Taylor spent the summer preparing a fall campaign while trying to drive the Seminoles from the north central portion of the peninsula. Harney led several reconnaissance parties between the lower Withlacoochee and St. John's Rivers but found no Indians.[32] This duty proved exhausting, though, and having been in the field for a year, Harney asked for and got four months leave. Late in August he went home to St. Louis again, this time to see little Elizabeth Brown Harney, his newly born second daughter.[33]

By the time Harney returned to Florida early in January 1839, Taylor had decided to divide the territory north of the Withlacoochee into twenty-mile squares and place a twenty-man garrison of regular troops in each. This and his earlier decision to dismiss most of the territorial militia upset Floridians, who complained that his measures would not end the conflict. Secretary of War Poinsett grew so exasperated that in March he decided to accept Jesup's advice and postpone removal. Accordingly, he sent Gen. Alexander Macomb to Florida with instructions to arrange a truce and do whatever else might be necessary to stop the fighting. The uniqueness of Macomb's participation underscored Poinsett's frustration. This marked only the second time since the reorganization of the army in 1821 that the commanding general, who normally acted only as the principal coordinator of army administration, had assumed a field command.[34]

On April 5, 1839, Macomb arrived at Garey's Ferry southwest of Jacksonville, conferred with Taylor, and immediately sent out runners asking Seminole chiefs to attend a council at Fort King on May 1. Macomb also ordered Harney, then in southeastern Florida with "knowledge of hostile parties" there, to invite those Indians to the meeting. Assembling the chiefs took longer than Macomb expected, but by the time the council convened on May 18, Harney had arrived with several, including Chitto Tustenuggee (Snake Warrior), a representative of Arpiucki. As the dignitaries sat around an American flag spread over the ground, Macomb arranged an unwritten peace agreement. In addition to requiring both sides to stop fighting, it permitted the Seminoles to remain unmolested below Pease Creek, roughly the southwestern quarter of the peninsula, "until further arrangements could be made." The agreement also required the army to build a trading post there. On May 20, Macomb proclaimed a cessation of hostilities and returned to Washington confident that now the government could resolve the Seminole question peacefully. The *Washington Globe* considered it done. The paper announced that the Indians had been pacified and no more blood would be spilled.[35]

Macomb had made two grave errors, however. First, he had purposely not mentioned emigration during the council, thus allowing the Indians to perceive the arrangement as permanent. Second, he had failed to consider public opinion and the disunity of the Seminoles, many of whom had not been represented at the conference. Both mistakes helped destroy the accord. When announced publicly, the Fort King agreement enraged Floridians, who thought the government had given up on removal. The *Tallahassee Floridian* denounced the armistice as insane and called on its subscribers to shoot Indians on sight, while the *St. Augustine News* urged whites to unite in protest. Then suddenly in mid-June the papers printed excerpts of official correspondence revealing that the government considered the agreement temporary. Whites welcomed this news, but it alarmed the Seminoles.[36]

Meanwhile, despite the public outcry, the army implemented the agreement. Macomb wanted the trading post built at either Charlotte Harbor or some point on the Caloosahatchee, the southernmost river on Florida's Gulf Coast. At Fort King, Chitto Tustenuggee and several other Indians had asked to have Harney stationed in the Pease Creek district with them. The request seemed logical, as he had treated the Seminoles kindly at Fort Mellon two years earlier, and so Macomb ordered him to choose a site and erect the post. After a trip to Key Biscayne, where he held cordial talks with Arpiucki and secured the old chief's promise to abide by the peace agreement, Harney proceeded to the Caloosahatchee with six dragoons early in June. There, approximately fifteen miles upriver on the north shore, he selected a site in a pine forest, and being a loyal Jacksonian Democrat, he christened it Fort Van Buren in honor of the president. He then continued on to

Tampa Bay, where he asked Taylor for two companies for a guard detail. Much to Harney's chagrin, Taylor refused to assign troops to the trading post until the Indians arrived there. Knowing that the general had been instructed to provide assistance, Harney took offense at Taylor's unexpected brusqueness and complained to Macomb that it seemed a deliberate attempt to undermine the peace.[37]

Left on his own, Harney sent for twenty-two unmounted dragoons whom he had left at Key Biscayne, started building a store at Fort Van Buren, and chose James B. Dallam of Tampa Bay as post trader. Between late June and mid-July, while Harney traveled back and forth from the Caloosahatchee to Key Biscayne and Tampa Bay on various errands, Indians began to frequent the tiny new post. They traded, seemed friendly, and voiced satisfaction with the truce.[38] Thus everything seemed in order on July 21, when Harney returned from one of his trips and decided to go early the next morning to Sanibel Island, near the mouth of the Caloosahatchee, and shoot wild hogs for the soldiers' mess. An avid hunter, Harney chased swine throughout the day before returning exhausted about 10:00 P.M. During his absence, he had left the usually dependable Sergeant Bigelow in charge, and having faith in him, Harney carelessly gave in to fatigue. He strode directly to his tent, took off his boots and pants, and fell into bed.

At dawn on July 23, 1839, rifle shots and yelling Indians awakened the sleeping camp. Harney bounded to his tent door and saw bedlam. Some 160 warriors, led principally by Chakaika, chief of the so-called Spanish Indians, descendants of a Seminole precursor group in Florida, and Holato Mico (Billy Bowlegs), swarmed over the post. Amid shouts of "Run to the water," most soldiers raced to the river, where they made poor targets. They could not escape, though, for Indians lined both banks. Wearing only his underclothes and shirt, Harney dashed out of his tent just as several attackers entered it from the rear. He started to join his men in the river but saw that they had no weapons. A corporal reported later that another noncommissioned officer, probably Bigelow, had neglected to pass out ammunition for the dragoons' Colt rifles. Realizing that he could not help two dozen unarmed soldiers against scores of Indians but determined not "to die without making a struggle of some sort," Harney ran into the woods.

After pausing to blacken his face and underclothes with mud to help avoid detection, he walked to the coast, treading gingerly in his stocking-feet through sharp-bladed saw palmettos. En route he met a private who had also escaped, and together they located a canoe that Harney had left at the mouth of the river. They put to sea in the craft and soon hailed a small sloop in which seven dragoons and two sutler's assistants had fled during the early moments of the raid.

Thus reunited with some of his troops, Harney returned to the post after dark to survey the damage. As Indians slept on the opposite shore, he and the eight dragoons, with only two guns among them, crept quietly into the ransacked camp. There they found buzzards roosting in the trees above the mutilated bodies of six soldiers and two civilians, one of them Dallam. Two weeks later, a burial party found two more survivors and five other bodies, and the death toll rose to sixteen, including three men whom the Indians carried away and killed elsewhere. Meanwhile Harney's poking around in the dark succeeded only in arousing the sleeping Indians across the water, and so he and his ragged little party made their way swiftly downriver and took the sloop to Key Biscayne.[39]

The attack incensed Harney, and he remained that way for a long time. He could not have been angrier even if he had known that years later Holato Mico would boast, "O, yes–I make him run like hell, one time!" Harney could not understand why the Indians had broken the Fort King agreement and attacked the post. Ignoring his own culpability for not checking camp defenses, he felt certain he had not been at fault, and he did not intend to take the blame. Both privately and in his official reports, he maintained that the attack would not have occurred if Taylor had furnished troops to protect the trading house, or if Bigelow, who had been told to post sentinels and remain alert, had followed orders. Eventually Harney concluded that Sandy, a black interpreter at the trading post, had incited the assault, but that does not seem plausible, for reportedly the attackers killed him, too. Significant responsibility for the disastrous incident rested with Poinsett and Macomb. They failed to recognize that the peace accord could not succeed unless every group of native people in Florida accepted it, and then they misled those who did. Chakaika had not attended the Fort King talks, but regardless of whether he approved of the peace arrangements, news that the whites considered the removal reprieve temporary created motivation for revenge.[40]

The Caloosahatchee River attack wrecked the uneasy truce and dashed hope for a peaceful settlement of the war, now nearly four years in progress. Within days, fighting resumed throughout Florida, and on August 3, the *St. Augustine News* proclaimed, "The War Renewed!" Immediately Taylor launched another campaign to drive the Seminoles out of settled areas, and the War Department sent Twiggs and his six Second Dragoon companies back to the peninsula, authorized additional militiamen, and approved experiments with Cuban bloodhounds to track the Indians.[41]

While the fighting increased north of the Everglades, Harney remained at Key Biscayne and commanded the southeastern military district. Humiliated by the Caloosahatchee calamity, he grew rancorous and contemplated revenge of his own. In an effort to "get the Indians at war with each other," he held a series of talks with Chitto Tustenuggee and Arpiucki in August and September and promised them meat and corn if they would help him capture the leaders of the attack on Fort Van Buren. For several weeks, while feigning interest in Harney's proposal, the two chiefs and their followers loitered around Key Biscayne and Fort Lauderdale. Then late in September, Chitto Tustenuggee lured two soldiers and an interpreter into his camp, ambushed them, and disappeared into the Everglades. This sent the volatile Harney into a rage. He had held his last council with a Florida Indian. Writing heatedly to Taylor, he declared, "Our humane efforts to save a portion of the Indians from extermination have only led to another exhibition . . . of malice and disregard of their pledges. . . . There must be no more talking—they must be hunted down as so many wild beasts. . . . Let every one taken be hung up in the woods to inspire terror in the rest."[42] His wrath reflected both the growing frustration of many officers with the war and the way in which their attitudes toward Indians could waiver according to circumstances.

Despite his agitation, Harney also offered several well-reasoned suggestions about how the army could be more effective. He declared that too many officers, especially captains, had absented themselves on leave and detached service, thus placing too much responsibility on lieutenants "too green to command." Ending "the separation of the staff from the line" and developing "a provision for superannuated officers," he asserted, "would remedy this evil and have a highly beneficial influence upon the whole army." So would, he suggested, implementing a system of "awards and punishments" to "insure the removal of the drones, and encourage the active and enterprising to make great efforts to gain distinction." He also pointed out, like Jesup earlier, that the army lacked adequate maps of Florida and "very few of our superior officers understand the detail of Topography." Thus Harney recommended that the War Department send "half the corps of Topographical Engineers" to map the entire peninsula. Additionally he proposed that troops receive training and equipment for catching Indians, not merely fighting them. He advocated giving soldiers athletic exercise, target practice, instruction in woodsmen's skills, and dozens of strong, light canoes with which to pursue Indians in the Everglades. With eight to ten "light, fast boats," he declared, the army could patrol the southern coastal waters and prevent the Seminoles from trading with West Indian fishermen. The navy had been trying to blockade the coast for several years, frequently under army supervision, but Harney considered "Naval cooperation" an "unproductive business."[43]

Harney had correctly identified some key problems and unmet needs that slowed the army's overall efficiency and hindered its Florida operations in particular. Large numbers of line officers served, as he once had, in staff positions on detached service. Lack of a retirement system kept senior officers on duty far too long. New officers received little or no instruction in tactics that had practical application in Florida, and enlisted men received no physical training or shooting instruction. The army had neither trained nor equipped its troops for guerilla warfare. And the Seminoles had been obtaining guns and ammunition from offshore smugglers for years. Despite his lack of formal military training and his ineptitude as a desk soldier, Harney had good insights into how the army functioned and might improve. He also held a heroic view of officership that emphasized physical courage and achievement in battle.[44]

Unfortunately, Harney's recommendations went unheeded, and illness forced him temporarily to give up his search for Chakaika and Holato Mico. Having been unwell for several weeks, Harney began coughing up blood, and army doctors advised him to go to Cuba for a lengthy recuperation. Coincidentally, the medical staff in Florida at that time included Harney's brother Benjamin, who had arrived in August and now served as director. The War Department granted Harney an immediate furlough, and he sailed to Havana aboard the steamer *William Gaston* early in December. As he left, the *St. Augustine News* proclaimed, "No man has more willingly encountered every peril to close this war. Brave, almost to recklessness . . . he never ordered where he would not lead. We shall rejoice to be the chronicler of his return." Mary and the children joined him in Cuba, and with rest his health improved. Late in May 1840, he returned "fresh and vigorous" to Florida and found that little had changed except that Taylor had resigned his command and Walker K. Armistead had replaced him.[45]

Trying a different strategy, General Armistead established a line through Fort King across the top one-third of the peninsula, assigned militiamen to defend north of it, and sent the regulars south to harass the Seminoles and destroy their crops. This kept Harney and several companies of dragoons busy throughout the summer. They ranged from Fort King to Fort Mellon, pursuing small hunting parties and burning Indian corn, pea, and potato fields. Harney wanted to dress his men in Indian clothing to help avoid detection during their patrols, but Armistead would not allow it.[46]

As the weeks passed, thoughts of the Caloosahatchee River attack continued to gnaw at Harney. His frustration mounted in August, when Chakaika and his warriors killed horticulturist Henry Perrine at Indian Key, thirty miles off Florida's southern tip.[47] Harney could do nothing at that moment, but he began forming a daring plan. In November, he obtained permission to go to Key Biscayne "in consequence of indisposition." Shortly after arriving there he learned that a young black man then in military confinement could lead him to Chakaika's camp. In return for his services, Harney promised the man, named John, one dollar a day and his freedom. Next, the enterprising dragoon looked around for boats and eventually obtained sixteen canoes from a marine detachment on Indian Key. Finally, he wrangled sixty-nine Third

Artillerymen, twenty-one Colt-armed Second Dragoons, and four officers from Forts Lauderdale and Dallas. On December 6, Armistead,
unaware of his supposedly ill officer's activities, ordered him to return
north "if your health will permit." But Harney had already gone after
Chakaika.[48]

A cold rain fell as he and his cobbled command launched their canoes into the Miami River and set out through the Everglades on the
evening of December 4, 1840. The adverse weather continued through
the following day, as the men spent several hours dragging their craft
through mud and grass. For a time Harney questioned John's reliabil-
ity, but eventually he led the troops to a half-mile-wide spot of dry land
covered with papaya trees. The party camped here, and December 6
dawned beautiful and sunny. Again disregarding Armistead, Harney
and the other men in lead craft disguised themselves as Indians, and
the expedition proceeded southwest through a "boundless expanse of
saw-grass and water, occasionally interspersed with little islands."
Two days later they saw their first Indians—two warriors and their families also traveling in canoes. Harney ordered Lt. James Rankin to pursue them with four canoe-loads of troops and then climbed a tree to
watch the chase. The soldiers "made their boats fairly jump out of the
water," and as they overtook the Indians, Harney "made the Island ring
with his cheering." Rankin's men caught all eight Indians, and with the
women and children watching, Harney did as he had vowed. He
hanged the two men "to the top of a tall tree." While neither justifiable
nor in accord with military policy, these executions did not constitute
an isolated incident. In subsequent years, particularly in the Pacific
Northwest, several commanders hanged Indian captives as examples
to other native people. However, few, if any, officers earned as much
notoriety as Harney for the cruel and summary punishment.[49]

With the gruesome deed done, John volunteered that Chakaika's Island lay nearby, and Harney decided to strike it at daybreak on December 10. Rain and a moonless night prevented the troops from
reaching the place until well after sunrise, but still they surprised the
Indians. Chakaika was chopping wood when the soldiers crept to the
edge of his camp and began firing. Aghast, the chief dropped his ax and
fled, but Private Calvin Hall raced after him, dropped him with a rifle

shot, and took his scalp. In the meantime the other troops killed another Indian and captured seven others. The fighting spread then to another island four miles away, but the native people on it escaped and warned their comrades elsewhere that soldiers had entered the glades. Shortly afterward the melee subsided. While the troops rested, Harney went back to the first island to recover Chakaika's body, and at the edge of the water he captured the chief's wife and children as they tried to slip away in a canoe. Late in the evening, before them and the other captives, he hanged two more warriors and sadistically strung Chakaika's body up alongside them.

Having penetrated deeper into the Everglades than any previous military expedition and secured his revenge on Chakaika, Harney now struck a course south to the Gulf. For the next four days, the troops threaded their way around other islands and down the Shark River, capturing more Indians along the way. After reaching the Gulf of Mexico on December 15, they proceeded leisurely on to Indian Key, where on the twentieth they obtained a sloop and started for Key Biscayne with thirty-six captives.[50]

Although the Second Seminole War was far from over, Floridians celebrated Harney's expedition lavishly. To the accompaniment of band music and cannon salutes, the citizens of St. Augustine illuminated their market house with a giant transparency inscribed "Lieut. Col. Wm. S. Harney–Everglades–No More Treaties–Remember the Caloosahatchee!–War to the Rope." The St. Augustine News, most likely recalling Harney's meetings with Osceola and the other chiefs at Fort Mellon in the spring of 1837, noted that early in the war Harney "evinced . . . a forbearance and humanity to those of the enemy who fell into his hands, which was considered by many as carried to an excess." But the attack on the Caloosahatchee had "opened his eyes," the paper declared, and his expedition to the Everglades represented "a meritorious act" by a "man who knows his duty to his country, and is not afraid to perform it." Even Armistead seemed pleased, and Secretary of War Poinsett called the news "highly gratifying."[51]

Harney wasted no time basking in this praise, for he had unfinished business. He wanted to kill or capture Arpiucki and Holato Mico, too. Unaware that Armistead had sent him orders not to reenter the glades,

Harney began organizing a second expedition. On this one, despite his low regard for joint ventures with the navy, he cooperated with naval forces. Upon learning of Harney's success and that he had a reliable guide, Lt. John Rodgers and John T. McLaughlin, long recovered from his February 1837 wound at Fort Mellon and now a navy commander, asked to join him. Accordingly on the evening of December 31, 1840, with McLaughlin leading the naval detachment and Harney commanding overall, 240 dragoons, artillerymen, sailors, and marines left Fort Dallas in five- and ten-man canoes and started across the Everglades toward the Big Cypress Swamp on the opposite side of the peninsula. To avoid detection they traveled only after dark, kept their canoes in single file about twenty paces apart, and communicated with whistled signals. These measures slowed their progress but apparently prevented the Seminoles from discovering them as soon as they might have otherwise. After three laborious nights the expedition found Chitto Tustenuggee's camp, but the Indians had abandoned it a short time earlier. Harney sent scouts in several directions, and during the next few days his forces killed or captured ten warriors. For several more days the soldiers, sailors, and marines searched for Arpiucki, and although they found his camp, too, he also eluded them. When that became clear, Harney returned with the soldiers to Fort Dallas, but the sailors and marines continued to the western coast and became the first white men to traverse the full width of the Everglades. The navy had been trying unsuccessfully to penetrate the area for more than six months, and so although Harney had not found either Holato Mico or Arpiucki, he had demonstrated to both services how to operate effectively in the swampy region.

During the next nine months, the navy increased its fleet of canoes in Florida to one hundred, double the previous number. Between October 1841 and April 1842, sailors and marines using Harney's riverine tactics crisscrossed the Everglades on numerous expeditions. They captured few Seminoles, but they destroyed villages and kept the Indians moving constantly. Through these efforts the navy significantly improved its ability to fight on inland waterways and established procedures for use in future wars.[52]

Meanwhile, the Second Seminole War dragged on with yet another change of command. In May 1841, after offering principal chiefs $5,000 each, lesser chiefs $200, and warriors $30 and a rifle if they would surrender for emigration, Armistead gave way to Col. William J. Worth. He continued to press Indian bands throughout the peninsula, and when Coacoochee agreed to leave, many other Seminole leaders followed his example. By the summer of 1842, federal officials believed that no more than three hundred native people remained in Florida, and on August 14, Worth announced that "hostilities with the Indians within this territory have ceased." By then the army had shipped almost three thousand Seminoles to Arkansas Territory.[53]

For Harney, the Second Seminole War ended long before Worth's announcement. On February 20, 1841, he received three months' leave, which the War Department extended subsequently to eighteen months because of recurring illness.[54] Still, he had spent almost four years in Florida. During that time he had demonstrated skill, daring, and ingenuity as a combat commander and tactician and contributed to such success as the army had in the war. He had also won widespread public and professional acclaim for both his military achievements and his revenge-driven brutality against native people. The citizens of St. Augustine had lauded him, the Florida legislature had voted him a sword, and the War Department had breveted him a colonel. Even Stephen Watts Kearny, with whom Harney had clashed at Fort Belle Fontaine, felt compelled to acknowledge his efforts, albeit grudgingly. Although Harney "has no more brains than a Grey hound," Kearny wrote another officer, "he has done more to impress the Indians with a fear of us and the desperate state of their cause, than all other commanders of Corps or Detachments."[55]

CHAPTER 6

The Road to Mexico City

"GOD DAMN your mean cowardly soul, you contemptible son-of-a-bitch," Lt. Col. William S. Harney roared at the soldier. "I knew you were a God-damned cowardly rascal." In midsummer 1844, long inactivity and isolation at Fort Washita, in present south central Oklahoma, combined to fuel Harney's vicious temper and bode ill for anyone who crossed him. Pvt. D. G. Williamson escaped with a tongue-lashing. Others did not fare as well.

On July 5 Musician J. H. O'Brien and Pvt. Sylvanus Bean insulted their supervising officer and refused to dig a latrine. Declaring, "I will put a stop to that," Harney strode to the work site carrying a cane. As soon as Bean and O'Brien saw him, they resumed their cursing and complaining, with the musician taking the lead. It proved a mistake. Harney seized O'Brien by the hair, threw him to the ground, and beat him repeatedly with the walking stick. The soldier spent a week recuperating in the post infirmary. Bean, who had protested less vigorously, received only slightly better treatment. Harney shackled him with an iron ball, chain, and spiked collar and assigned him twenty-seven days of hard labor.

Just two years earlier Winfield Scott, now commanding general of the army, had prohibited cruel and unusual punishment for enlisted men, although he did not rule out striking them in self-defense or putting them in irons. Many officers routinely disregarded Scott's order and continued administering whatever chastisement they could conceive. Harney devised a special punishment for troops who brawled. He goaded them into fistfights with one of several pugilistic slaves he kept at the post. However, when he provoked a fight between Musician Richard Shannon and a slave named Henry, the soldier got the best of it, and Harney displayed his ungovernable wrath before the entire garrison. From his perch on a three-foot-high porch, he called Shannon over, cursed him violently, and gave him a wooling in the presence of several witnesses. Wooling–grabbing a man by his ears and alternately yanking each up and down–had been one of Zachary Taylor's favorite punishments during the Second Seminole War, and usually officers got away with it. But this time Harney did not. His series of outbursts launched a long string of miscalculations and resulting imbroglios that nearly derailed his career before he managed, largely with the aid of luck and politics, to wiggle out of them.[1]

Harney's inactivity had commenced early in 1841, when he returned to Havana for his second health-related furlough within a year. Eventually his leave stretched to eighteen months and made a poor transition between public adulation in Florida and a series of routine and unexciting assignments in the Southwest. In part because the probate court had his father-in-law's estate under review, Harney spent some of this time in Missouri. Like many prominent St. Louisians, including other members of the Mullanphy family, Mary Harney had a large home in the fertile Florissant Valley about twelve miles north of the city. Named Harneywold, it overlooked the Missouri River and featured large maple trees shading a long access road. Often on summer Sundays well-turned-out gentlemen and fashionably dressed ladies assembled at neighbors' homes for news, gossip, and feasts of rum omelets and chicken gumbo served outdoors, and the Harneys joined those who entertained in this fashion.

After the court adjourned in December 1841, Harney followed a physician's advice and returned to Cuba, where he remained until March.[2] When he reported for duty in Florida, he found the Second Seminole

War almost over and the Second Dragoons ordered to Louisiana. He also learned that Congress was considering a bill to dismount the regiment. With the fighting winding down in Florida and tensions easing along the Canadian border, opposition to a standing army loomed large. Confident that he could dissuade the lawmakers, Harney obtained another leave of absence and went to Washington to lobby. His efforts proved futile, and on August 23, Congress reduced the army to its pre-1838 levels and converted the Second Dragoons to a foot unit. Disappointed, Harney used the rest of his furlough to return home and see his son, John Mullanphy Harney, born March 29, 1842.[5]

During the summer, Senator Lewis F. Linn tried to help Harney land the command of Fort Leavenworth. In addition to being nearer to his family, that assignment would have enabled him to follow the probate court more closely. The attempt failed, though, and frustrated, Harney reported to Baton Rouge Barracks, where he had received his first commission twenty-four years earlier. Returning now as a hero of the nation's longest Indian war, he would win even greater laurels during America's first foreign war by aiding Winfield Scott's triumphant march from Veracruz to Mexico City in 1847. The intervening years of 1843–46, however, proved anything but glorious. Harney's violent temper, arrogant manner, and opportunistic bent entangled him in almost constant controversy in Indian Territory, Texas, and northern Mexico, marred the professional accolades he had received in Florida, and for a time raised serious questions about his continued ability to command. These episodes demonstrated dramatically both his shortcomings and the contentious nature of the officer corps in general.

In Louisiana, Harney served briefly with his brother Benjamin before being assigned to command Fort Washita in June 1843. The army had established this post on the left bank of the Washita River just thirty miles inside the American border to prevent roving bands of Texas Indians from preying on the more sedentary Chickasaws and Choctaws in the southwestern United States. When Harney arrived at the isolated fort, he found troops from the First and the Second Dragoons living in log huts surrounded by a stockade. His own quarters formed part of a four-room, twenty-foot-square cabin, which he shared with his adjutant and Maj. Benjamin L. Beall. The other officers occupied similar buildings, while the enlisted men bunked in cabins consisting of two seventeen-by-nineteen-foot rooms. Such conditions existed commonly at posts throughout the western frontier. The army built them not to withstand Indian attacks but only to deter them, and not to house troops long term but only to shelter them temporarily until native people became pacified and white settlement dominated.[4]

Purpose and policy notwithstanding, Harney considered Fort Washita "entirely out of the reach of the civilized world" and resolved immediately to improve living conditions. He put the troops to work felling trees fifteen miles away, hauling logs, sawing planks, and erecting a permanent officer's quarters and recreation hall, which he furnished with ninepin alleys, a billiard table, and a bar. All officers and selected enlisted men had access to the hall, and when Insp. Gen. George Croghan visited in the summer of 1844, he predicted that the new facility would boost morale significantly. Croghan noted also that Harney's command raised an uncommonly large variety of vegetables in the post garden and enjoyed better food than men at most other frontier forts. Harney had also requested and received approval for an Episcopal chaplain to provide religious instruction to garrison children.[5]

Despite these efforts to make life at Fort Washita more bearable, here as elsewhere on the frontier, physical isolation and boredom brought out the worst in many soldiers, Harney among them. In addition to abusing enlisted men, he quarreled with fellow officers over matters ranging from installing a bar in the recreation hall to using post funds for a regimental band. A more serious clash occurred when Harney bought a stolen horse unwittingly and then traded it to Capt. Marshal S. Howe. Upon learning the truth about the animal, Howe wanted to void the trade, but Harney refused. This error in judgment, together with his boisterous manner, especially offended Lt. Abraham Johnston of the First Dragoons. He and several other young West Pointers in that regiment complained regularly about what they considered coarse and unprofessional behavior by older officers appointed from civilian ranks. In August 1844, Johnston charged Harney formally with "arbitrary and unmilitary conduct" detrimental to "good order and military discipline." To support those accusations, Johnston recounted the disputes about the bar and post fund and the cursing, wooling, and beating incidents involving Williamson, Shannon, O'Brien, and Bean. Once again Harney's uncontrollable temper, paired this time with sheer pigheadedness, had landed him in trouble.[6]

The army ignored Johnston's charges until April 10, 1845, when General Scott called for a court-martial. He appointed Bvt. Brig. Gen. Matthew Arbuckle, with whom Harney had clashed over pay procedures in 1835, to preside and ordered the accused arrested. This defied common practice, as the army conducted proportionally few courts-martial involving abuse of enlisted men. Harney's disobedience eighteen years earlier made it easier for Scott to select him as an example, but the commanding general's long-standing feud with General Gaines, commander of the Western Division, motivated him most. Earlier Gaines had declined to order a court-martial because he considered the charges against Harney a waste of time.

When the court convened at Fort Smith, Arkansas, on June 6, 1845, Harney pleaded not guilty and then sat through ten days of testimony before trying to win acquittal with calculated closing remarks. Portraying himself as a victim, he suggested that Johnston had made his charges partly to curry favor with First Dragoon commander Kearny, Harney's old "enemy." As for O'Brien, Harney contended that the musician had been a "decidedly mutinous" soldier who could not be disciplined by "milder means." The cursing, Harney said, is a "habit . . . which I regret, and one which I have in vain tried to correct," and while "my manner" is "naturally boisterous," the "men of my company are accustomed to it." Lastly, he expressed confidence that the court would treat him fairly, for the members "all know that it is my wish to serve my country to the best of my abilities, even if they should think that, in some instances, I have erred in my manner of doing it." Except for his language Harney made no apologies. He regretted only that the controversy had led to a court-martial.[7]

Although testimony concluded on June 18, several weeks passed before the court delivered its verdict. On orders from Gaines, Harney spent most of that time in St. Louis. While he awaited the decision, his sister-in-law Ann Biddle, who had assisted him before his trial for murder, became gravely ill and wanted to consult physicians in Philadelphia. Harney had no authorization to leave St. Louis, but with no one else available to travel with Ann, he took on the task. Despite his roughness, he had capacity for compassion as well as good reason to help out. They got only as far as Cincinnati, though, before she became unable to continue.[8]

In August, the court declared Harney guilty of both charges and sentenced him to an official reprimand in general orders and suspension from rank and command for four months. Because of his "long and gallant service," however, the court recommended that Scott remit the suspension. He did, but only because he considered the punishment too lenient for Harney's "vicious habits." The only other punishment available to the court was dismissal from the army, and evidently Scott would have preferred it. Harney had been "a conspicuous violator of law and morals," the commanding general asserted. The charges, the lengthy trial, and Scott's reactions all highlighted officers' proclivity for contentiousness.

Harney should have been grateful for his relatively mild chastisement. Instead, he felt insulted. His resentment festered for several months, and on January 19, 1846, he asked the War Department to court-martial Scott for "vilifying unjustly and contrary to truth, the general moral character of Bvt. Colonel W. S. Harney." It was a petty, vindictive request. Scott's admonition had been sharp, but never before in the history of the army had anyone filed charges against the commanding general for carrying out the sentence of a military court. In February, President James K. Polk glanced over the unprecedented accusations and dismissed them as unwarranted. Harney did not get the revenge he sought.[9] He also failed to recognize that eventually such peevish and unproductive behavior could ruin his reputation for effective combat leadership. During the next twelve months, as war gathered with Mexico, he continued to act rashly and embroil himself in needless controversy.

The United States and Mexico had been headed for a clash of arms for more than a decade. Their leaders bickered over international boundary lines, commercial relations, conduct of diplomats, and private financial claims of American citizens against the Mexican government. When war finally came, aggressive United States expansionism, above all else, proved responsible. As early as the 1820s, scores of

Americans had emigrated to Texas, and many had fought in its war for independence in 1836. Although Mexico refused to recognize the new Lone Star Republic, Americans talked of annexing it. The Mexican government warned that such a step would lead to war. Despite the United States' superior size, Mexican officials considered their army better trained and equipped than its American counterpart and therefore capable of defeating it easily.

Enmity between the two countries grew rapidly in the mid-1840s. In 1844 Polk, a Tennessee Democrat who years before had studied law with War Hawk Felix Grundy in Nashville, won the presidency on an expansionist platform, and early the next year Congress passed a joint resolution for Texas's annexation. To prevent a Mexican reprisal and press America's claim to the disputed 120-mile-wide border region between the Nueces River and Rio Grande, Polk ordered Brig. Gen. Zachary Taylor into southern Texas with four thousand troops. The president wanted California, too, and he sent emissary John Slidell to Mexico late in 1845 to offer American dollars for a favorable boundary settlement and cession of Mexican territory from Texas to the Pacific.

Mexican officials refused even to talk to Slidell, and early in 1846 Polk directed Taylor to move troops from Corpus Christi into the disputed territory. If Mexico resisted, the president intended to ask Congress to declare war. In March, Taylor occupied Point Isabel at the mouth of the Rio Grande opposite the Mexican city of Matamoros. When Mexican officials ordered him to withdraw, he blockaded the river. Not surprisingly, on April 25, Mexican troops attacked an American detachment, and on May 13, 1846, Congress issued a formal declaration of hostilities.[10]

While these developments unfolded, Harney waited north of the Nueces near San Antonio, fuming over both professional and personal concerns. Two years earlier, in April 1844, Congress had voted to remount the Second Dragoons, and now they formed part of Taylor's command. But when he entered the disputed territory, he left Harney behind, charged only with standing in reserve against a possible Mexican invasion and preventing Indian raids. Comanches and Wacos stole horses from area ranch corrals and army tethers regularly, and despite help from the Texas Rangers, shortages of men, horses, and equipment hampered Harney's efforts to capture the culprits. His ego still smarted from Scott's reprimand, too, and he devoted part of his time to drawing up his unprecedented charges against the commanding general. In addition, Ann Biddle died and left Mary Harney "considerable property," and although Mary usually took care of family finances, she repeatedly urged her husband to resign his commission and return to St. Louis. Harney considered that "out of the question," although on April 27, unaware that hostilities with Mexico had already begun, he tried to appease Mary by requesting a sixty-day furlough subject to cancellation if war occurred.[11]

As soon as news of Taylor's clash with Mexican troops reached Washington, President Polk, General Scott, and Secretary of War William L. Marcy devised a war strategy. While the navy blockaded Mexican ports, Taylor's army would invade central Mexico from the north via Monterey, Saltillo, and San Luis Potosí, and smaller columns of troops would drive west and southwest into New Mexico, California, and Chihuahua. To fill the ranks of these commands, the government once more employed the concept of an expansible army. Congress authorized eighteen thousand regulars and fifty thousand volunteers.[12]

Recruiting proved easy. Anticipating a short conflict, most Americans looked at the nation's first foreign war with a blend of enthusiasm for the effort and intense curiosity about the location. Many participated in the massive mobilization of ordnance, field, and transportation equipment. A combination of increasing literacy, cheaper newspapers, the telegraph, and the first use of war correspondents enabled people to follow military events more closely than ever before. American romanticism, an idealization of the past spurred in part by the romantic novels of Sir Walter Scott, heightened interest, too. During and after the war, hundreds of soldiers chronicled their experiences and perceptions, and people devoured histories, novelettes, plays, photographs, and moving panoramas about the struggle and the country where it played out.

Before fighting started, however, most officers felt little eagerness for it. Their reasons for reticence varied, but many feared that war would disrupt organizational structure and careers. Harney stood as an exception. He wanted to get involved. When he learned about the hostilities at the Rio Grande, he characteristically declined to await orders from either Washington or Point Isabel. Driven partly by patriotic zeal and partly by a desire for personal acclaim, he launched his own initiative against Mexicans. On May 2, 1846, eleven days before the American declaration of war, he announced that "all who owe allegiance to the Government of Mexico" must leave Texas within three days or "be treated as enemies to the United States." When Scott heard about the unauthorized proclamation in July, he ordered Harney to withdraw it. He complied but not before evicting an undetermined number of people from San Antonio, though "fewer than was anticipated."[13]

Lacking any knowledge of the War Department's plans for a coordinated effort, Harney now decided to invade central Mexico himself. Like Scott and Marcy, he realized that thrusting across the border southwest of San Antonio would reduce Mexican pressure against Taylor's Army of Occupation near Matamoros. Thus, on May 8 Harney wrote to Taylor, asking for permission to march twelve thousand volunteers into the Mexican interior and strike some of the enemy's "most flourishing towns." Taylor never acknowledged the request, but it mattered not. Harney plunged ahead anyway. Despite giving little thought to what kind of resistance the Mexicans might throw against him, he felt confident that the results would justify his conduct. So, just as he had done in Florida six years earlier, he proceeded without authorization. If he could not have two regiments of militia, then he would use whatever troops were available. Previously he had secured seven companies of volunteers to protect against Indian raids, and now he assembled them in San Antonio and called on Texas governor J. Pinckney Henderson for five more units for guard duty. He also recruited a company of Delaware Indians to act as guides and spies. By July 6, he had gathered nearly six hundred men including his dragoons, and satisfied with his plans, he sent Taylor a note informing him of the impending invasion.[14]

Two and a half weeks later, on July 24, Harney and his motley command set out for Presidio de Rio Grande, a small Mexican border community more than 150 miles southwest. Once across the Rio Grande, Harney planned to push south a similar distance to Monclova, and if

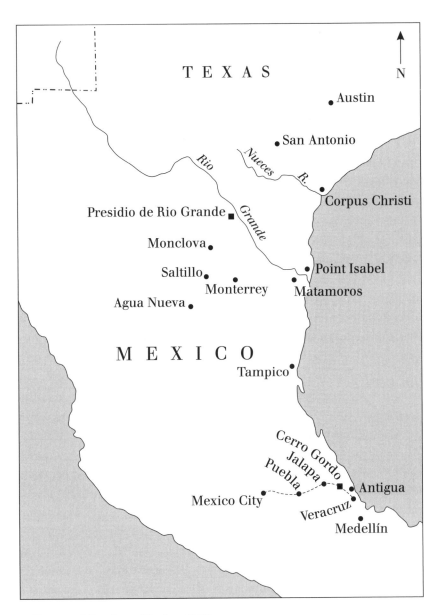

3. Texas and Northern Mexico, 1847

the Mexicans chose to fight, he would "give them enough of it." Before getting under way, he wrote a third time to Taylor, explaining, "I go for the good of the country" and "feel that I am acting in a manner that will meet with . . . [your] approbation."

Because of slow communication between San Antonio and Matamoros, which Taylor now occupied, he still had not received Harney's second note. Finally it arrived on the twenty-eighth, and too late Taylor ordered his determined subordinate to stay at San Antonio and await the arrival of Brig. Gen. John E. Wool, a stern man and capable officer whom the War Department had chosen to lead its planned invasion of Chihuahua. San Antonio had been designated the assembly point for the expedition, and even as Harney started for the Rio Grande, Wool had volunteer regiments from Arkansas and Illinois and more than $1 million worth of arms and other supplies en route to the Texas town. Both Wool and Taylor expected Harney to guard the war materiel as it accumulated, but when the supplies began arriving in early August, less than a dozen soldiers remained in San Antonio to receive and protect them.[15]

By then Harney was already halfway to the border, which he reached on August 12. He expected to find eight hundred Mexican troops at Presidio de Rio Grande, but the garrison there had never numbered more than two hundred, and these fled as the Americans approached. Leaving part of his force on the U.S. side, Harney crossed into Mexico with the rest to talk with the mayor and obtain corn and other badly needed supplies. The citizens gave Harney and his men a cordial reception, but while the soldiers rounded up provisions, water from recent heavy rains swelled the Rio Grande and made it uncrossable. By evening, still short of supplies and temporarily cut off from the rest of his command, Harney had second thoughts about the propriety of his actions and his chance for success. That night he penned another note to Taylor. This time he lied, but with little fear of contradiction. In contrast to his statements of July 24, Harney now maintained that he had marched to the border only because he had heard that Mexican troops had begun gathering there for an assault on San Antonio. By August 15, when he finally received Taylor's order forbidding the expedition, Harney had already decided to turn back.[16]

Meanwhile Wool arrived in San Antonio on August 14. Already irritated because flooded roads and a shortage of wagons hampered his efforts to move supplies inland from Port Lavaca on the Gulf Coast, Wool grew furious when he discovered what Harney had done. On the eighteenth Wool ordered him to consider himself under arrest for "abandoning your post without orders; leaving this place with a large amount of public property unprotected; and disobeying the positive orders of General Taylor."[17] Later, when he learned that Harney had not received Taylor's July 28 order before embarking on his adventure and had already started back to San Antonio, Wool substituted a tongue-lashing for the arrest order.

He believed that the premature march had hindered his own planned thrust into Mexico by wasting needed supplies and delaying efforts to find the best invasion route. In truth, Harney's expedition had little negative effect on Wool's. His supply problems stemmed from the weather, not Harney. Furthermore, as Taylor subsequently acknowledged, Harney had established the lack of resistance at the border, and eventually when Wool entered Mexico, he went along the same southwestward route that Harney had used.[18]

The impetuous lieutenant colonel's rash escapade harmed only his own deteriorating reputation as a commander. Although he did not know it, Scott had already decided that "Harney . . . is not fit for a separate command," and now his ill-conceived dash to the Rio Grande, despite the intelligence it provided, led Taylor to a similar conclusion. Only the army's need for experienced officers kept Harney in an important position. Even as he had tarried at Presidio de Rio Grande, the War Department announced that on June 30 he had been promoted to full colonel and assigned to command the Second Dragoons in place of Twiggs, who became a brigadier general. Once more Harney's career benefited from an expansion of the army.[19]

While preparations for Wool's expedition continued into September 1846, other American columns plunged deep into Mexican territory. In mid-August Col. Stephen Watts Kearny and his Army of the West occupied Santa Fe, where he laid plans for part of his force to meet Wool in Chihuahua. With most of the rest, Kearny set off to help Lt. Col. John C. Frémont and Commodore Robert F. Stockton consolidate American control in California. Meantime, Taylor's Army of Occupation moved southeast from Matamoros and captured Monterey.[20]

Wool started his first column, fourteen hundred troops, for the border on September 25 with Harney in charge. Despite Scott's and Taylor's assessments of his fitness, he remained Wool's senior subordinate. After launching a second column on the twenty-ninth, Wool pushed ahead and arrived at the muddy Rio Grande with the advance units on October 9. As soon as Harney's dragoons forded the river and scouted the area around Presidio de Rio Grande, the soldiers laid a pontoon bridge and began passing into Mexico. Moving 170 wagons and tons of supplies over the temporary structure took several days, and during this time Wool added a regiment of Arkansas volunteers to Harney's command.[21]

The Americans got under way again on October 16, and for two weeks they tramped unresisted through beautiful valleys and rugged mountain defiles. However, at Monclova near the end of the month, Wool abandoned his plans for a Chihuahua campaign. He could not move his large train there by direct route, and the Mexican defenders had already fallen back, making the effort pointless. Eventually, he got Taylor's permission to join the main Army of Occupation at Parras, about halfway between Monclova and Monterey.[22]

During the trek south, Harney had impressed at least one volunteer as "a good officer and . . . a perfect gentleman," but he remained aggravated about his own aborted invasion attempt. To distance himself from Wool, he requested and received permission to join the main concentration of Second Dragoons at Monterey. As he departed with an eighteen-man escort, a fellow officer could not resist joking that the Mexican commander at Presidio de Rio Grande had been promoted for defeating Harney's Texas volunteers. With face red and eyes glaring, the proud dragoon roared, "The scoundrel says he defeated me? By God if I hear of him on my way to Taylor, I will attack and lick him or die."[23]

On December 3, apparently in retaliation for his arrest, Harney filed a long list of misconduct charges against Wool. They included "Arbitrary, Illegal and Oppressive Conduct" for the arrest, "Neglect of Duty" for failing to conquer Chihuahua, "Misapplication of Public Money" for spending large sums in preparation for an expedition and then failing to complete it, and "Incapacity and Imbecility" for vacillation and destruction of "the confidence of the army under his command." Fortunately, Taylor's acting judge advocate recognized the charges as unsustainable and dismissed them. Further consideration would only have embarrassed Harney, for Wool had treated him leniently and had penetrated Mexico as far as Monclova without major difficulty.[24]

For the next several weeks, Harney kept out of trouble and performed effectively under Taylor, who now moved part of his forces southward to Saltillo, near the important Rinconada Pass into the interior. Beyond the mountains, Mexico's Gen. Antonio López de Santa Anna was gathering a large army, and in late December Taylor sent Harney and his dragoons through the pass to Agua Nueva, where they observed the Mexicans. This type of duty suited Harney, and he enjoyed it even though it lasted only a short time and placed him temporarily under Wool's command again.[25]

By the end of the year, other U.S. forces had captured the Gulf Coast port of Tampico and occupied most of Mexico's northern provinces. In Washington, President Polk decided that America could bring the war to a quick end by landing a large force at Veracruz, lower on the Gulf, and driving inland against Mexico City, and he chose Winfield Scott to command the effort. By late December, Scott had begun collecting men and supplies at Brazos, near the mouth of the Rio Grande. To the chagrin of Taylor, already piqued because he did not get the important Veracruz job, Scott transferred many Army of Occupation troops from Monterey and Saltillo to his own command. Their number included Harney and five companies of the Second Dragoons.[26]

Aware of the impending invasion and anticipating a chance at last to win glory on a Mexican battlefield, Harney arrived at Brazos in mid-January 1847. His keen expectation turned to shock and bitter disappointment on the twenty-second, however, when Scott directed him to turn his command over to his subordinate, Maj. Edwin V. Sumner, and report back to Taylor for some other assignment. Having clashed with the commanding general previously and knowing that he had a reputation for vindictive behavior, Harney should not have been surprised that Scott did not want him in his command. Desiring desperately to participate in the invasion, Harney complied with the order on January 23, and then requested its repeal. He asserted that he had looked forward to going to Veracruz, serving under Scott, and sharing "the dangers and privations of my regiment."

The following day, Harney received both a negative reply and the additionally dismaying news that upon his return to Monterey he might command only three or four companies. This he considered insulting because usually full colonels commanded regiments. Harney could think of only two courses by which he might retain command of the Second Dragoons. He could go to Monterey as ordered and appeal to the president for redress, which probably would entail a lengthy delay. Or he could disobey Scott's order, stay in Brazos, submit to arrest, and take his chances with a court-martial. The latter strategy would produce a decision more quickly. Both options risked alienating Scott further, but if a board would rule favorably, then the commanding general be damned. Confident that he understood the relevant military regulations, Harney informed Scott on the twenty-fifth that "as long as I am a colonel, I shall claim the command of my regiment; it is a right which I hold by my commission and the laws of the land, and no authority short of the President of the United States can legally deprive me of it."[27] As he expected, his immediate superior, Bvt. Brig. Gen. William J. Worth, charged him with disobedience of orders and insubordinate conduct. To avoid post-trial accusations about the fairness of the proceedings, Scott suggested that Harney select the members of the court, but for the same reason he declined.[28]

When the trial began on January 30, Harney pleaded guilty of disobeying orders but not guilty of insubordination. His chief defense rested on a complimentary endorsement that Worth had jotted on one of Harney's letters to Scott. At first Scott denied that Worth had made such a notation and refused to relinquish the letter, but at Harney's continued urging, the board secured it. Worth had written that Harney had frequently expressed a lively "anxiety for the success of General Scott's expedition" and a "deeper solicitude to serve under his orders."[29] On February 1, Harney rose for the fourth and last time in his career to defend himself before a court-martial. To the panel of eleven officers he complained of "injustice," "wounded pride," and lack of the "good fortune to participate in any of the recent actions with the enemy . . . which have covered our army with glory." No commander, he argued, had the right to relieve a subordinate because of "private revenge and personal hostility." After a brief deliberation, the court found Harney guilty of disobeying orders but not guilty of insubordination and directed only that he receive a reprimand in general orders. Eventually Scott remitted even that punishment.[30]

Although the trial had ended, Sumner remained in command of the Second Dragoons. Harney had no choice but to accept this, and so, "seriously and deeply lamenting that untoward circumstances" prevented his taking part in the Veracruz expedition, he asked Scott for further instructions about reporting to Taylor. This represented Harney's most mature acceptance of disappointment since the early days of the Second Seminole War. Scott regarded his tone as conciliatory and restored him to command of his regiment.[31] Harney's reputation for effectiveness in combat may have influenced Scott's decision, but belated intervention from the White House did not. Polk participated daily in managing the war, and when he heard about Harney's ouster, he became incensed. Having never gotten along with Scott, an avowed Whig, the president noted in his diary that Harney was "one of the most gallant and best officers in the service" and had been treated unjustly because he was a Democrat and "one of Gen'l Jackson's personal friends." Later Polk prevailed upon Secretary of War Marcy to rebuke Scott, but before Marcy did so, Harney had already returned to his regiment.[32] Now, both to his credit and Scott's, they put aside their mutual hostility and concentrated on their respective assignments.

During the court-martial proceedings, additional regulars and volunteers as well as rations, guns, ammunition, tents, wagons, medicine, and other supplies streamed into the Brazos army depot from numerous American Gulf and Atlantic ports. On February 15, Scott began moving men and equipment down Mexico's eastern coast to Lobos Island near Tampico, where he completed his plan of attack. Two weeks later, shortly after Taylor crushed Santa Anna's army at Buena Vista in northern Mexico, Scott's troop carriers and supply ships left Lobos and headed toward Veracruz.

After a stormy four-day passage of 180 miles, the vessels anchored off Anton Lizardo 12 miles below Veracruz, and officers and enlisted men busied themselves with last-minute preparations for the largest military operation and first amphibious assault that an American force had ever attempted. For the landing, Scott divided his army into three divisions ranging from twenty-five hundred to thirty-five hundred men each and led by Generals Worth, Twiggs, and Robert Patterson. Harney commanded all mounted regulars, which Scott held in reserve with his headquarters. All units stood ready on March 9, 1847, as dawn revealed clear skies and calm seas. Nine thousand troops, each carrying a haversack with two days' supply of bread and cooked meat, began exiting their transports onto schooner gunboats, which would move them closer to shore and provide covering fire. Completing this transfer and steering the warships into designated positions took most of the day. In late afternoon, the troops transferred from the gunboats into sixty-three specially constructed flat-bottomed surfboats. On these the invaders rode in successive waves to within a few hundred feet of the sandy beach and then splashed ashore with guns held high over their heads. Harney would have gloried in the scene, but an accident caused him to miss it. His transport, the *Yazoo*, carrying horses and a company of dragoons, grounded on a reef off Anton Lizardo, and the soldiers had difficulty rescuing the animals from the sea. Harney's own favorite horse, Buncombe, remained in the water several hours before being rescued.[33]

The Mexicans made no effort to resist the landing. Overwhelmingly outnumbered and protected in part by their walled city and the massive harbor fortress of San Juan de Ulúa, they chose to await reinforcements. Scott's troops ignored the fort and spent ten days establishing a seven-mile semicircular line around the rear of Veracruz and isolating it. Then on March 22, American artillerymen commenced shelling the besieged defenders.

While the heavy guns created a dense cloud of smoke overhead, U.S. mounted units scouted behind the siege lines. On the twenty-fifth, about nine miles south of Veracruz, Harney and four or five companies discovered several hundred Mexican troops in a wooded area near a stone bridge on the Medellín road. Daring as usual, he led a reconnaissance of the enemy position himself and approached within sixty yards of the Mexicans before they opened fire. When he saw that they had fortified the bridge, he fell back, called for artillery, and prepared to attack. After a brief bombardment and sharp skirmishing, he sent Capt. William J. Hardee and a group of dismounted dragoons shouting and lunging at the entrenched Mexicans. Then, as the defenders retreated and tried to regroup, Harney sent Major Sumner's mounted party charging through their hastily redrawn lines. The Mexicans fled toward Medellín, and the Americans chased them six miles along the road and through the town. Because the enemy had been moving food overland from Medellín to the coast and then by small boats into beleaguered Veracruz, this action would have assumed strategic importance in a lengthy siege. Having finally gotten into battle, Harney took great pride in what turned out as a minor victory.

After brief negotiations, U.S. soldiers occupied Veracruz on March 29. Scott declared martial law and immediately prepared to move most of his troops inland to higher elevations where they could escape yellow fever, a dreaded killer in low-lying coastal areas each spring and summer.[34]

Before the invaders could get under way, they had to find additional draft animals and food. Harney's command and others scoured the countryside for livestock and provisions. To keep citizens from selling goods to the Americans, Mexican army detachments garrisoned towns and harassed U.S. scouting parties. On April 1 and 2, Harney and several dragoon and infantry companies searched the area north of Veracruz for cattle and mules, and near Antigua they encountered several forty- to ninety-foot-thick log-and-brush barricades along the main road. When the soldiers pulled the obstacles down and entered the town, its fifty-man garrison fled. Already annoyed by the delay, Harney grew even more irritated when the citizens demanded exorbitant prices for their cattle and could produce no mules at all. Similar operations by other detachments fared no better, and eventually the Quartermaster Department brought draft animals and other supplies from New Orleans and Tampico.[35]

On April 8, the first U.S. troops marched out of Veracruz along the national highway toward Jalapa, about seventy miles northwest at a more healthful altitude of four thousand feet. By the twelfth, advance units had crossed the Rio del Plan just below the mountain pass at Cerro Gordo, where the Mexicans occupied strongly fortified positions. During the American landing and siege, Santa Anna had journeyed one thousand miles from the north to try to block Scott's route to Mexico City. Now the Mexican commander had more than twelve thousand soldiers situated strategically along both sides of the two-mile-long pass. On his right, south of the highway, he had nineteen guns atop three jutting ridges. To his left, north of the road, he had batteries on two conical hills, La Atalaya to the north and seven-hundred-foot El Telégrafo nearer the highway. Unfortunately for Santa Anna, the morale of his troops did not match the strength of his position. All his soldiers lacked water, many suffered from respiratory and digestive illnesses, and not a few considered the Yankees invincible.

Scott arrived at the Rio del Plan on the fourteenth and sent his engineers—among them Capt. Robert E. Lee and Lts. George B. McClellan, Joseph E. Johnston, and P. G. T. Beauregard, all future Civil War generals—to reconnoiter the enemy defenses. From their reports Scott concluded that a frontal assault would prove suicidal and that the river and its bluffs would prohibit his bypassing the Mexicans to the south. Subsequently, however, Lee discovered a path that would allow the Americans to skirt the enemy's northern flank, and Scott prepared an appropriate plan of attack. While Maj. Gen. Gideon Pillow's troops feigned an assault south against the three ridges on the Mexican right, most of the other Americans would follow Lee's route north around the enemy left and attack from the rear.

On the morning of the seventeenth, Scott's eighty-five hundred soldiers maneuvered into position. Trudging over boulders and through mesquite and cactus, the men of General Twiggs's division, with Harney substituting as a brigade commander, moved toward La Atalaya. They had orders to occupy the hill, approach the Mexican left near the highway, and be ready to attack when the rest of Scott's army got into position. About midmorning, Mexican lookouts on La Atalaya spotted Twiggs's column. Santa Anna rushed reinforcements to the hill, and shortly after noon they opened fire on the Americans. Twiggs then ordered Harney to drive the Mexicans from the lower heights and hold them. He and his brigade charged up La Atalaya, cleared it of enemy

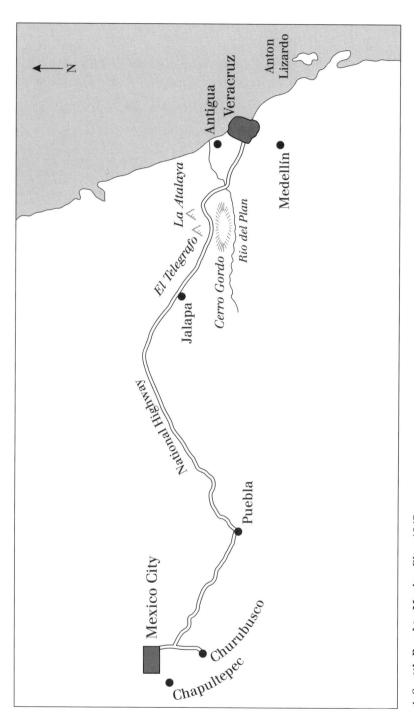

4. Scott's Road to Mexico City, 1847

troops, placed an American battery on it, plunged down the opposite slope, and got partly up El Telégrafo before heavy Mexican fire forced them to fall back.[36] As darkness approached, Harney and his men huddled on La Atalaya and gazed toward the crest of El Telégrafo, only a few hundred yards away, where the Mexicans worked furiously to strengthen their positions.

The next morning, April 18, Scott's artillery commenced firing on the Mexicans before daylight. Then Pillow began his deception on the Mexicans' right, and Twiggs started Brig. Gen. James Shields's and Bvt. Col. Bennet Riley's brigades around the Mexican left toward the national highway. Simultaneously, the American battery on La Atalaya opened fire on El Telégrafo. Enemy guns returned the blasts in kind. For a brief time Harney and his command of detachments from the Rifle, First Artillery, and Third and Seventh Infantry regiments lay under the cover of dense brush and listened to the fearful shriek of incoming grapeshot.

About 7:00 A.M. Harney sent Maj. William W. Loring and six rifle companies into a gorge to strike the Mexicans' right flank and divert their attention from the rest of the troops, whom he planned to send directly up the east slope of El Telégrafo. Before Loring got into position, however, Harney saw more enemy reinforcements approaching along the highway and decided to attack immediately. He shucked his coat, rolled up his sleeves, drew his saber, yelled, "Come on, boys," and leaped forward. Cheering loudly, the Americans dashed down La Atalaya's western side, across a ravine, through tangled mountain shrubbery, and up El Telégrafo. Firing at will, they moved steadily but swiftly through a costly torrent of enemy bullets. Harney led the way shouting. Sixty yards from the crest they halted momentarily to rest. Then they stormed the Mexicans' stone breastworks and, with swords and bayonets, drove the enemy soldiers from the hill. Quickly the attackers turned captured cannon on the fleeing Mexicans, who rushed headlong into Shields's and Riley's brigades near the national road. Routed, the remnants of Santa Anna's army raced pell-mell westward along the highway to Jalapa, leaving behind nearly three thousand men, including five generals, as prisoners. One disgruntled second lieutenant claimed later that Harney had inadvertently given Loring an incorrect maneuver order that exposed his men unnecessarily to deadly enemy fire and caused some to get lost. Those, the subaltern said, then detected the approaching Mexican reinforcements by chance and delayed them while Harney swept the heights. No official reports mentioned such an error.[37]

By 10:00 A.M. the fighting had ceased. Scott's army had overcome the greatest obstacle it would face on the road to Mexico City. At the center of the victory stood Harney, whose command had captured the enemy's strongest position at a cost of 28 dead and 161 wounded. "I cannot speak in too high terms of the conduct of Colonel Harney," said Twiggs, applauding the tall Tennessean's "indomitable courage" and "cool judgment" in battle. Even Scott praised his leadership as "brilliant and decisive." In three years in the American Southwest and Mexico, Harney had been involved in one controversy after another. He had vented his uncontrollable temper repeatedly before both officers and enlisted men, invaded Mexico without authorization, quarreled with Scott, suffered two courts-martial, and temporarily lost command of his regiment. On La Atalaya and El Telégrafo, however, he had won the glory he craved. More important, he had contributed invaluably to the climatic campaign of the war, and he had shown once again that he was a highly effective combat officer. For his sparkling performance in the Battle of Cerro Gordo he received a brigadier general's brevet.[38]

Harney never got to play another crucial role in the war, but he provided steady, useful service as the Americans pushed on toward the Mexican capital. His mounted troops led Scott's long column, reconnoitered the enemy, and foraged for supplies. After Cerro Gordo, Scott moved most of his force rapidly forward to Puebla, more than two-thirds the distance to Mexico City, and then paused to await reinforcements and replacements for volunteers whose enlistments had expired. Ten weeks dragged by before he completed this reorganization, but by early August he had an army of fourteen thousand. On the seventh he started again for the capital, approaching from the south. Large lava fields and terrain broken by huge irrigation trenches kept Harney and his mounted troops out of much of the fighting, and often his brigade separated into detachments for service with other units.

On August 20 at Churubusco, a fortified position five miles south of

Mexico City, elements of Harney's command carried out several widely scattered assignments, and he spent most of his own time "rallying fugitives" from various engagements. Late in the day, upon seeing Mexicans retreating in disorder on one of the causeways, he "collected all the cavalry within my reach" and raced after them with drawn saber. More than two companies joined in the chase, and when Harney ordered recall, Capt. Philip Kearny, nephew of Stephen Watts Kearny, failed to hear it. Dashing too near the city gates, he got entangled in fierce fighting and it cost him his left arm.[39]

After driving the Mexicans out of Churubusco, Scott rested his army a few days while U.S. negotiator Nicholas Twist and Santa Anna held fruitless surrender talks. Then, on September 8, the Americans attacked Molino del Ray. The cavalry saw heavy duty in the bloody battle, but Harney became ill and could only watch the action. Finally, on September 13, U.S. troops broke through Chapultepec, the last major obstacle barring entry to the capital, and Harney carried out one last action with which his name became forever linked. A number of officers and soldiers wrote about it later, but most of those who described it did not see it themselves and embellished it unnecessarily. The actual event proved gruesome enough.

Earlier at Churubusco, the army had captured seventy-two American deserters known as San Patricios. Mostly Irish immigrants with no strong attachment to the United States, they had gone over to fight with the Mexicans. Two military courts tried them and sentenced seventy to hang. Scott pardoned five of those and reduced the sentences of fifteen others to fifty lashes and branding with the letter D. The army hanged sixteen on September 10 and four more the following day. Harney received orders to hang the remaining thirty. Early on the thirteenth, he arranged them in a line atop boards laid across the backs of wagons pulled side by side under a long gallows. With their arms and legs bound and nooses looped around their necks and tied to the beam above them, the condemned men stood for more than two hours while their captors observed the battle in the distance and the wagon teams strained at their harness amid the thunder of battle. Curious citizens watched, and monks from a nearby convent tried to intercede for the prisoners, but reportedly Harney had declared that as soon as the

American flag rose over Chapultepec they "will have seen the last of earth." When the Stars and Stripes appeared, he gave the order and teamsters moved the wagons forward, leaving the prisoners choking to death. When asked later about cutting them down, Harney replied coldly, "I was ordered to have them hanged, and have no orders to *unhang* them."[40]

Their resistance smashed, the Mexicans surrendered on the fourteenth. Scott rode triumphantly into Mexico City's spacious Plaza de Armas under a brilliant sun, and Harney and his dragoons led the procession as a mounted band blared "Yankee Doodle." Although many officers shared the scene, after years of squabbling Scott and Harney—different in rank and command but equal in size, ego, and determination—basked together in the spotlight of victory. More than 90,000 American regulars and volunteers had participated in the war. Nearly 1,600 had been killed in the fighting, and approximately 11,300 more had died from accidents, disease, and other causes. For many who survived, there followed long occupation duty while diplomats thrashed out the details of a peace agreement giving the United States most of the territory it wanted between Texas and California. Other troops waited only briefly for permission to return home to families and friends.

Harney stayed in Mexico City six weeks, just long enough to visit with his brother Benjamin, who was Scott's medical director, demonstrate continuing callousness toward enlisted men, and get into one more scrape with his superiors. Navy Commander John T. McLaughlin, who had assisted Harney in his Everglades expedition, had died in Washington in July, and his brother, a dragoon private who only now learned the news, requested leave to return home. Harney responded heartlessly, "I do not think the reason given sufficient to entitle him to a Furlough." Later, when a French citizen assaulted the Mexican wife of an American by the name of Hall, Harney mistook the assailant as one of the many Mexicans harassing local women who married or cohabited with Americans. In typical swaggering fashion, Harney turned the man, Marie Courtine, and his accomplice over to Mr. Hall and the soldiers who had captured them and said, "There is my backyard, you can take them in and do with them what you please, I shall not interfere." The resultant beating of Courtine produced a protest from the French ambassador to the United States and earned Harney a written censure from President Polk.

On November 1, 1847, Harney left the Mexican capital to escort a train of 702 army wagons and carriages to Veracruz. From there he traveled via New Orleans home to St. Louis, and in both cities he received a hero's welcome. He had escaped another series of professional difficulties brought on by irascibility and personal ambition, and in the process he had again proved his talent for effective combat leadership and garnered public acclaim.[41]

CHAPTER 7

"Prince of Dragoons" in Texas

A S THE side-wheeler *Aleck Scott* lumbered downriver toward New Orleans the last week of November 1850, the stench of dung from a herd of cattle on deck competed with river smells, and engine noise drowned the sound of paddleboards slapping against the muddy Mississippi. Col. William S. Harney, his brother Maj. Benjamin F. Harney, and other passengers who boarded at St. Louis knew the dangers inherent in steamboat travel. Sparks and embers from the wood-burning vessels' smokestacks could ignite roofs and decks in seconds, and log snags in the water could rip open hulls just as quickly. The previous year, a fire on the steamer *White Cloud* had leaped ashore and roared through the city's waterfront, destroying twenty-three vessels and fifteen blocks in the commercial district. None of the travelers knew, however, that the *Aleck Scott* carried deadly cholera bacteria, which had killed several hundred people in St. Louis during the summer.

Having little else to do, the passengers spent their time in conversation, and Colonel Harney entertained them with stories about the Second Seminole War. The listeners included Father Pierre-Jean DeSmet, a Jesuit missionary active among

Indians on the Great Plains, and he and Harney formed a lasting friendship. When the boat docked at Memphis, Harney went ashore, hired a fifer and a violinist, and brought them aboard to play for an evening of dancing. "We enjoyed ourselves pretty, thanks to the liberality of the colonel," wrote Edward Wortley, an Englishman making a summerlong tour of America. When the journey resumed, the river wound through the delta country of Arkansas and Mississippi, and Wortley noted the sharp contrast between slave cabins and masters' homes on cotton plantations visible from the boat. By this time, deck passengers had begun to fall ill with cholera. A crewmember died of the disease, and as more passengers grew sick, the trip became tedious. Finally about four miles above the Crescent City, the boat stopped briefly while the crew unloaded the cattle and washed the nasty cargo deck. On December 2, the *Aleck Scott* docked in New Orleans, and its able passengers, DeSmet, Wortley, and the Harney brothers among them, disembarked.[1]

Hundreds of boats like the *Aleck Scott* carried passengers and freight up and down the Mississippi, but Harney traveled little while stationed in Texas between late 1848 and late 1854. On this occasion he was returning to duty after one of only two trips home during the entire six years. He saw Mary and their three children almost as much in the year before he went to Texas as during the remainder of his life. After returning from Mexico toward the end of 1847, Harney spent several weeks with them in St. Louis before the War Department called him east to perform inspection duties in January and February 1848. In Washington, he examined new types of saddles and tents to determine their desirability for army use, and at Carlisle Barracks, Pennsylvania, he inspected post grounds, quarters, and stables and suggested repairs and improvements. Afterward he spent several more weeks visiting Philadelphia and New York City and then joined his family in the resort community of Cape May, New Jersey, to spend the summer and await a more permanent assignment.

In the fall, the War Department ordered Harney and the Second Dragoons to southern Texas, where the army needed additional troops to guard frontier settlements against Indian raids and to control smuggling along the Mexican border.[2] Now forty-eight, Harney had mellowed little with age, but he avoided major controversy during the next six years, got along well with three commanding officers, led the Eighth Military Department on an interim basis himself on three occasions, and became the darling of the Texas people. More important, despite continuing to contend with and argue against military tactics not suited to Indian operations, he carried out government aims in Texas as successfully as possible with the limited number of troops available for duty there. However, his long absences, together with ongoing disagreements over Mary's money, led eventually to estrangement from his family.

By the time Harney arrived in Texas, the army had dropped to its prewar level of about ten thousand troops, and these proved insufficient for its many new responsibilities. In addition to exploring and mapping new territories, improving old roads and building new ones, and aiding westward migration generally, the army had to deal with different kinds of terrain—vast plains and rugged mountains—and with different kinds of Indians—aggressive, nomadic horsemen. Rather than removing native people beyond the so-called "Permanent Indian Frontier," west of the ninety-fifth meridian, now the army had to operate within that region, and it had two different charges. On the central plains it had to protect emigrants and other travelers using the nation's transcontinental trails, and on the southern plains it had to protect existing and new frontier settlements. Those tasks became more complicated after 1849, when Congress created the Department of the Interior and gave it control of the Indian Bureau with responsibility for all nonmilitary aspects of Indian affairs. Military and civilian authorities disagreed often about policy, and army officers frequently felt thwarted by bureau officials.

The problems seemed especially complex in Texas, where the state retained control over its public domain and prevented federal officials from establishing reservations. Washington also lacked jurisdiction over trade with Texas Indians, yet the state expected the federal government to keep them peaceful anyway. Additionally, in accord with the Treaty of Guadalupe-Hidalgo, which ended the war with Mexico, that country expected the United States to prevent American tribes from crossing the international border.[5]

During the late 1840s and 1850s, increasing numbers of white settlers pushed into the Texas interior, where Indians traditionally roamed and hunted. Railroad and land surveyors and travelers to California gold fields followed. Eventually the whites destroyed Texas buffalo herds, and the Indians often had to plunder or starve. Unscrupulous traders in both Texas and New Mexico inspired even more looting and killing by swapping beads, cloth, and blankets, as well as liquor, knives, guns, and ammunition for stolen items of all kinds. Indians from outside Texas inflamed the frontier further. Some, such as Seminoles, Kickapoos, and Delawares, wandered into the state from Indian Territory, while others ranged across the border from Mexico. With only about fifteen hundred regular troops available to patrol a combined northern, western, and southern frontier line of more than twelve hundred miles, the army could not prevent clashes. It could only try to reduce the frequency of them and hope to forestall full-scale war.[4]

Bvt. Maj. Gen. William J. Worth commanded the Eighth Military Department, encompassing most of Texas, when Harney reported for duty there in late 1848. Immediately Worth put him in charge of the Frontier District, a line of posts along the westernmost reaches of settlement from Eagle Pass on the Rio Grande to the West Fork of the Trinity River in northern Texas. In addition to overseeing troop movements, Harney inspected the posts regularly and, whenever necessary, established new ones such as Fort Graham on the upper Brazos River in north central Texas.[5] When Worth died suddenly in early May 1849, Harney became interim department commander. Just then Indian raids increased throughout the state. They "are playing the devil all over the country and I have not the means to check them," he lamented. Harney wanted more mounted troops for greater mobility. Already he had personally bought four mountain howitzers for the Second Dragoons, and in contrast to Mexican War configurations, he had the weapons mounted on special four-wheel carriages that transported both guns and ammunition. This relieved horses from carrying ammunition in packs, enabled faster traveling gaits, and allowed soldiers to move both guns and ammunition more quickly from place to place.[6]

The situation had not improved in July when Bvt. Maj. Gen. George M. Brooke, an infantry officer, arrived to assume command. Almost

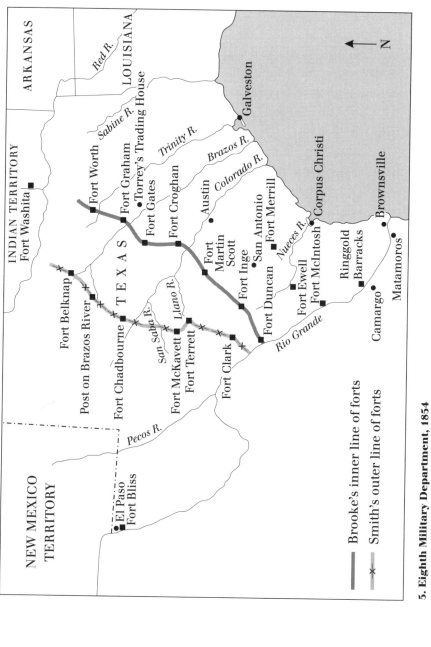

5. Eighth Military Department, 1854

Legend:
—— Brooke's inner line of forts
—×— Smith's outer line of forts

N

ARKANSAS

LOUISIANA

INDIAN TERRITORY
Fort Washita

NEW MEXICO
TERRITORY

T E X A S

Red R.
Sabine R.
Trinity R.
Brazos R.
Colorado R.
San Saba R.
Llano R.
Pecos R.
Nueces R.
Rio Grande

Fort Worth
Fort Graham
Torrey's Trading House
Fort Gates
Fort Croghan
Austin
Fort Belknap
Post on Brazos River
Fort Chadbourne
Fort McKavett
Fort Terrett
Fort Clark
Fort Martin Scott
Fort Inge
San Antonio
Fort Merrill
Fort Duncan
Fort Ewell
Fort McIntosh
Ringgold Barracks
Camargo
Matamoros
Brownsville
Corpus Christi
Galveston
El Paso
Fort Bliss

immediately he and Harney disagreed about the best way to defend the frontier. Both men wanted to build more forts, but Brooke wanted fewer than Harney and planned to garrison them with both dragoons and infantrymen. Brooke argued that while mounted troops rode out to scout and pursue Indian raiders, the infantrymen could protect the forts against attack. Harney, on the other hand, considered foot soldiers "useless" against Indians. The native people were excellent horsemen, he observed, and unless the army utilized sufficient mounted troops, raiding parties could easily slip through the line of forts and strike settlements. Further, he doubted that the Indians would attack an army post, except in a general war, and he maintained that stationing large numbers of infantrymen in distant forts would increase supply and transportation costs unnecessarily. He thought those troops could be used best on escort and garrison duty in the interior.[7] Although Adj. Gen. Roger Jones considered Harney's ideas "clever," Winfield Scott, still the commanding general and still committed to old methods, favored Brooke's plan and ordered it implemented. Texans agreed with Harney, however. The *Texas State Gazette* at Austin declared him "a model of the true soldier" and predicted that if "he had his own way . . . we might reasonably hope for security throughout our borders."[8]

Military officials other than Brooke and Harney also contemplated new posts and weighed the relative merits of foot and mounted soldiers. At the War Department, some authorities thought the army should scatter small temporary garrisons of mounted men throughout the nation's vast frontier and pursue every Indian raiding party. Others wanted to build a few permanent posts from which to send roving columns through Indian country each spring and summer to show the flag and intimidate the tribes. The army never adopted either strategy formally, but its practices resembled the former. In New Mexico, for example, Col. Edwin V. Sumner established a defense system much like the one Harney advocated.

Although they disagreed about strategy, Harney and Brooke remained on friendly terms, and when the raids increased dramatically in August 1849, Brooke reconsidered some of Harney's proposals. Near Laredo on the Rio Grande, Indians plundered pack trains, ranches, and small farms, raped at least three women, and stole several Mexican children. Other Indians spirited horses away from the army post at San Antonio, and still others killed five men near Corpus Christi and destroyed cornfields and butchered settlers' hogs north of Austin.[9] These incidents demonstrated clearly that existing posts stood too far apart to keep raiding parties out of settled areas. Brooke erected Fort Gates in central Texas and called for mounted volunteers, but these halfway measures had little effect. The Texas legislature reported that by the end of the year, Indians had killed 171 whites and run off or destroyed more than $100,000 worth of livestock.[10]

The raids continued into 1850, and the scattered army detachments could do little to stop them. The defense system "is but a mockery," the *Texas State Gazette* chided. Brooke kept Harney and his dragoons active on the northwestern frontier through the spring, and in the summer he sent Capt. William J. Hardee with four mounted companies and a group of Texas Rangers south to drive Indians out of the Nueces country. These operations dispersed some marauding bands but did not end the threat to settlers and travelers. In September, the *Gazette* declared that the Indians must be "driven back or exterminated." More constructive suggestions also emerged. Secretary of the Interior Thomas Ewing urged Congress to extend federal trade and intercourse laws to Texas tribes in order to curtail traffic in stolen goods. And echoing a recommendation from his predecessor, Robert S. Neighbors, Indian Agent John H. Rollins called on the state to set aside land for a reservation. Neither the United States nor Texas acted on these recommendations in 1850.[11]

Harney missed much of the year's struggle. In May, the War Department ordered him to Fort Leavenworth, Kansas, to preside over a court-martial, and on his way back to Texas he stopped in St. Louis for a lengthy visit with his family. Following his return trip down the Mississippi on the *Aleck Scott*, he reached his headquarters in Austin a few days before Christmas, and the *Texas State Gazette* welcomed him as a "favorite of the Texian people," declaring "no one is more deserving of their confidence and good wishes."

Shortly before Harney returned, Agent Rollins met the Comanche chief, Buffalo Hump, and representatives of half a dozen other tribes about a hundred miles northwest of Austin and negotiated a lengthy agreement with them. They expressed peaceful intentions, promised not to come inside the line of military posts or go into Mexico, and said they would surrender captives, stolen property, and troublesome warriors. In return, Rollins told the Indians that the United States would build trading houses for them and send them blacksmiths and teachers.[12]

Rollins's agreement had little impact. The Indians neither ceased their raids nor returned white captives, and in February 1851 Brooke planned to send Harney and Hardee to the upper Brazos to punish all the tribes and seize their prisoners. Before Brooke could set his scheme in motion, however, he died from complications of a hernia, and in March Harney went to San Antonio and took command of the Eighth Department again. He decided immediately to implement his earlier suggestions for frontier defense and asked the War Department to return four Second Dragoon companies then in New Mexico and increase all ten units to one hundred men each. He intended to distribute the dragoons among the outermost posts in western and northwestern Texas and station the infantry and mounted volunteers at interior forts and along the Mexican border. The War Department denied both requests.[13]

During the next few months Harney made good use of the troops he had and gave Texans better protection than they had enjoyed in two years. In April, he sent Hardee and two hundred men with Indian Agents Rollins and Jesse Stem to the Llano River west of Austin, where they persuaded Comanche and Lipan bands to release seventeen Mexican captives and one American. Next, he declared trading houses that received stolen property "the most fruitful source of trouble on the frontier" and warned the proprietors that he intended to stop them.[14] To combat depredations along the border, he allowed Col. Juan Maldonado of the Mexican army to pursue raiding parties into the United States. In mid-May, Harney ordered Fort Mason erected on the Llano and instructed the commanders of all nine garrisons with mounted troops to send out at least one scouting party every week. This, he hoped, would keep most Indians from penetrating the interior and trap those who did. Finally, he met with a group of Comanches and Lipans at Fort Martin Scott near Fredericksburg and told them that he would "chastise them severely if they did not in future conform strictly to all treaty stipulations, and conduct themselves in a friendly manner toward whites." Earlier he had "regarded a general Indian war as inevitable." Now he felt "satisfied" that "suitable activity and perseverance on the part of the troops" could "in a great measure, if not entirely," prevent widespread fighting.[15]

Harney continued to press the Indians throughout the summer. In a variation of the roving columns strategy debated in Washington, he kept Hardee, Maj. Henry H. Sibley, and their dragoon detachments constantly in the field visiting Caddos, Wacos, Kichais, Tawakonis, and other tribes. In communications with the War Department, Harney referred to the Indians as "savages," yet now at the westernmost posts he gave them expired army provisions, because "many of these unfortunate people are in a suffering condition and both humanity and policy will . . . be served" by this plan.[16] His comments reflected both prevailing white attitudes and his own ambivalent feelings. He could denigrate native people and sympathize with their condition at the same time. His decision to feed the Indians reduced their need to raid white settlements, and by July, Harney exuded "high spirits" and had become even more popular with Texans. One unidentified citizen declared, "He has lived amongst us; we like him, not only for his gallantry as an officer, his independence, energy and decision of character, but . . . for his noble and generous qualities as a man." The War Department recognized Harney's success, too, and Secretary Charles M. Conrad praised him for his "accustomed activity."[17]

Despite having made the Texas frontier more secure, Harney did not retain command long. Even before Brooke died, the War Department had planned to put Bvt. Maj. Gen. Persifor F. Smith in charge of the Eighth Military Department, and he arrived in September 1851. Harney returned to supervising scout and patrol activities, and Smith erected another series of forts west of the existing outer line. The new posts included Fort Phantom Hill on the Clear Fork of the Brazos, Fort Chadbourne on a tributary of the Colorado, and Fort McKavett on the San Saba. Instead of garrisoning them with dragoons, as Harney would have done if given approval, Smith manned them with infantry companies and thus committed the same error that Brooke had made in 1849. Sometimes foot soldiers trapped raiding parties between the inner and outer lines of forts, but frequent mounted patrols between the exterior posts could have kept more Indians out of the settled areas.

In the summer of 1852, drought diminished food supplies, and Indian forays increased sharply.[18] Coincidentally, Smith became ill, and in December he traveled to Philadelphia for medical treatment. Harney then became temporary department commander for the third time, and although scarcity of mounted troops prevented him from changing defensive arrangements, he adopted a sterner posture toward raiders. Disgusted with their "defiant manner," he declared vindictively that only "severe and summary punishment" would make them "respect us."[19]

In January 1853, Harney decided to make examples of Lipans who allegedly had attacked a ranch near San Antonio and Caddos who had raided settlements north of Austin. To both detachments of pursuing troops, he gave the same instructions, "Reclaim the stolen property, demand the persons who committed the unlawful acts, and if they should not be surrendered . . . exterminate all the men and make the women and children prisoners." These measures had little effect on plundering. They only reflected the frustration that Harney and many other officers elsewhere felt in trying to protect the frontier with insufficient manpower.[20]

When General Smith returned to Texas in mid-1853, little had changed. Most of the state's twenty-five thousand native people wanted only "lands . . . to live upon . . . and clothes to keep us warm," and their agents continued to call for permanent reservations. Finally, early in 1854, Texas authorized the federal government to survey 53,136 acres of unclaimed state land for Indians. By late 1855, many Texas tribes had moved onto two selected tracts on the upper Brazos River, but others, as well as bands from Indian Territory, New Mexico, and Mexico, continued to plague the state's settlers for years.[21]

Along the Mexican border the army had more problems than Indian raids. After the war, Mexico imposed high tariffs on American imports, particularly cotton fabrics, but Mexican people continued to buy Yankee products. Citizens from both countries smuggled goods across the Rio Grande and sold them in Mexico for a handsome profit. After 1850, the Mexican government tried to curb the illegal trade with military force, and many residents of northern Mexico loathed both the import duties and the officials assigned to collect them. Late in 1851, José María Carvajal, a Mexican visionary who wanted both a lower tariff and various constitutional reforms, launched a revolution to achieve them. When Carvajal recruited a group of interested Americans, including John S. "Rip" Ford and other former Texas Rangers, President Millard Fillmore ordered the army to prevent U.S. citizens from leaving the country to interfere in Mexico's internal affairs. On October 21, 1851, Smith instructed Harney to keep Americans from shipping supplies to Carvajal and repel any revolutionaries who tried to escape into the United States.[22]

Harney gathered several dragoon companies and set out at once for Ringgold Barracks on the lower Rio Grande. Like many regimental commanders, he had molded his unit to his own personality, and at least one observer thought that in manner and bearing the Second Dragoons resembled cocky European hussars. When they rode into Ringgold Barracks on November 4 with early morning sunlight glistening on their sabers and carbines, they created "quite a stir," according to Theresa Vielé. The wife of a young West Pointer, she declared that "a more dashing, well-drilled set of men" could not be found, and their strong-willed, athletic-looking colonel seemed the "prince of dragoons." He had "come down from Northern Texas," she observed, "to administer 'jesse' . . . to all delinquents, and let the community . . . feel that he was 'about.'" He assumed command of all U.S. forces along the border and then conferred with Mexican officers from Camargo, just across the river. The meeting ended poorly, though. While Harney talked with the foreign officers indoors, one of the dragoons stole several expensive pistols from the Mexicans' saddle holsters. The following day, when guards caught the guilty soldier on the barracks veranda, Harney grabbed him by the neck "like a kitten" and, according to Vielé, "administered a good shaking and moral lecture combined." Another Texan remarked to her that Harney was certainly "one of your high flung fellers."[23]

In the meantime, Ford and about thirty other ex-Rangers had joined Carvajal, and his combined army of some five hundred had captured the small Mexican town of Reynosa. Carvajal had then proclaimed new tariff duties for northern Mexico and besieged Matamoros. Despite ten days of cannon barrages, intermittent street fighting, and devastating fires, the city had refused to surrender, and the revolutionaries had moved up the south bank of the Rio Grande under harassment by Mexican regulars. In mid-November, Carvajal and many of his band fled into Texas to prepare another campaign. While they lurked somewhere between the Rio Grande and the Nueces River, Harney placed guards at major border crossings and dispatched patrols to search for insurgents. To prevent sympathetic Americans from aiding them, he urged Smith to ask the president to declare martial law along the border, but Smith refused, declaring the situation insufficiently threatening to "the national existence or its vital interests."[24]

Despite Harney's efforts to grab them, Carvajal and his followers slipped back into Mexico on February 20, 1852, and attacked Camargo the next day. However, partly because dragoon patrols had hindered the rebels' preparations, Mexican regulars defeated them easily. For the next day or two, American troops plied the Rio Grande in small boats looking for stragglers, and finding none, Harney concluded that Carvajal's rebellion had been squelched "for the present." On March 8, Lt. John Gibbon arrested the revolutionary leader and eleven of his men in Brownsville, Texas, but when civil authorities released him on $5,000 bail, Harney feared a resumption of the revolt. Consequently, he recommended that the government negotiate a reciprocal tariff with Mexico, particularly on cotton goods, and station more mounted troops along the border. The latter measure, he pointed out, would also reduce Mexican Indian raids. Smith believed "the personal efforts of General Harney" chiefly responsible for curtailing Carvajal's activities and thought Washington should consider his ideas. He has "valuable information in relation to the present and future prospect of this frontier," Smith wrote. The War Department paid no attention, however, and Carvajal remained an irritant along the border, although a lesser one, for several more years before focusing his revolutionary interests elsewhere in Mexico.[25]

Even though officials in Washington ignored Harney's suggestions for frontier defense, he reveled in accolades from Texans and enjoyed his service in the Southwest. When not in the field dealing with Indian matters and policing the border, or in San Antonio acting as interim commander of the Eighth Department, Harney made his headquarters in Austin. He went to extraordinary lengths, including spending large sums from Mary's inheritance, to make life there comfortable for himself and his troops. When he arrived in Austin in 1848, he considered the post too small to house his dragoons adequately, and so he bought a block of land next to the military compound, built a 20-by-150-foot barracks and a stable, and donated them rent-free for army use. Later, he installed a billiard table for the soldiers' recreation, provided quarters for a regimental band, and located and wrangled from storage in Philadelphia 445 experimental hats with floppy wide brims that would protect his dragoons from the hot Texas sun. A variation of these covers became the standard cavalry campaign hat of the 1870s. For his personal use, Harney purchased a hundred-acre tract and house, "a pretty place, upon an eminence," seventeen miles outside of town.[26]

Family life went less well for him. With only two trips home, albeit lengthy ones, in six years, he did not see his children grow up. While he remained in Texas, his daughters, Ann and Elizabeth, passed through their middle teen years, and young John incurred a crippling illness. Harney's marriage deteriorated, too, in part because he took advantage of Mary's wealth. After refusing to pay a $1,000 debt for him in 1849, she complained to a family member that he had "never shown any interest [in the money] only spending all he could lay hold of." In the meantime, Harney asked his brother Thomas to act as his personal financial agent. "My wife is unjust and unreasonable in relation to '*her money*,'" Harney declared heatedly, "and *I will not submit to* such conduct any longer!" For several months, he and Mary refused even to write to each other, and he received no news of the children.[27]

In addition, Mary made what Harney regarded as "foolish charges about women" and contemplated leaving him. She based her allegations in part on a story that Capt. Charles F. Ruff told in St. Louis in 1849. Motivated by a personal grudge over lack of a brevet promotion, Ruff asserted publicly that during the Mexican War Harney had "carried with him throughout Mexico that vicious and *notoriously* abandoned prostitute, Mrs. Shepherd." The evidence neither supports nor refutes Ruff's tale, but Mary believed it. Harney grumbled that she was a "*bigoted* Roman Catholic," and then on New Year's Day 1850, while "drinking freely of egg nog," he wrote her a long conciliatory letter. She agreed to forgive him and "begin anew."[28]

After Harney visited St. Louis later that year, however, they saw each other only twice more. The first time, in late 1852, he received several months of leave that he managed to get extended through the end of the year. During that time, he even tried unsuccessfully to secure a transfer closer to St. Louis. In his petition he cited the "anxiety a Father must feel to be with his family" when "daughters are fast growing into womanhood." Despite that pitiful-sounding plea, Harney apparently used part of his furlough to travel to New York City, where he rejected an invitation from Tammany Hall Democrats to speak in opposition to Winfield Scott's Whig candidacy for president. Unlike Scott, Harney and most other officers considered the army apolitical. "While holding a commission in the army of the United States," he wrote his solicitors, "I have always, from a sense of propriety, withheld any active participation in political contests." He declared, "My vocation is at the bidding of the constitutional authority" because "the framers of the constitution made the military subordinate to civil power." Except for that, he asserted, it would have afforded him "the highest satisfaction" to "bear testimony" to the "statesmanlike ability" of Franklin Pierce, the Democrats' standard-bearer.[29]

The following summer, after Harney returned to Texas, John's health worsened, and Mary took him and the girls to live in Paris, where he could get special medical care. In France, Ann and Elizabeth studied music and language, and in the autumn of 1854, Ann, then eighteen, became engaged to Viscount Louis de Thury, a naval officer. As soon as Harney learned of the couple's intentions, he obtained a six-month furlough and went to Europe, where, according to one of his in-laws, he intended "to whip the Frenchman, who *dared think* of marrying *his* daughter." The wedding took place before Harney arrived, though, and a short time later Elizabeth married a French citizen, too, Count Ludovic de Noue, an army officer. Whatever effect Harney's long absences had on his relationship his family, it did not deter his daughters from pursuing matrimonial courses similar to their mother's.[30]

Harney tarried in France only until Christmas Eve 1854, when at the request of Secretary of War Jefferson Davis, he departed for the United States to command a major expedition against Sioux Indians in Nebraska.[31] As Harney recrossed the Atlantic, he could not have avoided thinking about both his new assignment and the improbability of seeing his wife and children again in the foreseeable future. While serving mostly in a subordinate position in Texas, he had sacrificed irretrievable family moments. But he had also done at least as much as his three commanding officers to provide a measure of protection to frontier settlements, and he had overseen a partial restoration of order along the Mexican border. These achievements had further enhanced both his public and professional reputations. Throughout his Texas service, he had also maintained correctly that with more men, especially mounted troops, the army could be more effective. Now he had to worry about having adequate support to carry out his duties on the central plains.

CHAPTER 8

"*Great White Chief*" on the Plains

T HE ALARMING incident began with a wagon train of Danish Mormon emigrants, a lame cow, and a band of hungry Indians. It ended with thirty-one men dead or dying and authorities in Washington considering new strategies to ensure peace on the Great Plains.

On August 18, 1854, the lodges of more than fifteen hundred native people stretched three miles along the south bank of the North Platte River in present eastern Wyoming. Under terms of an 1851 treaty, various bands of Sioux had been camped there several days waiting for a new federal agent to arrive at nearby Fort Laramie and release food and other annuity goods from storage. As the wagon train rumbled westward past seemingly endless rows of tepees, the cow strayed from its emigrant owner into a Brulé camp, where High Forehead, a visiting Miniconjou, caught and butchered the hapless animal. The fearful Mormons said nothing and continued on to the fort, where they reported their loss a few hours later.

While the post commander, Lt. Hugh B. Fleming, considered how to respond, his second-in-command, Lt. John L. Grattan, a year out of West Point and anxious to prove himself, clamored for permission to take troops to the Sioux camp and seize High Forehead. Fleming should have waited for the agent to arrive and replace the cow with one from the Indians' annuity herd. Instead, he gave in to Grattan's pleading. Accompanied by a drunken French interpreter, two noncommissioned officers, and twenty-seven infantrymen traveling in wagons, Grattan paraded boldly into the Brulé camp the next afternoon, unlimbered two artillery pieces, and demanded that High Forehead surrender. When he refused, Brave Bear and Little Thunder of the Brulés, together with Man Afraid of His Horse, an Oglala leader, urged Grattan to wait and let the agent handle the matter. After arguing and posturing for forty-five minutes, Grattan grew impatient and ordered his men to shoot. Both sides opened fire, and Brave Bear fell mortally wounded. Hundreds of warriors rushed the soldiers, who sent poorly aimed howitzer blasts sailing harmlessly over the Indians' heads and through the tops of their lodges. Recognizing their situation as hopeless, the troops turned to flee, but Spotted Tail's Brulés and Red Cloud's Oglalas cut off their retreat and rode them down. Only one soldier escaped to Fort Laramie, and he died of wounds a few days later. Before they stopped, the incensed Sioux raided the warehouses of traders James Bordeaux and Pierre Chouteau and threatened to overrun the fort. Afterward the Indians assembled north of the Platte and declared war on all whites.[1]

Known popularly as the Grattan Massacre, this collision shook government officials from Nebraska to Washington. Many realized that responsibility for it rested squarely on the army, and on Fleming and Grattan in particular, but President Franklin Pierce and Secretary of War Jefferson Davis blamed the Sioux. Convinced that the Indians had provoked Grattan's attack deliberately as an excuse to plunder the warehouses, Pierce and Davis decided to send a military expedition to punish the Indians and restore order. According to Davis, the president considered this "the only measure that could be relied on to stay the [Indians'] hand of violence." Thus on October 26 Davis wrote to Col. William S. Harney and asked him to cut short his visit in France, return to the United States, and lead the campaign. While Davis waited for Harney to receive the message and cross the Atlantic, Indians harassed other whites regularly along the emigrant route. In a major raid on November 16, a Brulé war party ambushed the Salt Lake stage, killed three men, and escaped with a mail sack and a strongbox containing $10,000 in gold.[2]

As in Texas during Harney's service there, the problems on the Great Plains stemmed in part from the acquisition of vast new territories following the Mexican War. Small numbers of Americans had been traveling overland to settle in Oregon since the 1830s, and others had discovered gold in the lower Sacramento Valley in 1848. Now thousands streamed westward each year. Some followed the Platte River across what is now Nebraska and eastern Wyoming, took the South Pass through the Rocky Mountains, and then trekked northwestward through southern Idaho to fertile Oregon farmland. Others followed the same route as far as South Pass and then journeyed southwestward across present Utah and Nevada to mineral-rich California. Both routes took the travelers through Indian country, making clashes inevitable. As a further complication, in 1854 Congress passed the Kansas-Nebraska Act, formally organizing those two territories and repealing outmoded provisions of the 1834 Trade and Intercourse Act, which had established a "Permanent Indian Frontier." This drew more settlers into the region.

Also as in Texas, these Indians had horses, which made them formidable. The federal government, particularly the army, considered the potential for major hostilities great. Military men worried especially about the Arapahos, Cheyennes, Comanches, Kiowas, and Sioux. Early in 1846, Congress created the Mounted Rifle Regiment to protect travelers on the overland trails, and immediately after the Mexican War, units of that regiment founded Fort Kearny on the Platte River in present south central Nebraska and Fort Laramie on the North Platte. Other troops constructed forts farther south to protect traders on the Santa Fe Trail, and in 1853 the army built Fort Riley in what is now north central Kansas. That same year the War Department reorganized its western commands and created the Department of the West, extending from the Mississippi River to the Rocky Mountains and from Texas to Canada. Unfortunately, the new command lacked sufficient troops to police its vast reaches. In 1854, for example, the army could assign only about seventeen hundred men to the entire department.

The government tried other strategies, too. Indian Bureau officials

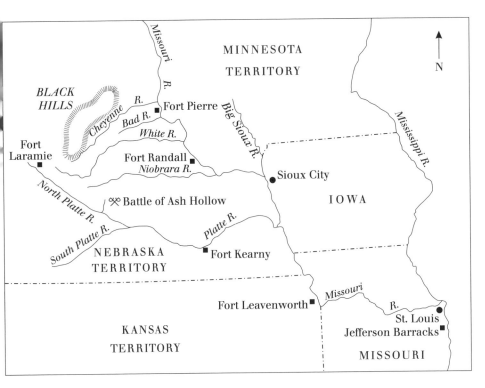

6. Platte River Country, 1855

concluded peace treaties with most plains tribes at Fort Laramie in 1851 and Fort Atkinson in 1853. Despite knowing little about native political structures, decision-making processes, and tribal relationships, government representatives distributed enormous supplies of merchandise, food, and domestic animals at the councils and promised more gifts annually for fifty years. With little understanding of the white man's papers, the Indians signed them, attesting more to their own sometimes conflicting council speeches than to the written words. In doing so, they agreed to let the government build roads and forts in their country and promised not to molest travelers or make war with each other or the United States. The northern tribes–including the Arapahos, Cheyennes, and Sioux–consented also to remain within certain broad geographical boundaries.[3]

Although the principal tribes totaled as many as fifty thousand souls, and the War Department estimated that the Sioux alone could muster seven thousand warriors, federal officials had considered the transcontinental routes secure until the Grattan incident. Passing out treaty annuities at forts along the emigrant road had only drawn Indians to it and made hostilities more likely. Now, without sufficient troops to protect the road and pursue all the hostile parties, the army could not stop the raids. Davis informed Winfield Scott about the anticipated punitive expedition in December. "A mere demonstration . . . will be useless," the commanding general warned. "To strike an effective blow, an effective force in discipline, instruction and equipment as well as numbers, is necessary."

The Grattan incident marked the beginning of more than three decades of determined Indian resistance to white westward movement across the northern Great Plains, and Harney's expedition became the first major campaign, and one of the most dramatic ever, against principal tribes. He could not have anticipated that it would make him the army's best-known active Indian fighter or that it would become the aspect of his career for which historians remember him most. But that is what happened. His campaign served notice that the army intended to take a new, harder line against hostile groups and if necessary wage total war, punishing warriors and noncombatants alike. Because it aimed at particular Indians in response to specific events, the expedition differed from the more general roving column strategy that military officials had debated for a decade. Nevertheless, it drew upon that concept and provided a pattern for similar undertakings later. These included Col. Edwin V. Sumner's Cheyenne campaign in Kansas in 1857, Col. Benjamin L. E. Bonneville's Apache expedition in New Mexico that same year, and Capt. Earl Van Dorn's Comanche campaign in northern Texas in 1859. Harney's expedition also helped set a precedent for winter warfare, such as Col. Patrick E. Connor waged against the Shoshones in Idaho in 1863. Finally, the difficulties that Harney experienced with Indian Bureau officials both during and after his campaign illustrated vividly the ongoing struggle between the army and civilians for control of federal Indian affairs.[4]

Just as usually they left most departmental activities to individual commanders, Davis and Scott left the "particular plan of operations" and timetable for the Sioux campaign to Harney. When he returned early in 1855, they gave him only general instructions and urged him to commence "as early in the season as may be found practicable" and make the expedition "short and decisive." To help him accomplish that, they assigned him to command in his brevet rank of brigadier general and gave him four companies from the Second Dragoons, all the Sixth Infantry, a detachment from the Second Infantry, and the Light Battery from the Fourth Artillery. These units constituted approximately twelve hundred men, or nearly 10 percent of the entire army. With them, Davis and Scott expected Harney "to operate against the hostile Indians" and protect "the Western frontier of Nebraska, and Kansas, and the emigrant routes leading from the Missouri river to the West," an area covering ninety thousand square miles. So that troops would be "encumbered with as little baggage as possible," Davis and Scott suggested that Harney use three principal supply depots and as many subordinate ones as necessary. The three primary posts were Fort Laramie, Fort Kearny, and Fort Pierre, a recently purchased former American Fur Company trading post at the confluence of the Missouri and Bad Rivers in present South Dakota. Scott suggested further that Harney divide his command and position some of his forces at Fort Pierre to confront any Indians who might go to the upper Missouri to escape his main column.[5]

Despite the War Department's preliminary preparations, myriad organizational tasks remained for Harney, and some proved maddening. Logistical difficulties plagued military operations regularly in the 1850s because neither congressional appropriations nor staff services kept pace with the army's growing geographical responsibilities. But knowing that other officers faced similar problems gave Harney no comfort. After he set up temporary headquarters in St. Louis on April 1, 1855, only two staff officers reported on time, and outbreaks of cholera and smallpox menaced several companies of the Sixth Infantry at nearby Jefferson Barracks. He complained to Washington about the shortage of officers and moved the infantrymen to Fort Leavenworth. In the meantime, Q.M. Gen. Thomas S. Jesup decided that instead of hauling expedition supplies 600 miles from Fort Leavenworth to Fort Laramie, it would be cheaper and more efficient to send them up the Missouri to Fort Pierre and then overland, a distance of only 325 miles. To supply the expedition via Fort Pierre, Harney needed to get shipments out immediately, but unusually low water prohibited normal steamboat traffic, and so he recommended that the army purchase a light-draft vessel for upriver use.[6]

Meanwhile, numerous other details demanded attention. In April, Harney visited the St. Louis arsenal and selected three hundred long-range Sharp's rifles and other ordnance stores. In May, he went to Fort Leavenworth and arranged for detachments of the Sixth Infantry and Fourth Artillery to move ahead to Forts Kearny and Laramie. And to save time and money on additional winter shelter at cramped Fort Laramie, he ordered the commanding officer there to buy lodges from friendly Indians.[7]

As summer approached, more delays and setbacks hampered preparations. Although Maj. Benjamin Harney begged for and received assignment as the expedition's chief medical officer, by late May the staff remained incomplete. For a time it included neither an adjutant nor an aide-de-camp. More important, the dragoon companies at Fort Leavenworth lacked sufficient recruits, and water in the Missouri River remained low, preventing Harney from inspecting Fort Pierre personally.[8]

When finally the first steamboats started upriver with troops and supplies early in June, the *Australia* sank with its cargo of public stores. By mid-June the army had modified two steamers to operate on the upper Missouri, but Harney feared that too little time remained for a full-scale campaign in 1855. Blaming Congress for failing to provide the necessary resources, he informed the War Department that while he remained confident he could achieve "a victory in the technical sense of the term" this season, the Indians would feel defeated only if "we destroy more of them than they do of us." They "must be crushed," he wrote, "before they can be conquered."

Privately to Davis, Harney added, "Only let me get into the field, & I will be 'at home'" and "in pursuit of those rascally fellows."[9] Like so many times before, especially when he left the monotony of Fort Belle Fontaine to go on Atkinson's expedition in 1825 and when he escaped the "infernal" paymaster's job for the Florida wilderness in 1837, he preferred doing rather than planning, the outdoors rather than desks. Also, as his Texas years had demonstrated, he preferred almost any active military enterprise to idleness in St. Louis. He seemed most at home when farthest from it.

While red tape and transportation problems delayed the campaign, warriors from several tribes continued to strike mail parties, cattle drivers, and emigrant trains in the central plains and Rocky Mountain foothills. Many white families packed their belongings and fled to more settled areas.[10] Harney angrily blamed much of the trouble on the Indian Bureau. Like many officers, he considered the civilian officials generally inept and often dishonest. He also believed that some Indian agents had given their charges ammunition for hunting and they had used it on whites instead. As he had in Texas, he also blamed traders for the continuing attacks. "They do not hesitate at anything that may promise to fill their pockets," he asserted, and "they indirectly encourage . . . depredations . . . by becoming recipients of the spoils." He suggested that the government restrict trade with Indians, dismiss the agents, and assign their duties to post commanders. Davis agreed with these recommendations, but he had no authority to implement them.[11]

On July 3, the War Department instructed Harney to disregard the lateness of the season and "strike a blow" against the Indians any time he could achieve a "decided result." After further preparation, he left St. Louis aboard a steamer and arrived at Fort Leavenworth on the eighteenth. By then portions of the Second Infantry had reached Fort Pierre, and so Harney decided to march first to Fort Laramie and then proceed northeastward between the White and Cheyenne Rivers, where a detachment from Fort Pierre would join him. He believed he had sufficient force "to attack any body of hostile Indians which I can overtake or may chance to encounter." If parties of warring Sioux refused to fight, he reasoned, at least they would have to abandon their families who "would be obliged to surrender themselves or incur the risk of starving" during the winter.[12] Thus, by either defeating Sioux warriors in battle or imprisoning their women and children, Harney expected to force the Indians to sue for peace.

Following common army procedure he had used before, Harney tried to hire friendly Indians–Delawares and Sac and Foxes–as scouts and hunters. They refused to help, however, because they believed, mistakenly, that they would lose their annuities if they aided soldiers. Although he had no proof, Harney insisted that Indian Bureau officials encouraged that thinking because Indian Commissioner George Manypenny opposed the punitive operation. Manypenny denied interfering, but at least one of his subordinates, Agent Benjamin F. Robinson, told the Delawares early in August that they "ought not to enlist in this expedition until they hear what their great father in Washington has to say."[13]

On August 4, Harney and the six hundred troops he had assembled at Fort Leavenworth started for Fort Kearny without Indian scouts and without Maj. Benjamin Harney, who remained behind due to illness. Each day they followed the same schedule. Reveille sounded at 4:00 A.M. and by 6:30 A.M. horses, mules, and men had been fed, tents struck, wagons hitched and loaded, and columns started. As the soldiers and their supply trains crossed the rolling prairie, heavy rains pounded them, and they struggled along muddy trails and across flooded streams. The bad weather soon put Harney in a foul temper, and he vented his anger on the expedition teamsters. When he saw one of them whipping a mule as the command crossed the swollen Big Blue River, he unleashed what one soldier described as "the greatest volley of oaths we had ever heard." Afterward some of the drivers feared him so much that in camp they walked an extra half-mile just to avoid passing his tent.[14]

While the expedition made its way across the plains, newly appointed Indian Agent Thomas S. Twiss arrived at Fort Laramie and launched his own investigation of the Sioux disturbances. Erroneously concluding that neither the Brulés nor the Oglalas had committed any robberies or murders during the past year, he proclaimed the North Platte a boundary between friendly and hostile native people. Then he assembled about four thousand peaceful Indians, including Brulé and Oglala Sioux, Cheyennes, and Arapahos, in camps south of the river. Most of the Brulés and all of the Miniconjous remained north of Twiss's boundary, however. Those included Little Thunder's Brulé band, some Oglalas, and a few Miniconjous who camped on Blue Water Creek, a small tributary of the North Platte about 150 miles east of Fort Laramie. Their lodges stood within five miles of the emigrant road, where previously warriors had harassed white travelers.[15]

Meanwhile, Harney's column reached Fort Kearny on August 20. Two days later, his topographical officer, Lt. Gouverneur K. Warren, arrived from Fort Pierre with news that most of the Brulés were somewhere between the Niobrara and Platte Rivers. Although uncertain of their exact location and still concerned that he had too few troops, Harney decided to continue westward along the emigrant trail and attack any apparently hostile bands in his path. On the twenty-fourth he set out for Fort Laramie, and during the next ten days the expedition pushed 180 miles across land now hot and dry. Late in the afternoon on September 2, the troops reached Ash Hollow on the south bank of the North Platte. Here the prairie gave way to a ravine dotted with stunted ash trees and wild cherry and plum bushes. On the opposite bank the Blue Water Creek, a clear, sandy-bottomed stream twenty to thirty feet wide and two to three feet deep, spilled into the river. Less than six miles north, in the gorge of the small stream, stood forty-one Brulé and eleven Oglala lodges housing about 250 Indians. Harney had learned of their presence two days earlier.[16]

Although traders had warned Little Thunder of the approaching troops, he had made no attempt to move his lodges. The Sioux claimed later that they had been hunting buffalo and could not leave until the meat had dried. However, according to Capt. John Todd of the Sixth Infantry, the Indians showed no fear of the soldiers and sent Harney word that "if he wanted peace he could have it, or if he wanted war . . . he could have that." Whatever the case, Harney knew that these Indians had participated in the Grattan affair and harassed travelers, and he prepared to attack them at dawn the next morning. Because high bluffs extended along both sides of the Blue Water, he decided to send his cavalry against the Indians' rear and lead his infantry directly up the creek against their front. This necessitated a risky night march by the mounted force, but Harney felt confident the plan would produce the kind of punitive blow that Pierce, Davis, and Scott wanted.[17]

Just past midnight on the morning of September 3, 1855, night guards roused officers and soldiers with hushed voices and reminders not to light pipes or cigars or make unnecessary noise. At 3:00 A.M., Col.

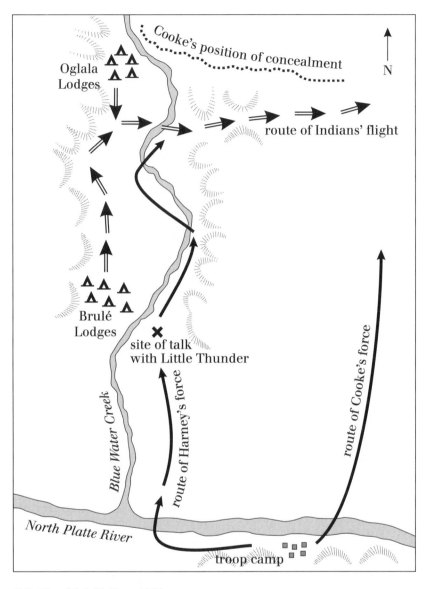

Oglala
Lodges

Cooke's position of concealment

N

route of Indians' flight

Brulé
Lodges

✖ site of talk
with Little Thunder

route of Harney's force

route of Cooke's force

Blue Water Creek

North Platte River

troop camp

7. Battle of Ash Hollow, 1855

Philip St. George Cooke led two dragoon companies, the light artillery battery, and a company of mounted infantrymen quietly across the North Platte River just below Ash Hollow. Guided through the darkness by trapper Joseph Teason, they skirted twelve miles around the Blue Water gorge and just after sunrise dismounted and hid in the grass along a ridge one-half mile northeast of the northernmost lodges. In the meantime, five companies of the Sixth Infantry under Maj. Albemarle Cady forded the river at 4:30 A.M. and trudged along the winding creek bank toward the Sioux camps. Harney and his staff accompanied them on horseback.

The infantrymen covered only a mile before the Brulés realized the gravity of their situation. They had not expected Harney to attack this early, if at all, and unaware of the cavalry in their rear, they struck their lodges and retreated up the gorge in confusion. To gain time for their women and children to get away, Little Thunder, Spotted Tail, Iron Shell, and several other leaders mounted their ponies and galloped forward to parley, but Harney refused to talk. The Indians rode away, then returned a few minutes later with a white flag. This time Harney decided to stall and give the cavalry more time to get into position. He halted the troops, dismounted, and walked ahead to meet Little Thunder, who raced his mount full speed to within ten yards of the general. He stood unflinching, and when Little Thunder leaped to the ground and extended his hand, Harney refused to shake it. Sternly he stated the government's grievances against the Sioux, said that he had not "come out here for nothing," and demanded the surrender of all Indians responsible for the Grattan affair and the mail robbery. The chief protested that he did not want war, but Harney told him that the "day of retribution" had come and the Indians "must fight." Bewildered by Harney's unyielding attitude, Little Thunder mounted his horse and returned to his frightened people.[18]

As soon as the native leaders disappeared from sight, Harney ordered the infantry to charge. When Colonel Cooke heard them firing, he sent the cavalry dashing into the northern end of the gorge to block the Indians' escape. Seemingly trapped, men, women, and children abandoned their belongings and scrambled up the western slope, where many sought refuge in small caves along a steep rock wall. The crevices afforded little protection, and the Indians' weapons proved useless against the soldiers' long-range rifles. With the cavalry and infantry closing in on them from opposite directions, some of the Indians tried to escape through a narrow ravine leading out of the eastern side of the gorge. From the rim above, dismounted dragoons poured a murderous volley on them, and many failed to reach the prairie. Mounted troops raced after survivors, including Little Thunder and Spotted Tail, and chased them more than five miles across the plains. At 9:00 A.M., Harney, who watched the melee from a ridge, commanded his bugler to sound recall, but some of the horsemen had ridden out of earshot and did not return until noon.[19]

As the bugler's notes drifted over the battlefield, eighty-six Indians and four soldiers lay dead or dying. Camp equipment, clothing, buffalo meat, and dead horses and mules littered the gorge and adjoining prairie. Screams and moans from women and children filled the air. "The sight . . . was heart-rending," Lieutenant Warren observed afterward. Near the crevices, where at least seven women and three children died, he discovered an unconscious twelve-year-old girl with bullet-riddled feet and a small boy who had been shot through both calves and thighs. "I took him in my arms, said Warren, and "he had enough strength left to hold me round the neck." With the help of several officers, army doctors treated the wounded, while the troops rounded up about seventy prisoners, mostly women and children, and collected six wagonloads of meat, hides, lodge poles, and other items from the Indians' camp. The plunder included two scalps from white women, clothing taken during the Grattan fight, and letters seized during the November 1855 mail robbery.[20]

"The result was what I anticipated and hoped for," Harney reported vengefully, for the Indians "were retaliated upon fully for their hostile acts towards our people and the wildest consternation seized those who escaped." Both Davis and Scott commended Harney for the "gallantry, zeal and efficiency of his command." From a military standpoint he deserved their praise, for he had planned and executed the attack masterfully. No one could recall when any force, white or Indian, had destroyed such a large Sioux camp or killed and captured so many of their people in a single clash. They held him in awe for more than a decade afterward, and according to Maj. Gen. Oliver O. Howard, who gained national distinction following the Civil War, Harney became "the most renowned Indian fighter that we had." He had shown that even if the army could not stop Indian hostilities everywhere on the Great Plains, it could conduct effective offensive operations against particular groups of native people.[21]

Harney's success rested in part upon his and the War Department's willingness to wage total war–to engage the Indians in battle with little concern for the safety of their noncombatants, destroy all their possessions, and demoralize them. The army utilized such tactics increasingly in subsequent years, but Harney's actions marked him more than most officers as a killer of women and children.[22] Although Washington officials who ordered the punitive expedition must share blame for the slaughter, Harney carried out the assignment with uncommon ferocity and vindictiveness. The soldiers would have killed fewer women and children if Little Thunder had moved his people out of the gorge before Harney's troops reached Ash Hollow, or if during the battle some warriors had not taken refuge in the caves. But neither of those things occurred. That other officers in other times and circumstances employed similar tactics does not reduce Harney's responsibility either. In contrast to some of his subordinates, he expressed little regret about the Indians' losses. "Yours was the first band of Sioux I met when I came to fight," he told Little Thunder later, "but if I had met any other band it would have been the same."[23]

Although Harney wanted to resume the campaign as quickly as possible, various chores kept his troops busy on the Blue Water for several days. Callously leaving the bodies of slain Indians for wolves, the soldiers buried fallen comrades near their Ash Hollow camp and then sorted the spoils of victory. Keeping only usable items such as lodge poles and buffalo robes, they destroyed everything else in a huge bonfire. Afterward they threw up a sod embankment that Harney called Fort Grattan and garrisoned with a company of the Sixth Infantry. He hoped it could provide whatever further protection wagon trains and mail parties might require between Forts Kearny and Laramie. Finally, on September 9 he sent part of his force back to Fort Kearny with the prisoners and continued westward toward Fort Laramie with the rest of the troops.[24]

Upon arriving there six days later, Harney found a number of Indian leaders waiting to offer "earnest protestations of friendship." Shocked by Harney's severity, they sought to appease him. He "had done right" to Little Thunder, they declared, because he "had been told . . . to keep off the emigrant trail." Harney held the Indians in suspense about his plans while turning his attention first to gun traffickers. Having found large quantities of powder in Little Thunder's camp, he concluded that white traders had sold guns and ammunition to the Indians. Consequently, on September 18, he ordered that all Sioux trade be conducted near military posts, where army officers could oversee the transactions.[25]

On September 22, Harney met Man Afraid of His Horse and several other Brulé and Oglala leaders at a noon council. The conquering general was fifty-five now, and his once-auburn hair had turned white, matching the neatly trimmed beard and mustache that he had worn since his Texas years. In spite of his age, he remained robust and commanding in appearance, and because of his bearing and reputation, the Sioux referred to him variously as "Mad Bear" and the "Great White Chief." Harney played the role grandly, assuming "all the austerity I could put on." Already his restriction on trade seemed to increase the chiefs' distress, and now, he reported, they "begged piteously to be spared." They had as much ability as Harney to exaggerate their feelings in the council had they chosen to do so, but Agent Twiss considered them stunned. "The affair on the Little Blue Water . . . was a thunder clap to them," he wrote a short time later. Their entreaties surprised Harney, for he had expected to fight "many serious encounters" before causing such apparent consternation. Therefore, he offered the Indians what he considered a "just . . . opportunity to prove their desire for peace." If they wanted to avoid further fighting, he told them, they must surrender the warriors who had attacked the mail stage, return all animals stolen from whites, and stay south of the Platte River road.[26]

While the chiefs who attended the Fort Laramie conference promised to comply with Harney's demands, he doubted that they would, and whatever their intentions, they did not speak for the Miniconjous,

Hunkpapas, and other Sioux bands, or even all the Oglalas and Brulés. Harney realized that he had intimidated only a portion of the Sioux, and those perhaps only temporarily. Thus, despite misgivings about marching his troops to Fort Pierre during the cold plains autumn, he decided to follow his original plan and sweep through the heart of Sioux country. "I would lose much of my prestige by not doing so and . . . the results would more than compensate for any loss of animals and the temporary exposure of my men," he explained to Davis.[27]

After instructing Col. William Hoffman, the new commander of Fort Laramie, to receive any individuals or property the Indians might surrender, Harney and his reduced force of about 425 troops departed on September 29. Guided by twenty-five mountainmen, the column swung south of the Black Hills, spent two days reconnoitering the upper Niobrara River country, and reached the White River in present southwestern South Dakota on October 2. Then as sharply dropping temperatures, high winds, and occasional snow chilled the troops, they tramped a hundred miles down the White and through the deep, tortuous gullies of the Bad Lands, where they tarried briefly to collect fossils as souvenirs. Harney kept his scouts ranging far on each side of the main party, but they saw no Indians. In fact, all signs indicated that most had fled to the Black Hills. Certain by mid-October that "there were no Indians within my reach," Harney sent three companies back to Fort Laramie and proceeded directly to the Missouri River with the rest of his force. Exhausted and nearly frozen, they arrived at Fort Pierre during a driving sleet and snowstorm on the twentieth and warmed themselves with whiskey that Harney, who used alcohol with restraint, provided "to preserve the[ir] health." Despite having seen no Indians, they had demonstrated that an army column could operate effectively in the West during winterlike weather.[28]

Since August the Sioux expedition had covered two thousand miles, according to Harney's calculation, but the troops found no comfortable quarters at Fort Pierre. The small, decaying post consisted largely of crude log structures not intended for military use. Troops who had come upriver from St. Louis during the summer had arrived in time only to put up a few flimsy, prefabricated wooden cottages, each designed for thirty men. But even with those, the fort could not house all the command, which now swelled to nine hundred. All the kitchens remained unfinished, and the post had only two latrines. Located 250 yards from the nearest buildings, both privies sat in a mire of filth, and the soldiers refused to go near them. Human excrement littered the ground, and a foul odor hung over the camp. In addition, low water in the Missouri had prevented shipment of sufficient forage, and because the post stood on a barren plain, the troops had to travel more than twenty miles to obtain hay and wood. Both could be had across the river, but the soldiers had only one small boat to transport them.

Harney had expected problems, but the dilapidated conditions, lack of forage, and apparent negligence of officers who had been in command infuriated him. "I have never visited a post where so little had been done for the comfort, convenience and necessities of the troops," he complained to the War Department. He wanted to know whether the buildings acquired from the fur company matched the descriptions in the sales contract, and he appointed a board of officers to find out, though it mattered little now. Tackling the more immediate problem of getting the soldiers settled for the winter, he assigned two Second Infantry companies to garrison the fort and sent the remaining units to the nearby wooded areas. There the men built log huts for themselves and gathered bark from young cottonwood trees to feed their horses.[29]

The troops had scarcely begun those tasks when twenty-five Miniconjous came to the fort early in November and asked for peace. A party of Sans Arc Sioux followed a week later, and in both instances Harney treated the Indians coolly, refusing even to shake their hands. Like the Brulés and Oglalas whom he had met at Fort Laramie, they appeared "in a pitiable condition, suffering for everything" and, in Harney's view, pleading for their lives. This convinced him that most of the Sioux feared him now and that by acting quickly he could conclude his mission before spring. Accordingly, on November 9, he sent a message to each Sioux band. If they wanted to avoid war, he told them, their principal men must attend a council at Fort Pierre on March 1, 1856. He did not say that he expected them to sign a treaty in which they would agree to surrender all stolen animals and accused murderers and guarantee safe passage for travelers along the emigrant route.

Although the War Department had given Harney latitude to conduct the expedition as he saw fit, he did not have authority to make a treaty. Realizing that implementation would depend upon acceptance in Washington, he outlined his proposed terms and asked for permission to proceed. He still planned a spring offensive, but he warned that if the Indians responded by dividing into small bands and using guerilla tactics, "we will have another Florida war on our hands and it will be for them to fix the peace." From his years in Texas he knew well the plains Indians' ability as mounted warriors, and he did not want to give them an opportunity to regain their confidence. Now, Harney argued, offers "the *time* and the *circumstances,* best calculated . . . to restore quiet and security" to the frontier. Davis agreed, and after consulting President Pierce, the secretary authorized Harney to complete a formal accord based on the terms he had suggested. Apparently both Davis and Harney expected the Bureau of Indian Affairs to go along with this plan, but neither communicated with those officials. They considered Harney's activities an invasion of their own treaty-making prerogative, refused to cooperate, and became a major stumbling block.[30]

Agent Twiss proved particularly troublesome. Immediately after the Battle of Ash Hollow, he had reported to his superiors that he and Harney had "the best understanding" in "all matters relating to Indian Affairs." But he had lied. He had been clandestinely swapping stolen annuity goods and other public property to Indians for horses and buffalo robes, and he feared that further military involvement would disrupt his illegal business. Thus he opposed any measure that promised more efficient regulation of trade. His attitude first became apparent following the surrender of Spotted Tail, Red Leaf, and Long Chin, three Brulés who had robbed the Salt Lake stage. On October 18, 1855, the trio had donned their finest war costumes, ridden into Fort Laramie singing death songs, and submitted to arrest. Immediately afterward, Twiss had expressed satisfaction that the Sioux had met all necessary conditions for peace, and he had called for restoration of their trading privileges.

Now the agent attempted to obstruct Harney's treaty plans. In December, several Brulé and Oglala chiefs showed Twiss their invitations to the spring council and asked him whether they should go. He dared not advise them to ignore the conference, but he tried to prevent their leaving the vicinity of Fort Laramie in time to attend it. On the sixteenth he sent Harney a note inquiring whether, in view of Spotted Tail's surrender, the general still wished to confer with the Brulés and Oglalas.[31] Twiss hoped the Indians would remain near Fort Laramie until Harney's answer arrived. Then it would be too late to go. Twiss's letter reached Fort Pierre in February 1856, almost simultaneously with a report from Hoffman about the agent's illicit trading. Enraged, Harney ordered Hoffman to confine Twiss to quarters and bar him from communicating with the Sioux. A few weeks later, Harney suspended the agent from duty. As a military officer, he lacked authority to issue such an order, but he had the power to enforce it. Naturally his directive further antagonized Indian Bureau officials.[32]

While waiting for the council to begin, Harney and his troops struggled to survive the cold South Dakota winter. In November, snow began to fall regularly, and ice formed thick enough on the Missouri River to support a wagon. During the next few months, the temperature plunged often to forty degrees below zero. Hoarfrost covered the pasteboard-thin walls inside the portable cottages, and the soldiers tried to insulate them by banking earth around the exteriors. Those men who lived in log huts burned green cottonwood to warm themselves, but the smoky fires turned the frozen dirt floors around the hearths into quagmires and had little effect against cold wind that swept through poorly covered doors and windows. Forced by lack of mess rooms to store and consume rations in their quarters, the soldiers took their haversacks to bed each night to keep their food from freezing. Even when they put on all the clothing they had, they could not avoid frostbite, and several had to have a hand or foot amputated. Most endured the cold only with the help of buffalo robes and deer and beaver skins they bought from Indians and sewed into coats, mittens, and caps. The cavalry horses suffered, too, for their brushwood shelters afforded little protection. More than one-third of the animals died.

Despite their miserable situation, some of the soldiers found cheer in visiting small parties of friendly Indians who occasionally pitched their lodges near army camps. Using sign language, the troops taught the warriors card games and played with their children. A few men even joined the Indians in feasts of roast dog. Other soldiers broke the monotony of the long winter by gambling, reading, and taking music lessons from members of the expedition band, and all sang a little doggerel that expressed their feelings about Fort Pierre:

Oh, we don't mind the marching,
nor the fight do we fear,
But we'll never forgive old Harney
for bringing us to Pierre.
They say old Shotto [Chouteau] built it,
but we know it is not so;
For the man who built this bloody ranche,
is reigning down below.[33]

Harney could do little to improve the troops' living conditions. In midwinter, when scurvy killed several men and left many others weak and listless, he managed to get a few potatoes and onions hauled up from Council Bluffs to supplement their diet, but chiefly he concentrated on arranging early shipment of supplies for spring. He sent three staff officers to St. Louis to procure goods and again urged the War Department to buy light-draft steamers for use during low water. No vessel purchased the previous summer had, in his opinion, proved suitable for that purpose.

Harney also took time to search out other potential locations for forts along the Missouri. In January, traveling only with his adjutant, an assistant surgeon, and an eleven-man escort, he trudged 230 miles downriver to Ponca Island, where he recommended that the army build a post to ensure continued open communication with Fort Pierre. And though he did not visit the sites personally, he also suggested new posts about a hundred miles upriver from Fort Pierre and on the Big Sioux River in present eastern South Dakota. These locations, he thought, would give the army control of key "positions where the Indians can congregate."[34]

While Harney remained confident that he could bring peace to the central and upper plains, waiting through the long winter made him cross and more volatile than usual. To relax and keep fit, he went for a morning walk or ride as often as the weather permitted. One day, as he strolled about Fort Pierre in civilian clothes followed by an orderly leading his favorite mount, he happened unobserved upon a teamster flogging an army mule. Already convinced that muleteers were "careless and worthless," Harney seized the unsuspecting man by the back of the neck and beat him savagely with a riding whip. As he wielded his weapon, Harney unleashed a blast of profanity that, according to one witness, would have made "the average cowboy . . . ashamed of . . . his choicest vocabulary."

Afterward, soldiers speculated about why their commander, who had led a calculated attack against an Indian village filled with women and children, had once again become so emotional about a man whipping a mule. Did Harney, because of some "peculiarity of his nature," feel more compassion for mules, they wondered, than for the innocent children at Blue Water Creek? The soldiers thought so, and in an over-simplified manner, they judged him correctly. However, the incidents with the children and the teamsters differed in one important respect. Harney brought harm to the children in calculated battle. He beat the teamsters during spontaneous outbursts of anger. Theresa Vielé had observed in Texas that despite Harney's "impetuous passions," he seemed "tender-hearted in the extreme toward [both] children and animals." Numerous instances in his career confirm that he had significant capacity to care about the welfare of native people, both children and adults, in peaceful conditions. But he also had enormous capacity for callous vindictiveness in war and at any other time when he took personal offense. Harney never revealed any remorse about killing and injuring children at Ash Hollow, for there he had sought retribution consistent with both his orders and his convictions regarding punishment. The children had been caught up in battle. He also never expressed any regrets about beating the teamsters, for in those instances he had responded instinctively to behavior that he considered inappropriate and offensive. In all three episodes, he demonstrated that he could be dangerous.[35]

Whispering about the muleteer episode at Fort Pierre had scarcely subsided when large groups of Sioux arrived at the post in late February. Because of Twiss's interference, no Oglalas came, but representatives of nine other bands traveled great distances through snow and ice to meet the Great White Chief. With them came their women and children, and by the end of the month nearly a thousand tepees dotted the prairie around the post. Although the Indians seemed peaceful, they outnumbered the soldiers, and recalling what had happened at the Caloosahatchee trading post in Florida, Harney cautiously doubled the number of sentries, issued extra ammunition, and ordered his troops to stay away from the Indian camps.

In the meantime, he finished writing his treaty. Its provisions and his subsequent report to the War Department revealed that despite his brutal and punishing attack at Ash Hollow, he sympathized with the difficult circumstances in which white encroachment placed Indians. Harney's proposed solution to their "many sufferings, consequent to the domain of our people on the soil of this continent" had a long and popular history among both military and civilian authorities. He intended to protect the Sioux from unscrupulous white traders and adventurers and to encourage them to forsake hunting for farming. This would make the Indians dependent upon whites and ensure the latter's access to native land without interference. Harney believed his plan would "very much simplify our relations with these Indians, and at the same time render our control over them effectual." He also stressed the necessity of keeping agreements with them. "They have been deceived so often," he concluded, that if whites break future pacts, the Indians will "never again give them their confidence." Before he promised assistance, however, he intended to seek further redress for white grievances.[36]

At noon on March 1, 1856, Harney convened the Fort Pierre council on a knoll outside the stockade. In this vicinity nearly thirty-one years earlier, he had joined other Sioux in a feast of boiled dog on the Fourth of July, prior to a treaty council led by Henry Atkinson and Benjamin O'Fallon. Now Harney and several other officers, along with clerks and interpreters, sat on a low platform facing another group of chiefs and headmen, who took seats on the ground. Not unlike Atkinson and O'Fallon, Harney planned to dictate, and he intended that his listeners consent. The Indian dignitaries included Long Mandan of the Two Kettle band, Bear Rib of the Hunkpapas, Fire Heart of the Blackfeet Sioux, Crow Feather of the Sans Arcs, and Little Thunder of the Brulés. All listened attentively as the interpreter repeated the towering general's conditions for peace and rules for future relations. First, the Great White Chief explained, the Indians must return all stolen property to the nearest military post and surrender all persons guilty of crimes against whites. Second, they must promise to stay away from emigrant routes. And third, they must make peace with the Pawnees and other neighboring tribes. In return, the government would prosecute whites who committed hostile acts against the Sioux, release Indians currently imprisoned, and restore the annuities discontinued after the Grattan affair. Harney pledged further that if the Indians would give up their roving habits and "raise stock . . . corn, [and] pumpkins," the United States would plough their land and assist them with planting and harvesting. If the Sioux "do as I tell them," he stated emphatically, "they will find me the best friend they ever had; but if they don't do it, they will find me the worst enemy they ever had." On this threatening note Harney recessed the conference to give the Indians time to weigh his words.

When the council resumed on March 2, Little Thunder expressed sentiments shared by all the assembled chiefs. Haunted by painful memories of Blue Water Creek and aware that he must appease Harney, he declared, "I don't wish to fight you; what I want with you is to shake hands." Harney replied sternly that he would not clasp the Indians' hands until they signed the treaty, but as a gesture of goodwill, he said he would release the Brulés captured in the Battle of Ash Hollow. The Indians cheered that proclamation, but when Harney tried to awe them further with a demonstration of the "great power of the white man," they laughed at him. After declaring, in his usual blustery manner, that his people could "kill and bring to life again," Harney instructed an army surgeon to chloroform a dog. While the Indians watched silently, the physician administered the anesthetic, and as soon as the animal lay still, the Great White Chief invited his guests to satisfy themselves that the victim was dead. When they had done so, Harney directed the surgeon to perform a resurrection. To both officers' dismay, the dog did not revive. "Medicine too strong, too strong," the Indians cried in amusement.[37]

Despite Harney's needless attempt to show off, the talks continued for five days, and after he finished coaxing and scolding the chiefs, they consented to everything he asked of them. "Your manners are very hard, very severe," Two Bears, a Yanktonai, remarked before signing the treaty. Harney, like most if not all of his treaty-making predecessors, did not understand that in signing such documents the Indians merely acknowledged the discussion in which they had engaged. Also like other white treaty makers, he ignored the organization of Sioux bands and families, their multiple levels of leadership, and their manner of making decisions by consensus. In addition to the proposals set forth on the first day of the council, the final document contained traditional government provisions to centralize authority among the Indians for the convenience of the United States. At Harney's insistence, each Sioux band selected a principal chief and several subchiefs subject to his approval, and he told them they must take responsibility for their respective groups' relations with the federal government.

To help the principal chiefs exercise their authority and carry out treaty terms, Harney also suggested that each maintain a special police force of fifty to one hundred warriors. Later he urged the War Department to give these units rations and uniforms. "The expense would be trifling," he thought, "and their young men would be stimulated and encouraged to seek these positions." He added that "the dress should be durable and gaudy, particularly the head-dress; (they are fond of feathers)." The government showed little interest in Harney's novel recommendation to support tribal police among the Sioux, but after the Civil War the idea emerged again, this time among reformers and agents in a variety of locations. In 1878, Congress approved funding for agency-based Indian police, and by 1890, fifty-nine agencies had them in place among numerous tribes, including the Pawnees, Klamaths, and Navajos.[38]

On March 5, Harney distributed written commissions to the officially recognized chiefs. "I give you my hand as a friend," he said as he presented Little Thunder his paper. Then, optimistic that he had laid a foundation for peace on the northern plains, the Great White Chief wished all the Sioux well and adjourned the council. The following afternoon, one enlisted man recalled later, "Two thousand Indians marched to the stockade, where General Harney had his headquarters, and saluted his appearance" by beating on drums and "blowing on reed musical instruments made from willows," raising a "curious noise . . . heard for miles around."

Harney began immediately to implement the treaty. Even before the visiting delegations had struck their lodges, he sent word of the proceedings to the Pawnees, Cheyennes, and Arapahos and warned them that if they did not stay away from Sioux country and emigrant trails, he would "sweep them from the face of the earth." On March 8, he advised Davis of the council results and predicted that "with proper management a new era will dawn" in Indian-white relations. Finally Harney urged Davis to send another large force into Sioux country during the summer "to convince them of the ability and intention of the government to enforce obedience to its commands, whenever occasion shall require it."[39]

Representatives of the Oglalas arrived at Fort Pierre on April 19, and they, too, signed the treaty. Shortly afterward, Davis advised President Pierce that Harney had "brought to a successful termination the hostilities which had disturbed the peace of the frontier, and destroyed the security of the emigrant routes." The government then began calculating the cost of the agreement. This task fell as usual on Interior Department and Indian Bureau officials. Twiss and Manypenny, both still miffed with Harney, drove the estimate as high as they dared, and Interior Secretary Robert McClelland raised it further, to $100,000 per year. Believing the document merely an administrative plan that did not require confirmation in the Senate, Pierce sent it to the House of Representatives for funding, but that body, jealous of the Senate's sole authority in treaty ratification, delayed appropriations for it until 1858.[40]

While Washington authorities debated the treaty, expedition soldiers continued their garrison duty on the upper Missouri, and in compliance with the peace terms, the Indians surrendered several prisoners and dozens of stolen horses. Harney kept busy planning for permanent military occupation of the region and searching for the best Missouri River site for a new fort and supply depot. Ultimately he decided on a point thirty miles above the confluence of the Niobrara and Missouri Rivers. On June 30, he recommended naming the new post Fort Randall and advised the War Department that he would remain there until he received further instructions.[41]

Those orders had already been written. There would be no summer campaign. On June 20, satisfied that "the objects for which the sioux [*sic*] expedition was created, have been accomplished," Davis ordered Harney to complete the arrangements for the new post and report to Fort Leavenworth to await reassignment. The army had sent him to punish the Sioux for the Grattan affair and subsequent depredations, and according to Indian Agent Alfred J. Vaughn, Harney had "produced more terror and dismay among" them "than anyone could have imagined or dreamed of." Most Sioux abandoned the emigrant trail, and eventually, in 1858, the Indian Bureau began distributing the goods Harney had promised them. In the meantime, Cheyennes began harassing overland travelers, and in 1857, with Harney then occupied elsewhere, Davis sent Colonel Sumner to chastise the new troublemakers. Sumner followed Harney's example, as did other commanders afterward, for he had demonstrated clearly that the army could use large columns to wage total war against hostile Indians regardless of the season. However, the army remained too small and too poorly organized to respond to all crises in such force, and Indians and whites continued to struggle for supremacy on the Great Plains for most of the rest of the century, until native people could no longer forcibly resist.[42]

CHAPTER 9

Return to Riverine Warfare in Florida

I N EARLY 1856, fear swept across southern Florida like a tropical storm. When Lt. Loomis L. Langdon found the bodies of two oystermen near their charred boats in the Florida Keys on February 25, evidence at the scene implicated Indians. On March 3, a party of Seminoles burned a house and murdered a white man at Sarasota Bay. Three weeks later, a dozen Indians surprised an eleven-man water detail and killed two soldiers in Big Cypress Swamp. Sometime before April 6, an undetermined number of Seminoles attacked a physician's house on the Manatee River and carried off seven slaves and three mules. Shortly after that, an estimated eighty to one hundred dred Indians ambushed a column of 113 soldiers in the Big Cypress, killing one and wounding six.[1]

By then, seven Volusia County men had asked Maj. John Munroe to protect their wives and children, and cattle contractor James Stephens had requested an armed escort to help deliver beef to troops. Soon, terrified Floridians began to abandon their homes. Eighteen white families, about ninety people in all, huddled for mutual protection in a temporary camp sixteen miles outside Tampa, and others congregated nearby. Between eight and ten families assembled at Summerlin's Store, seven sought refuge at Camp Gibson, and twelve streamed into Soak-rum Settlement.[2]

Additional incidents heightened the panic. On May 4, a dozen Seminoles attacked the Bradley family home on the stage road between Tampa and Palatka and killed two children. The same band then struck a wagon train near Fort Brooke and killed three men accompanying it. Two weeks later, six to eight Indians hit another column in the same vicinity and killed two soldiers and a teamster. On June 14, thirty or more Seminoles attacked the Tillis residence about forty-five miles east of Tampa and killed three of seven militiamen who rushed from nearby Fort Meade to drive them off.[3]

In Hernando County, north of Tampa, John E. Turkett and nine other citizens gathered early in June and petitioned Secretary of War Jefferson Davis for "immediate assistance in consequence of the depredations committed by the Seminoles." "We have emigrated from different States of the Union," they wrote, and "we are poor and our little funds exhausted" and "our wives and children is [sic] exposed to the tomahawk and scalping knife of the merciless savage." Davis had already made Florida a separate military department, thereby according it greater attention, and in May he had instructed Major Munroe to call out five more companies of volunteers and send patrols deeper into the Big Cypress. Heavy rains had hampered those efforts, however, and now in mid-July, with Turkett's petition in hand, Davis turned once more to William S. Harney for help.[4] No officer knew Florida or understood the Seminoles' guerilla warfare better.

Harney had been idle at Fort Leavenworth only a few days when he received orders to report to the nation's capital. Although he had been on duty continually for eighteen months, he sought no leave. His family remained in France, distant in attachment as well as miles, and he rushed to Washington, where, in August, Davis handed him stacks of reports on the hostilities and requested recommendations for stopping them.

The government had left an estimated three hundred Indians in southern Florida at the close of the Second Seminole War, and ongoing friction with white settlers had led to the current crisis. After poring over the reports and petitions, Harney suggested innovative measures similar to those that had worked for him previously. He recommended assigning "not less than two *full Regiments of Regular* Troops" to the state and calling out a complementary cadre of volunteers. All these should operate "*almost entirely* in Canoes and Small Boats" and force the Seminoles "to abandon their hiding places in the Cypress Swamps of the Southern part of the Peninsula," he advised. In addition, eight to ten mounted companies should patrol areas north of the swamps to catch any Indians who slipped though the amphibious force. Each boat or canoe, he proposed, should carry no more than five to seven soldiers with enough meat, bread, sugar, and coffee for thirty days in order to reduce the number of supply depots. Finally, he advocated arming at least one hundred of the riverine troops with Samuel Colt's repeating rifles because soldiers had trouble loading "ordinary weapons" in canoes, and the rapid-firing rifles would produce a "moral effect" on the Seminoles.

"With a force not less than the above stated," Harney concluded, "I believe I can drive the Indians from Florida during the coming season if it is *possible* to drive them out at all, which I consider *very doubtful indeed.*" Although confident about his ability as a commander, he had reservations about the feasibility of the task. Davis agreed with both Harney's self-assessment and his recommendations and gave him the job of carrying them out.[5] As usual, Harney pursued his new assignment energetically and in accordance with his own personal convictions. He commanded the Department of Florida only six months before the government required his services elsewhere, but in that short time he demonstrated again his talent for unconventional tactics. The amphibious operations that he planned and put in place helped end the last armed conflict between Indians and whites east of the Mississippi River.

Decades of friction and the government's inhumane removal policy lay behind the Third Seminole War. Settlers and native people had clashed in Florida even before the United States took possession in 1821, and afterward neither removal treaties nor federal troops had produced lasting peace. Calm prevailed for a while following the long and costly Second Seminole War, but when Florida gained statehood in 1845, whites resumed their impassioned demands to remove all Indians. During the next four years, sporadic Indian-white skirmishes kept tempers inflamed. When a small party of Seminoles killed a white fisherman on Indian River near the lower eastern coast in January 1849, the Florida legislature panicked and asked the federal government to help avert a full-scale Indian uprising. Near the end of 1850, Brig. Gen. David E. Twiggs had seventeen hundred troops in the state, and he offered bonuses to entice chief Holato Mico (Billy Bowlegs to whites) and his followers to move to present-day Oklahoma, where most other southeastern Indians had already relocated. This induced only eighty-five Indians to leave the peninsula, and Holato Mico was not among them.[6] Little changed over the next several years, and neither more bonus offers nor talks with Holato Mico and other chiefs in Washington in 1852 altered circumstances. Settlers and Indians continued to skirmish and steal cattle and hogs from each other, and the legislature continued in an uproar.

On December 19, 1855, after discovering that Indians had burned Fort Shackleford, an abandoned post in the Big Cypress Swamp, Lt. George K. Hartsuff and a small surveying party destroyed a Seminole vegetable patch near Holato Mico's camp. The next morning, thirty-five Indians jumped Hartsuff's detachment, killed two men, and wounded four. This attack on federal troops elevated the level of hostilities, but due to growing military responsibilities in the West, the Florida command had dwindled to 871 men. Governor James E. Broome furnished three mounted militia companies to help pursue the Seminoles, and the federal government offered bounties ranging from one hundred to five hundred dollars for every Indian captured. Neither action helped, though, and 1856 brought the incidents leading to Harney's appointment.[7]

The War Department began at once to assemble troops and supplies for a fall and winter campaign. Davis assigned Harney the Fifth Infantry Regiment, ten companies of the Fourth Artillery, four companies of the First Artillery, and three companies of the Second Artillery, about twenty-two hundred men altogether and almost 13 percent of the entire army. He also authorized Harney to call on Governor Broome for eight to ten additional companies of volunteers. Q.M. Gen. Thomas S. Jesup located wagons from other commands, shipped more than 450 mules and horses to Tampa Bay, and ordered thirty-three eighteen-foot-long, light-draft boats built for Harney's use in Florida's marshlands. The department did not immediately order the Colt repeating rifles, however, because the company could not guarantee delivery before the start of the campaign.[8]

Harney made a quick trip to St. Louis in September for personal business, hustled to New York City in October to confer about boat construction, and then circled back to Washington for final consultation with Davis. What further inducements, Harney asked, could he offer the Indians to emigrate, and could he allow a dozen Seminoles to remain in Florida if they helped him remove the rest? Davis replied that each Indian who surrendered could receive the federal bounty offered for his or her capture and that if old Chief Arpiucki (Sam Jones) wanted to assist the government, he and his family could remain on a small Florida reservation suitable for farming and fishing. He would have to sign a formal treaty, however. Davis also informed Harney that on August 7 the western Seminoles and Creeks had signed an agreement that eliminated one of the eastern Seminoles' principal objections to removal. Previously the western Seminoles had shared a reservation with the Creeks without a corresponding voice in tribal government, a situation the eastern Seminoles found unacceptable. The new arrangement gave the western Seminoles their own reservation plus a $250,000 annuity and promised them an additional $250,000 when their eastern cousins joined them. In return the western Seminoles agreed to send a peace delegation to Florida to encourage emigration. Congress had yet to fund the treaty, though, and so Davis instructed Harney to wage a "most vigorous campaign." The War Department has "entire confidence in your zeal and capacity as a soldier . . . [and] in your special knowledge of both the enemy and the country," Davis wrote, and "you are left to the freest exercise of your discretion in the plans and conduct" of your operations.[9]

The new Florida commander interpreted this last comment literally. Early in November, he and his adjutant, Capt. Alfred Pleasonton, traveled south by train to Charleston and there caught a steamer to Key West. While waiting for transportation on to Tampa Bay, Harney directed several post commanders to send out white flags and encourage the Seminoles, especially Arpiucki, to come in for talks. On November 22, after finally reaching Fort Brooke aboard a revenue cutter, Harney ordered a cease-fire. Although ready to fight, he remained well aware of the difficulty of his assignment, and he wanted to try first to persuade the Indians "to emigrate . . . peacefully." If he did not succeed, at least the Seminoles would "fully understand the intentions of the Government" before the troops resorted to "extreme measures."[10]

While patrols posted white flags, Harney prepared to seal off the southern third of the peninsula. On November 25 he asked Governor Broome for seven new companies of mounted volunteers to complement the three units currently in service. Jesse Carter, the governor's special assistant, started recruiting men the following day and hoped to finish by December 20. Scouting parties reported that the Seminoles had retreated south of Lake Istokpoga, about eighty miles southeast of Tampa Bay, and so Harney planned to station the volunteers and three companies of regulars at nine points between Fort Brooke and the eastern coast. He expected those troops to protect white settlements to the north and free the remaining regulars to pursue the Indians into the Big Cypress Swamp and Everglades.[11]

By December 5, Harney doubted that any Indians would come in to talk unless a delegation of western Seminoles persuaded them. Accordingly he asked Washington to bring Otee-Ematular (Jumper), who had signed the August 7 treaty, and one hundred of his western brothers to Florida immediately. Only he can "go out to the Indians and inform them of my wishes to see them," Harney declared, and therefore "I shall reserve the action of the troops until after his services are exhausted." Davis and Interior Secretary Robert McClelland had already discussed the possibility of sending a few western Indians to help Harney, but until now Davis had not heard about the cease-fire, and he considered it an unnecessary delay. Angrily on December 10 he ordered Harney to reread his instructions for "vigorous prosecution of operations." He received Davis's message before December 26, yet stubbornly on the twenty-ninth he sent out several more patrols under white flags.[12]

While Harney waited for the Indians to respond, he wrestled with organizational details and petitions from citizens demanding increased military protection as far north as St. Augustine. Residents there asked for help after they heard rumors that Indians had murdered a family of settlers near New Smyrna, about thirty-five miles south. Harney asked Governor Broome for four additional companies of volunteers to patrol Florida's northeastern coast, but the state provided only one.[15]

In the face of these myriad pressures, Harney erupted into characteristic fits of temper. Second Lt. Oliver O. Howard, only recently out of West Point, reported to Harney at his temporary Fort Myers headquarters early in January and observed two outbursts almost immediately. Having heard that Harney could be "very severe in his style and hard to approach," the young lieutenant came unprepared for the "hearty welcome" and "cordial . . . manner" with which the veteran soldier received him in his office. "Why, Mr. Howard," Harney said, "I have long wanted an ordnance officer, and I am glad you have come! Take a seat and make yourself at home!" The two men chatted in a "companionable" manner until the evening mail arrived a few minutes later. Harney interrupted their conversation to open it, and one of the letters upset him tremendously. "His rough language corresponded to the heat of his passion," Howard wrote later, and "I was glad to make some excuse to retire from his presence. I saw then that Harney in quiet social life was one person but quite another when official matters ruffled his temper."

Harney remained irritated the next morning when, accompanied by Howard and Pleasonton, he boarded a small boat and headed out to the steamer *Fashion* for the return trip to Fort Brooke. After the boat crew set the mast improperly and one of the oarsmen locked paddles with his fellows on three successive strokes, Harney, who was steering, became "white with anger, seized a boat hook near at hand, and struck at the soldier," Howard recalled. The oarsman reacted playfully, dodging behind the mast and jeering at the general, who swung his weapon again in vain. A surgeon on board recognized that the man was delirious and calmed Harney. Once the boat got under way, he regained his composure. "I wouldn't hurt the lad," he said, but "the crazy fellow probably thought I wanted to kill him." Harney's protestation notwithstanding, he intended no little harm, and the incident increased his already widespread reputation for irascibility.[14]

Finally, on January 5, 1857, Harney gave up the notion of peaceful removal and ordered his troops to "make every effort . . . to capture or destroy the Seminoles." On January 8, he divided southern Florida into three military districts, placed a regimental commander in charge of each, and ordered them to keep scouting parties constantly searching for Indians. By January 14, he had land and amphibious troops either moving or preparing to move through the entire region in force. His plan provided for a more comprehensive and better coordinated sweep of lower Florida than any attempted during the Second Seminole War. In its thoroughness, relentlessness, and design to wear down the enemy, it anticipated campaigns that Brig. Gen. George F. Crook and Brig. Gen. Nelson A. Miles waged against the Apaches in the Southwest nearly thirty years later. Infantrymen would comb the western coast and adjoining lowlands in boats and canoes, while artillerymen and mounted volunteers raked the high country on foot and horseback. One amphibious company would patrol Charlotte Harbor north of Fort Myers, two would scour the upper reaches of the Big Cypress, and four would examine its lower waters and the Everglades. Three mounted volunteer units would patrol the area immediately north of the Big Cypress, and three artillery companies and two more volunteer units would cover the eastern side of Lake Okeechobee. Anxious as always to get into action himself, Harney intended to lead four foot and horse companies through the region between Lakes Istokpoga and Okeechobee and Pease Creek.[15]

By mid-January Harney had all his troops in motion with orders to investigate every Indian sign and burn every Seminole camp they discovered. Thus began a long and often arduous campaign in which the soldiers harassed Indians but captured few. On the sixteenth, Harney set out from Fort Brooke on his personal scouting mission. Leading only three mounted volunteer companies instead of four as he had planned, he marched eastward to the Kissimmee River, followed it south past Lake Istokpoga to Fort Bassinger, and then proceeded southwest to Fort Denaud on the Caloosahatchee, arriving finally at

Fort Myers on the coast by January 28. His party traveled light, doing without tents despite unseasonably cold weather and supplementing sparse rations with palmetto fruit and alligator tails. Occasionally the soldiers killed and ate an Indian hog, but they saw no Seminoles, only recently abandoned camps and villages. While searching the area south of Lake Istokpoga, one detachment discovered a thirteen-hut village in which the fleeing residents had left dogs, pigs, cooking utensils, and farm tools. Instead of pursuing the fugitives immediately, however, the volunteers returned to their own camp for supplies and the Seminoles escaped, leaving Harney seething.[16]

His other patrols saw no Indians either, and by the end of January he believed that most of the native people had moved south of Lake Okeechobee. Accordingly he decided to renew the search in the Big Cypress and Everglades and ordered Col. Gustavus Loomis and four Fifth Infantry companies to scour the swamp in boats while four other units moved along the coast and through the upper glades to seize any Seminoles seeking refuge there. Low water hampered these operations, and the troops found only one fresh Indian trail. It led southeast through dense growths of cypress and maple and then disappeared. Similar searches of the Florida Keys and Cape Sable also found nothing.[17]

Volunteer scouting parties north of Lake Okeechobee continued to produce negative results, too, and by February 20 Harney, now back at Fort Brooke, anticipated that his campaign would drag into summer. Events of the next few days seemed to confirm this prospect. On the twenty-eighth he learned that Congress still had not funded the August 7 treaty and no western Indians would reach Florida in time to assist him.[18]

Then on March 4 a Seminole woman seized near Lake Okeechobee reported that the Indians had separated into small parties after vowing to die fighting rather than emigrate. The woman also said that old chief Arpiucki was somewhere in the Big Cypress, and when Harney learned a few days later that two Fifth Infantry detachments had clashed with Indians southeast of Lake Okeechobee, he felt encouraged about chances for a decisive confrontation. News that finally the War Department had obtained one hundred Colt repeating rifles and sent them to Fort Brooke provided further cause for optimism. More importantly, reports on the Big Cypress incidents suggested that the Seminoles had initiated them. This indicated their continued willingness to show themselves when provoked. On March 8, Harney instructed Capt. Carter L. Stevenson, then on the upper Caloosahatchee, to "lose no time in pressing the enemy to some decided disadvantage." To support these operations, he ordered artillery and infantry units in the Everglades and on Cape Sable to proceed to the Big Cypress immediately. Convinced now that "the Indians are in force" in the swamp, he took the field again himself to direct the operations.[19]

During the next four weeks the soldiers fought a number of skirmishes with the Seminoles, captured several, and destroyed a number of abandoned Indian villages and gardens. Following the initial clashes, Harney returned to his temporary headquarters at Fort Myers and ordered further reconnaissance. On March 22, units of the Fourth Artillery from Cape Sable and Fifth Infantry from Chokoloskee entered the Big Cypress from the southwest, struck a fresh Indian trail, and followed it for four days. They discovered several recently extinguished campfires and destroyed some abandoned camp baggage and packs of bear and otter skins, but they saw no Seminoles. Scouting parties in the Everglades found no trace of Indians at all, but volunteers operating north of the Big Cypress detected fresh signs on both sides of Lake Okeechobee and clashed with about ten Seminoles.

Contrary to Harney's earlier assumption, the Indians now seemed scattered, and he believed that his persistent patrols had weakened them. Early in April, he intensified the search, concentrating again on the Big Cypress, where he still believed Arpiucki and Holato Mico were hiding, and in the Halpaticke and Ochlawaha swamps, north of Lake Okeechobee. Harney instructed his commanders to "act with energy" and follow "any recent sign" of the Seminoles "until they are overtaken." This "cannot but shake the confidence of the Indians in their efforts to avoid us," he assured Washington.[20]

Despite these redoubled efforts, Harney still longed for a delegation of western Seminoles and Creeks to speed removal. "The terror with which these Indians are inspired by my presence here," he declared to Davis, "prevents them from accepting any means of communication I can offer. They are ignorant of the generous intentions of the Government towards them, and will remain so, until confidence is restored to them by their own people." Although arrogantly self-serving, Harney's observation correctly assessed the need for mediation. Unwilling to wait any longer for Congress to act on the August treaty, he decided to try some other way to communicate with the Indians. On April 21 he hired Lewis Daugherty, a civilian, to deliver a message explaining removal conditions and the new reservation circumstances in Oklahoma. Before Daugherty could act, however, the War Department transferred Harney to Fort Leavenworth at the request of Robert J. Walker, the newly appointed governor of politically troubled Kansas Territory. Harney felt certain that his new duties would be "important," but he regretted "that the order was not delayed a month or two, as everything is progressing so well." On April 27, after suggesting that his existing "arrangements" in the department "not be disturbed," he relinquished command to Colonel Loomis.[21]

The Third Seminole War dragged on much longer than Harney had expected and concluded only after the government finally brought in western Seminoles and Creeks as he had requested. Almost immediately after Loomis assumed command, Adj. Gen. Samuel Cooper sent him a ten-point "Memorandum of the plan of operations proposed to be carried out by General Harney in the Department of Florida during the summer months" and instructed him to "conform, substantially" to it. Loomis agreed that confining the Seminoles to the Big Cypress and Everglades and harassing them constantly with mounted and amphibious patrols offered "the only practicable method of getting the Indians out of this State." However, the withdrawal of most regular troops for service in the West hampered his efforts.[22]

Relying heavily on volunteers, Loomis hounded the Seminoles as best he could and occasionally captured a woman or child. On August 30 he predicted that "the Indians cannot hold out much longer," and in December he reported that Holato Mico himself was urging the Seminoles to surrender. Some continued to resist, though, and in his annual report John B. Floyd, Davis's successor as secretary of war, expressed both the government's frustration with the military impasse and his own feelings of cultural superiority. "The country is a perpetual succession of swamps and morasses, almost impenetrable," Floyd noted, "and the Indians partake rather of the nature of beasts of the chase than of men capable of resisting in fight a military power. Their only strength lies in a capacity to elude pursuit."[23]

Finally on January 19, 1858, Elias Rector, superintendent of southern tribes in Indian Territory, arrived in Florida with a number of western Seminoles and Creeks, including Otee-Ematular, whom Harney had requested more than a year earlier. Loomis called in his patrols while the peace delegation contacted eastern Seminole leaders and arranged a council. In return for money and other inducements, Holato Mico consented to removal, and several other chiefs and headmen followed his example. In all, 124 Indians surrendered. Early in May, Rector escorted these and forty-one other captives to their new homes in Indian Territory.

On May 8, Loomis declared the war over. Those Indians who remained in Florida were widely scattered and posed no threat, he proclaimed. "The people can now return to their homes and usual avocations without fear of further molestation." By June, the War Department had transferred all but one company of regular troops out of the state. In December, Rector returned with Holato Mico, and by February 15, 1859, they had persuaded seventy-five more Seminoles to emigrate, leaving but a few in their homeland.[24]

The Third Seminole War represented one last major demonstration of the federal government's inhumane Indian removal policy and highlighted once again the army's difficulties in dealing with native warriors' unconventional fighting methods. A few hundred Seminoles, many of them women and children, occupied nearly three thousand regular and volunteer soldiers for almost two years, and the conflict resembled a mammoth reconnaissance operation more than a war. The government succeeded eventually in removing most of the Florida Indians only because Harney reintroduced the unconventional tactics he had originated during the Second Seminole War. His amphibious patrols and constant harassment of the Indians, which Loomis continued, accounted substantially for the success that Rector and the western Indians had in persuading the Seminoles to emigrate.

The war also provided another example of how circumstances significantly influenced the manner in which Harney treated Indians. His situation this time in Florida differed from the last years of his first service there and from the events surrounding his summons to Nebraska in 1854. With no personal score to settle and no charge to inflict a punitive lesson, he strained the patience of authorities in Washington by trying time after time to convince the Indians to leave peacefully because that seemed the most expedient alternative. Only after those efforts failed did he carry out his relentless pursuit.

1. William S. Harney, 1850s. *Courtesy of the National Archives (Brady Collection).*

2. *Col. Harney Storming the Citadel on the Summit of Cerro Gordo, April 18,*
1847. Woodcut by H. W. Orr. Courtesy of the Missouri Historical Society, St. Louis.

3. Brigadier General William S. Harney, late 1850s. *Courtesy of the National Archives.*

4. Little Thunder, Brulé Sioux. *Courtesy of the National Museum of the American Indian, Smithsonian Institution, negative no. 35111.*

5. Spotted Tail, Brulé Sioux, ca. 1872. *Photograph by Alexander Gardner. Courtesy of the South Dakota State Historical Society.*

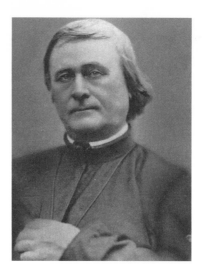

6. Father Pierre-Jean DeSmet, 1858. *Courtesy of the Jesuit Oregon Province Archives, Gonzaga University, negative no. 802.09.*

7. Lt. Gen. Winfield Scott, 1861. *Photograph by Matthew Brady.*
Courtesy of the National Portrait Gallery, Smithsonian
Institution, negative no. 79.41.

8. Indian Peace Commissioners, 1868. From left, Alfred Terry, William S. Harney, William T. Sherman, unidentified Indian woman, Nathaniel G. Taylor, Samuel F. Tappan, and Christopher C. Augur. *Courtesy of the National Archives.*

9. Indian Peace Commissioners at Fort Laramie, 1868. Harney is second from left, sitting on William T. Sherman's right. *Photograph by Alexander Gardner. Courtesy of the National Anthropological Archives, Smithsonian Institution, negative no. 3686.*

10. Railroad delegation at Fort Sanders, near present Laramie, Wyoming, 1868. William S. Harney stands tall in top hat and cape in right foreground. William T. Sherman stands to his immediate right, and Ulysses S. Grant has both hands on the fence left of the gate. Granville Dodge is at the extreme left, and Phillip Sheridan stands to his right in the foreground with hat in hand. *Photograph by Andrew J. Russell. Courtesy of the Golden Spike National Historic Site, National Park Service.*

CHAPTER 10

Civil Unrest in Kansas and Utah

L ATE IN the afternoon on Saturday, July 18, 1857, regimental bands struck up martial airs, and 650 Tenth Infantrymen marched past the quarters of Brevet Brig. Gen. William S. Harney, out of Fort Leavenworth, and westward toward Salt Lake City, Utah, twelve hundred miles distant. The next day, 70 men from a Fourth Artillery battery followed, and two days later 525 men from the Fifth Infantry tramped after them.

Setting out across the Great Plains this late in the summer constituted a significant gamble, and Harney had counseled against it. Unsuccessful in postponing the trek, he had issued detailed orders for its execution, covering everything from daily departure times for each unit to procedures for avoiding dust and picketing horses and mules at night. Traveling fifteen miles a day, each detachment had twenty-five days to reach Fort Kearny on the Platte River, twenty-five more days to march to Fort Laramie on the North Platte, and forty days to get from there to Salt Lake. They could rest five minutes every hour, all day every eighth day on the trail, and three days at each of the forts. Everyone walked except officers, drivers, those sick, and the mounted artillerymen. The latter could ride every other hour when on flat terrain.[1]

Thus began one of the two largest, and arguably most dramatic, pre–Civil War nineteenth-century uses of the army to support federal officials, enforce civil law, and preserve domestic order. The two efforts occurred almost simultaneously, and for a time Harney commanded both. As an anxious nation watched, he helped two territorial governors conduct peaceful, though inconclusive, elections in turbulent Kansas, where issues of slavery, land, and patronage created violent political factions whose actions portended national civil conflict. And he organized and twice commanded an enormous expedition sent to uphold the federal territorial system in Mormon-dominated Utah. In addition to illustrating the army's peacekeeping role, these undertakings highlighted the military's ongoing shortage of resources and its lingering inefficiencies in organizational structure.

In late April 1857, Harney traveled by steamer from Fort Myers via New Orleans to Fort Leavenworth, where he assumed "command of the troops serving in the Territory of Kansas." Although not ready to leave Florida, Harney anticipated a new kind of challenge and looked forward to the assignment "with pleasure." Had he known that the duty would be essentially administrative, he might have been less pleased, for as one observer of his Kansas years recalled later, war was his "trade" and peace his "aversion."[2] Harney himself had admitted that he felt happiest when conducting operations in the field.

The army's multifaceted peacekeeping responsibilities in the West required more, however. Besides protecting white settlers and travelers from hostile Indians, and peaceful Indians from hostile whites, the army also helped maintain order among whites themselves. The conditions that brought Harney back to Fort Leavenworth, launching site for his Sioux campaign, stemmed primarily, but not exclusively, from the question of slavery in the western territories. Two attempts, the Compromises of 1820 and 1850, had failed to settle the issue, and passage of the Kansas-Nebraska Act in 1854 had reopened it. The law divided the region immediately west of Missouri and Iowa into two new territories and, under the principle of popular sovereignty, allowed the citizens of each to decide for themselves whether to allow slavery. The legislation also opened Kansas to white settlement before the government extinguished Indian land titles and set up mechanisms for filing claims.

These circumstances, together with the usual frontier opportunities for political patronage and speculative enterprise, quickly turned Kansas into a literal and propagandistic battleground. Pro- and antislavery factions, within and outside the territory, struggled for control. Proslavery Missourians crossed into Kansas in the winter of 1854–55 and cast enough bogus ballots to ensure that the first territorial legislature, which convened at Shawnee Mission in July, adopted laws designed to protect slavery. The antislavery faction responded by forming the Free State Party, convening in Topeka in October, establishing their own territorial government, and writing a constitution that outlawed slavery. For the next two years, each of these two competing governments held its own elections and claimed to represent all Kansans.

Meanwhile antislavery forces as far away as Massachusetts urged people who opposed slavery to settle in Kansas. Proslavery Missourians raced to get there first and grab prime land. And tensions erupted into a series of violent and portentous acts that extended eventually to the floor of the U.S. Senate. In May 1856, armed proslavery men sacked the town of Lawrence and burned the Free State Hotel, two newspaper offices, and the home of Free State leader Charles Robinson. In retaliation, Connecticut-born radical abolitionist John Brown, his four sons, and three other men raided a proslavery settlement on Pottawatomie Creek, murdered five unarmed slavery proponents, and mutilated their bodies. In Washington, Massachusetts senator Charles Sumner denounced slavery and South Carolina senator A. P. Butler in a vituperative speech entitled "The Crime against Kansas." Two days later, South Carolina congressman Preston Brooks strode into the Senate chamber and beat Sumner savagely about the head and shoulders with a cane until he fell to the floor unconscious and bleeding.

The violence in Kansas continued throughout the summer, and on August 21 federally appointed governor Wilson Shannon resigned in disgust. Four days later, his interim successor, proslavery Territorial Secretary Daniel Woodson, declared Kansas in open rebellion. The new governor, John W. Geary, arrived in September and, with the help of federal troops from Fort Leavenworth, restored order temporarily. He then tried to arrange a permanent compromise between the warring factions and get Kansas admitted to the Union under the antislavery Topeka constitution. The effort failed, however, and Geary quit amid threats to his life.[3]

To succeed him, President James Buchanan, a Democrat who had won election in 1856 by sweeping southern and border states, selected Robert J. Walker. A short, balding man who had achieved distinction in the Senate and in President Polk's cabinet, Walker suffered from poor health, and his wife did not want to live in Kansas. Eventually, under pressure from Buchanan and Senator Stephen A. Douglas of Illinois, he accepted, but with several stipulations. In addition to requesting former Tennessee congressman Frederick P. Stanton as territorial secretary, Walker insisted on Harney as commander of federal troops assigned to maintain order. General Harney, Walker asserted, "is well known to the people of Kansas, and greatly respected by them." Walker also wanted Buchanan's assurance "that the actual bona fide residents of . . . Kansas, by a fair and regular vote" could decide for themselves "in adopting their state constitution" whether to permit slavery. The president consented to all three conditions.[4]

Pleased that in general the nation reacted favorably to his appointment, Walker went to Kansas confident of success. He considered the territory geographically unsuited to slavery-based agriculture, and he hoped to bring it into the Union as a free state. In his inaugural address at Lecompton on May 27, he pointed out that Congress recognized the proslavery territorial legislature as the region's legitimate government, and he promised that the June 15 election to choose delegates to a September constitutional convention would be conducted "free from fraud and violence."[5]

While Walker traveled around the territory repeating this message, Harney organized his command at Fort Leavenworth. His hair had grown thinner now, and sometimes he wore spectacles, but he remained straight in carriage and energetic in manner. To serve as adjutant he had brought along Capt. Alfred Pleasonton, a reserved and competent officer who had been with him since the Sioux campaign and in whom he professed "*perfect* confidence."[6] Harney had orders identical to those issued to Bvt. Maj. Gen. Persifor F. Smith, commander of the Department of the West. If Governor Walker found federal marshals inadequate to preserve the peace and enforce the law, he could requisition "a military force to aid him, as a posse comitatus." Under authority of the U.S. Constitution and the Calling Forth Act of 1795, federal troops in Kansas had performed that function many times during the previous fourteen months. In helping Governors Shannon and Geary break up armed bands of both proslavery men and Free Staters, thereby preventing civil strife in general, Col. Edwin V. Sumner had interpreted the army's role in preserving the peace broadly. What had begun as a charge to help marshals and sheriffs make arrests had evolved into an effort to police the territory. Now Walker and Harney started with that same broad view.[7]

And they started well. Although most antislavery men boycotted the June 15 election, Walker conducted it without incident, and as the days went by Harney housed territorial prisoners at Fort Leavenworth and provided a company of dragoons to help the Leavenworth County sheriff maintain order during a murder trial. On July 15, Walker asked Harney to send an entire regiment to Lawrence. A "dangerous rebellion" had occurred there, the governor wrote in alarm, and "if not speedily arrested," it would be "extended throughout the territory." His concern stemmed chiefly from the announced intention of antislavery citizens to establish a formal town government without a territorial charter and then urge Free State men in other communities to follow their example. Walker went to Lawrence to order the organizers to desist, and Harney sent Col. Philip St. George Cooke and seven companies of dragoons to support him. Upon arriving, they discovered that the governor had overestimated the danger of civil strife, but he continued to worry nevertheless.[8]

About this same time, a new cause for concern emerged, as Harney's future status in Kansas became clouded. On May 28, scarcely a month after arriving at Fort Leavenworth, he received word from his old nemesis, commanding general Winfield Scott, that he would "probably be designated to the command of a force to march to, and winter in, Utah." Seemingly contradictory to the bargain that Walker had made with Buchanan, this message reflected one of the army's major organizational problems in the 1850s. Despite being the nation's first major bureaucracy, and for many years the most professional, the army lacked well-coordinated, centralized leadership in Washington. The position of commanding general had never been well defined, especially in relation to the secretary of war. The latter had authority over all staff departments, from quartermaster and ordnance to adjutant general and paymaster, while in theory the commanding general had authority over all line officers, from infantry to artillery. However, the administrative department heads all exercised a high and often unproductive level of autonomy, and the secretary of war could and did communicate directly with line officers through the adjutant general. This system grew more cumbersome after Scott lost the presidency to his longtime rival, Zachary Taylor, in 1848. Miffed, the commanding general moved his headquarters to New York City and from there feuded openly with the War Department over organizational structure. Although Scott and departmental officials collaborated on some matters related to Utah, they did not communicate effectively about Harney and Kansas. Apparently Scott did not know about the condition under which Walker had accepted his appointment, and over the next six weeks Harney received a series of conflicting orders and directives from New York and Washington.[9]

The trouble in Utah Territory arose chiefly because the Mormons, members of the Church of Jesus Christ of the Latter-day Saints, resisted federal authority in various matters of territorial government. Organized by Joseph Smith in Palmyra, New York, in 1830, Mormons considered themselves "the one true church," exercising direct and complete influence over both the spiritual and temporal lives of members. Because of their sectarian religious beliefs and cooperative economic ventures, the Mormons encountered hostility almost everywhere they settled. In 1844 non-Mormons, outraged by the sect's political activities and newly announced practice of polygamy, killed Smith and his brother near Nauvoo, Illinois, and the majority of the faithful, about sixteen thousand, decided to move to the Rocky Mountains. Three years later, most settled in Salt Lake Valley, a region habitable for people willing to work hard, but too dry and isolated to appeal to many others. After two years, the emigrants formed a provisional government for the State of Deseret and asked for admission to the Union. Congress, preoccupied with the debate over slavery, refused this request but later created the Territory of Utah as part of the Compromise of 1850. President Millard Fillmore then appointed the Mormons' new leader, Brigham Young, governor.

That began a decade of almost constant bickering between Mormons and federal officials. The Mormons wanted to govern themselves without interference from any quarter, including Congress. Young, a determined and capable leader given to incendiary speech, quickly molded Utah into a desert theocracy in which the church controlled both elective political offices and local courts. Non-Mormons who settled in Utah objected strenuously to those practices, as did appointees sent from Washington to fill territorial offices. The latter increased the friction. Few proved capable, some had no scruples, and most stayed only a short time before hastening back east to describe Mormon excesses to Congress and the press.[10]

Polygamy exacerbated the controversy. Many national politicians considered the practice a "twin relic of barbarism" along with slavery, and some tried to make the Mormons an issue in the election of 1856. Slavery far overshadowed polygamy, but apparently the latter seemed serious enough to persuade President Buchanan that the Mormons constituted a political problem he should resolve quickly. Reports from various federal officials seemed to justify strong measures. For example, David H. Burr, newly appointed surveyor general of Utah, complained that church officials *"repudiate the authority of the United States . . . and are in open rebellion against the federal government."* Within a few weeks, Buchanan decided to replace Governor Young with a non-Mormon and give him sufficient military support to enforce federal law. The president doubted that Young would resist and assumed erroneously that most Mormons would welcome dismantling the theocracy.[11]

Scott's preliminary instructions to Harney reflected the administration's haste in deciding to send troops. At this point neither the commanding general nor the War Department had drafted any formal orders for the expedition. Scott could tell Harney only that his troops would include the Second Dragoons, the Fifth and Tenth Infantry regiments, and a battery of the Fourth Artillery and that he could not expect to have them available "until late in July, if that soon."

Having tramped across the plains and thrashed the Sioux two years earlier, Harney felt confident that he could deal effectively with the Mormons. And the prospect of taking 2,000 men, from the army's current 15,764 aggregate, into potential action appealed to him, too. However, he also recalled the logistical difficulties attendant to the Sioux campaign, and he doubted that an expedition leaving Fort Leavenworth in late July could reach Utah before snow fell and enabled the Mormons to block the narrow and strategic mountain defiles leading into Salt Lake Valley. I am "willing, if the President desires it," Harney informed Secretary of War John B. Floyd, "to go to Utah with such force as he may deem sufficient." The veteran campaigner preferred to go on his own terms, though, as opposed to those he had seen so far.

Within a week after hearing from Scott, Harney offered a number of observations and suggestions about the expedition. "In a military point of view," he opined, "nothing can be gained by forcing the troops into the valley this winter." He proposed, therefore, that the army assemble "one year's supply" at Fort Laramie, winter the expedition there, and enter Utah in the spring. He had information indicating that the Mormons had already begun gathering and arming men. Wintering at Fort Laramie would have a "moral effect" on them, he maintained, while avoiding being so close that "they can study our numbers, material, etc." In addition, blending expediency with a measure of opportunism, Harney proposed that Buchanan appoint him governor "with full powers to declare martial law." "The Mormons," he contended, "will never recognize the authority of any Governor except Brigham Young so long as he lives, unless that other has the *power* to *compel* them to do so." Finally, recalling his previous experiences with military bureaucracy, Harney urged Secretary Floyd to bring all expedition units to full strength, make Utah a separate military department, and place Forts Kearny and Laramie under his command at once "to avoid the inconvenience of referring matters of detail to Washington." Except for the governor's appointment, all these recommendations represented sound advice.[12]

Scott had already notified army department heads–quartermaster general, commissary general, chief of ordnance, and others–about the expedition so they could begin arranging for supplies and equipment. Even without formal orders, all knew this would constitute the army's biggest operation since the Mexican War and the largest force ever sent across the Great Plains. Gen. Thomas S. Jesup advised Harney on June 5 that although the Quartermaster Department would try to have all supplies ready by the anticipated departure date, Harney himself must take care of their transportation. Jesup, too, worried about the late start of the march. "I greatly regret," he said, "that we have not [had] the advantage of the two months just past to make our arrangements."

While awaiting further instructions and assisting Governor Walker as needed, Harney fleshed out preliminary plans. Earlier in the year, in hope of easing its increasingly difficult task of supplying far-flung posts, the army had granted the Kansas firm of Majors and Russell an exclusive contract to transport all military supplies west of the Mississippi. Accordingly, Harney consulted with Alexander Majors about the availability of wagons and teams. Since February, his company had dispatched 645 wagonloads of military goods from Fort Leavenworth in 48 oxen-pulled trains, and many of those remained en route to or from various posts. Thus the firm had a shortage of men, wagons, and draft animals. Because of that and the lateness of the season, it would be impossible, Majors told Harney, to get all expedition supplies to Utah before winter, though perhaps the company could transport enough to last until spring.[15]

This response, which seemed to confirm one of Harney's principal concerns, came almost simultaneously with alarming information from the West. Maj. Lewis Armistead reported from Fort Riley, at the fork of the Kansas River, that about 150 Indians had attacked an emigrant wagon train eighty miles northwest of there and killed four men. Also, a source that Harney described only as "authentic" informed him that the federal land on which his command probably would have to camp after reaching Salt Lake Valley was marshy, devoid of timber for huts, and nearly impassable in wet weather. Harney feared that Indians might "complicate" the expedition, but he worried more about the shortage of supply trains and the poor campground. Thus on June 12 he proposed another alternative. A single regiment of some six to seven hundred men might, he thought, be small enough to reach Utah by winter yet large enough to aid a new governor until reinforcements arrived the following season. Although addressed to the adjutant general in Washington, Harney's communication went ultimately to Scott in New York, where it arrived on June 22. By this time Jesup had informed Scott that "ample provision" had already been made for "trains and animals," and the commanding general thought the circumstances presented "no real difficulties." Scott observed that if the War Department would forward the orders he had now prepared for General Harney, his "doubts about transportation would be cured." In any case, Scott observed, "the proposition to risk one regiment alone, in Utah, for the winter, is utterly inadmissible."[14]

While Harney waited for responses from his superiors, he found time to give a party on June 23 for Governor Walker, his wife, and various officers and their spouses. One wife recalled later that a "courteous and deferential manner . . . invariably characterized" Harney "in the presence of ladies," but he had an "energetic mode of expressing himself" and sometimes ended up having to apologize for remarks. On one such occasion he boasted that when he got to Utah he would "hang Brigham first and try him afterward." The utterance typified Harney's swagger.[15]

By the end of the month the president, secretary of war, and commanding general had agreed on expedition orders. Scott notified Harney that in Utah, as in Kansas, he would help a new governor, Alfred Cumming, establish and maintain "law and order" by providing a posse comitatus whenever required. Buchanan still wanted troops in Salt Lake Valley by winter, but the War Department recognized the "lateness of the season" and granted Harney "a large discretion" in planning their movement. Scott cautioned him against being overly confident. Until the expedition got under way, Harney would command both the troops assigned to Utah and those ordered to stay in Kansas. After January 1, 1858, Utah would become a separate military department under either Harney or the senior officer present there.[16]

At this juncture Harney's forces still included far fewer troops than he had anticipated. He had at Fort Leavenworth 74 officers and 978 enlisted men from the Second Dragoons, Fourth Artillery, and Tenth Infantry regiments. Additionally, at least two companies of the Second Dragoons awaited his instructions at Fort Kearny, and he expected two more companies of Tenth infantrymen from Minnesota and the entire Fifth from Jefferson Barracks. Units he had requested from the Sixth Infantry had not been assigned to him, though, and most soldiers in the Fifth remained exhausted or ill after months in Florida's swamps. At least two hundred men had deserted that regiment upon learning that they had to march to Utah, and although recruits had arrived from New York to fill some of those and other vacancies, too little time remained to train them. No recruits at all had come for the dragoons, and only a few of the assigned staff officers had arrived. Reminiscent of the Sioux expedition, these problems mirrored, on a larger scale, difficulties that departmental commanders faced throughout the West and highlighted both the army's organizational difficulties and inadequate resources.[17]

The next few weeks proved especially frustrating and hectic for Harney, as he worked to get the expedition under way by the late July deadline. Congestion and confusion abounded at Fort Leavenworth. Situated on the Missouri River about twenty miles north of present Kansas City, the post boasted rows of red brick and white clapboard buildings on tree-lined streets and normally looked more like a peaceful New England village than a military installation. Now it overflowed with soldiers, horses, mules, wagons, and equipment of all kinds. The barracks could not accommodate all the troops, and Harney had them erect brush arbors along the river. In the almost unbearably hot weather, he assigned them as little other duty as possible. He also directed them to wear broad-brimmed hats and flannel shirts or frocks instead of dress coats on the march and to pack their extra clothing in knapsacks for transport by wagons. Several Majors and Russell trains would accompany each regiment and carry ammunition, rations, tools, kegs of horse and mule shoes, scores of new Sibley tents, grain for the livestock, desks for the officers, and other supplies.[18]

While overseeing these preparations and the purchase of hundreds of mules and horses, Harney worried about controlling the expedition once its men and trains became strung out along the trail. Impatient and annoyed that the War Department had not given him command of Forts Kearny and Laramie, he acted as he frequently did when he thought bureaucratic shortsightedness stood in the way of practicality. He disregarded normal military procedure and on July 11 telegraphed President Buchanan directly and asked him to have the necessary orders issued. "These measures are indispensable to the success of the movements to Utah," Harney asserted. The War Department complied immediately with his request, much to the chagrin of Scott, who reminded Harney sternly that he should have channeled his plea through the commanding general.[19]

In the meantime, on July 8 Floyd engaged former Texas Ranger Ben McCulloch to go to Fort Leavenworth, review Harney's preparations, and make certain that he had "every element of success . . . at his disposal." Eventually, after advance elements of the expedition had departed, McCulloch reported that Harney had everything he needed, including by July 21 a total of 2,099 troops, counting four companies of Colonel Sumner's Second Dragoons who would join up en route. McCulloch also surmised that Harney could remain at Fort Leavenworth until October 1 and still catch up with the expedition before it entered Utah.[20]

On July 15, the same day that Governor Walker rushed with Colonel Cooke to contain the anticipated Free State disturbances in Lawrence, Scott informed Walker by telegram of Harney's impending departure. The governor knew about the Utah expedition, of course, but he expected Harney to remain behind. To Walker's further consternation, Harney now advised him that once the expedition began, only a single infantry company might be left in Kansas. Walker felt certain that "some mistake must have been made by General Scott, and that such a course could never have met the approval of the President." Immediately Walker complained to Secretary of State Lewis Cass that he had taken the job in Kansas with assurance that General Harney would remain in the territory "until the danger was over." Without that promise, Walker reminded Cass, "I would never have accepted this office." The next day, the alarmed governor telegraphed his concern to Buchanan and attributed the trouble in Lawrence partly to rumors of Harney's impending departure. The following day, the general received instructions to commence the Utah operation but remain in Kansas himself pending further orders.[21]

With appropriate military pomp, Harney launched the expedition in three successive waves between July 18 and July 21. While his columns rumbled across the prairie, he stayed at Fort Leavenworth to command from a distance and oversee the Kansas peacekeeping effort. He did not consider the latter task pressing, though, and longed to join the march. On July 28, he ordered Capt. Stewart Van Vliet, an assistant quartermaster, to proceed ahead of the columns, identify potential forage along the route, and enter Salt Lake City. There he was to deliver a letter to Brigham Young as suggested by McCulloch, secure a suitable place for the troops to camp, and, if possible, contract for lumber and other materials for huts and stables. To Young, Harney wrote that Washington had decided to form a military department in Utah, he had been selected to command it, and he would appreciate help in obtaining forage for his livestock and rations for his men when they arrived.[22]

Young's reply could not be expected for several weeks, and as Harney waited, he could feel pleased. Despite his concerns about starting so late in the year, he had organized the expedition in just six weeks. As the days passed, memories of his success against the Sioux in 1855 welled further within him, and by August 8 he could barely contain his desire to get into the field. "My presence is at this time so necessary to the troops en route," he wrote Floyd, "that I am constrained to speak to you upon another subject—my early release from the service in Kansas—everything here is quiet, nor is there any probability that I shall be needed." Other officers could assist Governor Walker, Harney argued, "but with the troops marching on Utah it is not so—the service is new to the commanders as well as the troops, and my knowledge and experience of that country will do much towards smoothing the way for their arrival." But he did not get his wish. Walker still considered Kansas a tinderbox, and he continued to protest the transfer of federal troops from the territory.[23]

In the meantime, the expedition ran into difficulties, and once again Harney incurred the wrath of General Scott. On the same day on which he wrote Floyd, Harney learned that Indians had attacked his supply lines. All summer, Colonel Sumner and several companies of mounted and foot soldiers had been pursuing Cheyennes along and south of the Platte toward the Solomon River. He had orders to punish them, as Harney had chastised the Sioux, for depredations against travelers on the emigrant trail, and on July 29 his troops fought a brief but sharp battle with some 300 warriors on the Solomon's south bank. Afterward, while Sumner found and destroyed their hastily abandoned village, lodges, and personal belongings, the Indians scattered in several directions. On August 2, about 150 of them attacked two Utah expedition cattle herds approximately twenty-eight miles west of Fort Kearny, ran off all 824 head plus 18 of the drovers' mules, and killed a guard. A detachment of infantrymen sent from Fort Kearny the next day to look for stray animals rounded up only 43 cows.[24]

Harney blamed Sumner for the loss. Recalling Ash Hollow, he lamented that Sumner's men had killed so few Cheyennes—nine—that "his action was not attended by any moral consequences." If Sumner had made the Indians "fear for their families," Harney speculated, they would not have dared to attack the herds. Moreover, he felt that Sumner, who knew about the Utah expedition, should have sent two of his horse companies to protect its supply trains immediately after dispersing the Cheyennes.[25] Scott, on the other hand, blamed the loss on a "grave blunder" by Harney. The commanding general had instructed him to send the cattle ahead of the main body of the expedition so they could travel slowly and arrive in Salt Lake City in good condition at the same time as the troops, and Harney had complied. But he had assigned only nineteen men to escort them. Given his experience and his awareness of Sumner's operations, Scott had good cause for anger. Even though Harney had fewer troops in his command than he wanted, or had expected, he should have detailed more to protect the herds.[26]

Coincidentally, within days Harney found himself leveling similar charges of carelessness against one of his subordinates. In mid-August, he learned that Van Vliet had taken ten days to travel three hundred miles to Fort Kearny. At that rate he would not arrive in Salt Lake City until mid-September. He blamed his slow pace on "the very poor outfit that was furnished me." Livid, Harney reminded Van Vliet that he had made his own arrangements for the journey, that he should average fifty miles a day, and that he had the "most important and delicate" assignment connected with the expedition. If lack of scouting information brought "any disasters" to his troops, Harney railed, he would consider Van Vliet's "conduct . . . the chief cause." Although neither man knew it, the Mormons still had not decided precisely how to respond to the expedition, but Brigham Young spoke publicly about forcible resistance. He characterized Harney as a "blood-thirsty old villain" and declared that if he should enter Utah with a hostile army "we shall prepare to defend ourselves."[27]

Meanwhile, in late August, long before Van Vliet reached Utah, the War Department put Col. Albert Sidney Johnston, then en route from Washington DC, in command of the expedition. Having grown more nervous about Kansas, Buchanan wanted to ensure that Walker remained there and facilitated its admission to the Union, slave or free, as soon as possible. The president hoped that keeping Harney at Fort Leavenworth would calm the restive governor. On September 1, Secretary of State Cass informed Walker that the "President is determined" to retain "a sufficient military force" in Kansas "to resist every attempt . . . to disturb the peace and good order of society." Johnston assumed command of the Utah expedition on September 11. By now, in addition to the troops that had departed in July, two more companies of the Tenth Infantry and a contingent of Second Dragoons from Fort Kearny had also set out for Utah, and Johnston arranged for Colonel Cooke to depart with six more dragoon companies. With units of his command strung out over hundreds of miles, Johnston left Fort Leavenworth on September 26 optimistically proclaiming that he would overtake the advance parties and reach Salt Lake City by October 20, two days ahead of Harney's schedule.[28]

While Johnston labored to make good that prediction, Harney busied himself helping Walker. The governor had become so apprehensive about the upcoming elections that pleasing him proved difficult. Earlier in the month, when Utah's new governor had passed through Fort Leavenworth and requested a troop escort to Salt Lake City, Walker had objected vigorously to Harney's sending as few as fifty more soldiers out of Kansas. "Important as the affairs of Utah may be," Walker had opined, "they do not threaten the peace of the country, or the stability of the Government." Harney gave Cumming an escort anyway, but throughout late September and October, he also managed to comply with numerous requests for posses comitatus in Kansas.[29]

Walker worried most about territorial elections scheduled for October 5 and 6 to select county officials, a new legislature, and a delegate to Congress. Fearing that persons not qualified to vote might effect "a violent seizure of the polls," on September 21 he asked Harney to send at least one company of soldiers each to Council Grove, Emporia, Burlington, Hyattville, Atchison, and five other towns to maintain order. Harney provided them on September 22, and four days later he sent two other companies to assist territorial officials in Lawrence, where the Free State faction sought to enforce an illegal tax ordinance. By October 3, he had sent troops also to Shawnee Mission, Kickapoo, and Easton and positioned two companies in the town of Leavenworth.[30]

On election day, both pro- and antislavery men voted en masse despite wet weather. The rain, together with federal troops at many polling places, restricted violence to a few isolated fistfights, and on October 9 Harney asked Walker how much longer he would need federal troops. He replied that if order could be maintained until spring, military force would no longer be required. Walker expressed similar sentiments to Cass, along with "great obligations" to "General Harney for judicious advice, at all times, as to the location of the troops, a prompt and cordial co-operation, and a just and patriotic appreciation of the serious difficulties" in Kansas.[31]

Including troops who arrived shortly before the October elections, Harney now had more than thirty infantry, artillery, dragoon, and cavalry companies–some two thousand men–in Kansas, and nineteen of these units lacked quarters. Housing them during the winter became a major concern. Harney sent five cavalry companies to Fort Riley on the Kansas River, proposed to shelter four or five infantry companies on two steamboats brought up from St. Louis, and planned to build cottages for the remainder. The latter soldiers commenced work on their quarters, as well as on kitchens and mess rooms, early in November. To keep the other troops busy and get them all better prepared for duty, in December Harney directed each regimental commander to establish "schools of instruction" for both commissioned and noncommissioned officers and to conduct daily drills, weather permitting, for enlisted men.[32]

December and January brought more elections and more demands for troops to guard polling places. When delegates to the federally supported Lecompton constitutional convention, elected back on June 15, completed their work, they announced that on December 21, Kansans would not be permitted to vote for or against the constitution but merely on whether the document should allow additional slaves in Kansas. This infuriated Walker, who believed that popular sovereignty required a public referendum on the entire constitution and whether Kansas would allow slavery at all. When he learned that the Buchanan administration was prepared to go along with the election called by the convention, he resigned in a huff. In the meantime, Territorial Secretary Frederick P. Stanton called a special session of the new, predominantly antislavery legislature, and it provided for a referendum on the constitution on January 4. Before either election could be held, the new governor, James W. Denver, arrived and declared that he intended to conduct both peacefully. Harney provided troops on each occasion and prevented major disturbances.

On December 21, as on June 15, most antislavery voters stayed away from the polls, and the proslavery faction carried the day. But in the referendum on January 4, voters sent the Lecompton Constitution to resounding defeat. Buchanan refused to accept the latter outcome, though, and in February 1858 he urged Congress to approve the document and admit Kansas to the Union. The solons debated the matter heatedly all summer, and on August 2, 1858, they voted no. Kansas would have to endure additional conventions and referendums and wait two more years for statehood.

Altogether between 1855 and 1858 approximately fifty-five persons died violently in Kansas as a consequence of political controversy. Though alarming, that figure pales compared with the eventual carnage of the Civil War. But as Walker had rightly perceived, given the high emotional temperature of the issues and the national attention focused on Kansas, the potential for greater violence had remained ever present. Thus in that critical period of the territory's history, the army performed its role as peacekeeper fairly successfully, and much of the credit for that must go to Harney, along with Sumner before him.[33]

Following the January 1858 election, U.S. troops continued to help federal judges, marshals, and land office employees carry out their various civil responsibilities. In February, though, the War Department ordered Harney to Washington to preside over a board of officers examining two new Colt pistols, and he remained there two months before being sent back to Fort Leavenworth.[34]

The army returned Harney to Kansas because Albert Sidney Johnston had failed to push the Utah expedition into Salt Lake Valley before winter, and now President Buchanan and Secretary Floyd planned to send more troops across the prairie. Harney had been right, as had freighting contractor Alexander Majors. The march had started too late the previous year. When Van Vliet reached Salt Lake City on September 8, 1857, the Mormons, though still privately undecided about their course of action, convinced him that they intended to meet the expedition with force. After talking with Young and other church officials, Van Vliet toured the valley and confirmed what Harney already knew. Only one route led into it from the east. It passed through fifty miles of rugged mountains and narrow canyons, and Van Vliet speculated correctly that a small number of Mormons could easily stop federal columns there. Moreover, snow had already begun to fall at the eastern end of the pass, and in a few weeks deep drifts would block it. So in mid-September when Van Vliet, en route back to Fort Leavenworth, met Col. Edmund B. Alexander, commander of the expedition's advance columns, the concerned captain suggested that they winter in present southwestern Wyoming.[35]

Alexander had already reached a state of alarm on his own, and with good cause. He had made it to Utah Territory, but his troops, supply trains, and stock herds remained scattered several days apart along the trail and seemed tempting targets for Mormon raiders. Other expedition units, including the dragoons, lingered up to seven hundred miles behind him, and Johnston, his new superior, was still making his way across Nebraska. To make matters worse, on September 15 Young declared martial law in Utah and ordered the Mormons to prepare to defend themselves. This, combined with Van Vliet's report, so frightened Alexander that he stopped his columns at Ham's Fork on the Green River, about sixty miles west of South Pass. In a sentiment Harney surely would have echoed, one disgruntled expedition officer wrote his wife that "had the blockheads in Washington had an idea in their heads, or listened to those who were able to give advice, all this would have been avoided" and a more effective effort made in the spring.[36]

Eventually Johnston ordered Alexander forward to Fort Bridger, an abandoned trading post, but not before mounted Mormon militiamen slipped behind the federal columns and destroyed three relatively unprotected supply trains along the Green and Big Sandy Rivers. Hampered further by snow and subfreezing temperatures, Johnston informed the War Department in mid-October that he could not enter Salt Lake Valley until spring. For the next month, his remaining troops and trains struggled to reach Fort Bridger, while he established a winter camp he named Fort Scott. Governor Cumming reached it on November 19 and settled in with the troops.[37]

In Washington, Floyd and Buchanan deliberated about what to do next. The secretary of war remained convinced that the Mormons intended to secede from the Union. Proclaiming that their theocracy blocked "the great pathway . . . from our Atlantic states to the . . . Pacific seaboard," he called for five new regiments to suppress the "spirit of rebellion." In his annual message to Congress, the president declared, "We ought to go there with such an imposing force as to convince these deluded people that resistance would be in vain, and thus spare the effusion of blood." In January he authorized sending nearly four thousand additional troops to Utah, including recruits for units already at Fort Scott. Once united, the force would number fifty-six hundred men, nearly one-third of the U.S. Army in 1858.

During the next three months, the War Department sent replacement provisions to Johnston and put the Quartermaster's Department to work arranging supplies for the additional troops who would march in the spring. As conceived, operating columns alone would require more than 1,100 wagons, 6,400 mules, and 250 horses, not including mounts for the cavalry. The supply trains would require nearly 4,000 more wagons and 47,000 oxen. The undertaking grew so gigantic that

Floyd sought to finance it through private sources and on credit until Congress could pass a special deficiency appropriation bill, which it finally did in May.[38]

Having committed such enormous assets to Utah, the War Department assigned Bvt. Maj. Gen. Persifor F. Smith to lead the expanded expedition and head the new military Department of Utah. He retained command of the Department of the West as well, and Harney became his chief subordinate for the expedition. Until they arrived in Utah, Johnston would remain in charge on site. However, this arrangement lasted scarcely two weeks after Harney returned to Fort Leavenworth in early May. Shortly after midnight on the seventeenth, Smith died, and Harney took over "the military forces in and destined for the Department of Utah" and reported his action to Floyd in Washington. Harney did not assume command of the Department of the West, which, according to his understanding of previous orders, devolved on Col. Francis Lee of the Second Infantry.

These events embroiled Harney immediately in another dispute with Scott, who became peeved because Harney communicated with Floyd and not with him. The commanding general whined that Harney should send all future communications about Utah to him and contact Floyd only about matters related to the Department of the West. Further, Scott railed that Harney should have taken charge of that department and should not have assumed command of the Utah expedition until he arrived in that territory. Seeing "something more than rebuke" in Scott's admonition, Harney responded that he had not considered himself "at liberty" to take command of the Department of the West. Furthermore, he wrote, he had assumed the Utah position in complete accord with Smith's and his own original orders from the War Department, and he had left Johnston in command in the field. Not satisfied with that explanation, Scott had his adjutant endorse Harney's letter with a further record of his mistake as the commanding general interpreted it. In addition to continuing the friction between two strong personalities, this quarrelsome exchange highlighted the ongoing communication problems associated with Scott's residence in New York.[39]

While these two stubborn old enemies feuded, efforts to reinforce the troops in Utah moved forward. Most arrangements had been completed before Smith died, and so Harney had relatively little to do except secure more horses and wagons, arm the civilian teamsters, and issue marching orders for the available troops. He accomplished all of this in late May and early June. Smith had already dispatched one column, the Sixth Infantry, and Harney sent five others between May 21 and June 14. Each included four to six companies of soldiers and a supply train.[40]

On the same day that the sixth column left Fort Leavenworth, the army promoted Harney, at age fifty-seven, to the regular rank of brigadier general. News of his elevation sparked mixed emotions. In Missouri, the *Liberty Weekly Tribune* described him as "a bold, rough officer" who "will have no child's play with the Mormons." In Utah, a *New York Times* correspondent concluded that the appointment alarmed the Mormons and disappointed some troops who felt that Johnston should have been promoted and given the Department of Utah. "General Harney is disliked exceedingly," the reporter declared, as a "vulgar, ungentlemanly personage, who treats men with familiar brutality, and officers ditto. The 'Saints' look upon him as one who will provoke a collision if opportunity arises." Harney, of course, cared little what the Saints thought. With his promotion he became the army's fifth-most-senior officer, behind Maj. Gen. Winfield Scott and Brig. Gen. Thomas S. Jesup, Brig. Gen. John E. Wool, and Brig. Gen. David E. Twiggs.[41]

With a headquarters staff that included Pleasonton, plus future Civil War and Indian war notables Joseph E. Johnston, Don Carlos Buell, and Winfield Scott Hancock, Harney started for Utah on June 15, hoping to overtake the lead column in the vicinity of Fort Laramie. About six days out, Father Pierre-Jean DeSmet caught up with the group to serve, at Harney's request, as chaplain. They reached Fort Kearny on June 24, and Harney reported his troops "in good health" and the march proceeding "satisfactorily." Not everything went smoothly, however. Just as they had on the Sioux expedition, the teamsters gave Harney fits. Charles E. Bazin, himself a driver, later recalled seeing him curse one man until he exclaimed he would give the general "a thrashin' he would never forget" were he not an officer. At that, Harney leaped from his horse, took off his coat, and the two "went at it." The teamster prevailed, Bazin remembered, "but Harney took his trouncin' like a man."[42] It is difficult to conceive of Harney's peers resorting to such behavior, but he disliked teamsters intensely and had always been quick to defend his personal honor. Age had not diminished that impulse.

While the troops pushed toward Utah, authorities in Washington reconsidered their strategy for dealing with the Mormons. Following a major national economic depression—the Panic of 1857—further expenditures for a massive military campaign seemed increasingly difficult to justify, and Congress approved only two of the five new regiments Floyd requested. Public support for punishing the Latter-day Saints waned, too. Already, in April, Buchanan had appointed Ben McCulloch and former Kentucky governor Lazarus W. Powell peace commissioners to go to Utah and urge Young and his followers to accept federal authority in return for a pardon for sedition and treason. The pair arrived in Salt Lake City in June, met Young, and told him that the government intended to enforce obedience to federal laws and officials. The commissioners' firm stance, together with the size of the expeditionary force, convinced Young to accept the pardon and federal presence in the valley. Johnston's troops entered Salt Lake City without incident on June 26.

Harney learned about the agreement on July 8, when a messenger overtook him on the South Platte River approximately a hundred miles west of Fort Kearny. With the army as its primary instrument, the federal government had exerted its authority over Utah Territory, at least in principal, and Harney had played the most significant military role. For the second time in two years, however, he had anticipated leading a large force into Salt Lake Valley and been recalled. Putting disappointment aside, he now sent some of his troops to Utah and dispatched the others elsewhere, as directed. After pausing to talk with Cheyennes in the area, Harney trekked back to Kansas and arrived at Fort Leavenworth on August 2.[43] From there he went directly to St. Louis, where on the seventh he prepared to take up duties as commander of the Department of the West. The day before he arrived in the gateway city, however, Floyd had sent him instructions to report to Washington "with as little delay as practicable." The secretary planned a new military department in the Pacific Northwest and he wanted Harney to command it.[44]

The army's newest brigadier won no special accolades for his service in Kansas or with respect to Utah. However, Governor Walker credited Harney with maintaining civil order in Kansas Territory, and the *Atlantic Monthly* concluded that he had been well chosen for the Utah command. In March 1859, the magazine proclaimed him "an officer of a rude force of character, amounting often to brutality, and careless as to those details of military duty which savor more of the accountant's inkstand than of the drum and fife, but ambitious, active, and well acquainted with the character of the service for which he was detailed." As late as October 30, 1858, however, Scott blamed Harney for the army's failure to reach Salt Lake City in 1857. He "threw cold water" on the effort "at the outset," Scott complained, and "those under him were infected by discouragement."[45] Except for Harney's failure to protect the cattle herd adequately that first summer, Scott's biased assessment had no basis in fact. If he and Floyd had listened to Harney initially and delayed the expedition for a season, the government would have avoided considerable wasted expense. In any case, Harney organized the effort and got it under way on schedule in 1857 amid considerable logistical obstacles, and he launched the reinforcing columns successfully in 1858. Overall both phases of the undertaking proceeded as well as anyone could have expected given the limited military resources. When Harney left Kansas, he could be satisfied that he had played a key role in two of the army's most important pre–Civil War efforts to maintain domestic order by upholding civil law and federal authority.

CHAPTER 11

The Pacific Northwest, "No Ordinary Sphere"

O N SUNDAY AFTERNOON, July 31, 1859, three British war-ships lay off San Juan Island about midway between Seat-tle and Vancouver, British Columbia. Carrying nearly a thousand sailors and marines and sixty-two naval guns, they stood poised to rout Capt. George E. Pickett's vastly outnum-bered company of U.S. infantrymen camped on shore with two small brass cannon. Pleasure boats dotted the harbor, too. Cu-rious about all the military fuss, some five hundred residents of British-owned Vancouver Island had come to survey the scene. They swarmed over San Juan's tiny wharf, strolled among the buildings of a Hudson's Bay Company trading sta-tion, and milled about the American camp on a ridge about a half mile from the bay. Pickett, of subsequent Gettysburg fame, and officers from one of the British ships sat outside, in plain view of the gawkers, talking easily but settling nothing. For days afterward, American newspapers from San Francisco to Portland intertwined patriotic pride with calls for caution. Dip-lomats and other government officials from Washington to London considered potential solutions and consequences. And an international boundary commission continued its two-year-long effort to resolve ownership of San Juan and neighboring islands. Great Britain and the United States had disputed legal possession since signing the Treaty of Washington in 1846, but neither country's government had considered the contested territory worthy of military confrontation. Now, as crisis brewed, Brig. Gen. William S. Harney, commander of the Department of Oregon, stood squarely in the middle.[1]

This was not what Secretary of War John B. Floyd had in mind when he assigned Harney to the Pacific Northwest in late summer 1858. As the nation's most experienced Indian fighter, he had gone there to quell long-standing conflict between whites and native people. Ever since the discovery of gold in California in 1848, the federal government had been laboring to establish peace on the West Coast, where diminishing numbers of Indians resisted increasing white encroachment. Most of the remaining difficulties centered in Washington and Oregon territories, and so federal authorities separated those areas, except for the Rogue River and Umpqua districts immediately north of California, from the military Department of the Pacific and created a new Department of Oregon. In addition to present Washington and most of Oregon, it also included what is now Idaho and portions of Montana and Wyoming. Upon placing Harney in command, Floyd instructed him to exercise the "greatest possible vigor and activity" to conclude the military campaign already under way and leave all "hostile bands . . . thoroughly chastised."[2]

This was the kind of duty Harney liked most and had handled so effectively on the Great Plains. He commanded the new department almost two years, and during that time he enforced and solidified peace between intruding whites and native people and cooperated with Indian Bureau officials to prevent clashes among tribes. In his spare moments he also helped expand the army's Pacific road building program. And he clashed again with Winfield Scott, as well as with several subordinates who, together with Harney, carried on the tradition of almost continual quarreling within the officer corps. But most important, through a combination of impulsiveness, expansionist sentiment, and obstinacy, all leading to poor judgment, he came close to pushing the United States and Great Britain into a clash of arms.

Communication and travel between Washington DC and the Pacific

Northwest required three to four weeks, and so as Floyd and Harney discussed the new department in August 1858, they did not know exactly what conditions he would find upon arriving there. However, they did know that years of fighting and negotiating treaties had brought peace only to parts of the region. Many Indian groups inhabited the Pacific Northwest, and before 1850 most had retreated peacefully into the interior as whites settled on the coast and in major river valleys. After 1850, however, thousands more whites flocked to gold fields in northern California and southern Oregon, and increasing numbers homesteaded rich agricultural tracts elsewhere in the region. Indians no longer cleared out of the way quickly enough to avoid conflict. For several years California and Oregon volunteers used any excuse to wage wars of extermination against native people, and until the mid-1850s the army lacked sufficient troops and supplies to stop the fighting. Indian Bureau officials moved coastal tribes to new homes east of the Cascade Mountains, but they refused to stay there.

In 1854–55, Isaac I. Stevens, newly appointed Washington governor and superintendent of Indian affairs, negotiated cession treaties with most Puget Sound Indians and many of the interior tribes. As an energetic exponent of Pacific Northwest development, he wanted, like most other frontier entrepreneurs, to extinguish Indian land titles, put all native people on reservations, teach them to farm, and open the way for white settlement. Congress took three years to approve the treaties, though, and his efforts contributed little toward immediate peace.

By the fall of 1855, war seemed imminent. In Oregon, miners and settlers clashed with various Indian bands along tributaries of the Rogue, Illinois, and Klamath Rivers. In Washington, prospectors passing through Yakima country to new gold fields near the Canadian border irritated that tribe's powerful chief, Kamiakin, and he inflamed both his own and other groups. Hostilities followed on a broad scale in both territories. Brig. Gen. John E. Wool, commander of the Department of the Pacific, responded too slowly to suit many whites, and in Oregon fifteen companies of volunteers spent the winter combing trouble spots for warring tribesmen. That, together with regular army operations in the spring of 1856, brought peace to most of the territory. Unfortunately, it also devastated the area's native people. The fighting

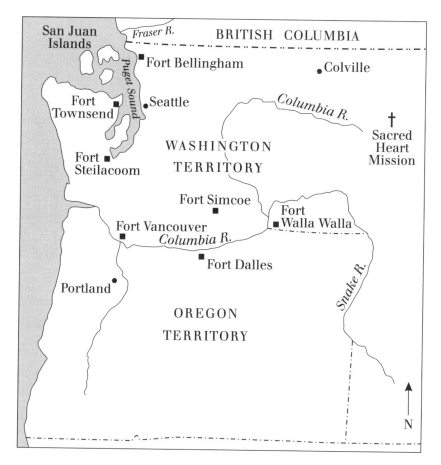

8. Department of Oregon, 1859

in Washington proved less conclusive. Wool easily restored calm around Puget Sound, but in the interior he had to content himself with establishing new military posts and banning additional white settlement east of the Cascades, except in the Colville gold region.

The potential for renewed hostilities remained high through 1857. Bvt. Brig. Gen. Newman S. Clarke replaced Wool, and the Interior Department combined the Oregon and Washington superintendencies and named former volunteer officer James W. Nesmith to the new position. Otherwise, little changed until early 1858. Then hundreds more miners traveled back and forth from the coast to Colville, in northern interior Washington, and the Fraser River, site of new gold discoveries in southern British Columbia. As they passed through Indian country, they provoked numerous skirmishes. Qualchin, chief of the Kittitas, led the opposition to the miners, and by March rumors spread that he and Kamiakin planned a general uprising. In response, Col. Edward J. Steptoe decided to march 164 men from Fort Walla Walla through the Palouse range to Colville and back again to awe the Indians and reassure the miners. About a thousand Upper and Middle Spokanes, Coeur d'Alenes, Palouses, and others attacked Steptoe's column on May 16 and inflicted heavy losses. In the weeks that followed, Clarke planned a campaign to punish Steptoe's attackers and either capture Kamiakin and Qualchin or drive them from the region.[3]

Floyd expected Harney to oversee the completion of those plans and wage total war, as he had done against the Sioux. The secretary instructed him to "capture" Indian families, "destroy" their animals, and make "no overtures of friendship . . . to any tribes" before punishing belligerent ones. Remembering the static between Harney and Scott over channels of communication during the Utah expedition, Floyd also directed his new appointee to send all reports straightaway to the commanding general in New York and provide copies to the War Department.

While Floyd and Harney conferred, army surgeon Benjamin Harney died at Baton Rouge Barracks on August 29, but General Harney's new assignment prevented his taking leave to help attend to his brother's affairs. After concluding his conversations with Floyd, he remained ten more days in the District of Columbia arranging for shipment of various supplies unavailable on the Pacific coast. Then, sometime before September 17, he went to New York City, where he conferred with Father Pierre-Jean DeSmet. The widely respected Jesuit had spent six years among Pacific Northwest Indians during the 1840s, and Harney asked him to return to facilitate peace talks.[4]

On September 20, 1858, Harney and DeSmet sailed with Capt. Alfred Pleasonton, Harney's faithful adjutant, aboard the steamer *Star of the West*. Carrying 640 passengers bound mostly for California and British Columbia gold fields, the vessel made Aspinwall on the eastern coast of Panama in eight days. Harney and his companions then crossed the isthmus by rail and took the steamship *John L. Stephens* to San Francisco. They arrived on October 16, having traveled nearly seven thousand miles from New York.[5]

The next day the boom city's *Daily Alta California* announced that "the Indian War in Washington Territory is at an end." Harney, the paper proclaimed, "will find all at peace." General Clarke, who had just arrived from Fort Vancouver, confirmed this surprising news. He informed Harney that in methodical, well-conducted operations in late August and September, Maj. Robert S. Garnett had captured a number of Yakimas and Palouses and executed five of them. Further, Col. George Wright had defeated several hundred Spokanes, Coeur d'Alenes, and other Indians, slaughtered nine hundred ponies, hanged fifteen native men, and arrested Qualchin. Kamiakin remained at large but had been wounded. Accomplished with precisely the kind of flourish Harney had been sent to achieve, these actions, together with the simultaneous intercessions of several Jesuit missionaries, had dispersed the Indians and restored calm to Washington and upper Oregon.[6]

Leaving Clarke in San Francisco, Harney and his traveling companions departed by boat on October 20 and reached the mouth of the Columbia River three days later. Father DeSmet observed that the area had changed considerably since he last saw it in 1844. Small towns and rich farms dotted the Willamette Valley, and growing settlements stood along both banks of the Columbia. About ninety-five miles upstream and thirty-five miles short of the Cascades lay the town of Vancouver, Washington, consisting of the military post, some one hundred houses, and a white frame Catholic church. When the travelers arrived on October 24, they found the townspeople still celebrating Clarke's campaign and, like whites throughout the region, delighted that Harney had arrived. Just two days earlier, the Olympia *Pioneer and Democrat* had expressed confidence that he would pursue a policy of "rough and ready, sledgehammer warfare."[7]

The veteran dragoon wasted little time getting to work. He sent immediately for Wright and instructed him to bring whatever official records, reports, and maps he might need to give a more detailed briefing than Clarke had provided. "We have nothing to apprehend," Wright reported. The Walla Wallas, Palouses, Spokanes, Coeur d'Alenes, Nez

Perces, and other tribes along the Columbia and its tributaries seemed "entirely friendly," he stated proudly. Official treaties had been made with all of them, and the only remaining difficulties appeared limited to the Colville region. After studying the situation, Harney concurred. An estimated forty-two thousand native people remained in Washington and Oregon, but when forwarding Wright's report and copies of several treaties to army headquarters, he wrote that "from all the information I can obtain . . . I am inclined to believe the Indians in this department can easily be controlled."[8]

If Harney regretted that now he had no opportunity to lead troops in the field, he gave no indication of it. Instead, he plunged into his duties as departmental commander. On October 28, he approved Father DeSmet's proposal to travel immediately to the Jesuits' Coeur d'Alene mission, eight hundred miles to the northeast, and talk with leaders of various tribes en route. All the Indians, DeSmet recalled later, "still retained their prejudices and an uneasiness and alarm which had to be dissipated." Harney directed DeSmet to tell the tribes that they must abide by the treaties and surrender Kamiakin and his brother Skloom. The commander of the Department of Oregon wanted the Indians to understand that no soldiers had left the territories and if forced to fight again they would "give no quarter." To ensure DeSmet's success, he ordered all post commanders to provide whatever guides, interpreters, escorts, animals, and other assistance the missionary might need.[9]

Harney felt so confident he could maintain peace that on October 31, without consulting Indian Bureau personnel, he rescinded the ban on white settlement east of the Cascades. This pleased Stevens, now Washington Territory's delegate to Congress, and most other whites. The Olympia *Pioneer and Democrat* hailed Harney's order as "the wisest . . . policy yet adopted," and the Salem *Oregon Statesman* viewed it as "Politic" and likely to "conduce to the ultimate benefit of the country." Superintendent Nesmith, on the other hand, thought Harney should have waited until all the recent treaties had been ratified and reservations formally established.[10]

Meanwhile, after approving the hanging of two Yakimas who had killed an Indian agent, Harney speculated about Indian relations in the Pacific Northwest and native people generally. In a long report to Scott, he predicted that Indians in Washington and Oregon would never attempt another coalition because their "different languages, interests, and jealousies" made collaboration too difficult. Further, he observed, "the red men of America will gradually disappear, about the same time, from the different sections of the country." Reservations and farming, he thought, offered their only hope for survival in the face of continually expanding white population. These resembled the conclusions he had drawn at Fort Pierre in 1856 and echoed beliefs he shared with many other officers.[11]

Harney next turned his attention to supplying and repositioning the nearly two thousand men in his command. Many lacked sufficient clothing for winter, and finding none for them in California, he asked Scott to speed the shipment of goods destined for Fort Vancouver in the spring. To improve troop placement, Harney planned a new post near Colville to protect miners and suggested building two others along the Oregon Trail in what is now southern Idaho. Scott passed Harney's recommendation on to Floyd, and the secretary replied that the War Department could not afford to build any more forts in the Department of Oregon. The government still had a large force to maintain in Utah and Indian trouble to curb on the Great Plains and in the desert Southwest.[12]

As Harney tended to logistical matters, Father DeSmet worked his way through the interior, talking to Indian leaders and sending back frequent reports on his conversations. He reached the Coeur d'Alene mission, in present northern Idaho, on November 21, having seen neither Kamiakin nor Skloom. The Jesuit's guides assured him, however, that Kamiakin no longer exercised any influence among the tribes. Confident now that "the Indians . . . are better disposed for peace than they have been for several years," DeSmet asked Harney if some of their leaders could travel back to Fort Vancouver with him, pay their respects, and give the general "some fine mountain furs" as tokens of friendship. Harney replied that he would "be glad to see" the Indians and "explain . . . the intentions of the government" toward them.

DeSmet remained at the Coeur d'Alene mission, snowed in, until mid-February. He then trudged further into the interior, visited the St. Ignatius mission, located Kamiakin and Skloom, and talked with them on several occasions over the next two months. Kamiakin admitted that he had participated in the attack on Steptoe and the battles with Wright but maintained that he had murdered no one. Finally, he agreed to accompany DeSmet and other native leaders to Fort Vancouver.[13]

While DeSmet and the chiefs made their way west to meet Harney, he assisted Indian Bureau personnel elsewhere. At the Warm Springs Reservation, he approved Indian Agent Ami P. Dennison's request for fifty surplus rifles and ammunition for Teninos to use to deter Northern Paiutes from stealing reservation livestock. And at the Yakima Reservation, he offered Superintendent Nesmith vacant buildings from now-closed Fort Simcoe. These experiences stood in marked contrast to Harney's difficulties with Agent Twiss earlier in Nebraska, but this spirit of cooperation did not last long.[14]

Flathead Agent John Owen, an erstwhile trader with several mountain tribes and a frequent critic of the Jesuits, decided to accompany DeSmet back to Fort Vancouver, take charge of the chiefs traveling with him, and assume credit for persuading them to meet Harney. Falsely claiming that Nesmith and Indian Bureau special investigator Christopher Mott had ordered him to arrange a council, Owen persuaded DeSmet to relinquish control of the peace party. To cover himself, the duplicitous agent informed Nesmith that Kamiakin and other chiefs had surrendered to him and asked him to take them to see Harney. When the delegation reached Fort Walla Walla on the thirteenth, Owen halted it to await Nesmith's approval to proceed, and DeSmet went ahead to Fort Vancouver. A few days later, Kamiakin stole away in the night. No one ever determined whether he merely became restless in DeSmet's absence or came under the influence of Nez Perce chiefs visiting the post. But certainly, without Owen's interference, DeSmet, who had won Kamiakin's confidence, would have taken him on to Fort Vancouver.

News of Owen's shenanigans infuriated Harney, for he had already reported Kamiakin's surrender to army headquarters. Now he could only send the chief a message and hope he would come in later. "Father DeSmet has told me of your good intentions toward whites, and your desire for peace," Harney wrote. "I am glad to hear this; it makes me forget the past, and inclines me to extend to you and your people my good will as long as they keep at peace with the whites." Kamiakin never responded to this or any other overtures, but he refrained from further hostilities.[15]

Harney met the remaining chiefs at Fort Vancouver on May 28. They expressed a desire for friendship, promised that they would never go to war again, and asked for reservations where they could live in peace. Harney assured them that the government would abide by the treaties negotiated previously. He expressed satisfaction with Kamiakin and gave Spokane Garry, Adolphus Red Feather, and Victor Happy Man letters proclaiming them "good" men and head chiefs of their tribes. When the talks concluded, DeSmet took the Indians on a three-week tour of white farms and towns before they returned to their homes in late June.[16]

His job in the Pacific Northwest done, DeSmet prepared to return via the Rocky Mountains to his regular duties in St. Louis. Before departing he suggested that the government establish, in northeastern Washington Territory, one huge reservation for all Indians in the region. The land is beautiful and filled with game, DeSmet noted, and "one single military post might suffice to protect them against all encroachments and infringements of evil disposed whites." Harney endorsed the idea. He knew that efforts to concentrate California Indians on large reservations in the Central Valley had failed earlier in the decade, but he believed that three circumstances, absent in the California experiment, made success likely in Washington. The area here afforded sufficient means of subsistence, did not seem in immediate demand by whites, and included a network of Jesuit missions. "From what I have observed of the Indian Affairs of this Department," Harney declared, "the Missionaries among them possess a power of the greatest consequence in their proper government and one which cannot be acquired by any other influence."

Whatever the merits of DeSmet's plan, it received no consideration in the East. In April, Delegate Isaac Stevens had persuaded Congress to ratify the 1855 treaties, which provided separate reservations for Umatilla, Yakima, Nez Perce, Coeur d'Alene, and other tribes. Those tracts, combined with General Clarke's campaign and Harney's and DeSmet's diplomacy, ensured an uneasy peace between whites and Indians in the region for almost two decades. Isolated clashes still occurred, but widespread fighting ceased. Harney continued to provide military protection for citizens and Indian Bureau officials who requested it and to assist the latter with transportation. Overall he cooperated more closely than ever before with Indian service representatives.[17]

As anxieties regarding native people eased, Harney turned his attention increasingly to transportation needs, especially as they related to supplying his command. When Congress had created Washington Territory in 1853, only about four thousand whites had inhabited it, and although the number of settlers, miners, and other emigrants had increased steadily since then, waterways and pack trails remained the most important avenues of travel. A federal wagon road from Walla Walla, in the extreme southeast, to Steilacoom, at the southern tip of Puget Sound, plus a few muddy private and territorial roads, principally around the sound, offered the only alternatives. Settlers, territorial officials, and military men all wanted more and better roads. In 1855, the army's Topographical Corps had opened a Pacific Wagon Road Office in San Francisco, and in each recent legislative session the Washington territorial assembly had enacted construction bills. In Washington DC, meanwhile, Isaac Stevens had been lobbying Congress for a road between Fort Walla Walla and Fort Benton at the head of navigation on the Missouri River. Now both civilian and military officials sought Harney's support for their ideas. In November 1858, Assistant Quartermaster Rufus Ingalls gave him a detailed plan for a military road between Fort Dalles and Salt Lake City, and in December, Washington's acting governor, Charles H. Mason, sent him copies of assembly resolutions advocating a road similar to the one Stevens had proposed. Harney liked both ideas. He forwarded Ingalls's proposal to army headquarters and informed Scott that he intended to explore the Utah route in the spring of 1859. If this road proved feasible, Harney reasoned, the government could supply troops in Utah much faster and at less expense from Fort Vancouver than by way of Fort Leavenworth.[18]

Within weeks, a flurry of road-building activity began. Congress appropriated $100,000 for construction of the road between Fort Walla

Walla and Fort Benton, and the War Department designated Lt. John Mullan, who had already helped survey part of the route, to build it. Floyd doubted the feasibility of the proposed Fort Dalles to Utah road, but he authorized Harney to explore it anyway. He assigned that task to Capt. Henry D. Wallen, gave him a detachment of engineers, two companies of dragoons, and one of infantry, and ordered him to commence in June. While Wallen prepared, the Topographical Corps in San Francisco planned a pack trail between Seattle and Whatcom in Washington Territory and a road between Astoria and Salem in Oregon.[19]

The Mullan and Wallen efforts proved by far the most ambitious undertakings. Mullan had almost autonomous authority, but he sent Harney regular progress reports. Starting in July 1859, the lieutenant and his men worked their way northeastward toward the Bitterroot Mountains, cutting down trees, removing rocks, grading slopes, and building bridges as they went. After wintering in the St. Regis Borgia Valley, they pushed forward in the spring of 1860 to the Hell Gate River in present western Montana and from there to Fort Benton. When completed, the Mullan Road never became either the strategic military highway that the War Department had envisioned or the significant emigrant road that Isaac Stevens and other frontier developers had expected, but it served as an important route for commerce between the Pacific coast and inland Northwest.[20]

Efforts to open a military road to Utah did not turn out as well. Slowed for a time by an overly large supply train, Wallen surveyed and mapped several hundred miles of terrain and discovered and named Lake Harney in southeastern Oregon. By late summer in 1859, he concluded that a military road would not be feasible, but Harney and Lt. Joseph Dixon of the Topographical Corps believed that Wallen had at least found a practical shortcut for part of the Oregon Trail. In January 1860, Harney planned a second exploratory expedition, but financial and other circumstances precluded it. Harney also recommended less ambitious road-building projects in the Department of Oregon, as did Stevens and the Topographical Corps, but Congress did not fund those either.[21] Nevertheless, Harney's support highlighted a significant way, beyond constabulary duties, that the army helped open the West to white settlement.

Whatever sense of relief and well-being Harney's Indian policies and road-building activities gave Pacific Northwest residents, the prospect of war with Great Britain over the boundary between Washington Territory and British Columbia disrupted. The border dispute had a long history, as did efforts to resolve it. The incident that brought the two nations to the brink of armed conflict occurred unexpectedly, however, and had relatively little importance until Harney reacted inappropriately to it.

For two decades at the beginning of the century, four nations—the United States, Great Britain, Spain, and Russia—had claimed the territory between California and Alaska. For two more decades, Great Britain and the United States had occupied the area jointly while negotiating about where between the 42° and 50° 40' of latitude to divide it. Democrats had even made "54° 40' or Fight" a slogan of James K. Polk's presidential campaign in 1844. Finally, in 1846, the claimants had agreed in the Treaty of Washington to split the region generally along the forty-ninth parallel. According to that document, the border continued from the mainland along 49° north latitude "to the middle of the channel which separates the continent from Vancouver's Island and thence southerly from the middle of the said channel, and of Juan de Fuca Straits, to the Pacific Ocean." The British received Vancouver Island, and both countries got free navigation rights to the channel, straits, and Columbia River south of the forty-ninth parallel.

Unfortunately, the treaty did not clarify the location of the "channel" and thus left undetermined the ownership of the dozen or so San Juan Islands twenty miles off the southeastern tip of Vancouver Island. The oversight did not go unnoticed long, and both nations claimed the insular territories. British diplomats cited Rosario Strait, on the eastern side of the islands, as the main channel referred to in the treaty, while American diplomats cited Haro Strait, on the western side of the islands, as the principal channel. However, except for an occasional fisherman or woodcutter, neither country attempted to occupy the islands until 1853, when the Hudson's Bay Company put thirteen hundred sheep on the largest, San Juan, and sent Charles John Griffin along to look after them. That sparked a chain of patriotic posturing on both sides, but no serious trouble occurred until 1855, when Whatcom

County sheriff Ellis Barnes took a posse to San Juan to collect local taxes on the sheep. Griffin, now a British magistrate, refused to pay, and Barnes seized thirty-seven of the animals and took them back to the American mainland for sale. James Douglas, chief factor of the Hudson's Bay Company, wrote immediately to Governor Isaac Stevens, and warned him that the San Juan Islands constituted British territory. When Stevens informed Secretary of State William L. Marcy what had occurred, he conferred with President Franklin Pierce and then instructed the governor to "abstain from all acts on the disputed grounds which are calculated to provide any conflicts, so far as it can be done without implying . . . concessions to Great Britain." No force or other effort should be used to exercise exclusive rights to the islands, Marcy continued, until title to them could be established through diplomatic channels. The secretary then informed British ambassador John F. Crampton of the instructions to Stevens and expressed hope that "collision may be avoided."[22]

The rival claimants remained generally calm for the next four years, but occasionally so-called northern Indians, from British Columbia and Alaska, raided American settlements along the upper reaches of Puget Sound. In 1856, as part of his effort to curtail Indian hostilities throughout northern Washington, General Wool established Fort Bellingham, on the bay of that name, and Fort Townsend, on the mainland southwest of Whidbey Island, but those actions did not stop the depredations.

Efforts went forward at the same time to fix the exact location of the international frontier. In the summer of 1857, the United States and Great Britain sent commissioners to negotiate the water boundary on site. Royal Navy Capt. James C. Prevost led the British contingent, while Archibald Campbell headed a large American delegation.

As the commissioners pursued their assignments, British and American population on San Juan Island slowly increased. By early 1859, at least twenty Americans had staked land claims there. Most had come from the Fraser River gold fields, and in addition to being frustrated by their failure to strike it rich, they harbored lingering animosity toward the Hudson's Bay Company over restrictions that Douglas, now governor of British Columbia, had placed on foreign miners. Brit-

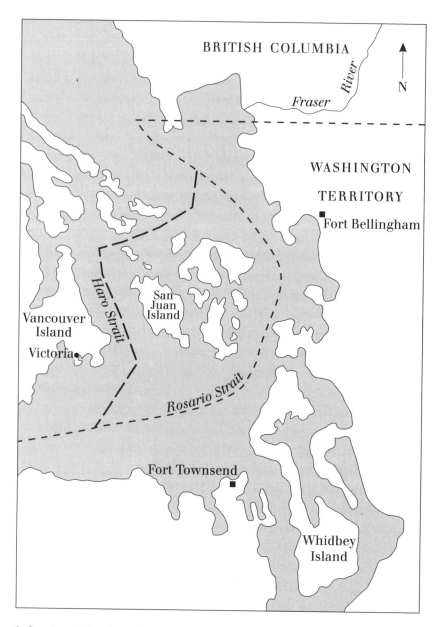

9. San Juan Islands, 1859

ish inhabitants included Griffin and fifteen Hudson's Bay employees, and they, along with Douglas, fretted about the influx of Americans.[23]

Those circumstances set the stage for trouble, and it arose over a pig. On June 15, 1859, Lyman Cutler, an American claimant who lived near the Hudson's Bay Company post on San Juan's southeast quadrant, arose to find the porker rooting in his potato patch. Earlier, when company animals had knocked down his fence, Cutler had protested to Griffin, and the magistrate had told him that he had no right to the land he lived on and would have to protect his crops himself. So this time Cutler grabbed his gun, chased the pig into the woods, and killed it. He then went to Griffin's house, told him what had happened, and offered to pay fair compensation. According to Cutler, Griffin became enraged and demanded $100. Cutler said he would not pay that much and went home. A short time later, Griffin and three other British officials, including A. G. Dallas, Governor Douglas's son-in-law, called on Cutler and threatened to arrest him if he did not pay the requested amount. Cutler declared that the pig was not worth even $10 and challenged Griffin's authority to take him into custody. After further argument, one of the visitors reportedly told Cutler, "You will have to answer for this hereafter," and then they went away. British officials later denied that they had threatened Cutler, but most Americans privy to his version of the incident accepted it.[24]

Harney stood among those. He first heard the story three weeks later, when he visited San Juan Island on a routine inspection tour. Traveling aboard the steamer USS *Massachusetts,* which the navy had placed under his authority, he and his staff left Fort Vancouver on June 28, spent two or three days each at Forts Steilacoom and Bellingham, and visited the boundary commissioners at Semiahmoo on the forty-ninth parallel. At Victoria on July 8 Harney called on Governor Douglas and enjoyed a courteous reception. No one mentioned Cutler or the pig. The next morning, July 9, Harney and his party crossed over to San Juan Island, where Paul K. Hubbs Sr., a U.S. customs officer, informed them of the incident, embellishing the story as he told it. Hubbs said the British had abandoned their intention to arrest Cutler only after he had threatened to shoot Dallas.

After further conversation with the locals, Harney left the island in time to visit Fort Townsend on July 10. On the eleventh, twenty-two Americans living on San Juan petitioned him in writing to protect them from northern Indians and the British. They stated that in April 1858 members of the Clallam tribe, then living on the island, had fired shots at Hubbs's house and three months later the bound bodies of two white men had washed ashore near the Indians' camp. Further, the petitioners claimed, residents had seen the Clallams kill a man that autumn, and another body had turned up on the beach in July 1859. The solicitors did not mention the Cutler incident, but they cited the Treaty of Washington and proclaimed their right to "American protection in our present exposed and defenceless position."[25]

From Fort Townsend Harney went to Olympia, where according to Isaac Stevens's son, Hazard, the former governor and the general dined together and discussed what to do about the situation on San Juan. Neither the elder Stevens nor Harney ever acknowledged such a conversation, but while continuing on to Fort Vancouver, the latter had time to think further about the recent developments on the island and its strategic importance.[26] About fifteen miles long and five to six miles wide with elevations up to one thousand feet, it had good stands of timber, plenty of grass, and, in Harney's opinion, an excellent harbor. By the time he reached his headquarters on the fifteenth, he had concluded that it "is the most commanding position we possess on the Sound" and he should send troops there to safeguard American interests.

The next day, July 16, Harney issued orders that escalated the San Juan dispute to a near international crisis. "For the better protection of the inhabitants of Puget Sound & its vicinity from the incursions of the northern Indians of British Columbia and the Russian Possessions," he directed Captain Pickett to move Company D of the Ninth Infantry, then at Fort Bellingham, to San Juan Island and establish a camp near the Hudson's Bay Company post. Harney also transferred the garrison of Fort Townsend to Fort Steilacoom and placed the *Massachusetts* under the command of Col. Silas Casey. He received orders to assign an infantry company to the steamer, convey Pickett's men to San Juan, and then keep the vessel on patrol among the islands to warn off Indians and, if necessary, assist the occupation force. On July 18, Harney informed Pickett that in addition to preventing Indian depredations, "Another serious and important duty will devolve upon you . . . arising from the conflicting interests of the American citizens and the Hudson's Bay Company." You will "resist" all British "attempts at interference . . . by intimidation or force" and tell British officials that any grievances they have against Americans must be settled in U.S. courts. Harney then reported his actions matter-of-factly to army headquarters in a summary of his inspection tour.[27]

This information did not reach Scott and other officials in the East for several weeks. In the meantime, American and British military forces in the Pacific Northwest moved dangerously close to a clash of arms. On July 27, Pickett landed on San Juan Island with some sixty men, announced his intention to establish a military post, and ordered "all the inhabitants" to report any Indian sightings. He declared in addition that "this being United States territory, no laws, other than those of the United States, nor courts, except such as are held by virtue of said laws, will be recognized or allowed." Later that same day John F. DeCourcy, recently appointed British stipendiary magistrate for the San Juan Islands, arrived aboard the HMS *Satellite* and demanded to know why and under what authority the Americans had come. When Pickett replied that he had landed under orders from his government, DeCourcy warned him that he was trespassing and would have to leave. Pickett then introduced Henry R. Crosbie, a Whatcom County official who had come along to serve as the Americans' justice of the peace, and cautioned DeCourcy against interfering with U.S. citizens.[28]

DeCourcy remained on the island while the *Satellite* carried news of Pickett's landing back to Victoria. Governor Douglas did not receive it calmly. He did not want to precipitate a fight, but he felt compelled to strengthen the British military position. Accordingly, he sent the twenty-one-gun *Satellite* back to the island, along with the thirty-one-gun frigate HMS *Tribune* and the ten-gun HMS *Plumper*, and on August 2 he prepared a formal protest against the American occupation. "The sovereignty of the island of San Juan and of the whole of the Haro Archipelago has always been undeviatingly claimed to be in the Crown of Great Britain," Douglas asserted. The following day he advised the

British Columbia legislative assembly of the steps he had taken and speculated correctly that Harney had acted "in ignorance of the intentions of the U.S. government."[29]

In the meantime, Colonel Casey sent the *Massachusetts* back to San Juan with Capt. Granville O. Haller and a company of infantry to reinforce Pickett. Although the American vessel posed no threat to the three British warships anchored in the harbor, its presence added to the growing tension. On August 3, the three British naval captains went ashore, handed Pickett a copy of Governor Douglas's protest, and repeated the question that DeCourcy had asked a week earlier. Under what authority had American troops occupied the island? Pickett replied that he had acted on orders from Harney, whom he assumed had appropriate authorization from the War Department. The British officers had difficulty believing that the U.S. government had approved Pickett's landing, and they suggested that British and American troops occupy the island jointly until further instructions could be obtained from London and Washington. Pickett said he could not enter into such an agreement and asked Capt. Geoffrey P. Hornby, the senior British officer, to put the proposal in writing for submission to Harney. That evening, with the three British warships still anchored offshore, Pickett hastily scrawled a note to Harney. Forwarding Hornby's suggestions and a copy of Douglas's protest, Pickett advised that the British could land on the island at any time and place they chose. "They have a force so much superior to mine that it will be merely a mouthful for them." He believed that "to maintain our dignity we must occupy in force, or allow them to land an equal force," and he requested that "an express be sent me immediately on my future guidance. I do not think there are any moments to waste." Pickett did not know that Hornby had already decided, independently of Douglas, not to try to disembark British troops for fear of weakening his country's diplomatic position.[30]

Harney responded on August 6. Having already erred in occupying the island, he now made a second mistake. He refused Hornby's reasonable suggestion of joint occupation by equal forces. At the same time he ordered Colonel Casey to the island with additional reinforcements and appealed to the senior American naval officer in San Francisco for ships of war. Harney also sent Pickett a note for Governor

Douglas, answering the question about who ordered the American military occupation. "I placed" troops there, he declared, as "commander of the Department of Oregon" in order "to protect American citizens." Harney cited Lyman Cutler's story that the British who had visited him on June 15 intended to arrest him, take him to British Columbia aboard a warship, and try him under British laws. That, Harney ranted, constituted an "outrage" and an "insult," and consequently he intended to keep troops on San Juan Island until he received "further orders from my government."[31]

The next day, Harney disregarded Floyd's admonition to send all reports to Scott and wrote directly to the War Department, forwarding a copy of Douglas's protest and a succinct report on what had happened since July 19. Repeating that he had acted to protect U.S. citizens from both northern Indians and the British, Harney asserted confidently that "while there is no one more desirous than myself for amicable settlement of the difficulties . . . I shall use all the means at my command to maintain the position that I have assumed." Contrary to what he had implied to Douglas, he sought neither approval nor advice about what to do next.

Officials in Washington had already discussed Harney's first report. Scott had called it to the attention of Acting Secretary of War W. R. Drinkard, who had taken it to James Buchanan. "The President was not prepared to learn that you had ordered military possession to be taken of the island," Drinkard wrote Harney on September 3. Buchanan decided to reserve judgment on the matter, however, until he had more information. In the meantime, he worried less about a clash of arms than about hampering the boundary negotiations. He wanted to know if Harney had conferred with Commissioner Campbell before landing troops, and he wanted Harney to assure British authorities that he was not trying to influence the outcome of the talks.[32]

Harney had not consulted Campbell. The commissioner had learned about the occupation by coincidence on July 26. Having stopped at San Juan Island while exploring the entire archipelago, he had seen the *Massachusetts* steam into the harbor that afternoon, and he had watched Pickett's troops disembark the next morning. Although surprised and uncertain whether Harney had acted alone or on orders,

Campbell had perceived no threat to the boundary negotiations. By August 14, though, he had begun to worry, and he wrote Harney that he would "be greatly relieved to learn that you have some authority from the government for the decisive step you have taken." Harney replied that he had received no instructions but had reported his actions and expected orders in due course. In any event, he maintained, "the relative claims of the two countries has had nothing to do in the assignment of the troops in question." Immediately after reading Harney's communication, Campbell reported all he knew about the matter to Secretary of State Lewis Cass.[33]

Buchanan reached a decision in mid-September. With his military forces already overextended and sectional animosity over slavery growing daily, he could ill afford either a military clash or a political debacle over a tiny group of remote islands. Accordingly he asked General Scott to go as soon as possible to Washington Territory, assume command of all U.S. forces on the Pacific coast if necessary, and attempt to resolve the dispute peacefully around Hornby's suggestion for joint military occupation of San Juan. Accompanied by his doctor, aide, and the assistant adjutant general, the seventy-three-year-old commanding general, still recovering from a recent fall, left New York City on September 20 aboard the *Star of the West.* Neither he nor Buchanan knew for certain that American and British forces had not already clashed or that they would not before he arrived. Scott had instructions in either event "not [to] suffer the national honor to be tarnished."

American West Coast newspapers echoed that sentiment. While abhorring war and urging circumspection, editors militantly asserted American ownership of the San Juan Islands and stood firmly behind Harney, as they erroneously assumed the administration did. The Olympia *Pioneer and Democrat* recommended a "moderate course" but warned, "Let it not be understood that we yield an inch to what we deem the intrusion of the British occupants of San Juan. Our right to that and the neighboring islands, under the treaty, we assert to be as clear as the sun at noonday." The Portland *Weekly Oregonian* maintained that its readers would "find no difficulty . . . in determining that General Harney was right in taking possession of the island, as it clearly belongs to the United States." He "will protect and defend it, regardless of the fuss and fury growls and swaggering of Gov. Douglas, Capt. Hornby or other British officials." In San Francisco, the *Daily Alta California* declared that "the watchword is "the Canal de Haro, or fight.' We trust that it will end more creditably to our politicians than did "Fifty-four-forty, or fight.'"[34]

By placing troops on San Juan Island, Harney had brought the nation to the brink of war. Almost every historian who has studied these events has concluded that he acted unwisely. However, neither they nor Harney's contemporaries agree about his motives. Years later, Gen. George B. McClellan speculated that Harney and others, including Stevens and Pickett, hoped to draw Great Britain into a war that would overshadow sectional issues, unite the American populace, and avert civil war. Conversely, Col. Granville O. Haller charged that Harney and other Southerners wanted to provoke a foreign war to enable the South to secede with little or no opposition. Some British observers thought Harney sought a way to win enough national attention to run for president. There is no evidence to support any of these theories. Harney's contemporary biographer, Logan Uriah Reavis, accepted his subject's own explanation, that he wanted only to protect American lives, property, and rights from northern Indians and the British. At least three historians who have examined the events from British and Canadian perspectives suggest that Harney recognized the strategic military importance of the islands and saw the Cutler incident as an appropriate excuse to seize control of them before the boundary commission could award them to Great Britain. This coincides with Hazard Stevens's view, although he maintained that his father had been "the master spirit" who "instructed General Harney as to the merits of the controversy." At least one historian attributes Harney's actions to disdain, which he shared with many Americans, for the Hudson's Bay Company. And finally, some students of the time and region contend that it is impossible to discern why Harney acted as he did.[35]

Upon further examination, however, it seems clear that three factors—impulsiveness, expansionist sentiment, and obstinacy—influenced Harney's actions. Almost always excitable, aggressive, and quick to react to any affront, insult, or attack, whether real or imagined, personal or professional, Harney behaved true to character when he occupied the island. He acted impulsively. Despite taking several days to reach his decision, he did not apply the same careful reasoning he had used in considering an appropriate frontier defense system in Texas in 1849, devising a coordinated campaign against the Seminoles in Florida in 1857, or recognizing the logistical obstacles facing the Utah expedition that same year. Rather, in this more immediately personal circumstance, he behaved as he had when, without authorization, he went after Chakaika in 1840 and invaded Mexico six years later. He did not allow time for either ongoing boundary discussions or other communication between his government and British officials to resolve the dispute, and he did not consider any potential consequences of armed conflict, other than defending American honor and territory. Clearly he viewed the British attempt to arrest Cutler as a slur against his country and against himself as commander of American troops in the area, and he allowed both personal outrage and expansionist sentiment to cloud his judgment.

As the army and its officer corps became increasingly professional during the course of Harney's career, fewer and fewer officers exhibited the bellicose expansionism of Andrew Jackson and others of his era. And those who retained such feelings generally subordinated them to their desire for organizational stability, which peace ensured. Harney proved a significant exception to this trend. Having grown up in Jackson's shadow, observed firsthand his dashing and headstrong tactics, assisted him in the official transfer of East Florida to the United States, and benefited several times from his personal assistance, Harney admired the man and his deeds and believed, as he did, in "the march of manifest destiny." This pushed him prematurely into Mexico in 1846, and it shaped his response to the events on San Juan Island.

Only a few months earlier Harney had used that exact phrase in one of two rambling, expansionist-tinged discourses about American economic development. In January 1859, he had shared his thoughts with both acting Washington governor Charles H. Mason and Oregon governor George L. Curry. "The knell of power was sounded in Europe," Harney wrote, "when the first pilgrim vessel sought a harbor on the western shores of the Atlantic," and now "Providence" has cast "the lot" of West Coast Americans "in no ordinary sphere." Marveling at future prospects of trade with Russia, Japan, and China, Harney declared that the Pacific Northwest's "natural harbors and magnificent forests tell us that this coast must be in future times, the Queen of commerce." In the meantime, the United States should "cover by a protectorate the entire country from the Rio Grande to the Isthmus of Panama," because "the organizations of the people occupying" those regions "cannot be considered as national, and they should not be permitted to interrupt or retard our intercourse." Further, he declared, "In the scale of civilization they are but one remove from the Indians occupying our own soil, and like the Indians, they must gradually disappear before the improvements of the age."

In his departmental inspection report, written three days after he ordered Pickett to land on San Juan, Harney repeated many of these same sentiments, noting that "Puget Sound is a most remarkable sheet of water and is destined to be eminent in the annals of commerce." In none of his writings did Harney advocate seizing territory, disputed or otherwise, but he had become so strong a proponent of economic expansion that, when presented with the opportunity to assert American ownership of the San Juan Islands, he did so. He could not abide allowing the British any unavoidable advantage in the region.[36]

Once Harney committed to occupying San Juan Island, obstinacy kept him wedded to that course. Convinced initially of his correctness and too stubborn later to see or admit his error, he continued to escalate tensions while officials in the national capital deliberated and Scott made the long journey west via Panama. On the morning of August 10, under Harney's orders and the cover of fog, Colonel Casey landed four more companies of soldiers and eight thirty-two-pound howitzers on San Juan. Once ashore, he began to fear that the British men-of-war might shell the island at any moment, and so he requested a meeting with Captain Hornby. From him Casey learned that Adm. R. Lambert Baynes had arrived at Victoria aboard the HMS *Ganges* and become the senior British military officer on the scene. Accompanied by Pickett and Campbell, Casey took the commissioner's steamer, the USS *Shubrick*, immediately to Esquimalt harbor and sought an audience with Baynes. Casey intended to request assurance that British forces would not actively oppose the American occupation, in return for which he planned to recommend that Harney withdraw his reinforcements. But Baynes refused to see Casey except aboard the *Ganges*. Unreasonably miffed because Baynes would not come to the *Shubrick*, Casey returned to San Juan, reported his efforts to Harney, and noted that "the British have a sufficient naval force here to effectually blockade this island when they choose." With the recent arrival of the corvette HMS *Pylades*, their fleet numbered 5 vessels, with 167 guns and 1,940 men.[37]

Neither Harney nor Casey knew that Baynes, like Hornby, had decided not to try to put British troops on San Juan or prevent further American landings. The admiral considered the occupation issue petty but potentially explosive, and he doubted that the absence of British soldiers would endanger British citizens or in any way weaken his country's claim to the archipelago. Governor Douglas remained incensed, though, and both the British Columbia provincial assembly and the Victoria newspaper, the *British Colonist*, demanded action. On August 13, Douglas appealed directly to Harney to withdraw his forces. Keeping them on disputed territory not only constituted a "marked discourtesy," Douglas contended. It also complicated chances for an amicable settlement of the boundary and seemed "calculated to provoke a collision between the military forces of two friendly nations in a distant part of the world." Douglas also sent Harney a copy of the letter that Secretary of State Marcy had written Ambassador Crampton in 1855 urging the avoidance of hostilities.

Harney replied that nothing short of instructions from the president would make him change his mind. However, he had not known about Marcy's plea for a peaceful resolution of the boundary until now, and so he began to worry that the War Department might disapprove his actions. To justify his decision further, on August 29 he sent Adj. Gen. Samuel Cooper another detailed description of the events that preceded the occupation. This time he embellished the accounts of Indian raids and added arrogantly that he had "carefully investigated the treaty of 1846, personally examined the premises in question," and concluded that "a stronger title cannot exist than that which the treaty . . . establishes for the United States." The British have "instituted a series of acts," he rationalized incorrectly, "aiming at the eventual sovereignty of San Juan Island in consequence of its paramount importance as a military and naval station."[58]

The situation changed little in the next two months, as each side moved cautiously. British forces remained alert while awaiting instructions from the Foreign Office. Casey and Pickett continued to organize, supply, and entrench American troops on the island. And Harney authorized the governor of Washington Territory to draw from Fort Steilacoom, in the event of war, one hundred thousand musket rounds and two thousand howitzer shells for volunteers. On September 14, still unaware of President Buchanan's reaction to the occupation but increasingly concerned that it might be unfavorable, Harney sent Scott copies of sworn affidavits, dated September 7, in which Cutler and Hubbs told their version of what had happened on the island on June 15. A few weeks later Harney received Drinkard's letter of September 3 inquiring whether he had consulted with Campbell before ordering the occupation. Harney replied that he had not but noted that he had communicated with the commissioner afterward. And once more the intractable officer attempted to justify his decision. "The facts of this case," Harney wrote, are that "the British government furnished five ships-of-war . . . to an unscrupulous colonial governor for the purpose of wresting from us an island that they covet. Such punic [*sic*] faith should never be tolerated, however plausible the pretext upon which it may be founded."[59]

After traveling more than four weeks, General Scott and his party arrived at Fort Vancouver in the early morning hours of October 21. The commanding general wasted no time signaling both his presence and his superior rank. From his cabin aboard the steamer *Northern,* he sent his aide, Col. George Lay, to tell Harney to report on board at 8:00 A.M. with copies of all correspondence and orders relating to San Juan Island. Harney received the colonel at 2:00 A.M. and offered to see Scott immediately, but Lay replied that the commanding general was sleeping and could not be disturbed. Harney and members of his staff reported unrested at eight o'clock, and Scott reviewed the requested documents for an hour before his steamer departed for Portland and a ceremonial welcome by city officials and other dignitaries. Harney rode along to continue the meeting, which lasted until shortly before noon. The ceremonies ran on for three hours, and afterward, at Harney's request, the two officers talked awhile longer. No one recorded the details of their conversations, but both men confirmed later that they had discussed a potential change of command for Harney and possible reorganization of the Department of Oregon. Given their proud and temperamental dispositions, the two veteran officers likely strained the limits of military courtesy as Scott conveyed the president's and his own considerable dissatisfaction. When the afternoon talk concluded, Harney went back to Fort Vancouver alone, and according to a journalist who saw him leave, "he indulged in one of his characteristic outbursts, but he was swearing at himself, and little notice was paid thereto." Scott returned later to spend the night before continuing on to British Columbia, but he said nothing more to Harney. For the remainder of his stay in the area, the commanding general communicated with his disgruntled subordinate only in writing.[40]

From Fort Vancouver Scott traveled to Fort Townsend and established temporary headquarters on the *Massachusetts*. Before leaving the former post he had learned from Pickett, there coincidentally to sit on a court-martial, that all the British warships except the *Satellite* had returned to their usual anchorage at Victoria and that "everything" appeared "quiet." Thus prospects for effecting a peaceful solution seemed good.

On October 25, Scott sent Lay to Victoria with a message for Governor Douglas. As a "basis for the temporary adjustment of any present difficulty" until their two governments could settle the boundary question diplomatically, Scott suggested that "without prejudice to the claim of either nation . . . each shall occupy a separate portion" of San Juan Island with a "detachment of infantry, riflemen, or marines, not exceeding one hundred men." After deliberating a few days, Douglas replied that he could not agree to such an arrangement without authorization from the Foreign Office, and he suggested a joint civil occupation instead. Scott responded that it would be unwise to entrust the peace to civil authorities not subject, in the case of the Americans, to the direct control of the president. Furthermore, either accepting or conveniently using one of Harney's stated reasons for the American occupation, Scott contended that the residents of San Juan "do in reality stand in need of troops for protection . . . against predatory bands of Indians." Douglas answered that as soon as he heard from London he would "be glad to co-operate . . . in arranging a plan for the temporary maintenance of order and protection of life and property upon the island." He offered in the meantime to withdraw all naval forces from the vicinity of the island if Scott would "divest" the American military force "of its menacing attitude." Additionally, Douglas insisted that the British would do nothing to "disturb the 'status'" of San Juan Island pending the outcome of the boundary negotiations.[41]

That proved enough for Scott. On November 5, he ordered all but one company of American troops, including Pickett's, off the island and instructed Casey to return his howitzers to the *Massachusetts*. Scott then informed Douglas and Harney of those orders and reminded the latter that until the sovereignty of the island could be determined, "British subjects have equal rights with American citizens" there.[42]

By November 15, Scott felt comfortable enough with the situation to return to New York. He recognized, though, that his temporary resolution of the crisis would endure longer if Harney left the area, too. So before leaving, pursuant to their conversation aboard the *Northern*, Scott sent Harney a conditional order to return to St. Louis and assume command of the Department of the West. Since discussing this possibility on October 21, Scott had come to believe that eventually the British might demand Harney's removal as a condition to accepting joint military occupation. "In such an event," Scott speculated to Harney, "it might be a great relief to the President to find you, by your own act, no longer in that command." Further, if Harney left voluntarily, his departure would be less likely to produce an outcry from his supporters in the region. In any case, Scott wrote, "If you decline the order, and I give you leave to decline it, please throw it into the fire."

Harney informed Scott immediately that he was "not disposed to comply with such an order." He could see no reason for Buchanan to be embarrassed or displeased, and he believed that combining the Oregon and Pacific departments under a commander headquartered in San Francisco would have a negative effect on discipline and Indian relations. Fearing that Scott might change his mind and reissue the order later, Harney sent his arguments against it to Adjutant General Cooper and urged him to submit them to the president. They had no impact, however, except to call more attention to Harney's self-important stubbornness.[43]

Little changed in the San Juan controversy over the next several months, but Harney had plenty of other disputatious activity to keep him occupied. While in the Department of Oregon he became enmeshed in more petty quarrels and potential court-martial cases than at any other time since the Mexican War. Although the incidents involved both enlisted men and officers, his disputes rested with the latter. Harney's own cantankerousness and vindictive bent contributed to the difficulties, but often the subordinates with whom he bickered seemed equally contentious.

Some of the difficulties centered on a hundred-acre farm that Harney, still benefiting from his wife's wealth, purchased for approximately $1,500 shortly after arriving at Fort Vancouver. Situated about a mile from the post, the property included a seven-room frame house, a stable, wagon sheds, and other outbuildings and provided both a place for recreation and an opportunity for financial speculation. It made an ideal location for gymnastic equipment that Harney used to stay fit, but it became more of a distraction than he had anticipated.[44]

In July 1859, not long after Harney sent troops to San Juan Island, he furloughed at least seven enlisted men, some for several weeks, to make improvements and cultivate a large garden on the farm. A number of officers objected to this, both because they questioned its propriety and because they could not properly account for the soldiers' whereabouts on monthly company and regimental returns. One officer, Lt. Henry V. DeHart, protested directly to Scott in New York. Infuriated, Harney placed DeHart under arrest and charged him with "contempt and disrespect" and "conduct unbecoming an officer and a gentleman." The commanding general ordered the charges dropped and DeHart released.[45]

A different kind of dispute arose in March 1860, when Harney arrested Lt. Henry C. Hodges and charged him with "neglect of duty" and "disrespect" for failing to address Pleasonton by rank in a written communication. Like DeHart, Hodges appealed to Scott, and this time he referred the matter to Secretary Floyd. "I am greatly mistaken," the commanding general asserted, "if an instance of tyranny so useless and vexatious ever occurred in our army before." Floyd freed Hodges, and he in turn charged Harney with "tyrannical conduct and abuse of authority." However, the War Department did not approve a court-martial. Given the almost constant bickering throughout the officer corps, Scott had exaggerated the uniqueness of the offense.[46]

By the spring of 1860, Harney realized that he needed a respite. He had not taken a leave of absence in five years, and in a few months he would celebrate his sixtieth birthday. Furthermore, Mary Harney and their children remained in France, and although he had not been anxious to return there, he now began to think more about them. He wrote to Mary twice, in what she described as "milder terms than usual," and requested twelve months leave with permission to go abroad.[47]

Before approval came, though, events on San Juan Island commanded Harney's attention again. Sometime after Scott returned to New York in the fall of 1859, the British government decided to accept his proposal of joint military occupation until the boundary dispute could be resolved through negotiation. Accordingly on March 20, 1860, Admiral Baynes informed Capt. Lewis C. Hunt, commander of the remaining American troops on the island, that a detachment of one hundred Royal Marines, under Capt. George Bazalgette, would land shortly "on the north point . . . for the purpose of establishing" such "occupation." When they arrived a few days later, Hunt notified Harney and sent him a copy of Baynes's letter.

This placed Harney in a quandary. Scott had not informed him about plans for a joint military occupation. Instead, disgruntled about having to travel to the Pacific Northwest in the first place and anxious to return home, Scott had only told Harney hurriedly that the British did not seem interested in dislodging the Americans from the island by force and that for the sake of cordial relations he had reduced the number of troops there. Furthermore, none of the selected Douglas correspondence that Scott had shared with Harney mentioned or even implied joint military occupation. On the other hand, Harney knew that the president and secretary of war did not approve of the way he had handled matters previously, and so he did not oppose the British landing.[48]

On April 10, 1860, however, Harney ordered Pickett back to San Juan Island to replace Captain Hunt, who had expressed uncertainty about who had jurisdiction over illegal liquor-trade cases. Harney directed Pickett to inform Bazalgette and Baynes that although Scott had left no instructions about joint military occupation, "nothing will be omitted in maintaining a frank and general intercourse . . . to establish a practical solution of the present misunderstandings." Had he stopped there, all would have been well. But Harney still stubbornly considered the island part of Washington Territory, and he declared that "any attempt of the British commander to ignore this right . . . will be followed by deplorable results." On April 30, Pickett relieved Hunt and sent Bazalgette a copy of Harney's instructions.[49]

Officials in both London and Washington reacted to Harney's actions with surprise and dismay. The British took particular exception to his insistence that the island lay within Washington Territory and British citizens must be subject to American laws. They complained to Secretary of State Cass and requested an explanation of why Harney had violated the arrangements that Douglas had made with Scott. This proved too much for the commanding general. "If this does not lead to a collision of arms," he wrote Floyd, "it will again be due to the forbearance of the British." Noting that he had doubted all along that Harney would follow instructions, Scott now recommended that he be relieved of command. After discussion with Buchanan, Cass informed the British minister in Washington that the War Department would revoke the orders to Pickett, give "full effect to the arrangement of General Scott," and make "a strict inquiry into the conduct of General Harney." On June 8, Adjutant General Cooper ordered the recalcitrant brigadier to turn over command of the Department of Oregon to his next in rank, "repair without delay to Washington city, and report in person to the Secretary of War."[50]

Harney relinquished command to Colonel Wright on July 5, 1860, and soon afterward started the long trip to the national capital with Pleasonton and Surgeon Joseph K. Barnes. Shortly after they arrived in mid-August, Harney learned to his surprise and chagrin that much of his and others' correspondence regarding the Department of Oregon had been printed for public and governmental review. Outraged, he complained to Floyd that Scott's remarks "are . . . injurious to . . . my good faith and reputation as an officer," and he requested and received permission to respond in writing.

In defending himself, Harney repeated many of the arguments he had submitted for referral to the president in November 1859. He added that the War Department had failed to advise him of former Secretary of State Marcy's 1855 assurances to Ambassador Crampton, that Scott had neglected to inform him about his proposal for joint military occupation of San Juan Island, and that despite those omissions he had not resisted the British marines' landing in March.[51] If, during his trip to Oregon, Scott had behaved less temperamentally himself and given Harney full and clear orders in writing, he might not have rekindled the controversy. Even so, as one of the nation's highest-ranking military officers, Harney should have acted less stubbornly and more cautiously. His persistence in proclaiming American ownership of the disputed territory was both unnecessary and irresponsible.

While he waited in Washington for Floyd's response to his defense, Harney learned that Mary had died in Paris on August 27. His series of poorly considered actions regarding San Juan Island had cost him the opportunity to see her again. With time to think further about his service in the Pacific Northwest, he could take pride in his contribution to military road building and in his successful efforts, with Father De-Smet, to render the peace achieved through General Clarke's Indian campaign more stable and lasting. However, he feared correctly that most people who subsequently recalled his duty in the Department of Oregon would associate him unfavorably with what eventually became known as the "pig war."

On October 26, 1860, Asst. Adj. Gen. Julius P. Gareschè informed Harney of Floyd's response to his version of what had occurred. In addition to abolishing the Department of Oregon, which action Harney had opposed, the secretary of war felt compelled, Gareschè wrote, to express "disapproval" of Harney's April 10 decision to send Pickett back to San Juan in disobedience of Scott's orders. "At the same time," Gareschè continued, Floyd "has no doubt of the good intentions of General Harney . . . and from his known high character and distinguished services he is not disposed to be severe in his condemnation."

Considering the potential that had existed for an international clash of arms, Floyd's reprimand seemed mild. Relieved, Harney immediately requested permission to take the year's furlough that Floyd had approved in March. This time, however, the secretary denied it.

Meanwhile, the San Juan water boundary remained unsettled until 1871. The Civil War and its aftermath delayed negotiations until 1868, and during that time Great Britain and the United States maintained the joint military occupation. Eventually the disputants agreed to a second Treaty of Washington. It declared Haro Strait the boundary and made the San Juan Islands American territory. Harney had at least predicted the outcome. When he had first seen the strait in June 1859, he had observed that "any fool could see" this is "the true boundary between the two countries."[52]

CHAPTER 12

"Loyal Soldier" in Missouri

A GAINST HIS better judgment, retired army officer William T. Sherman, recently installed as president of the Fifth Street Railroad, edged up Locust Street in front of his rented house shortly after noon on May 10, 1861. As he listened for the sound of musketry or cannon fire from the direction of Camp Jackson on the western edge of St. Louis, his seven-year-old son, Willie, tagged along. Earlier, Sherman's boarders, Charles Ewing and John Hunter, had urged him to join them in going out to the camp to "see the fun," but he had declined, noting that "in case of conflict the by-standers were more likely to be killed than the men engaged." Still, he remained curious to know what was happening in the standoff between Missouri secessionist volunteers in the camp and federal troops surrounding it. As Sherman and his son approached Olive Street, a man came running toward them yelling, "They've surrendered! They've surrendered!" On hearing that, Sherman moved farther along and soon came abreast of Lindell's Grove. There he saw a regiment of Union volunteers guarding a group of Camp Jackson prisoners, while a crowd, including Ewing and Hunter, milled about. A band played martial music, and onlookers cheered and taunted troops and prisoners. A few minutes later, as the military column began moving toward the center of the city, a shot rang out, and then more, and Sherman could hear balls cutting through trees above his head. Ewing reacted first and pushed Willie to the ground, and when Sherman saw troops reloading their weapons, he grabbed the boy and dove with him into a gully. They remained there until the shooting stopped, then arose unhurt. Others did not. At least twenty-eight people, including women and children, lay dead or dying and seventy-five others nursed wounds. In addition to the Shermans, Ewing, and Hunter, the unharmed witnesses included Ulysses S. Grant, present like Sherman as a private citizen and also like him a future great general. Brig. Gen. William S. Harney, who might have prevented the slaughter, did not see it because he had gone to Washington to try to regain command of federal forces in Missouri.[1]

The War Department had ordered Harney home to St. Louis in November 1860 to command the Department of the West, which encompassed most territory west of the Mississippi River and east of the Rocky Mountains, except for Texas. Despite the controversy he had stirred in the Pacific Northwest, his military seniority, years of experience in Indian affairs, and previous service in strife-torn Kansas all made him a logical choice for the appointment. But in moving Harney from Oregon to Missouri, his superiors had transferred him from one tinderbox to another, and now a new presidential administration had reservations about his loyalty. He had returned to Missouri amid a national crisis over slavery and speculation that the Southern states might secede from the Union. Missourians, like the citizens of other border states, stood divided on the issue, and Harney pursued a cautious strategy to keep them from coming to blows. Instead of taking firm action to ensure Union control, he tried to act as conciliator and allowed secessionists to arm themselves for the alleged purpose of helping maintain order. Consequently, Missouri became a battleground of the Civil War sooner that it might have otherwise, and authorities in Washington relieved Harney of command twice amid charges that he sympathized with the South. Although guilty only of questionable judgment, he could not overcome War Department doubts about his motives and continued ability to command.

Harney first assumed the Missouri post on November 17, just eleven days after Republican Abraham Lincoln, campaigning against the spread of slavery to new territories, won election as the sixteenth president of the United States. He had received no electoral votes from the fifteen slave states, and the South Carolina legislature had called a convention to vote on secession. Other Southern states seemed ready to follow that lead.

Missouri contended with a more complex political situation. Some of its citizens had strong family ties to the South, while others had binding economic links with the North. Moderate candidates had won nearly 90 percent of the vote in the August gubernatorial election and about 70 percent in the November presidential contest. These results indicated that most Missourians were conditional Unionists. While holding a variety of political opinions, they opposed both secession and the use of federal force to prevent it.[2]

Secessionists and unconditional Unionists constituted vocal minorities. Most of the former owned slaves and lived either in hemp and tobacco counties on the Missouri River or along the Kansas boundary. Compared with most other Southern and border states, Missouri had few slaves—about 115,000—and not all slaveholders considered secession necessary to preserve their way of life. Some believed that if they remained loyal to the Union, the federal government would protect their human property.

Unconditional Union feeling ran strongest in St. Louis, where European immigrants, principally Germans, accounted for more than half of the nearly two hundred thousand people. Most of the city's Germans had fled their homelands after unsuccessful revolutions against political and economic repression in 1830 and 1848, and they hated slavery. Unconditional Unionists found their chief spokesman in thirty-nine-year-old Francis P. Blair Jr., whose father had helped establish the Republican Party. Formerly a Missouri legislator and Free-Soil congressman, the younger Blair had fought the extension of slavery for more than a decade. During the recent elections he had utilized "Wide Awake" clubs of foreign-born residents to generate support for Republican ideas, and these groups remained a strong voice for the Union.

Missouri's newly elected executives held pro-Southern views. Governor Claiborne Fox Jackson, an experienced political strategist, headed the "Central Clique" of the state Democratic Party and favored extending slavery to the territories. His lieutenant governor, Thomas C. Reynolds, a native of South Carolina and former U.S. attorney, harbored secessionist sentiment.

Harney recorded no opinions about the growing state and national crises as he prepared for his new responsibilities. However, as a Southerner, slave owner, longtime Missouri resident, and veteran of forty-two years of dedicated service to the Union, he had the requisite background and experience to understand all the points of contention. He could see, too, how Missouri's geographic location and its standing as the richest and most populous slave-holding state would make it strategically important to both sides in the event of war. Still a key to inland commerce, St. Louis now served as an important east-west rail terminal, as well as a center of north-south steamboat traffic, and thick black smoke from its growing manufacturing enterprises hung over row after row of red brick commercial and residential buildings. Harney soon came to dread the potentially damaging human and economic consequences of a military struggle over these resources. He had little time to reflect about them in November and December, though.[3]

On November 21, the War Department ordered him to go to southeastern Kansas and "take summary steps" to "break up" a "lawless band" of abolitionists led by sectarian Campbellite preacher James Montgomery. Violence between pro- and antislavery men had troubled the Kansas-Missouri border for six years. Now, Montgomery had reportedly gathered as many as five hundred armed followers and publicly declared his intention to "destroy slavery." The federal judge at Fort Scott had closed his court and fled to Missouri, and residents throughout the region feared for their lives and property.

Harney hastened by train to Fort Leavenworth, ordered whatever troops could be spared from other Kansas posts to Fort Scott, and then rushed there himself with thirty dragoons. Capt. William Barry followed with two companies of light artillery, and Bvt. Maj. Henry W. Wessels and Capt. Nathaniel Lyon brought two companies of infantry from Fort Riley. Outgoing Missouri governor Robert M. Stewart provided a contingent of state militia from St. Louis under Brig. Gen. Daniel M. Frost.

Lyon and Frost brought opposing political philosophies to the hunt for Montgomery. Both had graduated from West Point and served with Harney in various locations since the Mexican War, but there the resemblance ceased. Married to Harney's niece, Eliza Graham, Frost had left the army to pursue entrepreneurial interests and manage the Graham family estate, Hazelwood, in the Florissant Valley. Although a Northerner by birth, he held strong proslavery views, and his acquaintances included lieutenant governor–elect Reynolds. Lyon, on the other hand, hated slavery and clandestinely aided persons who assisted fugitive slaves passing into Kansas on the "underground railroad." Although short and thin in statue and much less well known than Harney, Lyon possessed a similar reputation for hotheaded, vindictive violence.

Lyon had resented Harney's evenhanded peacekeeping in Kansas three years earlier and considered him a Southern sympathizer. Now, at the risk of court-martial, the impassioned captain determined to contravene Harney's efforts to stop Montgomery. On December 6, Lyon met secretly with the Free State leader and hatched a plan to hide him and another prominent abolitionist, Charles Jennison, when federal troops searched their homes. The plan worked perfectly, and Harney's men found neither "outlaws" nor rumored stockpiles of weapons. While Lyon laughed furtively, Harney concluded that he could do nothing more at the moment because a "large portion of the population on the border either belong to this organization, or sympathize with them" and rounding them up would take a larger force than he could readily acquire. Thus in mid-December Harney returned to St. Louis and recommended that the War Department give the governor of Kansas funds, and let him deal with Montgomery in his own way.[4]

Washington accepted Harney's decision. As the national political crisis grew, many other matters competed for attention, and no one asked why he did not try to augment his force and continue the pursuit. Persons familiar with Harney's career might logically have expected him to do so despite the conditions he cited. Had age dimmed his combative fire? Had his removal from command in the Pacific

Northwest made him suddenly more cautious? These would have been reasonable conclusions. After all, he was sixty-one now, and his rebuke in Oregon had been sharp and public. On the other hand, unlike previous situations in which he had acted impulsively, this one involved no perceived personal or national affront. Most likely for all those reasons, he measured it more carefully, determining that he neither could nor should do anything more. This concluded the Montgomery episode for Harney, Frost, and Lyon, but their paths soon crossed again in more momentous fashion.

A few days after Harney's return home, South Carolina seceded, and when the Twenty-first Missouri General Assembly convened in Jefferson City on December 31, the Palmetto State's decision dominated conversation. In his farewell address on January 3, 1861, outgoing Governor Stewart blasted the Republicans for opposing slavery in the territories, but he deplored secession and called for a compromise that would return South Carolina to the Union. Incoming Governor Jackson took a different stance. In his inaugural address, he expressed hope that the federal government would recognize the rights of slave states and declared that if it did not, Missourians would stand by the South. To determine the state's future relationship with the Union, Jackson asked the assembly to call a convention. And to get Missouri ready to fight, should war come, he asked the legislators to provide for reorganization of the state militia. The military bill failed to pass, but on January 21 the assembly authorized an election of delegates for the convention.

By then four more states—Mississippi, Florida, Alabama, and Georgia—had seceded. In three of them, as well as in South Carolina, state troops had seized federal arsenals and forts, and in Washington military officials worried about the safety of the arsenal in St. Louis. Situated in the southern section of the city, it held sixty thousand muskets and rifles, 1.5 million cartridges, ninety thousand pounds of powder, forty field pieces, and an assortment of other munitions. It was the largest federal arsenal in the South, and if secessionists captured it, they would have an initial advantage in a war.[5]

Anxiety grew in early February as Texas left the Union, and delegates from the six seceded states met in Montgomery, Alabama, adopted a constitution for the Confederate States of America, and elected Jefferson Davis, long a close acquaintance of Harney's, president. In mid-February, Brig. Gen. David E. Twiggs, another Southerner and Harney's former commanding officer, surrendered nineteen federal military posts and other property valued at $1 million to Texas authorities without a fight. In late January and again in early February, Winfield Scott, still commanding general of the army, instructed Harney to give his "personal attention" to strengthening the defenses of the St. Louis arsenal and if necessary to move recruits there from nearby Jefferson Barracks. On February 19, Harney reported that he had transferred three hundred recruits and that Maj. Peter V. Hagner, commander of the arsenal, had put it in "as complete a defensive condition as possible." The "apprehensions . . . of a demonstration" against it are "not well founded," Harney wrote, and it "is not at this time in danger." As he maintained this position over the next several weeks, Missouri Unionists became even more alarmed.[6]

On February 18, Missourians chose delegates to the state convention. Eighty-eight of the ninety-nine hailed originally from slave states, but most held either conditional or unconditional Union views. Further, in Missouri, unlike the six Confederate states, a decision for secession required ratification by popular vote. The convention opened at Jefferson City on February 28 and selected former governor Sterling Price, a conditional Unionist, as president. After two days in cramped quarters, the convention moved to the more spacious Mercantile Library in St. Louis. There on March 9, four days after the inauguration of President Lincoln, the attending delegates declared, by a vote of eighty-nine to one, their opposition to the use of federal force against seceding states and their belief that there existed "at present no adequate cause to impel Missouri to dissolve her connection with the Federal Union." After further debate and the election of a committee that could call it back into session at any time, the convention adjourned on March 22.

To some observers, Missouri's secession crisis may have appeared over or at least diminished. But it did not seem so to Frank Blair. Before the convention, Lt. Governor Reynolds had traveled to St. Louis and helped secessionists organize companies of minutemen to train for future service in the Missouri militia. Blair considered these units a constant threat to the Union and especially to the arsenal. A short time earlier he and like-minded colleagues had formed a Safety Committee, and now he speeded reorganization of German Wide Awakes and other Union men into home guard military units. Their ranks swelled quickly to more than fourteen hundred volunteers formed into sixteen companies. With the secret help of Lyon, whom the War Department had transferred to the St. Louis arsenal to boost defenses, the home guards drilled at night in deserted halls and warehouses.[7]

Despite the secessionists' state militia activities, Harney still considered arsenal defenses adequate, but Blair did not. His older brother, former St. Louis mayor Montgomery Blair, had been appointed postmaster general in Lincoln's cabinet, and Frank decided to take advantage of his family's influence in Washington. On March 11, he asked Secretary of War Simon Cameron to put Lyon in command of the arsenal. Blair had confidence in him, and he outranked Hagner, who served in his brevet rank. Cameron complied on March 13, but Harney, who did not trust Lyon and resented this interference, would not be outmaneuvered. He interpreted the secretary's order to mean that Lyon commanded troops at the arsenal while Hagner retained control of the arsenal's ordnance. Further, Harney instructed Lyon not to disturb the existing defenses without first submitting for approval "any considerations touching those subjects you may consider worthy of adoption."[8]

During late March and early April, Missourians and most others in the nation focused their attention on Charleston, South Carolina, where a handful of federal soldiers, besieged in Fort Sumter by Confederate forces, waited to see if President Lincoln would send relief. Harney, meanwhile, took care of a variety of routine departmental matters pertaining to the Dakotas, Nebraska, and other distant locations and entertained guests at his home on Fourth Street. At dinner on April 4, he received Col. Benjamin L. E. Bonneville, secessionist editor Samuel B. Churchill of the St. Louis *Bulletin,* and four officers from the arsenal, including Capt. Albert Tracy and Lyon. Churchill and Lyon argued most of the evening, Harney said little, and all seemed relieved at its conclusion.[9]

Despite such diversions, Harney realized that the likelihood of war increased each day, and now he took additional measures to protect the arsenal and other military stores. On April 6, he reversed his decision regarding Lyon, put him in charge of arsenal defenses, transferred all mounted artillery pieces and support equipment to his command, and directed him to throw up more earthworks and deploy whatever night guards he deemed necessary. Two days later, he refused to allow Lyon to go to Fort Leavenworth and face a court-martial for allegedly killing an enlisted man through imprisonment and starvation at Fort Riley the previous year. Harney considered it "very important" that Lyon not leave his command at the arsenal and suggested that the War Department convene the court at some future date in St. Louis. Next Harney ordered the commanding officer at Jefferson Barracks to transfer much of the munitions in his charge to the arsenal and place the rest under additional guard.[10]

On April 12, 1861, Confederate troops in Charleston fired on Fort Sumter. War had commenced. On the fifteenth, Lincoln called for seventy-five thousand volunteers to suppress the rebellion, and Secretary of War Cameron telegraphed a quota to the governors of all states still in the Union. He requested four infantry regiments, about three thousand men, from Missouri. Jackson replied on April 17. "Your requisition," he told Cameron, "is illegal, unconstitutional and revolutionary in its object, inhuman and diabolical, and cannot be complied with." Missouri will furnish "not one man," the governor declared, for "an unholy crusade" against the people of the seceded states."[11]

That same day Jackson called upon the Missouri General Assembly to convene in special session on May 2 for the purpose of reorganizing and equipping the state militia. He also directed all district militia commanders to mobilize their troops on May 3 for a week of drill. In the days that followed, Jackson enjoyed his greatest public support. In St. Louis, the *Daily Missouri State Journal* expressed the sentiment of many of the state's newspapers. "All honor to our noble, patriotic Executive!" it declared. "He reminds us of those stern patriots of the Revolution who hurled defiance into the teeth of despotism." Neither the editors nor Harney knew that Jackson had also sent secret envoys to Virginia, which had seceded on April 17, and to Jefferson Davis in Montgomery to request guns and other military assistance.[12]

Missouri's governor stood ready to fight, and so did Blair and Lyon. But not Harney. When Jackson declined to provide volunteers, Blair offered his home guards in their place, but Harney refused to swear them in or give them arms from the arsenal. When pressed to explain his actions, he said he had no authority to receive troops into federal service without direct orders from Washington. This enraged Blair. With the state militia mobilizing, he feared that secessionists would place batteries on hills behind the arsenal and shell it. Lyon declared that he would lead a sortie against any troops who appeared on the elevations, but Harney told him, "You will do no such thing." When Lyon persisted with the notion, Harney directed that "no patrols be sent outside the arsenal limits" without his permission. Lyon and other Union men thought Harney's responses defied reason. The Unionists included future secretary of war John M. Schofield, then a first lieutenant on leave to teach physics at Washington University and recently detailed by the War Department to swear in federal volunteers. While Schofield found Harney's "Union principles" not "quite up to the standard required by the situation," Lyon and others questioned his loyalty and interpreted his actions as delaying tactics designed to give secessionists time to prepare an attack. The skeptics did not know, however, that on April 16 Harney had advised General Scott that Jackson almost certainly intended to occupy the slopes overlooking the arsenal and, in the event of secession, demand its surrender. The 440 Union defenders could resist an assault by a greatly superior force, Harney reported, but "could not withstand the fire of . . . batteries" on the hills. "Under these circumstances," he concluded, "I respectfully request instructions for my guidance."[13]

Clearly Harney recognized the growing likelihood of a clash of arms. Further, he understood the military advantage of placing his own batteries on the overlooking hills and contemplated doing so, yet he hesitated to proceed without direction from Washington, just as he had declined Blair's urging that he accept the home guards into federal service. Harney considered both measures potentially provocative, and he hoped, however unrealistically, that even if Missouri seceded, fighting and its accompanying loss of life and property might somehow be avoided in the state. And if fighting did occur, he did not want the responsibility of precipitating it. A few days earlier he had even re-quested permission, which Scott denied, to leave St. Louis and go on "an expedition through the Department of the West."

Although not among those who thought Harney disloyal, Blair worried that the uncharacteristically cautious general's many pro-Southern friends and relatives had clouded his judgment. After talking to him on April 17, Blair began maneuvering to have him replaced. "I cannot say that he is not to be relied upon," Blair wrote the secretary of war, but he "is a southern man and has numerous property interests in Missouri and is I think afraid of the confiscation of his property by the state." Blair suggested that Cameron transfer Harney to some position that would not be "an embarrassment" to him and put Brig. Gen. John E. Wool or some other officer in command.[14]

Meanwhile, Lyon, again working without Harney's knowledge, pursued other ways to bolster arsenal defenses. On April 16, the resolute captain wrote Illinois governor Richard Yates and recommended that he confer with the War Department about holding his state's six volunteer regiments in readiness for service at St. Louis. Lyon suggested further that Yates request "a large supply" of arms from the arsenal. Weapons sent to Illinois would be safe if the arsenal fell to the secessionists. Yates complied, and on April 20 Cameron asked him to send "two or three regiments" to St. Louis with instructions to draw arms and ammunition for themselves plus ten thousand more weapons for other Illinois troops. Cameron also directed that the regiments remain at the arsenal to support its defense if needed. That same day, Harney wrote army headquarters requesting a replacement for Lyon. Although politely complimentary of Lyon's "zeal and fidelity," Harney still distrusted him and stated vaguely that "there are reasons, however, which, in my judgment," warrant a "change in the command . . . without delay." Simultaneously Harney moved his own headquarters to the arsenal in order to keep a closer watch on the entire situation and on Lyon in particular.[15]

In contrast to earlier years, when messages and orders could take days or weeks to reach their destination, information and instructions now sped almost instantly across the country by telegraph, and the wires buzzed with activity. On the same day that Cameron directed the

Illinois volunteers to the arsenal and Harney requested a replacement for Lyon, news spread that secessionists from Clay and Jackson Counties had captured the small federal arsenal at Liberty, Missouri. If Cameron needed any additional encouragement to remove Harney, that provided it. The next day, April 21, the secretary decided to relieve him of command and have him report to Scott, now in Washington. Even as the War Department formalized and transmitted Cameron's orders, Lyon and Blair prepared to enlist and arm the home guards at the arsenal that evening under the cover of darkness. They had already started when they received a late-night telegram from Cameron advising them of Harney's removal and instructing them to muster in and arm four regiments. Harney received his orders just after noon the next day and reported dutifully that he would leave immediately for the national capital. He had cause for both relief and regret, but for the moment he kept his thoughts to himself.[16]

Harney departed St. Louis by train on the evening of April 23, and the trip proved more eventful than he could have anticipated. About 2:00 A.M. on April 26, Virginia state troops, having learned that Harney was passing through Harper's Ferry by rail, stopped and boarded his train. After a thorough search of the cars, three officers found "a fine looking, elderly gentleman in civilian's clothes but of military air" asleep on a bench in the night coach and recognized him immediately. They awakened him and asked him to come with them. "By what authority do you make this arrest?" Harney asked. "In the name of the state of Virginia," came the reply. "Then it is heedless to make resistance," he answered. "I yield of course. Will you take my sword?" Confederate Capt. Thomas Marshall answered, "No. Keep it yourself." He then asked Harney for his baggage check and escorted the prisoner off the train. After securing his gear, the Confederates took Harney under military escort to Richmond, where Governor Robert Letcher apologized for the incident and released him. Letcher also urged him to resign his commission and accept a Confederate command, as had Robert E. Lee, P. G. T. Beauregard, and Joseph E. Johnston, all of whom had served with Harney in the Mexican War. He refused politely and resumed his journey.

The episode delayed Harney only a day or two, but it prompted him to reflect on his career and the national crisis. Writing from Washington to his friend John O'Fallon on May 1, Harney noted that rumor had him joining the Confederacy. The idea appalled him, and he declared:

> Forty-two years I have been in the military service of the United States, and have followed, during all that time, but one flag–the flag of the Union. I have seen it protecting our frontier, and guarding our coast, from Maine to Florida. I have witnessed it in the smoke of battle, stained with the blood of gallant men leading it on to victory, planted upon the strongholds and waving over the capital of a foreign foe. . . .
>
> Twenty stars, each representing a State, have been added to that banner during my service, and under its folds I have advanced from the rank of Lieutenant to that which I now hold. . . .
>
> The flag, whose glories I have witnessed, shall never be forsaken by me while I can strike a blow in its defense. While I have breath I shall ever be ready to serve the Government of the United States, and be its faithful and loyal soldier.

Harney wrote that he had watched the recent "course of events . . . with painful interest," and "so long as . . . hope of peaceful settlement . . . could be indulged," he had felt it best "to forbear any exertion of force." He hoped that Missouri would not secede, because doing so would "be her ruin." The state would lose "protection of her slave property" and "all hope of a Pacific railroad." He implored his "fellow citizens" in Missouri "not to be seduced by designing men to become the instruments of their mad ambition by plunging the State into the vortex of revolution."[17]

Blair had been right about Harney's loyalty but only partly correct about the reasons for his moderate military course. In Harney's mind, civil war threatened both the country's white population and its manifest destiny. Certainly, preventing war would serve his personal and family economic interests, but he believed it would also serve Missouri's and the nation's. He wanted to avoid the bloodshed and destruction that would come with fighting, and this was not a new or unique attitude for him. The same determination to pursue peaceful resolution had driven his insistence on peace talks prior to his coordinated campaign against the Florida Seminoles in 1857. He would fight like a fiend and glory in it when ordered to, when provoked, or when exerting or defending national interests against a foreign foe, but he had also proved that on occasion he could exercise restraint. Now, facing the most critical situation in his career, he had done so again, in the extreme.

While Harney conferred with Scott in Washington, rival factions in Missouri pushed closer to a military clash. The St. Louis *Missouri Democrat* reported on April 27 that Union recruits poured into the city every day. Crowds of spectators filled the parks to watch them "marching, wheeling, counter-marching, performing the maneuvers of the dress parade, or running and leaping in the Zouave practice" to the accompaniment of "martial music." By the thirtieth, Lyon had enlisted and armed 3,082 men, won election as general of their volunteer regiments, and occupied the hills overlooking the arsenal. He and Blair, who had been elected a colonel despite his lack of military experience, felt the need for still more troops, though, and with Montgomery Blair's encouragement and President Lincoln's approval, Cameron ordered the enrollment of up to ten thousand. He also authorized Lyon to declare martial law in the city if necessary and instructed him to remove all surplus arms and other military stores from the arsenal to Illinois. Unknown even to Cameron, Lyon had already clandestinely dispatched eleven thousand weapons across the river, in addition to those requisitioned previously by Yates.[18]

These measures, particularly removal of the arms, should have made the arsenal less attractive as a target, but if Governor Jackson knew about them, he remained undeterred. He expected Arkansas, Tennessee, Kentucky, and North Carolina to leave the Union within a few days, and he intended to take Missouri out with them. First, though, he wanted to prepare state troops for what would follow. The arms seized at Liberty on the twentieth would help, and so would two twelve-pound howitzers and two thirty-two-pound guns that President Davis had en route for an "attack on the arsenal." But the secessionists needed more. When the Missouri General Assembly convened on May 2, Jackson renewed his request for a military bill to reorganize and supply the state militia. To buy time for the legislature to act, he spoke publicly about keeping Missouri neutral in hopes that the Union might yet be preserved. Although his words amounted merely to stalling rhetoric, most of the state's newspapers applauded them. After all, Kentucky, also a border state, had been pursuing a policy of neutrality, and the federal government seemed to accept it.[19]

On May 6, while the assembly debated, General Frost began gathering his St. Louis militiamen ostensibly for their annual summer encampment. The troops congregated at various armories and then marched to Lindell Grove on the western edge of the city, stirring large clouds of dust and attracting crowds of curious onlookers as they went. By nightfall, 892 had arrived and pitched 240 tents, and their camp, named "Jackson" for the governor, had taken on the appearance of a small community. Some St. Louis residents speculated that Frost planned to attack the arsenal, but the pro-Union *Missouri Democrat* assured its readers that half the militiamen "would never draw a sword or pull a trigger against the Stars and Stripes and no one knows that better than Frost or Jackson."

That pronouncement did not comfort Lyon. Although the arsenal now held far fewer weapons and could withstand any assault Frost could mount, Lyon considered the militia camp a threat to the peace. He became further alarmed on Friday, May 9, when he learned that Frost had received guns and ammunition, as promised, from Davis. Seized from the federal arsenal in Baton Rouge and concealed in ale barrels and in wooden crates marked "Tamaroa" marble, the munitions had arrived the night before aboard the sternwheeler *J. C. Swon*, and Jackson men had spirited them to the militia camp in the dark of night. To see firsthand what Frost planned, Lyon borrowed a carriage, recruited a black driver, disguised himself as Blair's mother-in-law, and clutching a pair of pistols under his lap robe, rode undetected through Lindell Grove in midafternoon. There he saw temporary streets marked "Davis" and "Beauregard," small Confederate flags flying from tent poles, and the unopened "Tamaroa marble" crates. These sights convinced him that Frost intended to strike the arsenal. Upon returning to his headquarters, Lyon learned that Scott, reassured about Harney's loyalty, had reinstated him, and he would arrive back in St. Louis by train on Sunday evening. This news only spurred Lyon to work faster. He intended to chastise the secessionists before Harney could get back and thwart him. When night fell, Lyon summoned the Safety Committee formed earlier by Blair, told them what he had observed, and requested their support for an attack on the camp. Some suggested that Lyon merely serve Frost a writ of replevin for government property, but a majority approved the attack.[20]

Lyon worked through the night, and early in the morning on May 10, his home guard units began assembling. When Frost learned about their movements, he sent Lyon a letter of protest. "I am greatly at a loss," Frost wrote, "to know what could justify you in attacking citizens of the United States who are in the lawful performance of duties . . . under the Constitution in organizing and instructing the militia of the State." Before he replied, Lyon surrounded Camp Jackson with more than six thousand regular and volunteer troops and several artillery pieces. Then, in midafternoon he informed Frost that his command held contraband federal military goods and appeared "hostile towards the Government of the United States." He had "one-half hour's time" in which to surrender. Frost had no choice but to comply. He was vastly outnumbered, most of his men had fewer than five rounds of ammunition, and the supplies from Baton Rouge remained in their barrels and crates.[21]

The events that followed threw the entire city into a frenzy. Lyon, surprised by the easy surrender, had not planned what to do with the prisoners, other than take them to the arsenal. Although some militiamen had left the camp that morning and a few had managed to escape as Lyon arrived, he had 689 in custody. Elated with his achievement, he rushed excitedly about trying to determine his next moves. When he passed too close behind an artillery officer's horse, the animal kicked him square in the stomach and sent him reeling to the ground unconscious. While everyone stood around waiting for Lyon to come to and issue instructions, hundreds of civilians rushed to the camp to watch the spectacle. Some brought picnic lunches and a number carried rifles and shotguns. All lined the hillsides and streets leading away from the camp. William T. Sherman, his son Willie, and Ulysses S. Grant stood among the gawkers. This was precisely the kind of dangerous situation that Harney had hoped to avoid, but Lyon, once he regained consciousness, determined to make a show of force by marching his prisoners directly through the throngs. When his column stepped forth on Olive Street toward the arsenal with band playing and flags flying, the movement electrified the crowd. Some onlookers shouted, "Hurrah for Jeff Davis" and "Damn the Dutch." Others hurled rocks and clods of dirt at Union soldiers. Then someone fired into one of the German volunteer units. Pandemonium broke out, and shooting spread the length of the column. Both home guards and civilians fired indiscriminately in panic and anger.[22]

News of the debacle and its twenty-eight deaths and scores of wounded spread quickly through the city, inciting intense reactions. Mobs of angry men filled other streets yelling anti-German slogans, raiding gun stores, and threatening to destroy the presses of the *Missouri Democrat* and German-language *Anzeiger des Western.* Union troops with fixed bayonets rushed to guard the newspaper offices, and saloonkeepers closed their doors to prevent whiskey from bolstering the rioters further. Unrest continued through the night. Many residents boarded up their homes, and some fled to the country. The next day an exchange of gunfire between civilians and home guards in northern St. Louis left at least seven more people dead. Meanwhile, Lyon detained Frost's militiamen overnight and released them only after they swore "not to fight against the United States during this war."[23]

Depending upon their political allegiances, Missouri newspapers blamed either Lyon and Blair or Frost and Jackson for the bloody two days. Clearly Lyon could have avoided them. Given the weakness of Frost's camp and Lyon's overwhelming superiority in personnel and weaponry, he had acted precipitously. Characteristically he refused to accept any responsibility for the civilian losses. Rather, he blamed their suffering on their own curiosity. Harney, who felt compelled to uphold federal authority in order to suppress further violence, later said publicly that he approved of Lyon's decision to take Camp Jackson. But Lyon had set off precisely the chain of events that Harney had hoped to avoid. Many conditional Union men now went over to the secessionists. Former governor Sterling Price denounced Lyon and the Camp Jackson shootings to a St. Louis crowd that same night and set out early the next morning for the state capital to offer his services to Jackson. As soon as the governor learned about the disaster, he burst into the legislative hall to inform the General Assembly. Within minutes the members empowered him to reorganize the Missouri militia into a state guard and use it as he saw fit to "repel . . . invasion" or "put down . . . rebellion."[24]

As reports of these developments sped across the nation by telegraph, Harney made his way home from Washington. When he arrived in St. Louis a day early on Saturday, May 11, confusion still prevailed, and he proceeded deliberately in restoring calm. Mayor Daniel Taylor and others pressed him to disband the home guards, and he went to see Blair to discuss that possibility. Blair opposed it vehemently, and so Harney directed 250 regular troops into the streets to help maintain order. He then went home to consider what to do next. On Sunday morning, retired general Ethan Allen Hitchcock, former St. Louis mayor John F. Darby, and Judge John R. Krum called on Harney to express their concern about "the awful crisis." He assured them that he intended to protect "the lives and property of the good people of this city." Darby recalled later that Harney spoke with "deep feeling and emotion . . . as if prompted by a resolution and decision of mind that bespoke his unflinching purpose." In their presence, Harney then wrote a public proclamation. "I have just returned to this post," he announced, and "I most anxiously desire . . . to preserve the public peace." Recognizing that most Missourians had long been conditional Unionists and opposed federal coercion, he promised that he would not "exercise . . . any unnecessary powers," but he did not rule out the possibility of martial law. Finally, he called upon residents "to pursue their peaceful avocations, and to observe the laws and orders of the authorities, and to abstain from the excitements of public meetings and heated discussions."[25]

Almost everyone welcomed Harney's return. City papers had posted the news on their bulletin boards before he arrived, and according to the St. Louis *Missouri Republican,* it was "received by the community with the liveliest satisfaction." In obvious reference to Lyon, the secessionist *Daily Missouri State Journal* declared with relief that Harney "is a firm advocate of Union . . . but he is not a cut-throat, nor an uncivilized, unprincipled mercenary." Even the pro-Blair *Missouri Democrat* expressed confidence that now "Harney will do his duty." At the arsenal, the troops reportedly responded "with loud shouts of rejoicing," but Lyon grumbled to the War Department that Harney's homecoming jeopardized the "safety and welfare of the Government."[26]

On Monday, Harney had a secessionist flag pulled down from Frost's headquarters, where it had been flying for several weeks, and ordered searches conducted for contraband weapons. He also continued to review the events of the past few days, and he read the new military legislation with particular alarm. The following day, May 14, he issued a second, much longer proclamation. He began by declaring the "military bill" unconstitutional. It "cannot be regarded in any other light than an indirect secession ordinance," Harney said, and "cannot and ought not to be upheld . . . by the good citizens of Missouri." He argued further that Missouri's "geographical position, her soil, productions, and, in short, all her material interests" dictate that the state "must share in the destiny of the Union." For benefit of those citizens still angry about the Camp Jackson affair, Harney pointed out that Frost's men had been engaged in "openly treasonable preparations," and he reaffirmed his intention to maintain the "supreme law" of the land and "suppress all unlawful combinations of men, whether formed under the pretext of military organization or otherwise." To help accomplish this, Harney asked the War Department to provide ten thousand more stands of arms, send nine thousand volunteers from Iowa and Minnesota, and allow him to raise a regiment of Irish volunteers in St. Louis. The latter, he hoped, would help allay prejudice against present federal troops, most of whom were of German ancestry.[27]

Reactions to the proclamation proved extreme. Unionists applauded it, and secessionists damned it. The *Missouri Democrat* thought it would give "the quietus–the final and finishing blow–to rebellion in Missouri," while the *Daily Missouri State Journal* proclaimed that Harney had become the servant of "military despotism." Artist George Caleb Bingham wrote from Kansas City that the proclamation would act "as a salutary check upon our rabid fire-eating element," but Abraham C. Myers, a Confederate observer in Montgomery, declared Harney "a veritable traitor" who "has joined Lincoln in his crusade against the South."[28]

Those pleased with the proclamation included Frank Blair, for, as he wrote his brother, it suggested that Harney had begun "to see daylight." Blair still did not trust him, though, and had already initiated efforts to have him replaced permanently. This time, through his agent Franklin A. Dick, Blair took his case directly to the president. Dick arrived in Washington at 10:00 A.M. on May 16, stopped briefly at Montgomery Blair's office, and then went with him to the White House. There with Lincoln they found Cameron, Attorney General Edward Bates, and Secretary of the Interior Caleb Smith. Dick explained Frank Blair's reservations about Harney's Southern background and property interests in Missouri and argued that circumstances demanded more forceful leadership than Harney could give. While Dick talked, Blair drafted for Lincoln's signature a memorandum for an order removing Harney and replacing him with Lyon. Lincoln started to sign it, but Bates asked him to wait. Frost had sent agents to Washington, too, and one of them, Hamilton R. Gamble, was Bates's brother-in-law. Gamble and his colleague, James E. Yeatman, wanted the War Department to investigate the Camp Jackson incident and reprimand Lyon, and Bates thought that Lincoln ought to talk to them before relieving Harney. The president responded by directing his secretary to take the memorandum to General Scott and return immediately with his opinion of it.

With that the meeting broke up, and Montgomery Blair went to see Scott, while Dick, confident that he had "killed Harney effectually," went to Cameron's office to await Lincoln's decision. That afternoon, with the concurrence of his principal advisers, the president decided as Dick expected, and he and Blair rushed to Adj. Gen. Lorenzo Thomas's office to pick up the formal order. It relieved Harney of command of the Department of the West and placed him on leave until further notice.[29]

The next day Montgomery Blair sent the document to his brother along with a word of caution about its use. Noting that for the moment Harney's "*public* course . . . seems reasonable enough," the elder Blair suggested that Frank hold the order in abeyance until whatever time he judged appropriate to deliver it. Cameron and Lincoln urged discretion, too. By the eighteenth, the president had second thoughts and wrote to Frank Blair with "a good deal of anxiety . . . about St. Louis." Lincoln stated, "I was not quite satisfied with the order when it was made, though on the whole I thought it best to make it; but since then

I have become more doubtful of its propriety." He fretted that the public would accuse him of "vacillation" in the matter, but he worried more about retaining the border states in the Union and feared that the order might cause Harney to join the secessionists. "We better have him a *friend* than an *enemy*," Lincoln warned. "Still," he concluded, "if in your judgment" the order "is *indispensable*, let it be so."[30]

Unaware of the Blairs' machinations against him, Harney continued trying to maintain order in Missouri. On May 16 at Potosi, about sixty-five miles south of St. Louis, federal volunteers arrested fifty-six secessionists and confiscated two lead smelting furnaces, 425 ingots awaiting shipment to the South, and a quantity of cloth being made into Confederate uniforms. Later that same day at nearby DeSoto, volunteers broke up a meeting of fifty armed men and seized "some firearms and a secession flag." Because of incidents such as these and the likelihood that continuing efforts to strengthen the state guard would lead to others, Harney agreed to a conference with Sterling Price, whom Jackson had appointed guard commander. Price had also called upon Missourians to keep the peace, and Harney hoped that by cooperating they could achieve that goal.[31]

With Governor Jackson's approval, Price took a train to St. Louis on May 20 and met with Harney the following day. They conversed amicably and released a signed agreement. Price, representing the state government, accepted chief responsibility for maintaining order in Missouri, and so long as he succeeded, Harney promised not to "make military movements, which might . . . create excitements and jealousies between state and federal forces." Perhaps anticipating protest from Blair, he also issued another proclamation. It emphasized that the agreement did not prevent the use of federal troops whenever warranted. "If necessary to put down evil-disposed persons," Harney declared, "the military powers of both Governments" would be utilized. Although in effect the agreement recognized Jackson's public policy of armed neutrality, Harney considered it a logical way to avoid another episode like the one at Lindell's Grove. Naively he expected Price, and thus the governor, to abide by it. However, they had assented to the pact only to gain time to build up the state guard, arrange for military assistance from the Confederacy, and reassemble the state convention for passage of a secession ordinance.[32]

Public response gave Harney cause for optimism, for all factions seemed to like it. The *Missouri Democrat* praised it for ensuring "a peace which keeps Missouri in the Union," while the *Daily Missouri State Journal* lauded it for guaranteeing the state's "dignity and honor." The *Missouri Republican* predicted that the agreement would restore "peaceful relations throughout our borders." And the *Liberty Weekly Tribune* proclaimed that because of it "business is brighter . . . and everybody is rejoiced!"[33]

Private response varied, even among Unionists. Safety Committee member James O. Broadhead and attorney Thomas T. Gantt worried that Price and Jackson would not keep the agreement. Gantt wrote Montgomery Blair that although Harney had acted "in perfect good faith," he provided "no match" for Price and Jackson "in cunning or sharpness." On the other hand, Frank Blair, while disgusted, seemed to accept Harney's assurances that he would enforce the pact "to the fullest extent." If he did, Blair informed Cameron, then it would be "satisfactory."[34]

But Harney did not enforce the agreement to the fullest extent, at least in Blair's opinion. Both men continued to hear rumors and receive reports about Southern sympathizers either plotting or committing acts of violence. From southwestern Missouri came word that secessionists had seized fifteen thousand pounds of lead and seventeen kegs of powder in Lebanon. And from the Kansas border came a report that a mob had gathered in front of the St. Joseph post office, hauled down the American flag, and ripped it to pieces. On May 24, Harney heard that Confederate troops had begun moving from northwestern Arkansas into Missouri, and he wrote to Price for confirmation. "Is such the case?" Harney asked. If so, he intended to send a federal regiment to stop them. "I am satisfied that your information is incorrect," Price replied. Moreover, he cautioned, sending Union soldiers to the border would cause unnecessary excitement. As for the incidents in Lebanon and St. Joseph, Price told Harney that they had been "attended to." Harney's apparent acceptance of Price's reassurance exasperated Blair. He had now "lost all faith and nearly all hope," he told his brother, and would give Harney only a few more days to make the agreement work.[35]

Harney seemed to recognize that the end of his tenure as commander of the Department of the West might be near, and he considered how he might exit gracefully. During a reflective moment, he confided to Blair that he had considered requesting reassignment to California and implied that he would welcome assistance in securing it. Harney wanted to make certain, though, that there would be no public announcement that he had initiated the request. "In the name of all that is good and holy," Blair wrote his brother, "let this be done." Meanwhile, Harney continued to investigate reports of attacks against Union men and threats of invasion from Arkansas. On May 27, he sent Price a flurry of letters and telegrams about violent incidents in Springfield, Hannibal, St. Joseph, and Kansas City and an encampment of Confederate troops at Union Springs, Arkansas, only two miles from Missouri. Harney stressed that he considered his information about these developments reliable and they caused him "no little embarrassment." Consequently, he believed he might have to "afford protection" at those places himself, perhaps using home guard units, and he hoped that Price would not regard that as an "infraction" of their agreement.

As before, Price told Harney that his informants "must be mistaken." If violence had occurred, said Price, it had sprung from "irresponsible individuals," not from "meetings or organizations of any kind." Furthermore, he declared, if any Arkansas troops tried to enter Missouri, he would "cause them to return *instanter.*" Any attempt, Price continued, to use home guards would violate the agreement and "undoubtedly precipitate civil hostilities."[36]

This placed Harney in a quandary. He could either trust Price and do nothing or he could take military precautions that might plunge the state into war. Because he so intensely desired to avoid destruction of lives and property, Harney chose the first of these alternatives. On Wednesday, May 29, he reported to the War Department that "Missouri is rapidly becoming tranquilized, and I am convinced that by pursuing the course I have thus far . . . peace . . . will be fully and permanently restored." But, he continued, "I shall watch carefully the movements of the State authorities . . . and any attempt at rebellion will be promptly met and put down."[37]

The decision to continue trusting Price proved Harney's final undoing. Adjutant General Thomas had just mailed him a scorching message expressing Lincoln's concern about depredations against Union men. The president wanted them ended. "It is immaterial whether these outrages continue from inability or indisposition on the part of the State authorities to prevent them," Thomas noted. "It is enough that they continue to devolve on you the duty of putting a stop to them." Frank Blair shared those sentiments. He could wait no longer for Harney to act and now sent him the May 16 order relieving him of command.[38] Harney stepped down immediately, but when Thomas's letter arrived the next morning, he believed for a time that the president had changed his mind and voided the removal order. Gantt, a Blair associate who knew how the directive originated, explained that it superseded the letter.[39]

Although chagrined about the manner of his removal and its implications about his loyalty, Harney accepted the order calmly. At some other time in his career he might have raced irately to Washington and demanded to see the secretary of war or the president, but he had met with Scott, Cameron, and others once already, and he recognized the futility of protesting further. His increasingly difficult struggle to enforce federal authority in Missouri had ended, and with that came a measure of relief. A transfer would have accorded him a more satisfactory conclusion, but now he could only submit to the inevitable and reaffirm his loyalty to the Union. In a long letter to Thomas, he reiterated his confidence in his agreement with Price and his desire for "a bloodless victory" in Missouri and declared that the War Department had "inflicted unmerited disgrace" upon him. Nevertheless, he hoped he "may be spared to do my country some further service that will testify to the love I bear her." He asked specifically for command of the Department of California, unaware that it had recently been merged with the Department of Oregon to create the Department of the Pacific. Earlier to his brother, Frank Blair had confessed, "I have . . . never doubted General Harney's loyalty and devotion to his flag whilst I have differed with him in policy." Harney would have appreciated hearing those sentiments even though they changed nothing.[40]

Meanwhile, according to the *Missouri Republican*, Harney's removal caused "a good deal of surprise," because ever since the Camp Jackson affair the public perceived that he had been gradually restoring order in the state. The news did not surprise Lyon, of course. He had hoped desperately for it, and he immediately assumed command of the department and began preparing for the fighting he regarded as inevitable. Price, on the other hand, had not anticipated the order. He issued a proclamation in which he attempted to reassure people that Lyon would abide by the Price-Harney agreement. But he also instructed his district commanders to get ready for war.[41]

In a final effort to avoid general hostilities, several prominent citizens arranged for Price and Jackson to confer with Lyon and Blair in St. Louis on June 11. They met at the Planter's House and talked for more than four hours. Jackson promised to curb violence and curtail his reorganization of the militia if Lyon and Blair would disband federal home guard units and form no new ones. Lyon wanted to organize more and station them and federal troops throughout Missouri to ensure order and prevent a Confederate invasion. The discussion proved futile, for neither side trusted the other or genuinely wanted to compromise. Finally Lyon became angry and shouted that rather than concede anything to Jackson and Price, he would "see . . . every man, woman and child in the State, dead and buried!" He then declared, "This means war," and ordered Jackson and Price escorted to their train.[42]

On their way back to Jefferson City, they stopped only to cut telegraph lines. The next day Jackson called for fifty thousand volunteers to repel what he dubbed a federal "invasion" of Missouri. On the thirteenth, after hearing that Lyon had dispatched two thousand troops up the Missouri River, Price and Jackson abandoned the capital and withdrew to Boonville, about fifty miles to the northwest. Lyon occupied Jefferson City on June 15, and two days later, just east of Boonville, his command routed a state force under Col. John B. Marmaduke. The Civil War had come to Missouri.[43]

Harney probably could not have prevented war in the state no matter what he did, but he might have postponed it for a considerable time, and possibly rendered it less severe, if he had acted more force-fully. Although Jackson talked of "armed neutrality," Harney had actu-ally sought it. He never used the term or compared Missouri's situation to neighboring Kentucky's, but he resisted adamantly any action that might spark hostilities between secessionists and Unionists. Con-sequently he made two mistakes that allowed the former to strengthen themselves politically and militarily. First, he failed to protect the St. Louis arsenal adequately in February and March. If he had fortified the hills overlooking it and bolstered its defenses in other ways earlier in the year, he most likely would not have been recalled on April 21, and the Camp Jackson affair, for which Lyon must take the principal blame, would not have occurred. That incident encouraged support for secession and guaranteed passage of Jackson's military bill. Second, Harney entered into the agreement with Price and then trusted him to adhere to it. Although the pact seemed to calm many in the state, it lim-ited Harney's ability to establish order and federal authority. The se-cessionists continued organizing their military forces without fear of intervention.

Harney remained loyal to the Union throughout the war. Despite Lincoln's concern, he never once contemplated aiding secession or joining the Confederacy. Yet the War Department never entrusted another command to him. It ignored both his request for reassignment to California and a subsequent plea, made in November 1861, to return to the Department of the West. In August 1862, the governors of Iowa and Minnesota asked the government to send Harney to quell an out-break of Sioux hostilities, but officials sent Brig. Gen. John Pope in-stead.[44]

In August 1861, Congress passed the army's first retirement law. Sim-ilar in intent to a recommendation Harney had made in 1839, it allowed military boards to examine officers and recommend unfit ones for re-tirement. A subsequent law in 1862 allowed the government to retire of-ficers who had served forty-five years or reached the age of sixty-two. Under this legislation the War Department retired Harney and several other veteran officers on August 1, 1863, to make room for younger ones. All the retirees remained on full pay and from time to time per-formed some "light duty." Harney reported in writing to the adjutant general every month until the war ended, and he traveled to Washington on at least two occasions to sit on courts-martial. However, he divided most of his time between polite society in St. Louis and a thousand-acre stock farm that he bought about twenty-five miles west of the city and named "The Hermitage" after the home of his hero, Andrew Jackson.

Thus situated, Harney could only watch as officers such as Sherman and Grant prosecuted the war with the same kind of uncommon ferocity he had displayed in the Everglades and on the Great Plains. One of Mary Harney's distant relatives described his situation poignantly: "During all this fighting General H. is disgraced by both parties and has nothing to do but look on and feel what his middle course has brought him to." Harney never indicated any regret about not participating in the war, but others missed his presence. After the disastrous first Battle of Bull Run, fought in Virginia in July 1861, Missouri soldier Anthony W. Smith declared to his parents that now "Uncle Abe will begin to see that politics and war are two different things. They have thrown overboard good officers such as Wool and Harney to make room for a set of political popguns."[45]

Smith's observation proved prophetic regarding command in Missouri. In July 1861, the Blairs arranged for the reorganization of the Department of the West and had the inexperienced Lyon pushed aside as commander in favor of family friend John C. Frémont, the renowned "Pathfinder of the West" and son-in-law of former U.S. Senator Thomas Hart Benton. But Frémont lasted only one hundred days before he, too, ran afoul of Frank Blair and alienated Missouri's new pro-Union provisional government. The War Department removed Frémont amid charges of ineffective leadership and reorganized its Missouri-based command yet again. A succession of appointed leaders followed, and although Missouri remained in the Union, its citizens endured greater loss of life and property than any other slave-holding state that did not secede.[46]

CHAPTER 13

"Our Old Friend" as Peace Commissioner

A
S DAWN broke over southeastern Colorado on November 29, 1864, approximately seven hundred heavily armed mounted men separated into three groups and hurried into assault positions along both banks of Sand Creek. During the night Col. John M. Chivington, a former Methodist preacher with an insatiable appetite for military glory, had pushed these hundred-day volunteers all the way from Fort Lyon, forty miles south. Now, more like a hunter than a militia commander, he gazed across the nearly dry creek bed from atop a ridge and prepared to strike his unsuspecting quarry. Below, on the north bank of a sparsely wooded bend in the stream, stood more than one hundred Indian lodges. Among them some five hundred Cheyenne men, women, and children, together with a few dozen Arapahos, stirred awake. Several weeks earlier, they had separated themselves from hostile bands and expressed peaceful intentions to army officers at Fort Lyon and to Governor John Evans in Denver. Now they awaited formal acknowledgment and hoped for desperately needed provisions.

At first believing they had nothing to fear, the Indians watched with growing apprehension as Chivington's men deployed four howitzers on the ridge and galloped their horses across the creek at both ends of the camp, encircling it and separating it from grazing pony herds. Black Kettle, the Indians' principal leader, hoisted American and white flags above his tepee and then stood in front of it urging his people to remain calm. Seventy-five-year-old White Antelope ran toward the intruders waving his arms and begging them not to shoot, but his pleading fell on callous ears. The treacherous Chivington and his motley command had come to kill Indians, and they wasted no time commencing.

One of the volunteer units sent to seal off the Indian pony herds initiated the shooting, and immediately the attackers advanced en masse on the camp. A hail of bullets cut down White Antelope, and women and children ran screaming for cover while warriors tried to make a stand amid a row of lodges fronting on the creek. Deadly howitzer fire tore quickly through them, and one hundred other defenders took better positions upstream behind a bank and depressions in the sand. Chivington led attackers through the streambed on foot, while mounted men stormed through the camp.

More a massacre than a fight, the terrifying struggle raged through much of the day. When resistance ceased, Chivington's men ranged over the camp and its surrounds seeking out and killing those wounded and hiding. The attackers slashed women with knives, smashed children's heads with rifle butts, and scalped scores of people without regard to age or sex. Many victims still clung to life and screamed for mercy as steel blades sliced through their flesh. The slaughter concluded only when every native man, woman, and child still in the vicinity of the camp lay dead. Black Kettle and some others managed to escape, but at least nine chiefs did not. Estimates of the dead ranged from one hundred to Chivington's claim of five hundred. Whatever the number, reports agreed that two-thirds were women and children.

A few weeks later, a Denver theater proudly displayed more than one hundred Indian scalps, and many city residents hailed Chivington and his butchers as heroes. But when word of the atrocity spread over the rest of the Great Plains and the nation, the news produced shock, anger, and far-reaching consequences. Before the end of the year, fifteen hundred Cheyenne, Northern Arapaho, and Oglala and Brulé

Sioux warriors gathered with their families on Cherry Creek in north-eastern Colorado and committed to all-out war on whites. United States military officials disassociated themselves from the Colorado militia and the massacre. Religious and humanitarian reformers assailed American mistreatment of native people with renewed vigor. And leading officials in Congress and the Department of the Interior contemplated new treaty-making efforts and modifications in federal Indian policy.[1]

For all concerned, Sand Creek highlighted rapidly changing Indian-white dynamics on the Great Plains and signaled an urgent need for new approaches to peaceful coexistence. The circumstances and events that spawned and followed the shameful affair led eventually to a new federal plan to concentrate all Indians on reservations and force them to adopt white people's ways. This approach evolved most directly from a series of peace initiatives in which Bvt. Maj. Gen. William S. Harney, who had been accorded this additional rank in March 1865 for long and faithful service, assumed the role of Indian friend and advocate. Emerging from his forced retirement, he drew on his lifetime of experience with native people and personal acquaintance with many tribal leaders and served with quiet dignity on three major peace commissions between 1865 and 1868. For a year afterward, he managed a huge reservation that he helped create. In these capacities he represented a link between old and new federal Indian policies and between the army of his generation and that of William T. Sherman, Phil Sheridan, and other post–Civil War leaders.

While Harney sat idle during the nation's great internal conflagration, western settlement proceeded apace. In the late 1850s and early 1860s, mineral strikes, principally in present Colorado, Nevada, Idaho, and Montana, drew increasing numbers of miners to western spaces that whites had previously ignored. These new populations required new and expanded transportation and communication routes, and entrepreneurs and technology accommodated. Stagecoach roads, telegraph wires, and railroad tracks marched across the Great Plains and through mountain passes, and growing numbers of steamboats pushed up the Missouri River and its tributaries. The new settlers organized themselves politically, too. Between 1861 and 1864, Colorado,

Dakota, Arizona, Montana, and Idaho became territories, and Nevada became a state. As white population grew, areas where Indians could live in their accustomed manner shrank. Early in Harney's career, the government had focused on removing Indians to lands west of the Mississippi River in order to make room for advancing whites. Then in the late 1840s and 1850s, when settlers began crossing the Great Plains for Oregon and California, the government had worked at keeping Indians away from emigrant routes. Now both those options stood closed as means to avoid clashes.

New opportunities for Indian-white contact brought new potential for violence. As the Civil War unfolded and white migration continued unchecked, federal authorities maintained mostly peaceful conditions on the Pacific coast and in Utah and Nevada. In Arizona and New Mexico, the army contained Navajos and Mescalero Apaches, but it had mixed success against Comanches and Kiowas and none with Western Apaches and Yavapais. In southwestern Minnesota, the Santee Sioux ravaged white settlements and sparked retaliatory expeditions that engaged various bands along the upper Missouri River. These events alarmed whites everywhere but none more than Governor Evans, who already sought an excuse to sweep all Cheyennes and Arapahos from Colorado. Chivington's treachery at Sand Creek in 1864 proved the direct result. In the weeks that followed, the Indians who had gathered at Cherry Creek made good their declaration of war. In early 1865, they raided and burned the town of Julesburg, then ranged 150 miles through the South Platte Valley attacking stage stations, tearing down telegraph lines, ransacking wagon trains, burning ranches, stealing cattle, and killing more than fifty whites.[2]

Throughout the winter and into spring, federal authorities contemplated appropriate responses to the storm gathering across the Great Plains. Maj. Gen. Grenville M. Dodge, commander of the Department of the West, and other military men wanted to smash all hostile tribes in a massive, multipronged campaign. But various circumstances, including the end of the Civil War and the chaotic influx of thousands of supposedly helpful but unmounted reinforcements from the East, combined to postpone and scale down those plans. In the meantime, Congress, revulsed by the Sand Creek Massacre and concerned about charges of corruption in the Bureau of Indian Affairs, created a joint committee to investigate the condition of the tribes and make recommendations regarding their treatment by civil and military authorities. Headed by Senator John R. Doolittle of Wisconsin, the committee called attention to the high cost of fighting Indians and to current opportunities for negotiating formal peace treaties with southern plains groups. Meanwhile, Dodge and his subordinates pressed a summer campaign against hostile Sioux and northern Cheyenne and Arapaho bands in the Powder River country of northeastern Colorado and southeastern Montana. The effort accomplished little except to underline further the alarming cost of such undertakings, as well as their potential for producing more incidents like the Sand Creek disaster.[5]

Coincident with all these developments, the federal government sought also, as part of post–Civil War Reconstruction, to redefine relationships with Indian tribes that had aided the Confederacy. Thus, by late summer 1865, the country stood ready for major peacemaking efforts with native populations. Officials completed two such undertakings before winter, and Harney participated in both. He did not play a leading role in either. But no living army officer had longer, broader, or more successful experience in Indian affairs, and President Andrew Johnson and Secretary of the Interior James Harlan wanted both his informal advice and, more importantly, his presence as someone the Indians would recognize and respect.

Members of the Southern Treaty Commission assembled at Fort Smith, in northwestern Arkansas, early in September with Commissioner of Indian Affairs Dennis N. Cooley as chair. In addition to Harney, attending members included Col. Ely S. Parker, a Seneca Indian and member of Gen. Ulysses S. Grant's staff, and Charles E. Mix, chief clerk of the Indian Bureau and the commission. Occupying post buildings for quarters and meeting space, the officials opened their council on September 8 with more than one hundred delegates and interpreters representing both Union and Confederate factions among the Cherokee, Chickasaw, Choctaw, Creek, Osage, Quapaw, Seminole, Seneca, Shawnee, and Wyandot tribes. A few additional delegates arrived later.

The proceedings went quickly. Over the first two days, Cooley laid out the government's purpose and requirements. Foremost, he declared, each tribe must renew allegiance to the United States through a new treaty "for permanent peace." In addition, Cooley wanted the tribes to repudiate slavery and agree to consolidate under one Indian Territory government. Some delegates maintained that they had allied with the South "to save our lives" and "our hearts were not in the business, but with the north." None objected to new pledges of allegiance. Some strongly protested Cooley's secondary requirements, though, and ultimately the commission decided to delete those provisions in order to secure full participation, which it obtained. By September 21, all except the Chickasaws and Choctaws had signed loyalty treaties, and after making arrangements to secure their signatures later, the commission adjourned subject to Harlan's recall and left Cooley's secondary agenda for another day.[4]

Sometime before October 3, Harney traveled to Council Grove, Kansas, near the mouth of the Little Arkansas River, to meet with the southern plains tribes. Fellow commissioners included longtime trader and Indian Agent William Bent, Col. Kit Carson, Indian Agent Jesse H. Leavenworth, Southern Superintendent of Indian Affairs Thomas Murphy, Brig. Gen. John B. Sanborn, and James Steele of the Indian Bureau. Though not a commissioner, Jesse Chisolm, later linked forever with the Chisolm Trail, assisted with communication. Thanks to diligent preliminary work by Leavenworth and Sanborn, various Apache, Comanche, Kiowa, and southern Cheyenne and Arapaho chiefs and head men, Black Kettle among them, had already signed agreements promising to refrain from violence and attend the council to arrange "perpetual peace." They showed up as expected, and the deliberations proceeded according to plan.[5]

On October 14, pursuant to a motion by Harney, the commissioners elected Sanborn president. He greeted the assembled native leaders and apologized for Sand Creek. "Great wrongs have been committed," he said, and the commission has come to "make good this bad treatment" with reparations. The Indians received this declaration with skepticism. Black Kettle remarked, "Friends, I have never seen you before," except General Harney when "I don't know how small I was." Despite the Indians' concerns, over the next four days the commissioners persuaded them to sign treaties in which they pledged to live in a

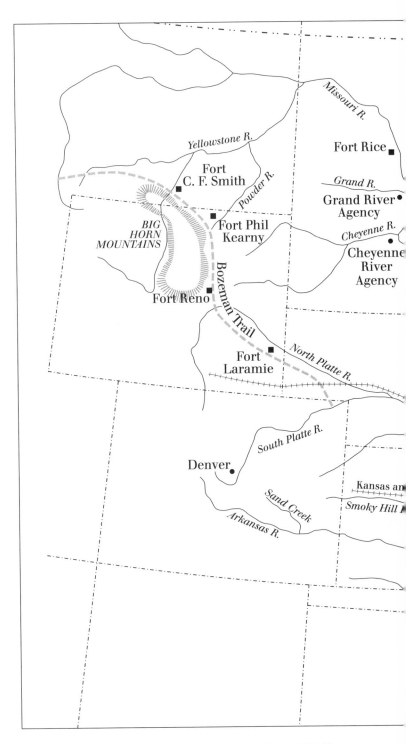

10. The West of the Indian Peace Commission, 1867–68

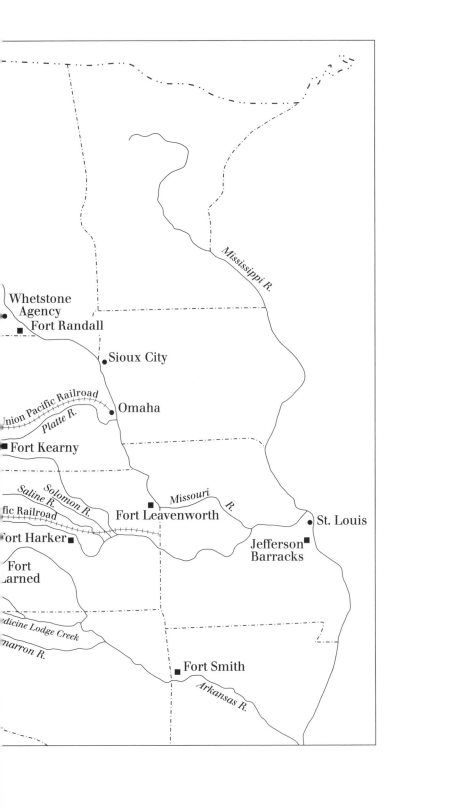

specified area south of the Arkansas River and avoid all white travel routes, settlements, and military posts. In return, the government promised annuities for forty years, with the Cheyennes and Arapahos receiving nearly three times as much as the other tribes in partial compensation for Sand Creek.[6]

While Harney and his colleagues met on the Little Arkansas, Northern Superintendent of Indian Affairs Edward B. Taylor and five others met with upper plains Indian leaders at Fort Sully on the Missouri River near present Pierre, South Dakota. These chiefs of the Miniconjou, Lower Brulé, Two Kettle, Sans Arc, Hunkpapa, Oglala, and Upper and Lower Yanktonnai Sioux all promised, in exchange for annuities, to keep away from emigrant routes. Unfortunately for the commissioners' purposes, almost none of these leaders represented the Indians that continued to threaten settlers and travelers in the Powder River region. The Senate had a bundle of treaties to ratify, and Indian Bureau officials and reformers could feel good about the various conversations and promises, but everyone soon discovered that peace remained elusive.

In the spring of 1866, the government sent commissioners back up the Missouri and over to Fort Laramie to get signatures from chiefs who had not affixed their marks to Taylor's treaties the previous October. At about the same time, the army strengthened defenses along the old Platte River road to Utah and the relatively new Bozeman Trail, which extended northwest from Fort Laramie east of the Big Horn Mountains and into the mining country of southwestern Montana. When Col. Henry B. Carrington established Forts Phil Kearny and C. F. Smith on the middle portions of the route, the Indians interpreted their construction as a hostile act and decided to destroy them. They struck their principal blow outside Fort Phil Kearny on December 21, 1866. Between fifteen hundred and two thousand Sioux, Cheyenne, and Arapaho warriors hid in ravines along both sides of a ridge, while a few of their number attacked an army wood train passing on the road above. When Capt. William J. Fetterman and a relief column of eighty men rode out from the post, the concealed Indians sprang upon them. A second relief column found no survivors, only stripped and mutilated bodies.

Like the Sand Creek affair, the Fetterman disaster produced shock waves that swept across the nation in early 1867. President Johnson sent a commission, headed by Brig. Gen. Alfred Sully, to investigate. The Doolittle Committee published its long-awaited report, which blamed whites for most Indian trouble and emphasized reconciliation. Congress debated transferring control of Indian affairs back to the War Department. And Lt. Gen. William T. Sherman, now commanding the Division, formerly Department, of Missouri, planned military operations against both northern and southern plains tribes.

None of these activities resolved anything. Sully's commission talked only with friendly Indians, and its presence restricted Sherman's military options. The Doolittle Report highlighted corruption once more and fueled the growing sense of crisis but sparked no prompt legislative action. The House of Representatives staved off Senate efforts to transfer the Bureau of Indian Affairs, but debate called further attention to the expense of continued fighting. Cost estimates ranged from $1 million for one week of military operations to $1 million for each warrior killed. On the northern plains, the army spent the summer on the defensive, as Indians harassed travelers, express riders, and work parties in Dakota Territory, attacked railroad surveyors and builders in Wyoming, and struck haymowers near Fort C. F. Smith and woodcutters at Fort Phil Kearny. On the southern plains, Maj. Gen. Winfield Scott Hancock succeeded only in disrupting reasonably peaceful circumstances and touching off chaos all along the Arkansas, Smoky Hill, and Platte Rivers. He agitated most in April, when with questionable necessity he burned a hastily abandoned village containing 251 Cheyenne and Sioux lodges and all the Indians' related trappings. For weeks afterward, white settlers, travelers, stage drivers, and railroad workers paid for the deed in terror from the Indians' revenge.[7]

With tensions rising, the nation could wait no longer for solutions, and on July 20, 1867, Congress acted, despite significant preoccupation with matters of Southern Reconstruction and the prospect of impeaching President Johnson. Sidestepping the question of which executive department had what authority in Indian affairs, the lawmakers created the Indian Peace Commission and empowered it to concentrate native people on reservations. The legislation called for seven commissioners to meet with all hostile tribes and negotiate treaties that would bind them to specific lands, keep them away from transportation and communication routes, resolve any just causes for complaint, and provide for necessary subsistence. The Indians would have no choice but to comply. In case any did not, the law gave the president, and through him the secretary of war, authority to call out four thousand mounted volunteers to help suppress dissenters. To support the commission's work, Congress provided $150,000 for expenses and $300,000 for aid.

The act named four civilian commissioners and allowed President Johnson to appoint army generals to the other three slots. All four civilians had strong humanitarian inclinations. John B. Henderson of Missouri chaired the Senate Committee on Indian Affairs and had introduced the bill that created the commission. Samuel F. Tappan, a well-known Indian rights exponent from Colorado, had chaired a military committee that investigated Chivington's conduct at Sand Creek. Nathaniel G. Taylor, a former Tennessee congressman and newly appointed federal commissioner of Indian affairs, devoted much of his time to Methodist preaching. And Minnesotan John B. Sanborn, an attorney and retired Civil War general of volunteers, had served on previous commissions. To this group, Johnson added two military men already on the scene: General Sherman, ranking officer in the Great Plains region, and Brig. Gen. Alfred H. Terry, a bookish forty-year-old former trial lawyer and Connecticut volunteer officer who now commanded the Department of Dakota. For the final slot the president selected Harney. Not only did he have peace commission experience, but Henderson, who suggested him, considered him "the only man up to the present day who has ever successfully waged war" against the Indians and, therefore, someone who could gain their attention.[8]

Commissioners and supporting officials wasted no time getting started. By July 29, Secretary of the Interior Orville H. Browning had scheduled the group's first meeting for August 6 at the Southern Hotel in St. Louis. In the intervening days, Harney received and acknowledged his appointment without comment. Sherman, whose plans for spring offensives had not gone as anticipated, regretted being selected for a peace initiative but resigned himself to it. He did not expect Terry, then on the upper Missouri, to make the first meeting, and thought that "I and Harney will be but two to the four Civil Commissioners" and "can hardly expect" to change their "conviction that Indians can best be managed by traders and agents." Much like Harney in 1855, the strong-willed Sherman preferred force first and then talk, but he had one primary idea compatible with the commission's charge to concentrate the Indians. He had already suggested relegating all southern plains tribes to territory below the Arkansas River and all northern tribes to territory above the Platte and punishing any that strayed.[9]

The press greeted Congress's creation with mixed reactions. Opinions did not follow strict geographical lines, but eastern editors tended more toward hope than westerners, who in some cases fumed. The *New York Times* welcomed the commission as an indication that the "Government intends to work a reform in the treatment of the Indians." Reservations are "the only practical method" of "guaranteeing alike security for the Western pioneers and justice to the red man." *Harper's Weekly* predicted that native people could be "much more cheaply taken care of as . . . pensioners than antagonists." A "sensible commission," the magazine declared, could easily induce "all the belligerent tribes . . . to remove to more remote hunting-grounds" for "a few millions in trinkets and annuities." In contrast, the *Nebraska City News* exhorted, "For God's sake, send us men for protection, and we will discuss Peace Commissioners afterwards." The peacemakers are no better than "agents and speculators," the *Montana Post* proclaimed. All are vampires "sucking treasures from the Government and blood from the people." The *Union and Dakotaian,* which six months earlier had favored the idea of reservations where Indians would be compelled "to work and learn–or die," now clamored for the Harney of old. "Peace commissioners" only "confirm the Indians in their mistaken belief that the government is afraid of them," its editor wrote. "Harney was the best 'peace commissioner' ever sent among the Indians. The 'peace' he made among them at Ash Hollow in 1855 was salutary and effective, and . . . the threat that he will again be sent against them is more potent for good, than the visitation of all the latter day peace commissioners in christendom."[10]

While editors speculated and vented, the commissioners assembled in St. Louis, elected Taylor as their president, and set their agenda and schedule. They projected two major councils, one at Fort Laramie with the northern Indians in mid-September and one along the Arkansas River with the southern Indians in mid-October. In the meantime, they determined to proceed up the Missouri, gather information about potential reservation sites, meet preliminarily with as many officials and tribal leaders as possible, and send runners to inform hostile groups about the councils. Taylor and Sherman dispatched a series of orders informing Indian agents and army officers of the plans and directing their cooperation, and Browning made certain their authority rang clear. While in the field the commission would have "control of all matters relating to the Indians, and all officers civil and military" must "extend to it all the aid and facilities in their power."[11]

Heading up the Missouri aboard the steamboat *St. Johns,* the commission stopped first at Fort Leavenworth on August 12. There they met initially on the post and then at the Planter's House in town. General Hancock joined them, and members questioned him at length about Indian affairs in general and his spring campaign in particular. Like Sherman, he favored reservations but believed that permanent peace depended on the Indians being "subdued." The commissioners also talked with Jesse Leavenworth, Thomas Murphy, and others, including Harney's old Jesuit friend and counselor, Father DeSmet, whom they asked to join them later farther upriver. Compared with Henderson, Sanborn, Sherman, and Taylor, Harney said little for the record in these early meetings, and that remained a pattern for his future participation in formal proceedings. However, when finally the commission began talking with tribal leaders, his mere presence, together with his interaction with them between formal councils, lent crucial credibility, as Henderson and others had anticipated.

As they moved farther north, the commissioners conducted more information-gathering interviews aboard the steamer and at the Herndon House in Omaha. They also elected Sanborn as their vice president.[12] On August 31, at Fort Sully, near the middle of present South Dakota, they began identifying the complaints of Indian leaders available to talk. These discussions continued periodically through September 20, as the commission returned south past the Yankton, Ponca, and Santee

Indian agencies to Omaha and then traveled by rail to North Platte, Nebraska. All along the way, the chiefs singled out Harney almost exclusively as a familiar face. He had been a fierce enemy, but they now accorded him a measure of respect the other commissioners had not earned. "I heard he was dead" and "I felt like a child and was ready to cry" upon seeing him, said Red Eagle Plume, an Oglala. "General Harney is our old friend," declared Big Horn of the Minneconjous. "Old Fort Pierre . . . is where I saw him first." Several Indians displayed chief's certificates that Harney had given them in 1856. He "tried to put sense into my head," remarked Long Mandan, a Two Kettle. "He whipped it into me. I have been studying that," and "I have had that paper for twelve years, and there is not a speck of dirt on it yet."

When asked what they wanted, the Indians replied almost uniformly. Provisions, agricultural tools, clothes, and guns and ammunition for hunting topped the list, followed closely by honest agents and interpreters. Most claimed they had been trying to farm, none felt they had received all the annuities promised them, and few understood the distinction between commodities sent upriver to their agencies and supplies shipped to military posts for soldiers. Obviously the "great father" had goods. What happened to their portion, they asked. "I want my wife and children to live as well as you do," said Long Mandan, expressing a shared sentiment. Then "you must adopt the same customs and habits as the white man," Henderson told them. He suggested that if they did, the government "would then send General Harney up here as Governor of the entire Indian Country, so that you would have your old friend always with you."

The Brulés and Oglalas at North Platte, among them Spotted Tail of Ash Hollow experience, complained especially about the lack of arms for hunting and cited the Bozeman Trail as a primary source of conflict. Sherman responded that the commission would neither provide weapons nor give up the trail so long as hostilities persisted. And he warned them, this is "also a War Commission." His colleagues gave the North Platte delegation ammunition anyway, and before concluding their trip the commissioners also designated funds for immediate relief of the upper Missouri Indians. Then, upon learning that the tribal leaders invited to Fort Laramie had not come in, the peacemakers postponed the first of their major councils and planned to reconvene in early October.[13]

In the meantime, Sherman traveled to Washington, where President Johnson, having recently dismissed Secretary of War Stanton and further fueled the fires of impeachment, implored him to accept the vacant cabinet post. To fill in for Sherman on the commission, Johnson appointed Bvt. Maj. Gen. Christopher C. Augur, commander of the Department of the Platte, and he continued with the group even after Sherman, who declined the president's offer, returned. During his absence, Harney acted as the commission's senior military officer, commanding the troops at its disposal.[14]

Early in October, the commissioners gathered at Fort Leavenworth and took Union Pacific cars to Fort Harker in central Kansas. From there they journeyed by army ambulance southwest to Fort Larned and then south seventy miles to Medicine Lodge Creek for their meeting with the southern tribes. With them went nearly a dozen newspaper correspondents, including Henry M. Stanley, whose future travels in Africa and Asia captured international attention. Altogether the entourage numbered about six hundred, including the military escort and drovers for more than 175 wagons carrying supplies and annuity goods. Dragging a battery of Gatling guns, the train lumbered across the plains for several days, and the reporters found Harney organized, practical, and clear of mind regarding Indians and the commission's task. Stanley described him as towering "above his associates like another Saul" possessing "a wonderful power of vitality and passion despite his old age." His and Sanborn's practice of giving the correspondents brandy with their noon meals did not diminish the writers' assessment.

They witnessed Harney's passion early on. During the afternoon of October 12, as Satanta, a Kiowa chief, rode with Harney in his ambulance, the train passed a herd of buffalo grazing in the distance. These magnificent beasts always constituted a stirring sight on the plains, and a number of soldiers, relief drivers, and others rode into the herd, slaughtered animals, and returned jubilant with bloody tongues hanging from saddle horns. Satanta became enraged at this waste of resources so critical to his people. Harney, equally furious over the insensitivity of such a scene immediately before peace talks, terminated the hunt.

The commissioners' column drew near Medicine Lodge Creek in midmorning on October 14. Before it descended into the wooded basin, Harney ordered the outriders and infantry ambulances to the rear, wisely ensuring a nonthreatening posture. Ahead, more than 450 Indian lodges stretched across the valley, and thousands of ponies grazed on the surrounding hills. Superintendent Murphy, accompanying the commission, estimated that five thousand Arapahos, Cheyennes, Kiowas, Comanches, and Apaches had lodges in the vicinity. When the column came to a halt, Harney and his colleagues alighted, went forward on foot, and greeted the chiefs with handshakes and embraces. Upon learning that most of the Cheyennes had not arrived, the commissioners dispatched a message urging them to come in, and Harney went about establishing camp. In a ring barricade of ambulances, orderlies pitched tents and started cook fires, while teamsters picketed draft animals in a wagon park. Later, all passed a quiet night broken only by army mules braying and Indian dogs barking.[15]

Over the next several days, Harney's knowledge of and comfort with native people contrasted sharply with both his civilian and military colleagues. While waiting for the remaining Cheyennes to show up, the commissioners took testimony from Cheyenne Agent Edward W. Wynkoop, two army officers, and various Indians concerning "causes that led to the existing troubles . . . on the Plains." Stanley noted that as interpreters repeated "the talk," Henderson seemed buried in deep study, Tappan read reports, Terry doodled, Augur whittled, and Sanborn picked his teeth. In sharp contrast, Harney, who knew better how to judge the Indians' reactions, sat "with head erect" and "watched with interest each . . . face of the Indians around the tent." Later, as he and others stood on the edge of the compound, Grey Head, Tall Bull, and fifty more mounted Cheyenne warriors wearing paint came trotting across the creek chanting. While others watched apprehensively, Harney recognized the lead riders and stepped out to embrace them. Gray Head produced a "friendship" commendation that Harney had given him after leaving the Utah expedition in July 1858. The next day, Sanborn asked a military witness if Satanta had been joking earlier when he boasted that the Kiowas were not afraid of whites. "I never knew Indians to jest," interrupted Harney. "In their boasts there is always a meaning."[16]

The absent Cheyennes still had not come in by October 19, and waiting no longer, the commissioners convened the council in a clearing amid a grove of tall elms. The Indian leaders and their interpreters sat on logs facing the commissioners, who situated themselves in a semicircle of chairs shaded by a cut-branch arbor. Reporters sat at tables behind them. Unlike the treaty councils of Harney's younger days, ceremony was minimal, and following introductions, Henderson led off and spoke briefly. "We have come here to hear all your complaints and to correct all your wrongs," he proclaimed. And we want to give you "all the comforts of civilization, religion, and wealth" including homes, lands, livestock, schools, teachers, and churches. He did not mention concentration, but the Indians knew the commission wanted them to live on reservations. They also understood the implicit threat that if they wanted much needed provisions and annuity goods they had to agree.

Talk went on intermittently over two days. "I made peace with General Harney, Sanborn, and Colonel Leavenworth" two years ago, said Satanta as he declared a reservation unnecessary and undesirable. "I love to roam over the wide prairie," and when I "settle down" I will "grow pale and die." Ten Bear, a Comanche, proclaimed of reservations and houses, "I do not want them." Poor Bear, an Apache, remarked simply, "I wish you would get through as soon as possible and let me and my braves . . . get our annuity goods" and go home. Kicking Bird, a Kiowa, maintained that annuities promised them two years earlier had not been provided, "and we are tired of waiting for them." When the Indians finished, Henderson summarized the government position. He said the buffalo will "not last forever," the whites are "settling up all the good land," and the papers have "been prepared." The commission expected the chiefs to sign the next morning, and they did. Though labeled for posterity as a council, the proceedings, like so many others before them, produced dictated, not negotiated, terms.[17]

Now the commissioners debated what to do about the still absent Cheyennes, who remained thirty miles away on the Cimarron River conducting "medicine" ceremonies in preparation for their talks. Black Kettle came into the peace camp on the evening of the twenty-first with three other chiefs and requested four more days to get ready. Henderson, whom the reporters noted always took a businesslike and sometimes impatient approach to council proceedings, wanted desperately to finish up and leave, and he did not understand the Indians' reasoning. Augur explained it as a matter of religion. When Henderson repeated that he could not wait, Harney seethed. Unable to contain his indignation, he exclaimed, "You cannot go home. We cannot do without you, and if you go I fear I shall have to arrest you." "Bah!" replied Henderson. "This medicine is all humbug." He stayed, but when the Cheyennes asked that the other tribes remain, too, he objected to the expense of feeding them four more days. Most lingered, however, with little objection from Henderson's colleagues.

On October 22, the Apaches asked to locate on a reservation with the Kiowas and Comanches, and the commissioners drew up an agreement to provide for it. Then they waited. Finally, a little before noon on the twenty-seventh, riders brought news that the Cheyennes would arrive shortly, and the commissioners discussed how to receive them. Ultimately Harney persuaded his reluctant peers to walk outside the compound and greet the Indians on the bank of the creek. There an earlier scene repeated with a larger cast. Several hundred painted warriors galloped in, and some among the whites grew nervous. But Harney led another round of handshaking, and concern subsided. That evening, the Cheyennes brought Harney a pony as a gift, and the following morning, attended by Arapahos and Kiowas, they sat down to talk. Henderson made essentially the same speech he had presented on the nineteenth and received similar responses. In a particularly defiant exception, Tall Bull, chief of the militant Cheyenne Dog Soldiers, noted that he had signed the peace agreement on the Little Arkansas in 1865. But "when we were treated as we were by General Hancock . . . I became blind with rage, and what I have done since, I am not ashamed of." Before the council closed, Satanta rose to speak one last time. Declaring himself "the white man's friend," he expressed gratitude for the opportunity to talk and receive annuities. But he regretted that the white man "now covers his face with the cloud of jealousy and anger and tells us to be gone, as the offended master speaks to his dog." He hoped that this time the government would keep its promises, but he harbored doubts. "We make but few contracts," he said, "and we remember them well. The whites make so many that they are liable to forget them."[18]

Throughout the council, after each group of Indians signed the "contracts," the commissioners distributed piles of cloth, blankets, army coats, and felt hats, together with boxes of beads, knives, gunpowder, and cartridges. At the end, their packhorses fully loaded and their travois literally bursting with gifts, the Indians departed into the plains, while the commissioners headed back to St. Louis bearing the signed treaties. The agreements concentrated the Indians on two large reservations, each consisting of several thousand square miles in the western portion of Indian Territory. The Kiowas, Comanches, and Apaches would go to one, and the Cheyennes and Arapahos to the other. With the land would come all the necessary trappings to turn the inhabitants into farmers and acculturate them—Indian agency facilities, schools, agricultural implements, sawmills and gristmills with personnel to operate them, a physician, a blacksmith, a carpenter, clothing, and other presents. Heads of families could have their own 320-acre tract as long as they cultivated it, and single individuals over age eighteen could have 80 acres. In return, the Indians relinquished all claims to nonreservation territory and promised not to oppose railroads and military posts or otherwise harm whites. The cultural gulf yawned so widely in the treaties that what one side regarded as generosity and progress, the other soon recognized as the road to subjugation and poverty. One participant in the Medicine Lodge drama, Capt. Albert Barnitz of the army escort, carried away a darkly prophetic notation in his journal: "We will certainly have another war sooner or later with the Cheyennes, at least, and probably with the other Indians, in consequence of misunderstanding of the terms of present and previous treaties."[19]

Upon reassembling in St. Louis the first week in November, the commissioners excused Henderson to return to Washington, and with Sherman back, they headed again to North Platte and beyond for the talks postponed in September. Once more, the principal Indian leaders did not come in, but Red Cloud of the Oglalas sent a message. He would not cease hostilities or talk until the army gave up Forts Phil Kearny and C. F. Smith and withdrew from the Powder River country. At Fort Laramie on November 12, the commissioners met with the peaceable Crows and concluded a treaty similar in structure to the southern agreements. This time Taylor opened the proceedings, giving a speech similar to Henderson's at Medicine Lodge. Responding much like their southern counterparts, the chiefs opposed a reservation and described previous harsh treatment. Bear's Tooth even recalled Benjamin O'Fallon pistol-whipping Crow leaders in the summer of 1825. "I was there and saw it done," Harney confirmed. The Crows also asked that the government abandon the Bozeman Trail and remove the forts along it. At North Platte two weeks later, the commissioners found only Spotted Tail, with whom they repeated September conversations. Before leaving, they joined him and other Brulés in a feast the Indians arranged to honor Sherman and Harney.[20]

In December, the commissioners convened in Washington, reviewed their findings, and detailed Taylor, Henderson, and Sherman to write a report to the president. Submitted January 7, 1868, the document acknowledged that the government had violated the boundary, annuity, and protection clauses of the treaties signed with most of the plains tribes at Fort Laramie in 1851. It decried Chivington's actions in 1864 and questioned Hancock's judgment in 1866. And it blamed Congress for not ensuring that all army officers understood and abided by treaty provisions. The report questioned the importance of the Powder River forts but refrained from suggesting abandonment, pending further talks with the northern Indians. And finally it recommended creating a cabinet-level Indian office independent of the War and Interior Departments, replacing all Indian service appointees, prohibiting state and territorial use of volunteers to combat Indians, enacting tougher Indian trade laws, and completing the concentration and acculturation policies contained in the treaties. Though not necessarily politically appealing or logistically practical, these suggestions reflected sound analysis of problems and admirable intent in solutions.[21]

In the spring of 1868, the commissioners returned to the plains and conducted another round of treaty making similar to that of the previous fall. They spoke with some of the same Indians on the northern plains and many different ones there and elsewhere, but in almost every instance the scenes, dialogue, and final act played out much the same. The commissioners told the native people what the government expected, the Indians shared their complaints and responses, and eventually leaders signed treaties that differed little from the Medicine Lodge documents, except in regard to places of concentration. During the commission's long recess, the army had made a major decision that helped facilitate this end. Ongoing hostilities over the Powder River posts had rendered the Bozeman Trail nearly useless, and now alternate routes seemed possible farther west, from along the Union Pacific railroad line. So the army decided that once hostilities ceased, it could abandon Forts Phil Kearny and C. F. Smith, as well as others in the region. This removed a major stumbling block to some northern Indians' acceptance of the treaties.

While Henderson remained in Washington for President Johnson's impeachment trial in the Senate, most of the commissioners reassembled at Cozzens' Hotel in Omaha the first week in April and divided up their work. Over the next four months they met in subgroups with Indians from Dakota to New Mexico. Harney, Sanborn, Tappan, Terry, and Augur treated with Brulé, Oglala, and Minneconjou Sioux at Fort Laramie in April. Harney and Sanborn remained there in May and secured signatures from Oglala Sioux, while Sherman and Tappan moved on to Bosque Redondo, New Mexico, and made an agreement with Navajos. In June and July, Harney, Sanborn, and Terry, with assistance from DeSmet, obtained signatures from Yanktonnai, Santee, Sisseton, Blackfeet, Hunkpapa, Sans Arc, and Two Kettle Sioux at Fort Rice on the upper Missouri. Meanwhile, Augur arranged a treaty with Snakes and Bannocks at Fort Bridger in southwestern Wyoming.[22]

Having been elected president pro tem of the commission, Sanborn directed the councils in which Harney took part, but the Great White Chief drew the Indians' personal attention. Displaying his Fort Pierre certificate, One Horn, a Minneconjou, said, "The proof that I think a great deal of you, General Harney, I have with me." Long Soldier, a Hunkpapa, exhibited his paper, too, and declared that seeing Harney made him "glad." Running Antelope, also a Hunkpapa, proclaimed, "I keep in my heart the talk that we had" at Fort Pierre, and "I never met a man of sense since, except Father DeSmet."

As on the southern plains, the chiefs spoke of broken promises and the need for guns and ammunition for hunting. In addition, the Brulés and Oglalas remained concerned about the Powder River situation. Red Leaf, a Brulé, said, "I hope there will be no more roads," and another, Iron Shell, maintained, "Those forts are all that is in the way" of signing a treaty. Sanborn told them that "if peace is made, we . . . shall within three months abandon the roads and withdraw the troops." But, he added, "If you continue at war, your country will soon be overrun." Harney, despite regretting that "you have been treated very badly for years past," retained his capacity for menacing edge and underlined Sanborn's statement. "I am afraid you do not understand why we want to make peace," the Great White Chief said. "Perhaps you think we are afraid. You can not be such fools as that, I hope." That remark held meaning for those who knew him. Man Afraid of His Horse, an Oglala who had clashed with Harney at Ash Hollow, recalled correctly that in the 1851 treaties the government had promised annuities for fifty years and discontinued them after ten. However, he expressed satisfaction with the army's decision about the Powder River forts and welcomed the news that Harney would remain on the Missouri "to protect our country."[23]

The Great White Chief left Dakota Territory, but only briefly. Having concluded their talks in sundry locations, the commissioners would have to reconvene in the fall, formulate their final recommendations, and produce a report. In the meantime, they had exhausted their funds, and the Senate had not ratified their treaties. While the lawmakers deliberated, Sherman took General Grant, now the Republican nominee for president, on a tour across the plains to Denver and back. They traveled whenever possible on the Kansas Pacific and Union Pacific railroad lines and conferred along the way with company officials, with whom they shared common interests. Army officers and railroaders alike wanted expanded rail transportation and peace in which to achieve it. With Sherman and Grant went both Harney and Maj. Gen. Phil Sheridan, commander of the Department of Missouri, which now encompassed only portions of the southern plains. By the time the officers returned, Sherman contemplated sending Harney back north, as Henderson had promised the Indians earlier.

Meanwhile, on July 25, the Senate ratified the Medicine Lodge agreements of 1867. That same day, Congress approved almost $173,000 to cover the commission's existing overexpenditures for feeding destitute native people, and two days later, the lawmakers appropriated an additional $500,000 to carry out the food and acculturation provisions of all the commission's treaties, ratified or not. Congress made Sherman responsible for administering the funds and in doing so gave the army, temporarily at least, control over plains Indian affairs. On August 10, using the treaties as his guide, Sherman formed reservation districts for all affected Indians and placed military men in charge. Bvt. Maj. Gen. William B. Hazen received command of the southern plains district and, as expected, Harney got the northern one, consisting roughly of present South Dakota west of the Missouri River. His and Hazen's authority extended only to Indian affairs, as military direction remained within normal army structure. "I cannot do better than to send General Harney" to the upper district, Sherman wrote the secretary of war, "with authority to collect the Indians . . . and make preparations to put them to work next spring." To accomplish this, Sherman allocated $200,000 of the $500,000 to Harney.[24]

On September 5, Sherman declared that he intended to use food, clothing, and other "inducements" to convince the Indians that "going to their reservations" served them better than "marauding and the uncertain results of hunting." But already the peace arrangements, problematic from the outset, had begun to fall apart. Ratification of the Medicine Lodge treaties with their attached annuity goods had come too late in the year, and Senator Henderson blamed Congress. If they "had let impeachment alone," he lamented to Sherman, and "attended to the business demanding attention we should be far better off." Reluctant to give up their nomadic habits, numerous restless Indians now demonstrated that, as usual, native people did not view treaties as legally binding like, in theory, whites did. On the southern plains, hostilities started with a number of lesser incidents north of the Smoky Hill River, and soon Indian raids spread west toward Denver and south into Texas. By the end of September, Sherman and Sheridan stood ready to wage total war against treaty violators, as Harney had done in 1855. Thus began a series of operations that raged all winter and into spring. Sheridan, whose command included Lt. Col. George Armstrong Custer and scouts William "Buffalo Bill" Cody and James "Wild Bill" Hickok, forced native people almost entirely out of the corridor between the Platte and Arkansas Rivers and south into Indian Territory. The many Indian casualties included Black Kettle, whose band Custer wiped out in a surprise attack almost exactly four years to the day after they had survived Sand Creek.[25]

The situation in the north proved calm by comparison, but Red Cloud provided an early sign of trouble. Despite sending messages that he would come in and sign a treaty once the army agreed to abandon the Bozeman Trail, he remained out until well after the commissioners had departed. Then in July, after the army finally packed up and left Forts Reno, Phil Kearny, and C. F. Smith, he burned the latter two. After that, despite the efforts of Father DeSmet, who was waiting at Fort Laramie to meet with him, Red Cloud went hunting and stalled until November before coming in and affixing his mark. Meanwhile, sporadic attacks on steamers, cattle herders, and small military detachments disturbed an area extending from Fort Buford, near the mouth of the Yellowstone, south toward northwestern Nebraska.[26]

Against this unsettled backdrop, Harney arrived at Fort Randall, on the Missouri River just above the Nebraska line, on September 7 and found that three thousand Sioux and mixed bloods awaited him on Whetstone Creek, about thirty miles upriver. The commissioners had selected this area earlier for an agency site, and most of the people here had come from the vicinity of Fort Laramie since June, when Harney and Sanborn had cut off government provisions there in order to force migration. Reportedly the new inhabitants liked the availability of wood, water, and grass along the creek and had already designated their new community Harney City in honor of the Great White Chief. Within a week, Spotted Tail and more than two thousand other Brulés and a contingent of Oglalas under Black Bear approached from the North Platte, but because they intended to continue hunting instead of farming, they remained west of the agency some thirty to sixty miles.

Even before reaching Whetstone Creek, Harney had already been at work in characteristic fashion. As he had done in other remote locations free from immediate oversight, he implemented his charge as he interpreted it and worried about consequences later. In this case, the intent of the treaties guided him. Having purchased and brought up two steamboat loads of supplies, he put Clark Chambers in charge of issuing all provisions and other materials to the Indians and of maintaining all related financial records in accordance with Sherman's orders establishing the district. By September 27, having finally read those instructions carefully himself, Harney realized that he had already overspent the amount credited to his account. Not at all contrite, he wrote Sherman explaining, "You are well aware of the great sympathy Entertained by myself for the Indians and how anxious I am to see them comfortably located." Thus, "I feel justified, and cannot but think that all who . . . are anxious to put an end to the perfidy and outrage which has generally hereto characterized the treatment of the Indian by the White Man will sustain me." Harney had experienced shortages enough during his previous stints on the plains. As long as he had authority to make purchases, he intended to meet the treaty provisions regardless of the cost.[27]

First, however, he had to attend the last meeting of the Indian Peace Commission. On October 7, with Sheridan's campaign on the southern plains in full swing, the commissioners assembled at the Tremont House in Chicago. Only Henderson could not attend. The members devoted the first day to reviewing reports about their summer talks with the various tribes, and then they spent two days reconsidering their January recommendation to merge the Indian functions of the War and Interior Departments into a separate cabinet-level unit. With Grant sitting in as an observer, Sanborn offered a resolution that "control of all Indian affairs be transferred to the War Department." Having made certain earlier that Augur would be present to vote for such a measure, Sherman now declared that the Indians must go to their reservations "and remain at peace else they must be killed." Taylor decried Sanborn's resolution and Sherman's point of view, proclaiming, "You have tried military management of Indian Affairs and it has proved a failure." Further, he said, "If it is desired and intended to exterminate" the Indians, "would it not be better first to count the probable cost?" If, he continued, it "required the army . . . seven years, at a cost of $35 million, to subjugate 1,500 Seminoles on the little pent-up peninsula of Florida, how long will it take, and at what cost, to exterminate over 300,000 Indians . . . roaming over the plains and mountains" of the interior? His arguments came to naught. On each and every resolution related to transfer, the five military members voted as a block, opposed only by Taylor and Tappan. Harney's sympathy for the Indians never wavered, but neither did his long-held view that the army could manage them best.

In addition to recommending that the Bureau of Indian Affairs be transferred from the Interior to the War Department, the commission offered several more proposals. Whether ratified or not, all commission-arranged treaties should be "considered to be and remain in full force," and the government should "feed, clothe, and protect" all Indians on the commission-arranged reservations. Southern tribes who committed "depredations" following the Medicine Lodge treaties should lose the right to roam and hunt outside reservation boundaries. And the army should use force to "compel" all tribes who signed commission treaties to move onto their reservations. Further, the government should cease recognizing Indian tribes as "domestic independent nations," except as required in existing ratified and unratified treaties, and it should hold all Indians individually accountable under the laws of the United States. With this, the commission adjourned, and Taylor submitted its formal resolutions to President Johnson early in December.[28]

Officials in Washington would need months to consider the recommendations and their implications, and in the meantime Harney returned to Dakota Territory to continue organizing the northern reservation district. Recognizing that the Whetstone agency could not accommodate all the Indians in his charge, he established two others farther up the Missouri. The most distant, at the mouth of the Grand River near Fort Rice, served primarily the Hunkpapa, Blackfeet, and Yanktonai Sioux, and the nearest, at the mouth of the Little Cheyenne River near Fort Sully, served mostly the Minneconjou, Sans Arc, and Two Kettle Sioux. That left the Whetstone agency to serve the Brulés and Oglalas. For reasons of economy and security, Harney ordered "all whites not legally incorporated with the Indians" off the reservation. Then, with military approval, he took advantage of 1866 legislation defining the post–Civil War army and formed a uniformed and mounted unit of up to 140 Indian "scouts" to help discourage "outrages" outside it. Enrollees functioned much like the Indian police he had recommended while at Fort Pierre twelve years earlier.[29]

On November 23, Harney took stock of what he had accomplished to date and what it had cost and sent Sherman a lengthy summary of both. Estimating that 28,000 Indians now resided on the reservation with more expected in the spring, Harney reported that he had erected agency buildings, warehouses, and a steam-powered sawmill on each of the three sites. In addition, at the Whetstone agency he had one hundred houses up and a church and a school under construction. At all three sites he had laid in supplies of flour, corn, bacon, coffee, sugar, and beef cattle, and at Whetstone he had also accumulated "a sufficient supply of work oxen and agricultural implements" to commence farming in the spring. To serve the entire reservation, he had hired six farmers. By this time Harney had 103 people on payroll, including 54 laborers and 14 herders. Having previously admitted overspending the allotted $200,000, he now estimated the excess at $485,784.21. "I took upon myself the responsibility" of making these purchases, he wrote confidently, "and I felt Congress would approve of my actions."

Already aware of Harney's mounting expenditures, Sherman revealed his concern to Augur that same day. "I hope Harney will play out this winter," he wrote, "when I can put some younger and better man there, but as long as he wants to stay there, I suppose it is best to bear his weaknesses." To Secretary of War John M. Schofield, Sherman acknowledged grudgingly that "General Harney has more influence over the Sioux than any man living, and if he cannot reduce them to subjection by peaceful means no man can." Still, it aggravated Sherman that "Harney never reads anything." He may not initially have read Sherman's orders regarding the $200,000, but he certainly knew the provisions of the commission's treaties, and he still considered his outlays necessary for giving the Indians "the blessings of civilization and Christianity" called for in the agreements. Furthermore, the expenditures supported effective strategy, Harney argued. In warring against the Indians, "Where have we gained any great victories? As relentless as death in their hatred and thirst for revenge, kindness secures their confidence."[30]

Paying for the overages and meeting future reservation needs required additional money, and that meant going back to Congress. Sherman sent Harney's full report to the War Department along with a request that lawmakers appropriate 1869 funds early enough to allow Harney to ship goods before summer. If the solons waited too long to act, low water on the Missouri would again force Harney to pay freight charges at twice the normal rate. Schofield sent both the report and Sherman's cover letter immediately to both legislative houses, and with his approval, Harney went to Washington to defend his purchasing decisions and advocate for more money. Although Sherman made it clear that he disliked the previous excesses, he hoped that Congress would "appropriate what General Harney wants" when he presented his case.[31]

Dr. Walter A. Burleigh, Dakota Territory's delegate to the House of Representatives, pleaded with his colleagues to provide adequate funding. "To fail to carry out the letter and spirit" of the treaties would rekindle "a long, cruel, and costly Indian war," he maintained, and cost "millions of dollars" more. The House Appropriations Committee examined Harney's report in detail. "No one can doubt the good faith of General Harney in what he has done, and his intention to act uprightly, if any one can be said to do so who attempts to expend public money without authorization of law," the committee reported. They understood both why he had purchased provisions for the Indians and why he had incurred abnormally high shipping costs. However, they did not understand why he had bought and shipped agricultural equipment when the season was already too late for planting. The explanation, of course, lay both in his lack of affinity for accounting and his zeal and haste to implement the treaties. Two days after the committee submitted its report, the Senate coincidentally ratified the northern Plains treaties, and on April 10 Congress approved $2 million to fulfill their stipulations, including funding Harney's $485,784.21 overage. The law also authorized the president to appoint an unpaid ten-member

Board of Indian Commissioners to supervise disbursement of the funds in conjunction with the secretary of the interior.[32]

Despite Congress's intentions, this act covered only part of Harney's overspending. He had run up a bigger indebtedness than he thought, and the government vouchers he had issued continued to drift in throughout the year. President Grant ordered $100,000 more of the $2,000,000 set aside for them, but they soon accumulated past that amount. Finally, in July 1870, pursuant to a request from Ely S. Parker, whom President Grant had appointed commissioner of Indian affairs, Congress approved an additional $120,000 to cover Harney's accounts. This brought the total appropriated for his overspending to more than $700,000. In the meantime, from April to June 1869, Harney and Parker squabbled over protocol and how much more of the $2,000,000 should go to the northern reservation. Harney estimated he would need $1,349,000, and Sanborn, who in the role of "late commissioner" submitted projections covering all the Peace Commission treaty stipulations, suggested $1,250,000. Parker came up with a figure of $720,000. Although he should have known which Sioux bands the Peace Commission treaties included, in May he asked Harney to clarify both those and the locations to which their goods should be shipped. Then in June, Parker "cautioned" Harney "to use the utmost care in your Expenditures, not to Exceed the amount made applicable to the Sioux." Harney fired back that he considered Parker's "language exceedingly impertinent" and warned him "not to presume" to use "that style" again.[33]

Operating variously from St. Louis and Sioux City, Harney worried incessantly about the late arrival of spring and summer supplies for the reservation. The Indians "are in a very critical position & serious trouble may result," he complained to Secretary of War John A. Rawlins. "I am now more fully convinced than ever that the Indian Affairs will not be properly attended to until they are transferred to the War Department." On June 12, this became a concern for him no longer. Rawlins and Secretary of the Interior Jacob D. Cox had agreed to appoint army officers as Indian agents at each of the three Sioux reservation agencies, and with Sherman's order appointing Harney set to expire on June 13 anyway, the army relieved him of duty.[34]

Harney expressed no regret about leaving. He had expected his responsibility to end in April following the $2,000,000 appropriation. Shortly after Capt. DeWitt C. Poole received his appointment as the Whetstone agent, he found Harney at his quarters in Sioux City's Northwestern Hotel and, having no experience with Indian affairs, sought "some valuable hints" as to his new duties. Poole asked Harney if he intended to visit the Indians on the reservation again before returning home. He replied that he did not because the Indians might expect to see him "with a quantity of horses, cows, and chickens," and he "had already made too many promises" he "could not fulfill." As for advice, Harney struck a chord reflecting both condescension and responsibility. "They are children," he said, "and you must deal with them as such." Many whites, especially Andrew Jackson, had used that paternalistic analogy numerous times to justify removing Indians from the path of white settlement and progress. For Harney now the comparison represented both a last link to his mentor and a more personalized way of explaining why, in his opinion, the government should expend greater effort to protect native people from further injustice.

When the new agents arrived at their assigned locations, they found generally peaceable folk receiving government food but anxious for their annuity goods. At the Whetstone agency, Poole found two warehouses filled with "substantial provisions," a well-stocked dispensary, and several hundred acres under cultivation, mostly by the seventy or so whites who had married Sioux women. Insects and heat plagued their meager crops, making the government stores vital. Poole also found logging carts, huge wagons known as "prairie schooners," and "an assortment of agricultural implements" that "clearly indicated the desire on the part of the purchaser for the speedy arrival" of the Indians "at a most advanced stage of scientific farming." Although Harney had bought the equipment while he had access to the money to do so, he held no such illusions. Only a year earlier, he had joined Sanborn in maintaining that "the Indians cannot . . . be self-supporting in less time than . . . one generation."[35]

Whatever time the federal government might need to effect its new policies of concentration and acculturation, Harney's role in the process had come to an end. Through reputation, physical presence, familiarity with native people and customs, and insistence on fair treatment backed by military firmness, Harney had helped the Indian Peace Commission complete its goal of treating with all the major plains tribes. More than any other person, he had influenced most of the Sioux to go to the northern reservation district. Through a blend of concern, carelessness, and arrogant defiance, he had wasted hundreds of thousands of dollars there, but he had helped keep those Indians reasonably peaceful through their first year of reservation life. And he had completed his public career by drawing usefully upon many of his earlier experiences on the Great Plains and elsewhere and by acting, as always, according to his own strongly held convictions.

As Harney entered a second period of retirement, the federal government continued to struggle with issues and challenges that the Indian Peace Commission had been created to help resolve, and either directly or indirectly key commission recommendations influenced many of those efforts. Although the Senate still had not ratified all the commission's treaties, in December President Grant reaffirmed its primary purpose and the course it had already launched. He announced a peace policy to place all nomadic tribes on reservations, teach them the tenets of white civilization and Christianity, and make them agriculturally self-sufficient. Eventually his plan failed due to a combination of factors, including continued incompetence and corruption in the Indian Bureau, but reservations and education remained foundation stones for future policy. In March 1871, Congress, pursuant to a Peace Commission recommendation, enacted legislation stipulating that the government would never again acknowledge or recognize a group of Indians as an "independent nation, tribe, or power with whom the United States may contract by treaty." The treaties Harney helped secure were among the last completed. Congress did not follow the commission's recommendation to transfer the Indian Bureau to the War Department. However, the Peace Commission succeeded in bringing a greater humanitarian tone to the nation's Indian policy and management, and in the next two decades a number of army officers, such as George Crook, O. O. Howard, and Nelson A. Miles, reflected it in word and deed. Despite all this, violent conflict between whites and Indians continued. On the southern plains especially, many Indians resisted concentration, and eventually war erupted again in the north, prolonging the conflict between contrasting and competing cultures through the rest of Harney's life. To the extent that the Indian Peace Commission affected the course of these developments and events, Harney stood among those members most responsible for its work and its impact.[36]

CHAPTER 14

A Time for Reflection

ONE MORNING in the early 1870s, a "striking scene" unfolded in the fashionable St. Louis neighborhood known as Lucas Place. An estimated forty Indians gathered for breakfast at the stately three-story red brick home of retired Bvt. Maj. Gen. William S. Harney. Time has obscured the date and reason for the native leaders' visit to their old friend, along with which tribes they represented, but they enjoyed a convivial atmosphere. Observing through the lens of polite society, the chronicler of the event noted only the Indians' "picturesque costumes" and their fondness for sweetmeats. Harney's servants had to beg his neighbors for half a bushel of stick candy to satisfy his guests' cravings, and his little "golden-haired" granddaughter Nettie served the treats on a silver platter.

The person who recorded those sparse details about the occasion did so because Harney's house "was the scene of much social activity," and this episode seemed unusual and amusing. The chronicler did not apprehend the feelings that passed between the host and his native visitors. She did not understand how his feting them in his home completed a circle begun some fifty years earlier on the upper Missouri when he dined for the first time with Indians as their guest. Nor did she know the details of his relationships with native people in the inter-vening period or comprehend where those associations and his mili-tary career fit in the story of the nation over that span. However, she captured a moment that allowed Harney to reach back and recall or connect to verses or chapters that carried particular meaning for him.[1]

Harney's retirement years accorded him considerable opportunity to reflect about the past, and he indulged himself to do so on more than one occasion. He also remained active farming, traveling, and com-municating with old friends. He even found time for romance, much to the dismay of his children. In addition to his house in the city, Harney owned two rural properties, one close in and one seventy miles west in the small town of Sullivan.[2] When not in St. Louis or traveling, he spent much of his time at the latter location. He first took note of the area while passing on the stage road between St. Louis and Springfield dur-ing his paymaster days, and he purchased nineteen hundred acres there following the Civil War. By 1870, serving as his own architect, he had converted a small existing residence into a federal-style sandstone and white pine mansion of some thirty rooms. He also built extensive stables from similar materials and planted eighty-five species of trees on the grounds.

In the ensuing years, Harney became a summer fixture in the small community and inspired long-remembered stories of colorful and gen-erous behavior. He went about the countryside in a coach drawn by "beautiful horses" and always wore a frock coat and silk hat in public. Often a crew of farm hands trailed along to handle various errands. Apparently, during the financial panic of 1873 he "practically supported this entire community" by hiring "an unusually large force" of work-ers. Harney regarded them with the same benevolent paternalism that he had shown Indians and his family. He "made merry" with them, the storytellers say, and helped them when he thought it appropriate, but he retained an authoritative detachment as well. Often in the guise of intended and ultimate kindness he enjoyed an insensitive but reveal-ing joke and hearty laugh at the workers' expense. Community tradi-tion held that Harney kept in his library "a battered trunk" always "well filled with greenbacks" and loved to call in employees, dismiss them "on false pretenses," rehire them on the spot, and give them a bonus from his cache. Here Harney's capacity for kindness traveled alongside his capacity for crudeness.

His coarser side surfaced on at least one other occasion in Sullivan, too, demonstrating that age had not lessened his vindictive impulses. After a local doctor sent a letter accusing him of "a breach of etiquette," Harney sought out and found the unsuspecting gentleman leaving the post office. Pulling a pistol from beneath his coat, the crusty old soldier handed the offending note to its author and forced him to eat it.

As always, Harney showed more patience with animals than with people who offended him. He liked to tramp about his property applying a small hand ax to low-hanging branches that blocked his way in the forests and caressing horses that followed him in the pastures. One day he bent over to inspect the foot of a horse that approached him limping. The animal knocked Harney's hat off, became frightened by the rolling chapeau, and tromped on Harney's foot. The horse recovered long before Harney could get around without a crutch, but he remained a devoted equine lover.

Sometime in 1872 or shortly afterward, Harney hired "a cultured lady" to reside in his Sullivan home, serve as his private secretary, and conduct a school for his employees' children. An attractive widow in her late forties, and coincidentally a second cousin of former paymaster general Nathan Towson, Mary St. Cyr soon "made herself so useful about the place" that Harney retained her as his "general manager." Employees called her "the madam."[5]

Despite the obvious pleasure that his Sullivan estate brought him, Harney retained a restless spirit born from a life of frequent travel and new experiences. In consequence of that, he sometimes journeyed to old haunts and contemplated new residences. On one occasion, in early 1870, he spent four months visiting New Orleans, Corpus Christi, Laredo, San Antonio, and Austin. On another occasion, in late 1875, he passed two months in the Rocky Mountains. He enjoyed that trip so much that in 1877 he approached the War Department about building a house on the military reservation at Fort Bridger in Wyoming Territory. By then he found the colder months in Missouri so disagreeable that he also investigated the possibility of establishing a winter residence at

Baton Rouge Barracks, provided that he could do so without placing "myself in the way of any troops" that might be there.[4]

As he grew older, Harney kept in touch with other retired officers, particularly Edward George Washington Butler, his old college classmate in Nashville, and Jefferson Davis, his friend at Fort Winnebago and onetime boss as secretary of war. Shortly before Robert E. Lee died in 1870, Harney honored his former Mexican War colleague by contributing funds to help endow the president's chair, which Lee held, at Washington College. Harney also corresponded with Ulysses S. Grant, who in the late 1870s tried unsuccessfully to lure him on a tour of old battlegrounds in Mexico. Grant quipped to an acquaintance that if Harney would go, he would be "set back about . . . ten years. The general I suppose admits to fifty-five now." In 1879 Harney bought a winter home on the Gulf in Pass Christian, Mississippi, where both Butler and Davis had residences. Mary St. Cyr joined him on sojourns there, and he enjoyed "many agreeable hours" talking over "old times and pleasant incidents" with neighbors and visiting friends, including P. G. T. Beauregard, with whom he had campaigned in Mexico.[5]

When Harney paused to think more seriously about the past, the images that sprang foremost to mind included recollections of Andrew Jackson, the Missouri secession crisis, and Indian affairs. Near the end of his Indian Peace Commission service, Harney received an invitation to a Washington banquet commemorating the Battle of New Orleans and the end of the War of 1812. He could not attend the event, but it stirred memories of his former mentor. Harney still revered Jackson as a "great patriot" and remained painfully aware of how differently their military careers had ended. Jackson had left the army under a hero's banner. Harney had been accused of disloyalty and dismissed, and it still troubled him. As late as 1872 he pleaded with the War Department for either formal permission or an order to file a "full statement of my course" in Missouri "up to the day on which I was so summarily relieved." He received neither.

Scarcely a year later, in May 1873, Father DeSmet, Harney's frequent partner in Indian affairs, died following a brief illness, and Harney stood among the hundreds of mourners at St. Louis University. The next day, the *St. Louis Times* singled him out as one of the famous Jesuit's closest remaining friends and perhaps the only one who "so thoroughly knew the Indian character." Harney could not have avoided recalling their several collaborative efforts among native people, but his most comprehensive reflections about Indian affairs came at the request of Congress in February 1874. The House Committee on Indian Affairs, still struggling with many of the same issues that the Indian Peace Commission had attempted to address, solicited his opinions on a variety of questions.

By this time, Harney's memory had dimmed to the point that he sometimes recalled dates more generally than precisely, but his convictions about Indian matters remained firm and consistent with actions and opinions he had evidenced throughout his career. In his last public act, he repeated the advice and counsel he had offered countless times before. The government could control native people in only two ways, he maintained, either through fear of punishment or through "kind treatment and *justice*." If whites would "keep . . . treaty stipulations with the Indians we would have no trouble with them." More than any other factor, Harney argued, agents and whiskey sellers "make the difficulty." Appoint army officers as agents and "hang the whiskey sellers or shoot them," he declared. He also urged the lawmakers to retain the reservation system and transfer the Indian Bureau to the War Department. The army can teach Indians agriculture and mechanical arts and manage Indian affairs better than civilians, he said, because officers "would have no interest except to do their duty." And finally, he pleaded, recognize that if it is necessary to fight Indians, the "cavalry alone can pursue and catch them." In short, Harney continued to believe and advocate that the government should use forthright, honest, protective, and dependable means to force native people to adopt white culture.[6]

As he had throughout his career, in retirement Harney spent more time with his military acquaintances than with his children. His daughters remained in France, and in the mid-1870s his son had retired there with his family as well. After they went abroad, Harney missed seeing his American grandchildren, and occasionally he corresponded with his daughter-in-law. In late 1875, he even mused about "poking over to France some of these times within a year or so," but he never went.[7]

By 1881 Harney's eyesight and hearing had begun to fade, and his health and family business matters prompted all his children to visit him. Before he knew their plans, he had rented out his Lucas Place home with the intention of spending the summer in the Rockies again, and so he had to rent another house to accommodate them. Their visit did little to strengthen their relationship with their father. Either during their stay or through some other means, they and he all agreed to borrow $380,000 against Harney's property and their mother's estate. The arrangement required that he and each of his children pay a proportionate share of the interest and the principal when due.[8]

The agreement came undone after Harney decided to marry Mary St. Cyr. Three days before the wedding, the two executed a nuptial settlement in which, for the sum of one dollar, he gave her one-half interest in his "entire real, personal, and mixed estate," including his "life estate in various and sundry valuable lands" that had belonged to Mary Mullanphy Harney. Accompanied by the bride's sister and daughter, Harney and Mary St. Cyr exchanged vows in a Catholic ceremony at St. Louis Cathedral on November 15, 1884. He was eighty-four. She was fifty-eight and, according to newspaper accounts, looked twelve years younger. Neither his family nor his friends had anticipated this development. Butler thought it "most fortunate," as "his children pay him no attention," and Harney seemed happy with his bride.

Unaware of the nuptial settlement, "a close connection of the Harney family" told one reporter that if the marriage did not affect Harney's heirs, "it was at worst only a very foolish affair." But it did affect his heirs, and they reacted negatively. His granddaughter Nettie H. Beauregard summarized their feelings years later when she recalled that Harney's "mind had been failing for some time—so he was an easy prey." Within months of the wedding, Harney's children sued him, his wife, and the insurance company. Charging that their father sought to escape his portion of their mutual debt, the petitioners asked the court to appoint a receiver to manage his property. Harney denied the accusation and in a cross petition requested and got a receiver for the entire estate. He then revised his will. Vindictively, Harney left five dollars to

John, five dollars to his daughter Elizabeth, nothing to his daughter Ann, and everything else to Mary St. Cyr Harney and her heirs.[9]

In February 1888, at home among his friends in Pass Christian, Harney celebrated the seventieth anniversary of his entry into the army. Neighbors dropped in to offer congratulations, children brought bouquets, and winter-dwellers came by to shake hands. A reporter interviewed him for the *New York Times*. Despite being "quite feeble of mind," Harney enjoyed the attention and had Mary bring his commission papers onto the veranda and display them to his guests. When the party ended and the reporter departed, Harney sat alone in the sun watching the water and listening to the birds sing.

A short while later, the Harneys purchased an "elegant home" on the south side of Lake Eola in Orlando, Florida, and lived there until he died on May 9, 1889, three months shy of his eighty-ninth birthday. Mrs. Harney took his remains by train to Washington DC, where two troops of cavalry met her at the Pennsylvania Railroad depot and provided an escort to Arlington National Cemetery. There on Sunday afternoon, May 12, eight army sergeants laid Harney's body to rest. In time, a tall gray monument marked the spot with this simple inscription: "Gen. William S. Harney–2nd Dragoons–1800–1889–Commissioned 1818–Black Hawk–Seminole–Mexican–Sioux–War of the Rebellion."[10]

Those words summarize Harney's service succinctly, and, as they should, they give the greatest weight to Indian affairs. For any observer more curious than his Lucas Place breakfast chronicler about his larger place in history, they provide only a starting point for understanding. But they mesh nicely with a more illuminating philosophy that Harney recorded in 1868: "The power of the sword in a free country is never to be invoked but to repel invasion, quell insurrection, & to enforce the law."[11]

Throughout his career, one of the army's two primary missions consisted of serving as a frontier constabulary. In carrying out this function, the army affected the settlement of the West in multiple ways, but none more dramatic than helping to implement federal Indian policy and trying to protect whites and native people from each other–in short, attempting to "enforce the law." Between the major reduction of personnel in 1821 and the start of the Civil War, eighteen officers held the unbreveted rank of brigadier general or higher at one time or another in the regular army. Among those only Winfield Scott, Thomas S. Jesup, John E. Wool, and David E. Twiggs served longer than Harney, and neither any of them nor any other officer in that era proved more effective in Indian-related military service. Further, having helped carry out both the removal policy before the Mexican War and the policy of protecting overland routes afterward, only Harney among the eighteen went on to take part in developing and implementing the concentration policy following the Civil War. All of these policies, of course, had the lamentable impact of destroying the freedom and way of life of America's native people.

Despite the cost and complexities of constabulary duty, the army's other primary mission, preparing for potential war with a foreign power, consumed almost all of the army's tactical thought and training energy. Consequently, no formal mechanism existed to teach officers to fight Indian warriors who used guerilla tactics. Commanders learned in the field, and Harney, born in a southern frontier society characterized by fighting, boasting, and short tempers, had the necessary drive and instincts to do so. Inspired by Andrew Jackson's example of an American military hero, Harney honed his skills over time on the waters of the Missouri, in the forests of Wisconsin and Illinois, in the swamps of Florida, and on the plains of Texas and Nebraska. He understood that defeating unorthodox fighters required innovative approaches, and he had a knack for developing them. A combination of innate ability, dogged determination, inventiveness, and experience eventually made Harney the most successful Indian fighter of his time. Peers and public alike recognized his ability. Acknowledgment flowed from fellow officers such as Stephen Watts Kearny, O. O. Howard, and William T. Sherman, from government officials like Jefferson Davis, John B. Henderson, and John M. Schofield, and from newspaper editors in towns from Florida to Oregon and from Texas to Dakota.

Harney contributed his first tactical innovations in the Second Seminole War. That long and wearying struggle exhibited numerous characteristics—guerrilla tactics, recurring fighting over a wide area, impenetrable swampy terrain, frequent changes of command, and high cost in dollars and personnel—that Americans would see more than a century later in another elongated countryside an ocean away. Harney introduced methods of amphibious riverine warfare that formed the direct conceptual basis for seek-and-destroy tactics that American forces employed in Vietnam.[12] But more important for his time, his use of light boats to pursue Seminole warriors enabled him and other army and navy officers who adopted his measures to conclude both the Second and the Third Seminole Wars earlier than they could have otherwise. Also in Florida, Harney experimented with new weapons to increase firepower, and he defied convention by dressing troops in Indian clothing to avoid early detection. Although the army failed in its ultimate goal of removing all the Seminoles to the West, no one did more to advance that effort than Harney.

He had less impact in Texas, but during three stints as interim department commander he accomplished at least as much as the three commanding officers under whom he served there, and he impressed Texans with his energy and his advocacy for greater use of mounted troops in frontier forts. He helped implement army policy to build additional posts in successive lines across the frontier, but unlike Gen. Persifor F. Smith, who is credited with doing most to develop that defensive concept in Texas, Harney advocated using mounted troops in the outer line of forts. Smith used them only in the inner line, and the strategy failed to maintain peace. Also in Texas, Harney increased the mobility of mountain howitzers by transporting ammunition on the gun carriages rather than on trailing pack animals. Of lesser importance but nevertheless illustrative of Harney's innovative bent, his Texas-based dragoons became the first army troops to employ a new, wide-brimmed campaign hat that eventually became the model for all cavalry units.

Harney's campaign against the Sioux in 1855–56 became the most remembered of his military endeavors. It followed a decade of debate about whether the government could maintain peace more effectively on the Great Plains through an extensive line of stationary posts in Indian country or by sending large roving columns through native people's homelands each spring and summer. It came also on the heels of failed treaties, increased violence along overland emigrant routes, and growing federal impatience with Indian resistance to white encroachment. Ordered to punish native bands responsible for the so-called Grattan Massacre, Harney carried out the task with an efficient and vindictive ferocity that plains Indians and whites recalled for years afterward. In the process he demonstrated that in response to specific incidents the army could and would send large columns against particular groups of Indians in summer or winter and would not hesitate to use them to wage total war involving combatants and noncombatants alike. As part of his peace arrangements with the Sioux, he attempted to establish a cadre of Indian police to help maintain order, but Washington did not support the idea. Others revived it after the Civil War, however, and congressional action in 1878 led eventually to the use of Indian police on reservations throughout the West.

The Sioux campaign and Harney's firm manner in the Fort Pierre talks afterward helped him earn a grudging respect among native people, and it carried forward to his influence with the Indian Peace Commission in the late 1860s. The deference accorded him stemmed also from his familiarity with Indians. Attitudes toward native people varied significantly among officers, just as the officers' individual backgrounds and experiences differed, but sadly and inappropriately most officers, including Harney, regarded Indians as culturally inferior to whites. Most officers, again including Harney, also modified their individual attitudes or moved back and forth between or among points of view in response to different or changing circumstances. Harney did not stand alone in his willingness to fight and kill Indians in one instance and his ability to express paternalistic concern for their well-being in the next. Few officers rivaled him, however, in personal familiarity with native people. From dining and sporting with Indians on the upper Missouri to fathering Mary Caroline Harney in Wisconsin and from sharing his sleeping quarters with Osceola in Florida to demonstrating cordiality and attentiveness at peace councils on the Great Plains, he evinced a degree of comfort and ease with Indians that few officers possessed. This made it easier for him to see at least some of the injustices inherent in removal, broken treaty promises, and corrupt bureaucratic practices. When combined with his military prowess, Harney's familiarity with native people and the knowledge that flowed from it lent weight to his words with both Indians and whites.

Although Harney made his most important contributions in the implementation and enforcement of federal Indian policy, the army's mission as a frontier constabulary involved other responsibilities, too. Through his service in Kansas and Utah in 1857–58, Harney contributed significantly to two of the army's largest and most important pre–Civil War efforts to preserve domestic order by enforcing civil law and federal authority. Had officials in Washington listened to his advice about delaying the start of the Utah expedition, the government might have expended fewer resources on it. Harney's concerns rested on timing, not dollars, for as he had demonstrated while a paymaster in the 1830s, he had little affinity or aptitude for accounting. He knew, however, that lack of personnel and equipment hampered military operations. He had seen how shortages of mounted troops hindered peacekeeping efforts in Texas, and he had overcome enormous obstacles in gathering troops and equipment for his Sioux campaign. These episodes illustrated that frequently the army lacked sufficient personnel and other resources as it tried to meet its broad peacekeeping responsibilities. These same episodes also showed that generally the army performed about as well as could have been expected with the tools available to it.

In addition to "enforce the law," two other phrases in Harney's 1868 comment about invoking the "power of the sword" help place him in the larger national story. American expansionist impulses caused the Mexican War, but Congress based its declaration on the need to "repel invasion" after Mexican troops crossed into disputed territory. Although the war with Mexico produced many heroes, Harney's effective command of the cavalry on the road to Mexico City and his attendant charge up Cerro Gordo rightfully cast him among those who stood out. Broader interpretation of that same phrase, "repel invasion," produced different career results when Harney occupied San Juan Island during his Oregon service. Expansionism prompted this use of the sword, too, but this time he alone felt that sentiment, and he very nearly produced a useless clash of arms with a friendly power. Harney's impulsive action and obstinate refusal to reconsider his chosen course also reflected poor political and military judgment, as did his failure to "quell insurrection" in Missouri in 1861. There he erred on the side of caution, both in delaying protection for the St. Louis arsenal and in not interpreting Sterling Price's activities as rebellion. As a result, Harney suffered the greatest humiliation of his career when Lincoln removed him from command and the War Department subsequently retired him. More than forced retirement, Harney hated the accompanying and erroneous implication that he had based his decisions on disloyalty to the Union.

Harney's 1868 statement does not provide any understanding about the bureaucratic structure of the pre–Civil War army or how Harney and his fellow officers behaved within it. That requires consideration of the officers themselves and Harney among them. The officer corps accommodated significant diversity except in race, but its members shared many attitudes and attributes. Harney resembled most of his peers in his intense interest in promotion, his use of political influence to gain it, and his propensity for peevish quarreling over petty matters. He differed in significant ways, too. Thanks largely to his relationship with Andrew Jackson, he enjoyed much greater success than most officers in utilizing favoritism, and accordingly he advanced more rapidly and farther than most. Although not the only officer to quarrel frequently and heatedly with Winfield Scott, Harney managed an uncommonly long string of disputes with the commanding general and became the first to file formal charges against him for carrying out a court-martial sentence. And few officers developed as much notoriety as Harney for profane language and vengeful violence, whether vented against enlisted men, civilians, or battlefield opponents.

In those ways and four others in particular, Harney stood apart in the bureaucracy. He loved the army and advanced its growing professionalism through example in Indian warfare, length of service, and avoidance of political activity. But he almost never hesitated to defy authority when he thought he knew a better way or when he believed circumstances warranted it. Unlike some officers, he also never expressed any interest in studying European methods, and except for his insightful analysis of organizational, training, and equipment needs during the Second Seminole War, he never wrote broadly about military life and activities, as many other leading officers did. And lastly, as his career grew longer and West Point graduates made up an ever-larger portion of the officer corps, he became increasingly conspicuous as part of a dwindling minority commissioned directly from civilian life.

History tends to recall Harney in almost stereotypical terms, as a hotheaded, two-fisted, Hollywood-style blood-and-guts Indian war campaigner and little more. In some important ways that reputation fits, but clearly he was more and deserves a better, fuller, more nuanced portrait that is at once harder in judgment and more generous in assessment. Individual attitudes, beliefs, and experiences always influence the perception and interpretation of historical evidence and create differences of opinion about impact and the presence or absence of personal merit. Even allowing for those variables, there is much about William S. Harney that should be remembered.

He should be remembered for his quick temper, foul mouth, violent nature, vindictive bent, and callous behavior. He should be remembered for abusing soldiers and committing a murder. He should be remembered for his impulsiveness, arrogance, quarrelsomeness, and obstinacy. He should be remembered for defying orders, nearly provoking hostilities over San Juan Island, and hesitating too long in the Missouri secession crisis. And he should be remembered as a willing and forceful instrument of white hegemony.

But Harney should also be remembered for his courage and boldness in combat and his innovative tactics. He should be remembered for his leadership of Scott's cavalry in Mexico, his effective service in Kansas, and his command of the Utah expedition in its formative stages. He should be remembered for his penetration into unexplored portions of Florida and his encouragement of road building in the Pacific Northwest. Despite his misjudgment and forced retirement at the beginning of the Civil War, he should be recognized and remembered for his unswerving loyalty to the Union. And he should be remembered for his familiarity with native people, his contributions to the work of the Indian Peace Commission, and his advocacy for fair treatment of Indians within the context of federal policy.

Finally, as his career is measured and his life tallied, William S. Harney should be remembered as one of the major American military figures of his time.

NOTES

These notes are limited chiefly to primary sources and do not always cite secondary works consulted for context and background information. See the selected bibliography for the most important of those sources.

ABBREVIATIONS

ACP	Appointment, Commission, and Personnel
AFS	*Armed Forces and Society*
AGO	Office of the Adjutant General
AJ	Andrew Jackson Papers
ALB	Atkinson Letter Book
AO	Army of Occupation
AOB	Atkinson Order Book
ARCIA	Annual Report of the Commissioner of Indian Affairs
ARSI	Annual Report of the Secretary of the Interior
ARSW	Annual Report of the Secretary of War
ASP:DLE	*American State Papers: Documents, Legislative and Executive*
ASP:IA	*American State Papers: Indian Affairs*
ASP:MA	*American State Papers: Military Affairs*
ASP:SPD	*American State Papers: State and Publick Documents*
BFP	Blair Family Papers

BHW	Black Hawk War Papers
BIA	Bureau (Office) of Indian Affairs
CSHSW	*Collections of the State Historical Society of Wisconsin*
DMSJ	*Daily Missouri State Journal*
DO	Departmental Order[s]
FHQ	*Florida Historical Quarterly*
GO	General Order[s]
HED	*House Executive Documents*
HQA	Headquarters of the Army
ID:SCIPC	Indian Division: Segregated Correspondence of the Indian Peace Commission, 1867–68
JAG	Office of the Judge Advocate General
KWH	*Kansas Weekly Herald*
LC	Library of Congress
LR	Letters Received
LS	Letters Sent
LWT	*Liberty Weekly Tribune*
MA	*Military Affairs*
MCC	Mary C. Clemens Collection
MD	*Missouri Democrat*
MFC	Mullanphy Family Collection
MHR	*Missouri Historical Review*
MHSB	*Missouri Historical Society Bulletin*
MMBC	Mrs. Mason Barret Collection
MOHS	Missouri Historical Society
MR	*Missouri Republican*
MW	Mexican War
NH	*Nebraska History*
NHB	Nettie H. Beauregard Papers
OB	Orderly Book[s]
OPMG	Office of the Paymaster General
OQMG	Office of the Quartermaster General
OSIA	Oregon Superintendency of Indian Affairs
PD	*Pioneer and Democrat*
PIPC	Proceedings of the Indian Peace Commission
RGP	Richard Graham Papers

RO	Regimental Order[s]
RRFIR	Regimental Returns for the First Infantry Regiment
RT	Regimental Return[s]
SAN	*St. Augustine News*
SDHC	*South Dakota Historical Collections*
SE	Sioux Expedition
SED	*Senate Executive Documents*
SHQ	*Southwestern Historical Quarterly*
SO	Special Order[s]
SW	Secretary of War
TKSHS	*Transactions of the Kansas State Historical Society*
TP	*Territorial Papers of the United States*
TSG	*Texas State Gazette*
UD	*Union and Dakotaian*
USAC	United States Army Commands
USACC	United States Army Continental Commands
WMH	*Wisconsin Magazine of History*
WR	*The War of the Rebellion*
WSH	William S. Harney Papers

Preface

1. Logan Uriah Reavis to George R. Taylor, May 14, 1887, George R. Taylor Collection; William S. Harney to Reavis, October 29, 1877, WSH; John M. Harney to Reavis, April 19, 1879, WSH; Patrick E. McLear, "Logan U. Reavis: Nineteenth-Century Urban Promoter," MHR 66 (July 1972): 567–88.

---

1. Son of Tennessee Pioneers

1. Robert V. Remini, *Andrew Jackson and the Course of American Empire, 1767–1821* (New York: Harper & Row, 1977), 165–73, 178–93; William M. Meigs, *The Life of Thomas Hart Benton* (Philadelphia: J. B. Lippincott, 1904), 73–80; John Wooldridge, ed., *History of Nashville, Tenn.* (Nashville: Publishing House of the Methodist Episcopal Church, South, 1890), 99.

2. Genealogy file, WSH; Robert M. McBride and Owen Meredith, eds., *Eastin Morris' Tennessee Gazetteer, 1843 and Matthew Rhea's Map of the State of Tennessee,*

1832 (Nashville: Gazetteer, 1971), 171; "An Act to Establish a Town by the Name of Haysborough, on a North Bluff of Cumberland River, in Davidson County," 1st sess., 3d General Assembly of the State of Tennessee, October 23, 1799; Thomas Harney to Andrew Jackson, November 5, 1808, AJ, microfilm, series 1, roll 4.

3. Genealogy file, WSH; Harney genealogy, NHB; Linda Harney MacDonald, "Heraldry," *Harney Update* 17 (January 1991): 11–13; Harney family genealogy, provided by Linda Harney MacDonald; Logan U. Reavis, *The Life and Military Services of Gen. William Selby Harney* (St. Louis: Bryan, Brand, 1878), 39–40; North Carolina Land Grants, books A-1:12, E-5:335–36, and B-2:106, Tennessee State Library and Archives; *Tennessee: Records of Davidson County; Land Records, 1788–1793* (Nashville: Works Progress Administration Historical Records Project, 1937), 389.

4. Wooldridge, *Nashville*, 214–25, 242–43, 300–302.

5. Genealogy file, WSH; Harney genealogy, NHB; *The National Cyclopaedia of American Biography* (New York: James T. White, 1900), 10:158–59; Reavis, *Harney*, 41–43.

6. Henry McRaven, *Nashville: "Athens of the South"* (Chapel Hill NC: Scheer & Jervis, 1949), 24; Reavis, *Harney*, 43; Edward George Washington Butler to Reavis, February 1, May 20, 1878, in Reavis, *Harney*, v–vi, 457–58.

7. Bertram Wyatt-Brown, *Southern Honor: Ethics and Behavior in the Old South* (New York: Oxford Univ. Press, 1982), 163–69; Michael Paul Rogin, *Fathers and Children: Andrew Jackson and the Subjugation of the American Indian* (New York: Alfred A. Knopf, 1975), 43, 134; Remini, *Jackson*, 193–217, 238–42, 257–85, 318–24; McRaven, *Nashville*, 35.

8. Alfred Leland Crabb, *Nashville: Personality of a City* (Indianapolis: Bobbs-Merrill, 1960), 172–74; George W. Cullom, *Biographical Register of the Officers and Graduates of the U.S. Military Academy at West Point, N.Y., from Its Establishment, March 16, 1802, to the Army Re-organization of 1866–67* (New York: D. Van Nostrand, 1868), 196–97, 200, 219, 238; William B. Skelton, *An American Profession of Arms: The Army Officer Corps, 1784–1861* (Lawrence: Univ. Press of Kansas, 1992), 117, 138.

9. Capt. Alexander Gray to John C. Calhoun, January 5, 1818, Maj. Richard Whartenby, Capt. William Christian, Lt. Robert L. Coomb, and eleven others, Recommendation for William S. Harney, March 25, 1818, and William Selby Harney to Gen. Daniel Parker, June 11, 1818, all in AGO:LR, M566, roll 107; General Order, April 30, 1818, USAC: South, Eighth General Order Received, vol. 450.

2. A Time for Learning

1. RO, May 15, June 13, 1818, Capt. William Laval OB, USAC:OB, vol. 74; Jefferson Davis to Reavis, January 1878, Reavis, *Harney*, iv; UD, November 30, 1867. Harney description based in part on 1840s color portrait owned by John M. Harney, artist unknown.

2. Remini, *Jackson*, 225–301, 321–60, 382–90; Lyle Saxon, *Lafitte the Pirate* (New York: Century, 1930), 214–17.

3. Davis to Reavis, January 1878, in Reavis, *Harney*, iv; Skelton, *Profession*, 68–72, 96–97, 120–25; Stephen E. Ambrose, *Duty, Honor, Country: A History of West Point* (Baltimore: John Hopkins Univ. Press, 1966), 56–57.

4. RO, May 15, 1818, Laval OB, USAC:OB, vol. 74; Gen. Eleazer W. Ripley to Wartenby, June 15, 1818, USAC: South, Eighth, General Orders Received, vol. 450; RO, June 25, 1818, Laval OB, USAC:OB, vol. 74; Beverly Chew to William H. Crawford, August 1, 30, October 17, 1817, ASP:SPD, 2:347–56; Harris Gaylord Warren, *The Sword Was Their Passport: A History of American Filibustering in the Mexican Revolution* (Baton Rouge: Louisiana State Univ. Press, 1943), 181–88.

5. Comdr. John Porter to Benjamin W. Crowninshield, June 28, 1817, ASP:SPD, 2:377; Ripley to Whartenby, June 15, 1818, USAC: South, Eighth, General Orders Received, vol. 450.

6. RO, June 25, 1818, Laval OB, USAC:OB, vol. 74; DO, July 7, 18, 1818, Amelung OB, USAC:OB, vol. 76.

7. DO, August 30, 1818, RO, November 14, 1818, and General Order, January 7, 1819, all in Amelung OB, USAC:OB, vol. 76; Company Detail, December 10, 1818, Laval OB, USAC:OB, vol. 74; DO, January 15, 1819, USAC: South, Eighth, General Orders Received, vol. 450; Skelton, *Profession*, 65–66, 193–94.

8. RO, December 12, 1818, OB, USAC:OB, vol. 76; RO, n.d., Laval OB, USAC:OB, vol. 74; Edgar Bruce Wesley, *Guarding the Frontier: A Study of Frontier Defense* (Minneapolis: Univ. of Minnesota Press, 1935), 28–30, 176–84; Frank Lawrence Owsley Jr. and Gene A. Smith, *Filibusters and Expansionists: Jeffersonian Manifest Destiny, 1800–1821* (Tuscaloosa: Univ. of Alabama Press, 1997), 172–80.

9. RO, n.d., and Detachment Order, December 29, 1818, both in Laval OB, USAC:OB, vol. 74; General Order, n.d., Amelung OB, USAC:OB, vol. 76; General Order, September 11, 1818, USAC: South, Eighth, OB of the Adjutant General, vol. 435; Garrison Orders, February 10, February 17, and March 29, 1819, and Detachment

Order, February 15, 1819, all in Laval OB, USAC:OB, vol. 74; "Courts-Martial," in John C. Calhoun to John W. Taylor, December 12, 1820, ASP:DLE, 2:268–74; Edward M. Coffman, *The Old Army: A Portrait of the American Army in Peacetime, 1784–1898* (New York: Oxford Univ. Press, 1986), 167–68, 191, 197–98.

10. William S. Harney to James Thompson Harney, February 9, 1819, WSH; Theophilus Rodenbough, ed., *Uncle Sam's Medal of Honor: Some of the Noble Deeds for Which the Medal of Honor Has Been Awarded, Described by Those Who Have Won It, 1861–1886* (New York: G. P. Putnam's Sons, 1886), 379–80.

11. Detachment Order, February 15, 1819, and RO, April 11, 1819, both in Laval OB, USAC:OB, vol. 74; Detachment Order, April 19, 1819, Garrison Orders, May 10, 20, 1819, and DO, May 22, 1819, all in Laval OB, USAC:OB, vol. 483.

12. RO, May 4, 1819, extract, and Garrison Order, June 30, 1819, both in Laval OB, USAC:OB, vol. 483.

13. "Recruiting Regulations" in Calhoun to Taylor, December 12, 1820, ASP:SPD, 2:261–63; Coffman, *Old Army*, 15–16, 138–45, 193–95.

14. Col. Robert Butler to Gen. Daniel Bissell, June 8, 1820, USAC: South, Eighth, LS, vol. 407; Lt. Levi Whiting to Harney, February 24, 1821, USACC: Western, Orders and Special Orders Issued, vol. 20; DO, June 1, 1819, Laval OB, USAC:OB, vol. 483; Coffman, *Old Army*, 184–85.

15. Harney to Calhoun, April 5, 1821, AGO:LR, M566, roll 140; Remini, *Jackson*, 388, 399–402; Russell F. Weigley, *Towards an American Army: Military Thought from Washington to Marshall* (New York: Columbia Univ. Press, 1962), 22–23; Calhoun to Taylor, December 12, 1820, ASP:MA, 2:188–93; Skelton, *Profession*, 126–29.

16. Andrew Jackson to John Quincy Adams, April 24, 1821, John Spencer Bassett, ed., *The Correspondence of Andrew Jackson* (Washington DC: Carnegie Institution of Washington, 1926–35), 3:52–53; Harney to Parker, dated April 1, written May 1, 1821, AGO:LR, M567, roll 140; Jackson to Governor José Callava, June 20, 1821, Bassett, *Jackson*, 3:72–74; Jackson to Gen. John Coffee, July 4, 1821, Bassett, *Jackson*, 3:89; Remini, *Jackson*, 404–6; RRFIR for July 1821, AGO:RT, M665, roll 1.

17. Orders of Gen. Jackson, July 10, 1821, AJ, microfilm, series 3, roll 63; Jackson to Callava, July 13, 1821, Bassett, *Jackson*, 3:98–99; *Niles' Weekly Register*, August 25, 1821; Remini, *Jackson*, 406–7, 417.

18. Whartenby to Adjutant General, August 22, 1821, AGO:LR, M566, roll 144; Harney to Lt. Robert B. Brent, September 23, 1821, and Brent to Col. James Gadsden, November 1, 1821, both in AGO:LR, M566, roll 140.

19. General Order no. 45, November 16, 1821, Orders Received by Atkinson, USACC: Western, vol. 42; Capt. Daniel E. Burch to Harney, May 21, 1822, USACC: Western, LS, vol. 1; RRFIR for February, March, April, May 1822, AGO:RT, M665, roll 1; Maj. Charles J. Nourse to Gen. Edmund P. Gaines, July 9, 1822, AGO:LS, M565, roll 6; Order no. 90, December 22, 1822, USACC: Western, Orders and Special Orders Issued, vol. 20; RRFIR for March 1823, AGO:RT, M665, roll 1.

20. William H. Ashley to Benjamin O'Fallon, June 4, 1823, 2:586–87; Gaines to Gen. Jacob Brown, July 26, 1823, 2:579; Col. Henry Leavenworth Order, June 18, 1823, 2:588, and O'Fallon to Gen. Henry Atkinson, July 3, 1823, 2:579–80, all in ASP:MA; Roger L. Nichols, "The Arikara Indians and the Missouri River Fur Trade: A Quest for Survival," *Great Plains Quarterly* 2 (spring 1982): 77–93; Roger L. Nichols, "Backdrop for Disaster: Causes of the Arikara War of 1823," *South Dakota History* 14 (summer 1984): 95–113.

21. Gaines to Brown, July 26, 1823, ASP:MA, 2:579, Gaines to Atkinson, USACC: Western, LS, vol. 1; Special Order no. 17, July 26, 1823, USACC: Western, Atkinson Orders, vol. 43; Atkinson to Gaines, September 5, 1823, ASP:MA, 2:584–85; RRFIR for September 1823, AGO:RT, M655, roll 1.

22. Calhoun to Gaines, August 14, 1823, ASP:MA, 2:581; Col. Henry Leavenworth to Atkinson, August 20, 1823, Doane Robinson, ed., "Official Correspondence Pertaining to the Leavenworth Expedition of 1823 into South Dakota for the Conquest of the Ree Indians," SDHC 1 (1902): 196–200.

23. Atkinson to Gaines, September 13, 1823, ASP:MA, 2:594–95; Roger L. Nichols, *General Henry Atkinson: A Western Military Career* (Norman: Univ. of Oklahoma Press, 1965), 86–87; Order no. 2, January 12, 1824, USACC: Western, Atkinson Orders, vol. 43.

24. Proceedings of a General Court-Martial Held at Fort Belle Fontaine, June 7, 1824, JAG: Courts-Martial, box 14, case file H-42; Dwight L. Clarke, *Stephen Watts Kearny: Soldier of the West* (Norman: Univ. of Oklahoma Press, 1961), 36–37, 73–75; Coffman, *Old Army,* 57, 66–67; Skelton, *Profession,* 51–59.

25. Proceedings of a General Court-Martial Held at Fort Belle Fontaine, August 26, 1824, JAG: Courts-Martial, box 2, case file A-80; Atkinson Order, September 1, 1824, USACC: Western, Atkinson Orders, vol. 43; Coffman, *Old Army,* 190–91.

3. Boatman, Woodsman, Indian Fighter

1. Journal of Stephen Watts Kearny, September 17–19, 1824, Stephen Watts Kearny Papers (hereafter Kearny Journal); RRFIR for September 1824, AGO:RT, M665, roll 1; Clarke, *Kearny*, 26–28; Roger L. Nichols, "Army Contributions to River Transportation, 1818–1825," MA 33 (April 1969): 245–46.

2. Atkinson to Gaines, August 19, September 13, 1823, ASP:MA, 2:582, 594–95; ARSW for 1824, ASP:MA, 2:689–99; Nichols, *Atkinson*, 87–91; *Statutes at Large*, 4:35–36.

3. Kearny Journal, September 20, 23, 24, 28, October 3, 10, 25, 31, 1824; Clarke, *Kearny*, 26–28.

4. Kearny Journal, October 26, 1824; Atkinson to Nourse, December 16, 1824, AGO:LS, M567, roll 9; Order no. 2, April 23, 1825, USACC: Western, Atkinson Orders, vol. 43.

5. Harney to Jackson, January 3, 1825, AJ, microfilm, series 1, roll 33.

6. Order no. 6, May 15, 1825, USACC: Western, Atkinson Orders, vol. 43; Henry Atkinson and Benjamin O'Fallon, "Journal of the Atkinson–O'Fallon Expedition," ed. Russell Reid and Clell G. Gannon, *North Dakota Historical Quarterly* 4 (October 1929): 10–11, entries for May 16–17, 1825 (hereafter Atkinson–O'Fallon Journal).

7. Atkinson–O'Fallon Journal, May 19, 21, 23, 25–26, 28–29, June 1, 1825; Kearny Journal, May 19, 23–24, 26, 28, June 4, 1825.

8. Atkinson–O'Fallon Journal, June 8, 1825; Kearny Journal, June 8, 1825; Atkinson and O'Fallon to James Barbour, November 7, 1825, ASP:IA, 2:605–9.

9. Atkinson–O'Fallon Journal, June 9, 1825; Kearny Journal, June 9, 1825; *Laws and Treaties*, 2:225–27; Raymond J. DeMallie, "Touching the Pen: Plains Indian Treaty Councils in Ethnohistorical Perspective," in Frederick C. Luebke, ed., *Ethnicity on the Great Plains* (Lincoln: Univ. of Nebraska Press, 1980), 38–53; Francis Paul Prucha, *American Indian Treaties: The History of a Political Anomaly* (Berkeley: Univ. of California Press, 1994), 208–34.

10. Atkinson–O'Fallon Journal, June 10, 1825; Kearny Journal, June 10, 1825; *Laws and Treaties*, 2:225–27.

11. Atkinson–O'Fallon Journal, June 14–15, 17–23, 1825; Kearny Journal, June 17, 1825; *Laws and Treaties*, 2:227–30; Henry Atkinson, "General Henry Atkinson's

Report of the Yellowstone Expedition of 1825," ed. Roger L. Nichols, NH 44 (June 1963): 70.

12. Kearny Journal, June 30, July 4, 1825; Atkinson–O'Fallon Journal, July 4, 16–18, 1825.

13. Kearny Journal, July 18, 20, 26, August 4, 1825; Atkinson–O'Fallon Journal, July 26–August 6, 1825; Atkinson and O'Fallon to Barbour, November 7, 1825, ASP:IA, 2:605–9; *Laws and Treaties*, 2:239–46; Nichols, *Atkinson*, 102–4.

14. UD, November 30, 1867; Reavis, *Harney*, 64–67; William B. Skelton, "Army Officers' Attitudes toward Indians, 1830–1860," *Pacific Northwest Quarterly* 67 (July 1976): 115–18.

15. Atkinson–O'Fallon Journal, August 6, 17, 20, 24–27, 1825; Richard M. Clokey, *William H. Ashley: Enterprise and Politics in the Trans-Mississippi West* (Norman: Univ. of Oklahoma Press, 1980), 164.

16. Atkinson–O'Fallon Journal, August 27–28, September 13–14, 1825; Kearny Journal, September 13–14, 1825.

17. Kearny Journal, September 19, 23, 1825; Atkinson–O'Fallon Journal, September 20, 1825; *Laws and Treaties*, 2:225–46, 256–62; Atkinson, "General Henry Atkinson's Report of the Yellowstone Expedition of 1825," 80–81; Army Register for 1826, ASP:MA, 2:203.

18. Kearny Journal, September 23, 1825, May 2, July 10, 1826; RRFIR for May to December, 1826, January to April, 1827, AGO:RT, M665, roll 1; Benjamin Harney to SW, April 23, 1827, AGO: Surgeons' Papers; Reavis, *Harney*, 68–69.

19. Lewis Cass to Barbour, July 10, 1827, TP, 11:1101–4; Col. Josiah Snelling to Atkinson, May 31, 1827, TP, 11:1082–83; *Laws and Treaties*, 2:74–77, 207–8, 268–73; ARSW for 1826, ASP:MA, 3:330.

20. John Marsh to Cass, July 4, 1827, TP, 11:1096–97; Cass to Barbour, July 10, 1827, TP, 11:1101–4; Peter L. Scanlan, *Prairie du Chien: French, British, American* (Mensasha WI: George Banta, 1937), 129–31; Nichols, *Atkinson*, 119–26.

21. RRFIR for August, September, 1827, AGO:RT, M665, roll 1; Nichols, *Atkinson*, 126–36; Thomas L. McKenney, "The Winnebago War of 1827," CSHSW 5 (1907): 178–83; Barbour to Gaines, TP, October 9, 1827, 1:1118.

22. RRFIR for September, November, 1827, January, 1828, AGO:RT, M665, roll 1; Harney to Brown, December 25, 1827, AGO:LR, M567, roll 20.

23. Thomas L. McKenney to Barbour, January 24, 1828, TP, 11:1157–58; ARSW for

1828, *ASP:MA*, 4:4–6; Maj. Gen. Alexander Macomb Order no. 44, August 19, 1828, quoted in Andrew Jackson Turner, "The History of Fort Winnebago," *CSHSW* 14 (1898): 71; RRFIR for March, April, July 1828, AGO:RT, M665, roll 1.

24. Maj. David E. Twiggs to Brig. Gen. Winfield Scott, October 7, 1828, AGO:LR, M567, roll 40; Twiggs to Scott, November 2, 1828, AGO:LR, M567, roll 32; Twiggs to Atkinson, December 29, 1828, quoted in Turner, "Fort Winnebago," 72–73; Francis Paul Prucha, *The Sword of the Republic: The United States Army on the Frontier, 1783–1846* (New York: Macmillan, 1968), 174–78.

25. Reavis, *Harney*, 74–75; Milo M. Quaife, "The Northwestern Career of Jefferson Davis," *Transactions of the Illinois State Historical Society* 30 (1923): 61; RRFIR for October 1829, July 1830, June 1831, AGO:RT, M665, roll 1; Satterlee Clark, "Early Times at Fort Winnebago, and Black Hawk War Reminiscences," *CSHSW* 8 (1879): 311.

26. Mrs. John H. Kinzie, *Wau-Bun: The "Early Day" in the North-West* (New York: Derby & Jackson, 1856), 29–30, 41–42, 121–22.

27. Affidavit of Juliette Grignou, October 5, 1838, roll 41, Affidavit of Robert Grignou and Alexander Grignou, September 28, 1838; roll 41, Charles H. Stewart to Simon Cameron and James Murray, October 18, 1838, roll 42, and John S. Hosmer to John Flemming, August 31, 1839, roll 41, all in Documents Related to Winnebago Claims, Territorial Papers of the United States, Territory of Wisconsin, 1836–1848, special files, BIA (Part 4), M236; T. Hartley to SW, March 21, 1840, TP, 38:164–68; *Laws and Treaties*, 2:345–48; Coffman, *Old Army*, 106–7; Sherry L. Smith, *The View from Officers' Row: Army Perceptions of Western Indians* (Tucson: Univ. of Arizona Press, 1990), 78–91; Sherry L. Smith, "Beyond Princess and Squaw: Army Officers' Perceptions of Indian Women," in *The Women's West*, ed. Susan Armitage and Elizabeth Jameson (Norman: Univ. of Oklahoma Press, 1987), 64–65, 69–74.

28. Jefferson Davis to Reavis, January 1878, in Reavis, *Harney*, iv.

29. Clark, "Early Times," 310–11; Reavis, *Harney*, 75–76.

30. Harney to Davis, March 15, 1879, Jefferson Davis Papers.

31. *Laws and Treaties*, 2:74–77; William T. Hagan, *The Sac and Fox Indians* (Norman: Univ. of Oklahoma Press, 1958), 92–105, 114–34; Gaines to Hugh L. White, July 6, 1831, ARSW for 1831, 22 Cong. 1 sess., HED 2, serial 216, pp. 186–89; Gaines to Maj. John Bliss, July 3, 1831, USACC: Western, LS, vol. 5; RRFIR for June, 1831,

AGO:RT, M665, roll 1; Prucha, *Sword,* 211–18; Roger L. Nichols, *Black Hawk and the Warrior's Path* (Arlington Heights IL: Harlan Davidson, 1972), 98–100.

32. Robert Stuart to SW, February 9, 1830, TP, 12:125–26; Col. Zachary Taylor to Gaines, May 14, 1830, AGO:LR, M567, roll 56; Joseph M. Street to William Clark, August 1, 1831, and Lawrence Taliaferro to Clark, August 8, 1831, both in ARSW for 1831, 22 Cong. 1 sess., HED 2, serial 216, pp. 192–93, 198; Hagan, *Sac and Fox,* 115–17; Patricia K. Ourada, *The Menominee Indians: A History* (Norman: Univ. of Oklahoma Press, 1979), 89–91.

33. "Journal of a Council Held with the Chiefs and Warriors of the Sac and Fox Indians at Fort Armstrong, on September 5, 1831," ARSW for 1831, 22 Cong. 1 sess., HED 2, serial 216, pp. 202–4; Donald Jackson, ed., *Ma-Ka-Tai-Me-She-Kia-Kiak: Black Hawk, an Autobiography* (Urbana: Univ. of Illinois Press, 1955), 115–17; Hagan, *Sac and Fox,* 136–39; Nichols, *Black Hawk,* 103–15; Anthony F. C. Wallace, "Prelude to Disaster: The Course of Indian-White Relations Which Led to the Black Hawk War of 1832," *Wisconsin Magazine of History* 65 (summer 1982): 276–85.

34. Macomb to Atkinson, March 17, 1832, AGO:LS, M565, roll 8; Hagan, *Sac and Fox,* 144–45; Prucha, *Sword,* 219.

35. Nichols, *Atkinson,* 157–61; Atkinson to Macomb, April 10, 1831, AGO:LR, M567, roll 66; Atkinson to Gaines, April 18, 1832, ALB, BHW.

36. Atkinson to John Reynolds, April 13, 1832, ALB, BHW; Atkinson to Macomb, April 27, 1832, AGO:LR, M567, roll 66; Jackson, *Black Hawk,* 121–22; Nichols, *Atkinson,* 157–61.

37. Atkinson Orders no. 8 and no. 9, May 8, 1832, and Atkinson Order no. 13, May 9, 1832, all in AOB, BHW; Albert Sidney Johnston Black Hawk War Diary, May 9, 15, 1832, MMBC.

38. Atkinson Order no. 12, May 9, 1832, AOB, Gen. Samuel Whiteside to Atkinson, May 12, 1832, ALB, and Whiteside to Atkinson, May 18, 1832, ALB, all in BHW.

39. Lucius Lyon to Micajah T. Williams, May 18, 1832, TP, 12:478; Nichols, *Atkinson,* 163–65.

40. Atkinson Orders no. 11 and no. 12, May 22, 1832, AOB, Atkinson to Macomb and Gaines, May 23, 1832, ALB, all in BHW; Whiteside to Atkinson, May 27, 1832, AGO:LR, M567, roll 66.

41. Atkinson to Reynolds, May 25, May 29, 1832; Atkinson to Macomb, May 30,

June 23, 1832, all in ALB, BHW; Phillip St. George Cooke, *Scenes and Adventures in the Army; or, Romance of Military Life* (Philadelphia: Lindsay & Blakiston, 1857), 157–58; John K. Mahon, "Militia in the Black Hawk War, 1831–1832," *Indiana Military Historical Journal* 8 (May 1983): 4–11.

42. Reavis, *Harney*, 84; Alfred Augustus Jackson, "Abraham Lincoln in the Black Hawk War," CSHSW 14 (1898): 118–37.

43. ARSW for 1832, ASP:MA, 5:18–25; Taylor to Atkinson, June 9, 1832, ALB, BHW; Jackson, *Black Hawk*, 133.

44. Atkinson to Macomb, June 15, 1832, AGO:LR, M567, roll 66; Atkinson to Scott, July 9, 1832, ALB, BHW.

45. Robert Anderson, "Reminiscences of the Black Hawk War," CSHSW 10 (1888): 170; Atkinson to Harney, July 11, 1832, and Atkinson to Scott, July 11, 1832, ALB, BHW; Johnston Diary, July 12, 1832, MMBC; ARSW for 1832, ASP:MA, 5:29–33; Nichols, *Black Hawk*, 130–32.

46. Atkinson to Scott, July 27, 1832, ALB, BHW; Johnston Diary, July 19, 1832, MMBC; Cooke, *Scenes and Adventures in the Army*, 179.

47. Atkinson to Scott, August 5, 9, 1832, ALB, BHW; Cooke, *Scenes and Adventures in the Army*, 178–79; Jackson, *Black Hawk*, 137–38; Hagan, *Sac and Fox*, 171–95; Nichols, *Atkinson*, 171–75; Skelton, "Army Officers' Attitudes," 121; S. Smith, *View from Officers' Row*, 71–72.

---

4. That Infernal Pay Department

1. Harney to Maj. Thomas J. Beall, September 10, 1832, AGO:LR, M567, roll 72; Harney to Atkinson, January 9, 1833, USACC: Western, LR by General Atkinson, box 2; Special Order no. 35, March 15, 1833, AGO:SO, vol. 3; Reavis, *Harney*, 90.

2. William E. Parrish, ed., *A History of Missouri* (Columbia: Univ. of Missouri Press, 1971–), vol. 2, *1820–1860*, Perry McCandless (1972), 131–37, 170–84; Edwin C. McReynolds, *Missouri: A History of the Crossroads State* (Norman: Univ. of Oklahoma Press, 1962), 434–44.

3. Harriett Lane Cates Hardaway, comp., "The Descendants of John Mullanphy: Saint Louis Philanthropist," typescript, MOHS, pp. 1–6, 8, 50–51; Alice Lida Cochran, *The Saga of an Irish Immigrant Family: The Descendants of John Mullanphy* (New York: Arno, 1976), 93–94; interview with John M. Harney, June 26, 1972; Harney to Col. Nathan Towson, October 1, 1834, OPMG:LR, box 211.

4. Army Register for 1833, ASP:MA, 5:143–46, 278; William S. Hamilton to Lewis Cass, February 10, 1833, AGO:LR, M567, roll 83; Towson to Harney, July 23, 1833, OPMG:LS, vol. 19; Reavis, *Harney*, 90; Skelton, *Profession*, 151, 197–98.

5. Annual Reports of the Paymaster General for 1833 and 1834, ASP:MA, 5:219–21, 428–30; Towson to Harney, July 26, 1833, and Receipt for Pay to William S. Harney, October 31, 1833, RGP; William B. Skelton, "The Army Officer as Organization Man," in Garry D. Ryan and Timothy K. Nenninger, eds., *Soldiers and Civilians: The U.S. Army and the American People* (Washington DC: National Archives and Records Administration, 1987), 66–68.

6. Harney Bond, July 10, 1833, OPMG:Bonds, vol. 1; Towson to Harney, July 23, 1833, OPMG:LS, vol. 19; Towson to Harney, July 26, 1833, Receipt for Pay to William S. Harney, October 31, August 31, September 30, 1833, Harney to Towson, November 1, 1833, and Towson to Harney, March 28, 1834, all in RGP.

7. Harney to Towson, November 30, 1833, and Harney Receipts, December 31, 1833, all in RGP; Harney Genealogy, NHB; Harney to Towson, March 10, 1834, OPMG:LR, box 211; Towson to Harney, March 28, 1834, OPMG:LS, vol. 20.

8. Harney to Towson, March 28, 1834, and Towson to Harney, March 28, 1834, both in OPMG:LS, vol. 20; Towson to Harney, March 29, 1834, and John DeMent to Harney, April 27, 1834, both in RGP; Harney to Towson, June 23, 1834, OPMG:LR, box 211.

9. Harney to Towson, April 26, 1834, OPMG:LR, box 211; Towson to Harney, May 12, 1834, RGP; St. Louis County Grand Jury Indictment, July 28, 1834, quoted in George P. Ihrie to Col. Samuel Cooper, July 29, 1860, AGO:LR, M567, roll 609; MR, *June 30, 1834.*

10. James Clemens Jr. to Harney, July 4, 1834, MCC; Clemens to Mary Harney, July 17, 1834, MCC; MR, June 30, 1834; St. Louis County Grand Jury Indictment, July 28, 1834, quoted in Ihrie to Cooper, July 29, 1860, AGO:LR, M567, roll 609; Clemens to Harney, August 1, 13, 1834, MCC.

11. Clemens to Harney, August 13, 1834, MCC; KWH, November 28, 1857; Arthur M. Schlesinger Jr., *The Age of Jackson* (Boston: Little, Brown, 1945), 88–94; Parrish, *Missouri,* 2:92–95.

12. Clemens to Harney, July 4, 1834, MCC; Maj. Timothy P. Andrews to Harney, August 7, 1834, RGP; Clemens to Mary Harney, July 17, 1834, MCC; Harney Bond, August 12, 1834, OPMG: Bonds, vol. 1.

13. Towson to Harney, July 15, 1834, OPMG:LS, vol. 20; Harney to Andrews, August 27, 1834, OPMG:LR, box 211.

14. Clemens to Maj. Richard Graham, September 16, 1834, RGP; Ann Biddle to Dennis Delany, January 3, 1835, MFC; Harney to Towson, October 1, November 19, 1834, OPMG:LR, box 211; Towson to Harney, October 30, 1834, OPMG:LS, vol. 20.

15. Application for Change of Venue, November 4, 1834, and Judge L. E. Lawless Order, November 5, 1834, both quoted in Ihrie to Cooper, July 29, 1860, AGO:LR, M567, roll 609; Harney to Towson, November 16, 1834, OPMG:LR, box 211; Circuit Court Record Book B, pp. 42–44, 20th Missouri Circuit Court, Circuit Clerk's Office, Franklin County.

16. Harney to Towson, November 19, December 28, 1834, both in OPMG:LR, box 211; Towson to Harney, December 15, 1834, OPMG:LS, vol. 20.

17. Towson to William B. Lewis, October 1834, RGP; Towson to Lewis, December 13, 20, 1834, OPMG:LS, vol. 20; Harney to Towson, November 16, 1834, OPMG:LR, box 211.

18. Biddle to Delany, February 19, 1835, MFC; W. V. N. Bay, *Reminiscences of the Bench and Bar of Missouri* (St. Louis: F. H. Thomas, 1878), 210–14; Circuit Court Record Book B, pp. 49, 52, 54, 80, 20th Missouri Circuit Court, Circuit Clerk's Office, Franklin County; Harney to Towson, March 19, 1835, OPMG:LR, box 211.

19. Towson to Harney, April 13, 1835, RGP; Towson to Cass, April 13, 1835, OPMG:LS, vol. 20; Harney to Towson, June 14, 18, 1835, OPMG:LR, box 211.

20. Harney to unknown, July 10, 1835, RGP; Skelton, *Profession*, 56, 195; Hardaway, "Descendants," 50.

21. N. Frye to Lewis, August 26, 1835, and Towson to Harney, July 31, 1835, both in OPMG:LS, vol. 20; Harney to Towson, August 15, 1835, OPMG:LR, box 211.

22. Harney to Towson, November 19, 1834, and Harney to Towson, June 28, 1835, both in OPMG:LR, box 211; Hardaway, "Descendants," 1–6.

23. Towson to Harney, July 31, 1835, OPMG:LS, vol. 20; Harney Receipts, August 31, September 19, 1835, and Towson to Harney, November 13, 1835, all in RGP; Harney to Towson, February 11, 1836, OPMG:LR, box 211.

24. Hardaway, "Descendants," 52; Harney to Towson, February 11, 1836, OPMG:LR, box 211; Harney to Thomas Harney, January 13, 1850, WSH; Harney to SW, April 1, 1836, AGO:LR, M567, roll 124.

25. Lewis F. Linn to President, May 17, 1836, AGO:LR, M567, roll 124; Theophilus

Rodenbough, *From Everglade to Cañon with the Second Dragoons* (New York: D. Van Nostrand, 1875), 17–19; *Statutes at Large*, 5:32–33; Jones to Twiggs, June 9, 1836, AGO:LS, M565, roll 9.

26. Towson to Harney, July 8, 1836, RGP; Harney to Towson, July 26, 1836, OPMG:LR, box 211; Jackson to Harney, August 15, 1836, AGO:LR, M567, roll 125; Reavis, *Harney,* 91.

27. Harney to Towson, August 16, October 6, 25, 1836, all in OPMG:LR, box 211.

28. John Mullanphy, *Last Will and Testament, February 27, 1830, with Alterations and Additions, November 23, 1831, July 3, 1833* (St. Louis: n.p., n.d.), 14–15; Albion K. Parris to Towson, November 8, November 22, 1838, OPMG;LR, box 211; Harney to Adjutant General, August 20, 1841, AGO:LR, M567, roll 231.

29. Army Register for 1837, ASP:MA, 5:1014–15; William B. Skelton, "Officers and Politicians: The Origins of Army Politics in the United States before the Civil War," AFS 6 (fall 1979): 29–33.

---

5. War to the Rope

1. Harney to Col. Roger Jones, January 27, 1837, and Col. Alexander Fanning to Jones, February 9, 1837, both in AGO:LR, M567, roll 144; Fanning to Jesup, February 12, 1837, ASP:MA, 7:831; Capt. John R. Vinton to Jones, March 25, 1837, AGO: Generals' Papers, Jesup, 1818–1838, LR, box 4; Reavis, *Harney,* 101; Edward W. Callahan, ed., *List of Officers of the Navy of the United States and of the Marine Corps from 1771–1900* (New York: L. R. Hamersly, 1901), 371. Wherever possible, spellings for Seminole names are taken from William A. Reed, *Florida Place Names of Indian Origin and Seminole Personal Names* (Baton Rouge: Louisiana State Univ. Press, 1934).

2. William B. Skelton, "Professionalization in the U.S. Army Officer Corps during the Age of Jackson," AFS 1 (August 1974): 455–62; James M. Denham, "Some Prefer the Seminoles: Violence and Disorder among Soldiers and Settlers in the Second Seminole War, 1835–1842," FHQ 70 (July 1991): 38–40; Samuel J. Watson, "Professionalism, Social Attitudes, and Civil–Military Accountability in the United States Officer Corps, 1815–1846" (Ph.D. diss., Rice University, 1996), 1184–95.

3. Rodenbough, *Second Dragoons,* 21–24; General Order no. 38, June 15, 1836, quoted in Rodenbough, *Second Dragoons,* 20–21; Jones to Twiggs, November 26, 1836, AGO:LS, M565, roll 10.

4. Jones to Brig. Gen. Thomas S. Jesup, December 31, 1836, AGO:LS, M565, roll 10; Harney to Jones, January 27, 1837, AGO:LR, M565, roll 143; Sidney Walter Martin, *Florida during the Territorial Days* (Athens: Univ. of Georgia Press, 1944), 181–85; John K. Mahon, *History of the Second Seminole War, 1835–1842* (Gainesville: Univ. of Florida Press, 1967), 109, 199.

5. Mahon, *Second Seminole War,* 138, 161–65, 186–87, 199, 325–26.

6. Mahon, *Second Seminole War,* 18–28, 30–31, 71–72; Edwin C. McReynolds, *The Seminoles* (Norman: Univ. of Oklahoma Press, 1957), 23, 48, 107, 115–16; Francis Paul Prucha, *The Great Father: The United States Government and the American Indians* (Lincoln: Univ. of Nebraska Press, 1984), 1:229–33; Kenneth W. Porter, "Negroes and the Seminole War, 1835–1842," *Journal of Southern History* 30 (November 1964): 427–50.

7. *Laws and Treaties,* 2:203–5; *Statutes at Large,* 4:411–12; Francis Paul Prucha, *American Indian Policy in the Formative Years: The Indian Trade and Intercourse Acts, 1790–1834* (Cambridge MA: Harvard University Press, 1962), 224–49; Ronald N. Satz, *American Indian Policy in the Jacksonian Era* (Lincoln: Univ. of Nebraska Press, 1975), 9–31.

8. Mahon, *Second Seminole War,* 69–86; *Laws and Treaties,* 2:344–45, 394–95; W. S. Croffut, ed., *Fifty Years in Camp and Field: Diary of Major Ethan Allen Hitchcock, U.S.A.* (New York: G. P. Putnam's Sons, 1909), 80–82.

9. Mahon, *Second Seminole War,* 69–86, 94–95, 99–107; Jackson Endorsement on Wiley Thompson to Elbert Herring, October 24, 1834, TP, 25:58–63; Bvt. Brig. Gen. Duncan L. Clinch to Jones, January 22, 1835, TP, 25:182–84; "Causes of Hostilities of Creek and Seminole Indians in Florida," ASP:MA, 6:561–62.

10. Mahon, *Second Seminole War,* 108–12, 136–68, 173–90; Benjamin F. Butler to Jesup, November 4, 1836, TP, 35:341–43; Lewis Cass to Martin Van Buren, March 8, 1836, AGO:LS, M565, roll 9.

11. Jesup to Butler, January 20, 1837, AGO:LR, M567, roll 144; Mahon, *Second Seminole War,* 190, 195–99; Fanning to Jones, February 9, 1837, AGO:LR, M567, roll 141.

12. Jesup to Butler, February 17, 1837, AGO: Generals' Papers, Jesup, 1818–1838, LR, box 4; "Capitulation of the Seminole Nation of Indians and Their Allies," ASP:MA, 7:834; Jesup to Jones, March 18, 1837, TP, 25:381–82.

13. Jesup to Col. Ichabod B. Crane, February 22, 1837, Jesup to Harney, March 15, 25, 1837, Jesup to Butler, March 15, 1837, and Lt. James A. Chambers to Harney, March 19, 1837, all in AGO: Generals' Papers, Jesup, LS, book 3.

14. Jesup to Harney, April 8, 26, 1837, AGO:LR, M567, roll 144; Jesup to Joel R. Poinsett, April 9, 1837, TP, 25:385–87; Jesup to Gen. Walker K. Armistead, April 15, 1837, AGO: Generals' Papers, Jesup, LS, book 3.

15. Chambers to Armistead, May 1, 1837, AGO: Generals' Papers, Jesup, LS, book 3; Harney to Jesup, May 1837, ASP:MA, 7:870–71; Jesup to Harney, April 26, 1837, AGO:LR, M567, roll 144; Skelton, "Army Officers' Attitudes," 113–24.

16. Jesup to Harney, May 11, 25, 1837, AGO: Generals' Papers, Jesup, LS, book 4; Harney to Jesup, May 1837, ASP:MA, 7:870–71; Hezekiah L. Thistle to David Henshaw, July 30, 1837, TP, 26:691–98.

17. Jesup to Jones, June 5, 1837, and Jesup to Macomb, June 28, 1837, both in AGO: Generals' Papers, Jesup, LS, book 4; Jesup to Nourse, July 11, 1837, AGO: Generals' Papers, Jesup, LS, book 5; Jesup to Poinsett, June 7, 15, 1837, ASP:MA, 7, 871–74; Poinsett to Jesup, July 25, 1837, ASP:MA, 7, 811–12.

18. Jesup to Harney, June 2, 1837, AGO: Generals' Papers, Jesup, LS, book 4; General Order no. 156, July 25, 1837, AGO: Generals' Papers, Jesup, Orders Issued from Headquarters Army of the South; Jacob Rhett Motte, *Journey into Wilderness: An Army Surgeon's Account of Life in Camp and Field during the Creek and Seminole Wars, 1836–1838,* ed. James F. Sunderman (Gainesville: Univ. of Florida Press, 1953), 112–13.

19. Capt. Julius A. de'Lagnal to Capt. Charles G. Merchant, August 16, 1837, AGO: General's Papers, Jesup, LS, book 6; Reavis, *Harney,* 117–18; Jones to Harney, October 3, 1837, AGO:LS, M565, roll 10.

20. Mahon, *Second Seminole War,* 214–18; Mark F. Boyd, "Asi-Yahola or Osceola," FHQ 33 (January and April 1955): 249–305; Jesup to Linn, August 29, 1842, in Reavis, *Harney,* 474–75.

21. Jesup to Poinsett, June 15, 1837, ASP:MA, 7:872–74; Jesup to Bvt. Brig. Gen. Abraham Eustis, October 29, 1837, AGO: Generals' Papers, Jesup, LS, book 6; Harney to Jesup, November 14, 1837, AGO: Generals' Papers, Jesup, LR, box 9; Mahon, *Second Seminole War,* 156, 219–20, 225–26.

22. Memorandum of Articles Required for an Advanced Depot, January 2, 1838, Jesup to Harney, December 25, 1837, and Jesup to Jones, December 30, 1837, all in AGO: Generals' Papers, Jesup, LS, book 7; General Order no. 43, December 24, 1837, AGO: Generals' Papers, Jesup, Orders Issued from Headquarters Army of the South.

23. Taylor to Jones, January 4, 1838, ASP:MA, 7:985–92; Holman Hamilton, *Za-*

chary Taylor: Soldier of the Republic (Indianapolis: Bobbs-Merrill, 1941), 128–34; Mahon, *Second Seminole War*, 226–30, 233.

24. Jesup to Jones, January 26, 1838, and Harney to Twiggs, January 25, 1838, both in AGO:LR, M567, roll 167; Rodenbough, *Second Dragoons*, 30.

25. Jesup to Poinsett, July 6, 1838, in John T. Sprague, *The Origin, Progress, and Conclusion of the Florida War* (1848; reprint, Gainesville: Univ. of Florida Press, 1964), 183–97; Jesup to Poinsett, February 11, 1838, Sprague, *Origin*, 199–201; Poinsett to Jesup, March 1, 1838, Sprague, *Origin*, 201–2; Jesup Memorandum, n.d., Thomas Sidney Jesup Papers, box 11, LC.

26. Jesup to Poinsett, July 6, 1838, in Sprague, *Origin*, 183–97; Skelton, *Profession*, 194–95, 200.

27. Jesup to Taylor, March 30, 1838, and Jesup to Jones, March 31, 1838, both in AGO: Generals' Papers, Jesup, LS, book 8; Lt. Richard H. Peyton to Jesup, July 11, 1838, AGO: Generals' Papers, Jesup, LR, box 2; Harney to Jesup, March 4, 1838, AGO: Generals' Papers, Jesup, LR, box 9; Special Order no. 30, March 27, 1838, AGO: Generals' Papers, Jesup, Orders Issued from Headquarters Army of the South; M. L. Brown, "Notes on U.S. Arsenals, Depots, and Martial Firearms of the Second Seminole War," FHQ 61 (April 1983): 447–48.

28. Harney to Jesup, April 4, 1838, AGO: Generals' Papers, Jesup, LR, box 9; Motte, *Journey*, 220–22; Skelton, *Profession*, 210–12.

29. Harney to Jesup, April 4, 6, 1838, and Harney to Twiggs, April 12, 15, 17, 1838, all in AGO: Generals' Papers, Jesup, LR, box 9; Jesup to Harney, AGO: Generals' Papers, Jesup, LS, book 8; Motte, *Journey*, 229.

30. Harney to Jesup, April 25, 1838, AGO: Generals' Papers, Jesup, LR, box 9; Motte, *Journey*, 230–35.

31. Harney to Jesup, April 25, 30, 1838, AGO: Generals' Papers, Jesup, LR, box 9; Motte, *Journey*, 235–37.

32. Order no. 118, Jesup, May 14, 1838, and Order no. 43, Taylor, July 18, 1838, both in USACC: Ninth, Orders Issued, vol. 2; Capt. Joseph H. LaMotte to Harney, July 16, 1838, AGO:LR, M567, roll 177; Mahon, *Second Seminole War*, 245–49.

33. Jones to Twiggs, August 6, 1838, AGO:LS, M565, roll 10; Twiggs to Jones, August 28, 1838, AGO:LR, M567, roll 177; Hardaway, "Descendents," 52.

34. SAN, December 15, 1838, January 12, 1839; Poinsett to Macomb, March 18, 1839, TP, 25:597–99; Mahon, *Second Seminole War*, 247–54; William B. Skelton, "The

Commanding General and the Problem of Command in the United States Army, 1821–1841," MA 34 (December 1970): 117–21.

35. Macomb to Poinsett, May 22, 1839, in Sprague, *Origin*, 229–32; Macomb to Harney, April 6, 1839, HQA:LS, M587, roll 2; Entries, April 5, 6, May 7–18, 22, 1839, in John T. Sprague, "Macomb's Mission to the Seminoles: John T. Sprague's Journal Kept during April and May, 1839," ed. Frank F. White Jr., FHQ 35 (October 1956): 144–46, 176–81, 183–87; Washington *Globe*, May 30, 1839; SAN, June 1, 1839.

36. Macomb to Poinsett, May 22, 1839, in Sprague, *Origin*, 229–32; SAN, May 25 and June 1, 15, 18, 1839; *Tallahassee Floridian*, June 1, 25, 22, 1839.

37. Macomb to Taylor, May 19, 1839, and Lt. Edmund Schriver to Taylor, May 24, 1839, both in AGO:LS, M565, roll 11; Harney to Macomb, July 15, 1839, AGO:LR, M567, roll 189; Harney to Francis L. Dancy, August 1, 1839, in Rodenbough, *Second Dragoons*, 38–39.

38. Harney to Dancy, August 1, 1839, in Rodenbough, *Second Dragoons*, 38–39; James B. Dallam to Francis J. Dallam, June 18, 1839, in William D. Hoyt Jr., ed., "A Soldier's View of the Seminole War: Three Letters of James B. Dallam," FHQ 25 (April 1946): 360–61.

39. Harney to Macomb, August 7, 1839, AGO:LR, M567, roll 189; Harney to Dancy, August 1, 1839, in Rodenbough, *Second Dragoons*, 38–39; Sergeant Haygood's Recollection, in Rodenbough, *Second Dragoons*, 504–5; *Niles' Weekly Register*, August 24, 1839.

40. LWT, June 25, 1858; Harney to Macomb, August 7, October 20, 1839; Harney to Taylor, August 20, 1839, all in AGO:LR, M567, roll 189; Harney to Dancy, August 1, 1839, in Rodenbough, *Second Dragoons*, 38–39.

41. SAN, August 3, 1839; Macomb to Taylor, October 17, 1839, TP, 25:643–44; James M. Covington, "Cuban Bloodhounds and the Seminoles," FHQ 33 (October 1954): 112–19.

42. Harney to Macomb, August 7, 1839, Harney to Taylor, August 15, 1839, Harney to Capt. George H. Griffen, September 12, 1839, Lt. Christopher Q. Thompkins to Harney, September 29, 1839, and Harney to Griffen, September 30, 1839, all in AGO:LR, M567, roll 189; Comdr. Isaac Mayo to James K. Paulding, September 17, 1839, TP, 25:634–35.

43. Harney to Griffen, September 30, 1839, AGO:LR, M567, roll 189.

44. Robert Fitzpatrick and William Wyatt to Col. William J. Worth, July 9, 1842, *tp*, 26:508–10; George E. Buker, *Swamp Sailors: Riverine Warfare in the Everglades, 1835–1842* (Gainesville: Univ. Presses of Florida, 1975), 47–48, 69–70, 92, 97–99; Skelton, *Profession*, 215, 221–22, 254–57, 318–20; Coffman, *Old Army*, 256–58.

45. Harney to Macomb, November 15, 1839, AGO:LR, M567, roll 189; Harney to Jones, January 2, 1840, AGO:LR, M567, roll 209; Jones to Maj. Benjamin F. Harney, August 22, 1840, AGO:LS, M565, roll 11; Order no. 6, December 5, 1840, USACC: Ninth, Orders and Special Orders Issued, vol. 2; SAN, December 5, 1839, May 20, 1840; Reavis, *Harney*, 147–48.

46. Armistead to Jones, May 18, 1840, USACC: Ninth, LS, vol. 1; Harney to Lt. Robert C. Ashton, June 5, 1840; Harney to Twiggs, June 26, 1840, and Capt. William W. S. Bliss to Harney, July 18, 1840, all in AGO:LR, M567, roll 201; Mahon, *Second Seminole War*, 274–76.

47. Order no. 23, Armistead, USACC: Ninth, Orders and Special Orders Issued, vol. 2; Lt. Comdr. John T. McLaughlin to Paulding, August 11, 1840, *tp*, 26:194–95; Jeanne Bellemy, ed., "The Perrines at Indian Key, Florida, 1838–1840," *Tequesta* 7 (1947): 73–78.

48. Bliss to Harney, November 10, 1840, roll 202, Bliss to Harney, December 6, 1840, roll 202, Harney to Bliss, December 29, 1840, roll 222, and Harney to SW, February 1, 1841, roll 230, all in AGO:LR, M567.

49. Harney to Bliss, December 29, 1840, AGO:LR, M567, roll 222; Anonymous, "Notes on the Passage across the Everglades," *Tequesta* 20 (1960): 57–65.

50. Harney to Bliss, December 24, 1840, AGO:LR, M567, roll 202; Harney to Bliss, December 29, 1840, AGO:LR, M567, roll 222; Anonymous, "Notes," 57–65; William C. Sturtevant, "Chakaika and the 'Spanish Indians': Documentary Sources Compared with Seminole Tradition," *Tequesta* 13 (1953): 50–55.

51. SAN, January 1, 1841; Bliss to Harney, December 30, 1840, AGO:LR, M567, roll 202; Poinsett to Armistead, February 1, 1840, *tp*, 26:250–51.

52. Bliss to Harney, December 30, 1840, AGO:LR, M567, roll 202; Harney to Bliss, January 22, 1841, AGO:LR, roll 230; SAN, April 2, 1841; Buker, *Swamp Sailors*, 98–104, 110–18, 124–37.

53. Armistead to Poinsett, January 16, 1841, AGO:LR, M567, roll 222; Message of John Tyler, May 10, 1842, in Sprague, *Origin*, 475–77; Order no. 18, August 14, 1843, in Sprague, *Origin*, 486; Mahon, *Second Seminole War*, 285–87, 297–309, 321.

54. Maj. Lorenzo Thomas Endorsement on David Levy to John C. Spencer, February 13, 1842, AGO:LR, M567, roll 252; Harney to Adjutant General, August 20, 1841, AGO:LR, M567, roll 231; Harney to Adjutant General, January 15, 1842, AGO:LR, M567, roll 252; Special Order no. 15, February 20, 1841, Armistead, USACC: Ninth, Orders and Special Orders Issued, vol. 2; Special Order no. 57, July 13, 1842, AGO: Orders, vol. 4.

55. SAN, January 29, 1841; Macomb to Poinsett, February 27, 1841, AGO:LR, M567, roll 233; Bliss to Thomas, May 10, 1841, USACC: Ninth, LS, vol. 1; Kearny to Maj. Ethan Allen Hitchcock, May 6, 1841, Hitchcock Collection.

---

6. The Road to Mexico City

1. Proceedings of a General Court-Martial Held at Fort Smith, June 2, 1845, JAG: Courts-Martial, case file EE-112; John D. Billings, *Hardtack and Coffee; or, The Unwritten Story of Army Life* (1887; reprint, Williamstown MA: Corner House, 1973), 143–57; Skelton, *Profession*, 270–73.

2. Harney to Adjutant General, December 11, 1841, AGO:LR, M567, roll 231; Harney to Adjutant General, January 15, 1842, and Endorsement, May 27, 1842, on Harney to Samuel Cooper, May 14, 1842, both in AGO:LR, M567, roll 252; William Clark Kennerly, *Persimmon Hill: A Narrative of Old St. Louis and the Far West* (Norman: Univ. of Oklahoma Press, 1948), 81, 178–80; Antoinette Douglas Schmitz, "Our Florissant," MHSB 24 (January 1968): 153–54.

3. Harney to Jones, March 19, 1842, and Harney to Cooper, May 14, 1842, June 16, 1842, all in AGO:LR, M567, roll 252; Jones to Harney, July 13, 1842, AGO:LS, M565, roll 12; Special Order no. 57, July 13, 1842, AGO:SO, vol. 4; *Statutes at Large*, 5:512–13.

4. Linn to John C. Spencer, May 27, 1842, AGO:LR, M567, roll 252; Benjamin F. Harney to Henry L. Heiskell, May 25, October 12, 1842, AGO: Surgeons' Papers, Personal Papers of Surgeons; Harney to Jones, June 12, 1842, AGO:LR, M567, roll 270; ARSW for 1841, 27 Cong. 2 sess., HED 2, serial 401, pp. 59–60; Rodenbough, *Second Dragoons*, 83–84.

5. George Croghan, *Army Life on the Western Frontier: Selections from the Official Reports Made between 1826 and 1845 by Colonel George Croghan*, ed. Francis Paul Prucha (Norman: Univ. of Oklahoma Press, 1958), 51–52, 68, 132–33; Harney to Jones, July 30, 1843, and Jones to James M. Porter, November 18, 1843, both in AGO:LR, M567, roll 270; Harney to William J. Sloan, September 6, 1844, AGO:LR, M567, roll 291.

6. Proceedings of a General Court-Martial Held at Fort Smith, June 2, 1845, and Lt. Abraham R. Johnston to Capt. James H. Prentiss, August 13, 1844, both in JAG: Courts-Martial, case file EE-112; Harney to Prentiss, January 28, 1845, AGO: Wars, MW, AO, LR, box 1; Coffman, *Old Army*, 197–201; Watson, "Professionalism," 754–87.

7. Skelton, *Profession*, 272; Jones to Gen. Matthew Arbuckle, April 10, 1845, AGO:LS, M565, roll 14; Proceedings of a General Court-Martial Held at Fort Smith, June 2, 1845, and Gaines to Johnston, September 13, 1844, both in AGO: Courts-Martial, case file EE-112.

8. Proceedings of a General Court-Martial Held at Fort Smith, June 2, 1845, AGO: Courts-Martial, case file EE-112; Cooper to Harney, May 12, 1845, and Harney to Jones, July 11, August 4, 1845, all in AGO:LR, M567, roll 299.

9. Lt. Samuel C. Ridgely to "General," August 4, 1845, AGO: Courts-Martial, case file EE-112; General Order no. 39, August 13, 1845, Harney to Lt. Henry H. Sibley, January 19, 1846, Jones Endorsement, February 20, 1846, and James K. Polk Endorsement, February 28, 1846, all in AGO:LR, M567, roll 316; Skelton, *Profession*, 57–58.

10. Justin H. Smith, *The War with Mexico* (1919; reprint, Gloucester MA: Peter Smith, 1963), 1:58–150; K. Jack Bauer, *The Mexican War, 1846–1848* (New York: Macmillan, 1974), 1–80; Thomas R. Hietala, *Manifest Design: Anxious Aggrandizement in Late Jacksonian America* (Ithaca NY: Cornell Univ. Press, 1986), vii–xii, 255–72; Charles G. Sellers, *James K. Polk, Continentalist, 1843–1846* (Princeton NJ: Princeton Univ. Press, 1966), 213–66; David M. Pletcher, *The Diplomacy of Annexation: Texas, Oregon, and the Mexican War* (Columbia: Univ. of Missouri Press, 1973), 1–5; K. Jack Bauer, *Zachary Taylor: Soldier, Planter, Statesman of the Old Southwest* (Baton Rouge: Louisiana State Univ. Press, 1985), 111–29; George Bancroft to Taylor, June 15, 1845, and William L. Marcy to Taylor, July 30, 1845, both in AGO:LS, M565, roll 14; "Message from the President of the United States Relative to an Invasion and Commencement of Hostilities by Mexico," May 11, 1846, 29 Cong. 1 sess., HED 196, serial 485, pp. 7–120.

11. *Statutes at Large*, 5:654–55; Jones to Taylor, August 6, 1845, AGO:LS M565, roll 14; Maj. Thomas T. Flauntleroy to Bliss, October 16, 1845, AGO: Wars, MW, AO, LR, box 1; Maj. John Hays to Harney, December 13, 1845, AGO: Wars, MW, Miscellaneous Papers, box 5; Harney to Maj. William W. S. Bliss, January 19, March 26, August 27, 1846, AGO: Wars, MW, Miscellaneous Papers, box 2; Harney to John F. Darby, July 16, 1841, Darby Papers.

12. ARSW for 1846, 29 Cong. 2 sess., *HED* 4, serial 497, pp. 46–48; J. Smith, *War with Mexico*, 1:190–92; Ivor Debenham Spencer, *The Victor and the Spoils: A Life of William C. Marcy* (Providence RI: Brown Univ. Press, 1959), 153–54; Skelton, *Profession*, 134–35.

13. Robert W. Johannsen, *To the Halls of the Montezumas: The Mexican War in the American Imagination* (New York: Oxford Univ. Press), 16–20, 45–55, 68–77, 108–14, 148–54, 186–89, 219–26; Samuel J. Watson, "The Uncertain Road to Manifest Destiny: Army Officers and the Course of American Territorial Expansion, 1815–1846," in *Manifest Destiny and Empire: American Antebellum Expansionism*, ed. Sam W. Haynes and Christopher Morris (College Station: Texas A&M Univ. Press, 1997), 68–114; Jones to Harney, July 18, 1846, AGO:LS, M565, roll 14; Harney to [Bliss], May 7, 1846, AGO: Wars, MW, AO, LR, box 2; William Elliot, Edward Williams, and twelve others to Harney, June 11, 1846, and William G. Crump, G. S. Wood, and twenty others to Harney, May 2, 1846, both in AGO: Wars, MW, AO, LR, box 4.

14. Harney to Bliss, May 8, 1846, and Harney to J. Pickney Henderson, May 2, 1846, both in AGO: Wars, MW, AO, LR, box 2; Harney to Bliss, July 6, 1846, AGO: Wars, MW, AO, LR, box 4; Henderson to Taylor, May 5, 1846, in Dorman H. Winfrey and James M. Day, eds., *The Indian Papers of Texas and the Southwest, 1825–1916* (1959; reprint, Austin TX: Pemberton Press, 1966), 3:39–40.

15. Harney to Bliss, June 6, 1846, AGO: Wars, MW, AO, LR, box 3; Harney to Bliss, July 24, 1846, and Wool to Taylor, August 15, 1846, both in AGO: Wars, MW, AO, LR, box 4; Taylor to Adjutant General, July 19, 1846, AGO:LR, M567, roll 318; Gen. John E. Wool to Jones, July 26, 1846, AGO:LR, M567, roll 330; J. Smith, *War with Mexico*, 1:166–270; Harwood Perry Hinton, "The Military Career of John Ellis Wool, 1812–1863" (Ph.D. diss., University of Wisconsin, 1960), 181–83.

16. Harney to Bliss, August 12, 1846, Wool to Taylor, August 15, 1846, Harney to Bliss, August 15, 1846, Wool to Taylor, August 18, 1846, and Wool to Taylor, August 23, 1846, all in AGO: Wars, MW, AO, LR, box 4.

17. Wool to Taylor, August 15, 1846, Wool to Taylor, August 18, 1846, and Wool to Harney, August 18, 1846, all in AGO: Wars, MW, AO, LR, box 4; Hinton, "Wool," 183–86.

18. Wool to Taylor, August 15, 24, 1846, AGO: Wars, MW, AO, LR, box 4; Special Order no. 4, August 26, 1846, AGO: Orders, General Wool's Orders, vol. 39; Taylor to Adjutant General, September 3, 1846, AGO:LR, M567, roll 328; Hinton, "Wool," 189–90.

19. Scott Endorsement, June 22, 1846, on Taylor to Adjutant General, June 2, 1846, AGO:LR, M567, roll 327; Taylor to Adjutant General, July 19, 1846, AGO:LR, M567, roll 328; General Order no. 36, August 12, 1846, AGO:GO.

20. Taylor to Adjutant General, October 9, 1846, 29 Cong. 2 sess., HED 4, serial 497, pp. 83–90; J. Smith, *War with Mexico*, 1:284–314, 331–46.

21. Order no. 78, September 24, 1846, and Order no. 88, October 9, 1846, both in AGO: Orders, General Wool's Orders, vol. 39; Wool to Jones, September 28, October 30, 1846, AGO:LR, M567, roll 330.

22. Wool to Jones, October 14, November 4, 1846, AGO:LR, M567, roll 330; ARSW for 1847, 30 Cong. 1 sess., SED 1, serial 503, pp. 46–47.

23. Wool to Taylor, November 1, November 20, 1846, AGO: Wars, MW, Miscellaneous Papers, box 5; Special Order no. 74, November 10, 1846, AGO: Wars, MW, Orders, AO, vol. 1; Adolph Englemann to parents, October 14, 23, 1846, in Otto B. Englemann, trans. and ed., "The Second Illinois in the Mexican War: Mexican War Letters of Adolph Englemann, 1846–1847," *Journal of the Illinois State Historical Society* 26 (April and July 1933): 393, 400–401.

24. Order no. 66, December 2, 1846, Harney to Bliss, December 3, 1846, and "Report upon the Charges against Brigadier John E. Wool," by Lt. Samuel C. Ridgely, January 18, 1847, all in AGO:LR, M567, roll 317.

25. Gen. William O. Butler to Bliss, December 28, 1846, and Order no. 20, December 28, 1846, both in AGO: Wars, MW, Miscellaneous Papers, box 7; Harney to Lt. Irvin McDowell, January 3, 1847, AGO: Wars, MW, Miscellaneous Papers, box 5.

26. ARSW for 1847, 30 Cong. 1 sess., SED 1, serial 503, p. 47; Order no. 23, January 8, 1847, 30 Cong. 1 sess, SED 60, serial 520, pp. 857–60; Taylor to Scott, January 15, 1847, AGO:LR, M567, roll 360; Charles Winslow Elliott, *Winfield Scott: The Soldier and the Man* (New York: Macmillan, 1937), 433–48.

27. Capt. Henry L. Scott to Harney, January 22, 1847, p. 867, Harney to Capt. Scott, January 23, 1847, pp. 867–68, Capt. Scott to Harney, January 24, 1847, p. 868, and Harney to Scott, January 24, 1847, p. 869, all in 30 Cong. 1 sess., HED 60, serial 520.

28. "Charges and Specifications Preferred against Colonel W. S. Harney," p. 870, Capt. Scott to Harney, January 28, 1847, pp. 870–71, and Harney to Capt. Scott, January 28, 1847, pp. 885, all in 30 Cong. 1 sess., HED 60, serial 520.

29. Proceedings of a General Court-Martial Held near the Mouth of the Rio Grande, January 30, 1847, AGO: Courts-Martial, case file EE-323; Capt. Scott to

Capt. William W. Mackall, January 30, 31, 1847, pp. 885, 886–87, and Worth Endorsement, January 24, 1847, on Harney to Capt. Scott, January 23, 1847, all in 30 Cong. 1 sess., HED 60, serial 520, pp. 867–68.

30. Proceedings of a General Court-Martial Held near the Mouth of the Rio Grande, January 30, 1847, AGO: Courts-Martial, case file EE-323; General Order no. 11, February 2, 1847, 30 Cong. 1 sess., HED 60, serial 520, pp. 887–88.

31. Harney to Mackall, February 3, 1847, p. 888, and Capt. Scott to Worth, February 3, 1847, p. 889, both in 30 Cong. 1 sess., HED 60, serial 520; Scott to William L. Marcy, February 4, 1847, AGO:LR, M567, roll 360.

32. Milo Milton Quaife, ed., *The Diary of James K. Polk during His Presidency, 1845–1849* (Chicago: A. C. McClurg, 1910), 2:385; Marcy to Scott, February 22, 1847, 30 Cong. 1 sess., HED 60, serial 520, pp. 874–75; Richard Bruce Winders, *Mr. Polk's Army: The American Military Experience in the Mexican War* (College Station: Texas A&M Univ. Press, 1997), 186–89.

33. Harney to Jones, February 21, 1847, AGO:LR, M567, roll 343; Scott to Marcy, March 12, 18, 1847, 30 Cong. 1 sess., SED 1, serial 503, pp. 216–17, 221–22; K. Jack Bauer, "The Veracruz Expedition of 1847," MA 30 (fall 1956): 162–69; Bauer, *Surfboats and Horse Marines: U.S. Naval Operations in the Mexican War* (Annapolis MD: United States Naval Institute, 1969), 63–82, 263–64; Reavis, *Harney*, 181–82.

34. Col. James Bankhead to Capt. Scott, March 24, 1847, AGO:LR, M567, roll 258; Harney to Capt. Scott, March 24, 1847, 30 Cong. 1 sess., SED 1, serial 503, pp. 250–52; Memorandum of Questions Asked of Ambrosio Valahaho, a Mexican Prisoner, Taken in an Action at the Puenta De Moreno, March 25, 1847, AGO: Wars, MW, Miscellaneous Papers, box 3; Harney to Noble A. Hardee, November 16, 1847, Thomas Butler King Papers; J. Smith, *War with Mexico*, 2:27–39.

35. Harney to Capt. Scott, April 4, 1847, 30 Cong. 1 sess., HED 60, serial 520, pp. 915–16; ARSW for 1847, 30 Cong. 1 sess., SED 1, serial 503, pp. 49–50; Erna Risch, *Quartermaster Support of the Army: A History of the Corps, 1775–1939* (Washington DC: Quartermaster Historian's Office, Office of the Quartermaster General, 1962), 291–93.

36. Harney to Lt. William T. H. Brooks, April 21, 1847, pp. 280–82, and Twiggs to Capt. Scott, April 19, 1847, pp. 274–77, both in 30 Cong. 1 sess., SED 1, serial 503; J. Smith, *War with Mexico*, 2:50–53.

37. Harney to Brooks, April 21, 1847, pp. 280–82, Scott to Marcy, April 19, 1847, pp. 255–59, and Twiggs to Capt. Scott, April 19, 1847, pp. 274–77, all in 30 Cong. 1

sess., *SED* 1, serial 503; J. Smith, *War with Mexico,* 2:51–59; Raphael Semmes, *Afloat and Ashore during the Mexican War* (Cincinnati: Wm. H. Moore, 1851), 177–84; Frederich Zeh, *An Immigrant Soldier in the Mexican War,* trans. William J. Orr, ed. William J. Orr and Robert Ryal Miller (College Station: Texas A&M Univ. Press, 1995), 32–34; [Daniel H. Hill], "Battle of Cerro Gordo," *Southern Quarterly Review* 21 (January 1852): 137–45; Dana O. Jensen, ed., "The Memoirs of Daniel M. Frost, Part III: The Mexican War Years," *MHSB* 26 (April 1970): 214–16.

38. "Return of the Killed, Wounded, and Missing of the Army under the Immediate Command of Major General Scott, in the Actions of the 17th and 18th of April, 1847, at Cerro Gordo, Mexico," pp. 265–74, Scott to Marcy, April 19, 1847, pp. 255–58, and Twiggs to Capt. Scott, April 19, 1847, pp. 274–77, all in 30 Cong. 1 sess., *SED* 1, serial 503.

39. Scott to Marcy, August 28, 1847, pp. 306–15, and Harney to Capt. Scott, August 24, 1847, pp. 346–47, both in 30 Cong. 1 sess., *SED* 1, serial 503; Lt. Philip Kearny to Lt. Col. Thomas P. Moore, August 24, 1847, *AGO:LR,* M567, roll 359.

40. Maj. Edwin V. Sumner to Mackall, September 9, 1847, 30 Cong. 1 sess., *SED* 1, serial 503, pp. 373–74; General Order no. 281 and 282, September 8, 1847, *AGO:* Wars, *MW,* General and Special Orders, vol. 54; "General Harney's Report of the Execution of the Deserters," September 13, 1847, *AGO,* miscellaneous file no. 45; William Austine to Cousin, November 1, 1847, Austine Papers; Charles S. Hamilton, "Memoirs of the Mexican War," *Wisconsin Magazine of History* 14 (September 1930): 82–82; Jensen, "Memoirs of Daniel M. Frost," 221–23; Dennis J. Wynn, "The San Patricios and the United States–Mexican War of 1846–1848" (Ph.D. diss., Loyola University of Chicago, 1982), 147–64.

41. Scott to Marcy, September 18, 1847, 30 Cong. 1 sess., *SED* 1, serial 503, pp. 375–84; J. Smith, *War with Mexico,* 2:164, 266–67, 318–19; Elliott, *Scott,* 551–52; Pvt. M. McLaughlin to "His Excellency The Commander in Chief," September 23, 1847, *AGO:* Wars, *MW, LR* from Officers, box 2; Reavis, *Harney,* 241–42; Marcy to Harney, December 11, 1848, in Reavis, *Harney,* 242–43; Harney to Jones, November 24, 1847, *AGO:LR,* M567, roll 345.

---

7. Prince of Dragoons

1. Wharncliffe Journal, Wharncliffe (Edward Wortley) Papers, 1850; William E. Foley, "St. Louis: The First Hundred Years," *MHSB* 34 (July 1978): 197; *TSG,* July 26, August 10, 1850.

2. Report of a Board of Inspection, January 11, 1848, and Harney to Jones, February 25, 1848, both in AGO:LR, M567, roll 378; Harney to Jones, July 12, October 12, 1848, AGO:LR, M567, roll 379; Jones to Harney, October 24, 1848, AGO:LS, M565, roll 16.

3. George D. Harmon, "The United States Indian Policy in Texas, 1845–1860," *Mississippi Valley Historical Review* 17 (December 1930): 379–81; Lena Clara Koch, "The Federal Indian Policy in Texas, 1845–1860," *SHQ* 28 (April 1925): 272–74; Prucha, *Great Father*, 1:354–61; Robert M. Utley, *The Indian Frontier of the American West, 1846–1890* (Albuquerque: Univ. of New Mexico Press, 1984), 37–41.

4. ARCIA for 1848, 30 Cong. 2 sess., HED 1, serial 537, p. 385; Harmon, "United States Indian Policy in Texas," 380–83; Averam Bender, *The March of Empire: Frontier Defense in the Southwest, 1848–1860* (Lawrence: Univ. of Kansas Press, 1952), 130–34; Rupert N. Richardson, *The Comanche Barrier to South Plains Settlement: A Century and a Half of Savage Resistance to the Advancing Frontier* (Glendale CA: Arthur H. Clark, 1933), 164–77; TSG, February 26, 1853.

5. Report of Capt. Edwin B. Babbitt, September 1, 1851, 32 Cong. 1 sess., HED 2, serial 634, p. 271; Worth to George T. Wood, February 15, 1849, in Winfrey and Day, *Indian Papers*, 5:36–37; Harney to Jones, April 19, July 19, 1849, AGO:LR, M567, roll 407.

6. William S. Harney to Thomas Harney, June 30, 1849, WSH; Harney to Ordnance Colonel, December 7, 1848, AGO:LR, M567, roll 401; Bender, *March of Empire*, 132.

7. Gen. George M. Brooke to Harney, August 5, 1849, AGO:LR, M567, roll 401; Harney to Jones, August 10, 1849, AGO:LR, M567, roll 407; Harney to Brooke, August 26, 1849, in TSG, June 15, 1850.

8. Jones Endorsement, September 13, 1849, on Harney to Jones, August 10, 1849, AGO:LR, M567, roll 407; Maj. William G. Freeman to Brooke, September 10, 1849, HQA:LS, M587, roll 3; TSG, September 1, 1849.

9. Robert M. Utley, *Frontiersmen in Blue: The United States Army and the Indian, 1848–1865* (New York: Macmillan, 1967), 53–58, 84–88; Lt. Egbert L. Vielé to Maj. George Deas, August 18, 1849, pp. 141–42, Capt. William J. Hardee to Deas, August 26, 1849, 146–47, and George Glascock, William Lackey, and 119 others to Harney, n.d., 145–46, all in 31 Cong. 1 sess., SED 1, serial 549; TSG, August 25, 1849.

10. Harney to Deas, August 26, 1849, and Brooke to Jones, August 31, 1849, 31

Cong. 1 sess., SED 1, serial 549, pp. 144–45, 143; Order no. 53, August 11, 1849, in TSG, August 25, 1849; R. Blake Dunnavent, "Years of Transition: The Texas Indian Question, 1848–1853," *East Texas Historical Journal* 35 (fall 1997): 14–16.

11. Brooke to Scott, May 29, 1850, AGO:LR, M567, roll 423; TSG, April 20, September 7, 1850; Nathaniel C. Hughes Jr., *General William J. Hardee: Old Reliable* (Baton Rouge: Louisiana State Univ. Press, 1965), 38–39; Harmon, "United States Indian Policy in Texas," 384–85; ARSI for 1849, 31 Cong. 1 sess., SED 1, serial 550, pp. 14–15.

12. TSG, May 25, December 25, 1850, January 11, 1851; Brooke to Volney E. Howard, December 26, 1850, BIA:LR, Texas Agency, 1847–1859, M234, roll 858.

13. Brooke to Harney, February 7, 1851, AGO:LR, M567, roll 441; Deas to Jones, March 9, 1851, AGO:LR, M567, roll 442; Harney to Jones, April 2, 1851, and Scott Endorsement, n.d., AGO:LR, M567, roll 447.

14. Order no. 31, April 20, 1851, BIA:LR, Texas Agency, 1847–1859, M234, roll 858; Order no. 34, April 22, 1851, and Hardee to Deas, May 28, 1851, AGO:LR, M567, roll 447.

15. Deas to Col. Juan Maldonado, May 1, 1851, Order no. 46, May 15, 1851, and Harney to Jones, May 17, September 2, 1851, all in AGO:LR, M567, roll 447.

16. Hardee to Deas, June 14, 1851, and Sibley to Deas, July 23, 1851, AGO:LR, M567, roll 447; Harney to Jones, July 21, 1851, AGO:LR, M567, roll 453.

17. Joseph La Motte to Ellen La Motte, August 21, 1851, La Motte–Coppinger Papers; TSG, August 2, 1851; ARSW for 1851, 32 Cong. 1 sess., HED 2, serial 634, p. 105.

18. TSG, March 22, 1851; Lt. George W. Lay to Col. Thomas F. Hunt, August 13, 1853, AGO:LR, M567, roll 490; Utley, *Frontiersmen in Blue*, 71–75.

19. Scott to SW, October 30, 1852, AGO:LR, M567, roll 472; Harney to Acting Adjutant General, January 23, 1853, AGO:LR, M567, roll 482.

20. Lt. Thomas J. Wood to Col. Phillip St. George Cooke, December 30, 1852, January 1, 1853, and Wood to Hardee, January 5, 1853, all in AGO:LR, M567, roll 482; Horace Capron to Luke Lea, January 23, 1853, and George T. Howard to Lea, March 1, 1853, BIA:LR, Texas Agency, 1847–1859, M234, roll 859.

21. Howard to Lea, June 1, 1852, BIA:LR, Texas Agency, 1847–1859, M234, roll 858; Robert S. Neighbors to George W. Manypenny, September 16, 1853, 33 Cong. 1 sess., SED, no. 1, serial 690, pp. 425–29; TSG, February 28, 1854; Prucha, *Great Father*, 1:362–66.

22. Ernest C. Shearer, "The Carvajal Disturbances," SHQ 55 (October 1951): 205–10; José María Carvajal to Capt. John W. Phelps, October 25, 1851, in TSG,

November 22, 1851; W. J. Hughes, *Rebellious Ranger: Rip Ford and the Old Southwest* (Norman: Univ. of Oklahoma Press, 1964), 100–105; J. Fred Rippy, "Border Troubles along the Rio Grande," SHQ 23 (October 1919): 94–97; Smith to Harney, October 21, 1851, AGO:LR, M567, roll 472.

23. Teresa Griffin Vielé, *Following the Drum: A Glimpse of Frontier Life* (1858; reprint, Austin TX: Steck-Vaughn, 1968), 171–73; Order no. 1, November 4, 1851, and Harney to Deas, November 27, 1851, AGO:LR, M567, roll 472.

24. Shearer, "The Carvajal Disturbances," 209–20; John Salmon Ford, *Rip Ford's Texas*, ed. Stephen B. Oates (Austin: Univ. of Texas Press, 1963), 199–204; Rippy, "Border Troubles," 94–99; Harney to Deas, November 17, 1851, Order no. 4, December 6, 1851, Harney to Deas, December 29, 1851, January 2, 19, 1852, and Deas to Harney, January 28, 1852, all in AGO:LR, M567, roll 472.

25. Harney to Deas, February 24, April 17, June 24, 1852, La Motte to Wood, February 21, 1852, and Smith to Jones, July 18, 1852, all in AGO:LR, M567, roll 472; Shearer, "The Carvajal Disturbances," 220–30.

26. Wood to Deas, March 29, 1851, and Harney to Jones, April 1, 1851, AGO:LR, M567, roll 447; Report of Maj. Edwin B. Babbit, September 1, 1851, 32 Cong. 1 sess., HED 2, serial 634, pp. 272–74; Harney to Bliss, August 26, 1851, USACC: Western, LR, box 5; Harney to Jones, June 28, 1852, AGO:LR, M567, roll 464; Joseph La Motte to Ellen La Motte, April 29, 1854, La Motte–Coppinger Papers; Richard Joseph Coyer, "'This Wild Region of the Far West': Lieutenant Sweeny's Letters from Fort Pierre, 1855–1856," NH 63 (spring 1982): 249; Randy Steffen, *The Horse Soldier, 1771–1943: The United States Cavalryman: His Uniforms, Arms, Accoutrements, and Equipments*, vol. 2, *The Frontier, the Mexican War, the Civil War, the Indian Wars, 1851–1880* (Norman: Univ. of Oklahoma Press, 1978), 15, 127.

27. Mary Harney to Ellen Anderson, January 13, 1850, Anderson Family Collection; Harney to Twiggs, November 26, 1852, AGO:LR, M567, roll 465; Mary Harney to Henry Boyce, February 12, 1849, MFC; William S. Harney to Thomas Harney, June 30, 1849, WSH.

28. Capt. Charles F. Ruff to Smith, September 2, 1848, and Ruff to James B. Bowlin, November 1, 1848, both in C. F. Ruff Papers; William S. Harney to Thomas Harney, January 13, 1850, WSH; Mary Harney to Ellen Anderson, January 13, 1850, Anderson Family Collection.

29. Special Order no. 128, August 28, 1852, AGO:SO, vol. 5; Harney to Twiggs, November 26, 1852, AGO:LR, M567, roll 465; Harney to Bliss, May 2, 1853, USACC:

Western, LR, box 9; Harney to a Committee of the New York Democracy, September 30, 1852, in TSG, October 27, 1853; Harney to Acting Adjutant General, August 25, 1854, AGO:LR, M567, roll 499.

30. Harney to Acting Adjutant General, August 25, 1854, AGO:LR, M567, roll 499; Davis Endorsement, September 5, 1854, on Harney to Acting Adjutant General, August 25, 1854, AGO:LR, M567, roll 499; Joseph La Motte to Ellen La Motte, September 30 and November 14, 1854, La Motte–Coppinger Papers; Hardaway, "Descendents," 52.

31. Reavis, *Harney*, 248; Samuel Cooper to Harney, October 26, 1854, AGO:LS, M565, roll 18.

---

8. Great White Chief

1. Lt. Hugh B. Fleming to Maj. Oscar F. Winship, August 30, 1854, 33 Cong. 2 sess., HED 63, serial 788, pp. 14–15; James Bordeaux to John W. Whitfield, August 29, 1854, and Whitfield to Alfred Cumming, October 24, 1854, 33 Cong. 2 sess., HED 1, serial 777, pp. 301–2, 304–6; Lloyd E. McCann, "The Grattan Massacre," NH 37 (March 1956): 1–25; George E. Hyde, *Spotted Tail's Folk: A History of the Brulé Sioux* (Norman: Univ. of Oklahoma Press, 1961), 48–56.

2. ARSW for 1854, 33 Cong. 2 sess., HED 1, serial 778, pp. 4–5; Cooper to Harney, October 26, 1854, AGO:LS, M565, roll 18; Jefferson Davis to Harney, October 26, 1854, BIA:LR, Upper Platte Agency, M234, roll 889; KWH, November 17, December 6, 1854; Utley, *Frontiersmen in Blue*, 114–15.

3. Cooper to Harney, March 22, 1855, AGO:LS, M565, roll 18; *Laws and Treaties*, 2:594–96; John D. Unruh Jr., *The Plains Across: The Overland Emigrants and the Trans-Mississippi West, 1840–1860* (Urbana: Univ. of Illinois Press, 1979), 175–89, 201–14, 386; Utley, *Frontiersmen in Blue*, 59–70, 108–12; Prucha, *Great Father*, 1:343–45; Prucha, *American Indian Treaties*, 208–12, 233–40; Catherine Price, *The Oglala People, 1841–1879: A Political History* (Lincoln: Univ. of Nebraska Press, 1996), 31–37.

4. Cooper to Scott, December 11, 1854, AGO:LS, M565, roll 18; Capt. Irvin McDowell to Cooper, December 14, 1854, AGO:LR, M567, roll 498; Cooper to Harney, March 22, 1855, AGO:LR, M567, roll 518; Utley, *Frontiersmen in Blue*, 62–63, 111–12, 121–25, 130–33, 155–57, 223–24, 345–47.

5. Cooper to Harney, March 22, 1855, AGO:LS, M565, roll 18; General Order no. 2,

March 28, 1855, AGO:GO; McDowell to Cooper, December 14, 1854, AGO:LR, M567, roll 498.

6. Cooper to Harney, March 22, 1855, AGO:LS, M565, roll 18; Harney to Cooper, April 5, 12, 1855, AGO:LR, M567, roll 517.

7. Cooper to Harney, April 17, 1855, AGO:LS, M565, roll 18; Harney to Thomas, May 12, 1855, and Winship to Col. William Hoffman, June 5, 1855, both in AGO:LR, M567, roll 517.

8. Harney to Thomas, May 13, 19, 1855, AGO:LR, M567, roll 517; Harney to Cooper, May 19, 1855, and Winship to Maj. Edmund A. Ogden, June 12, 1855, both in USACC: West, LS, SE, vol. 269; Special Order no. 95, May 23, 1855, AGO:SO; Capt. William G. Freeman, June 8, 1855, AGO:LS, M565, roll 18.

9. Harney to Thomas, June 2, 14, 1855, and Harney to Davis, June 16, 1855, both in AGO:LR, M567, roll 517.

10. Hoffman to Winship, May 8, 1855, and Lt. Henry Heth to Winship, May 27, 1855, both in AGO:LR, M567, roll 517; Mark W. Izard to Davis, July 3, 1855, AGO:LR, M567, roll 523.

11. Harney to Cooper, April 26, 1855, AGO:LR, M567, roll 517; Charles E. Mix to Robert McClelland, August 4, 1855, Harney to Thomas, July 24, 1855, and Davis Endorsement, August 11, 1855, on Harney to Thomas, July 24, 1855, all in AGO:LR, M567, roll 518; S. Smith, *View from Officers' Row,* 94–96, 121–25.

12. Cooper to Harney, July 3, 1855, AGO:LS, M565, roll 18; Harney to Cooper, July 14, 1855, and Harney to Thomas, July 30, 1855, both in AGO:LR, M567, roll 518; KWH, July 21, 1855; "Circular," August 9, 1855, and Winship to Commanding Officer of Fort Pierre, August 21, 1855, both in USACC: West, LS, SE, vol. 269.

13. Harney to Thomas, July 30, 1855, George Manypenny to McClelland, October 11, 1855, and Benjamin F. Robinson to Cumming, August 5, 1855, all in AGO:LR, M567, roll 518.

14. Harney to Thomas, August 23, 1855, AGO:LR, M567, roll 518; Winship to Maj. Benjamin F. Harney, August 31, 1855, USACC: West, LS, SE, vol. 269; D. C. Beam, "Reminiscences of Early Days in Nebraska," *Nebraska State Historical Society Transactions and Reports* 3 (1892): 300–301.

15. Manypenny to Thomas S. Twiss, March 12, 1855, BIA:LR, M21, roll 51; Twiss to Manypenny, October 1, 1855, 34 Cong. 1 sess., HED 1, serial 840, pp. 400–401; Alban W. Hoopes, "Thomas S. Twiss, Indian Agent on the Upper Platte, 1855–1861," *Mississippi Valley Historical Review* 20 (December 1933): 353–64.

16. Harney to Thomas, August 23, September 5, 1855, AGO:LR, M567, roll 518; Harney to Izard, August 28, 1855, and Harney to sw, November 10, 1855, both in USACC: West, LS, SE, vol. 269; Eugene Bandel, *Frontier Life in the Army, 1845–1861,* ed. Ralph P. Bieber (Glendale CA: Arthur H. Clark, 1932), 80–84; Emerson Gifford Taylor, *Gouverneur Kemble Warren: The Life and Letters of an American Soldier, 1830–1882* (Boston: Houghton Mifflin, 1932), 25–26.

17. Ray H. Mattison, ed., "The Harney Expedition against the Sioux: The Journal of Capt. B. S. Todd," NH 43 (June 1962): 110; Warren to Winship, September 4, 1855, and Harney to sw, November 10, 1855, both in AGO:LR, M567, roll 518.

18. Nathan A. M. Dudley to Robert Harvey, January 23, 1909, in R. Eli Paul, ed., "Battle of Ash Hollow: The 1909–1910 Recollections of General N. A. M. Dudley," NH 62 (fall 1981): 377–84; Warren to Winship, September 4, 1855, Cooke to Winship, September 5, 1855, Harney to Thomas, September 5, 1855, and Harney to sw, November 10, 1855, all in AGO:LR, M567, roll 518; Taylor, *Warren*, 25–27.

19. Harney to Thomas, September 5, 1855, and Cooke to Winship, September 5, 1855, both in AGO:LR, M567, roll 518; Mattison, "Harney Expedition," 113–15; Taylor, *Warren*, 27–28; Merrill J. Mattes, *The Great Platte River Road: The Covered Wagon Mainline via Fort Kearny to Fort Laramie* (Lincoln: Univ. of Nebraska Press, 1969), 321–28.

20. Taylor, *Warren*, 27–29; Mattison, "Harney Expedition," 114; Harney to Thomas, September 5, 1855, AGO:LR, M567, roll 518; Richard C. Drum, "Reminiscences of the Indian Fight at Ash Hollow," *Collections of the Nebraska State Historical Society* 16 (1911): 146–48; Beam, "Reminiscences of Early Days in Nebraska," 302–3.

21. Harney to sw, November 10, 1855, AGO:LR, M567, roll 517; Thomas to Cooper, September 29, 1855, 34 Cong. 1 sess., HED 1, serial 841, p. 51; Harney to Cooper, October 9, 1855, AGO:LS, M565, roll 18; Oliver Otis Howard, *My Life and Experiences among Our Hostile Indians: A Record of Personal Observations, Adventures, and Campaigns among the Indians of the Great West* (Hartford CT: A. D. Worthington, 1907), 1:74–77.

22. Utley, *Frontiersmen in Blue*, 345–46; S. Smith, *View from Officers' Row*, 67–74.

23. Harney Address, March 2, 1856, Council with the Sioux Indians at Fort Pierre, 34 Cong. 1 sess., HED 130, serial 859, p. 18.

24. Harney to Thomas, September 16, 1855, AGO:LR, M567, roll 518; Bandel, *Frontier Life in the Army*, 87–88.

25. Harney to sw, November 10, 1855, AGO:LR, M567, roll 518; Twiss to Commissioner of Indian Affairs, October 1, 1855, 34 Cong. 1 sess., HED 1, serial 840, pp. 400–401; Harney Circular, September 18, 1855, AGO:LR, M567, roll 539; Harney to Thomas, September 26, 1855, AGO:LR, M567, roll 518.

26. Augustus Meyers, *Ten Years in the Ranks of the U.S. Army* (New York: Stirling Press, 1914), 75; Harney to Thomas, September 26, 1855, and Harney to sw, November 10, 1855, both in AGO:LR, M567, roll 518; Taylor, *Warren*, 29–30; Twiss to Cumming, October 10, 1855, 34 Cong. 1 sess., HED 1, serial 840, pp. 401–5.

27. Harney to Thomas, September 26, 1855, and Harney to sw, November 10, 1855, both in AGO:LR, M567, roll 518.

28. Winship to Hoffman, September 28, 1855, USACC: West, LS, SE, vol. 269; Harney to Thomas, November 9, 1855, and Harney to sw, November 10, 1855, both in AGO:LR, M567, roll 518; Harney to Davis, August 20, 1856, SW:LR, M221, roll 178; Mattison, "Harney Expedition," 114–25; Davis to Reavis, January 1878, in Reavis, *Harney*, iv.

29. Harney to Thomas, November 9, December 14, 1855, and Field Return of the Sioux Expedition at Fort Pierre, November 9, 1855, all in AGO:LR, M56, roll 518; Order no. 12, October 21, 1855, Report of Fort Pierre Examining Board, October 24, 1855, and Order no. 19, November 1, 1855, all in Doane Robinson, ed., "Official Correspondence Relating to Fort Pierre," SDHC 1 (1902) 398–405; Meyers, *Ten Years*, 72–73.

30. Harney Circular, November 9, 1855, and Harney to sw, November 10, 1855, both in AGO:LR, M567, roll 518; Davis to Harney, December 26, 1855, 34, Cong. 1 sess., HED 130, serial 859, pp. 4–5.

31. Twiss to Commissioner of Indian Affairs, October 1, 1855, 34 Cong. 1 sess., HED 1, serial 840, pp. 400–401; Twiss to Cumming, November 14, 1855, BIA:LR, Upper Platte Agency, M234, roll 889; Harney to Thomas, November 21, 1855, Twiss to Harney, December 16, 1855, and Hoffman to Capt. Alfred Pleasonton, February 11, 1856, all in AGO:LR, M567, roll 518.

32. Hoffman to Pleasonton, February 9, 1856, AGO:LR, M567, roll 539; Pleasonton to Hoffman, February 19, March 6, 1856, AGO:LR, M567, roll 538.

33. Harney to Cooper, February 21, 1856, AGO:LR, M567, roll 538; Meyers, *Ten Years*, 90–95; Robert T. Athearn, *Forts of the Upper Missouri* (Englewood Cliffs NJ: Prentice-Hall, 1967), 42–46; Frederick T. Wilson, "Fort Pierre and Its Neighbors," SDHC 1 (1902): 264.

34. Harney to Cooper, January 14, 1856, and Pleasonton to Capt. Marcus Simpson, March 30, 1856, both in USACC: West, LS, SE, vol. 269; Harney to Adjutant General, January 20, 1856, AGO:LR, M567, roll 538; Harney to Thomas, February 27, 1856, AGO:LR, M567, roll 539; Meyers, *Ten Years*, 95–96.

35. Harney to Thomas, November 9, 1855, AGO:LR, M567, roll 518; Meyers, *Ten Years*, 75; George L. Miller, "The Military Camp on the Big Sioux River in 1855," *Nebraska State Historical Society Transactions and Reports* 3 (1892): 120; Vielé, *Following the Drum*, 173.

36. Harney to sw, March 8, 1856, 34 Cong. 1 sess., HED 130, serial 859, pp. 1–4; Meyers, *Ten Years*, 104–5.

37. Harney Address, March 1, 1856, 13–17, and Proceedings, March 2, 1856, pp. 17–22, both in Council with the Sioux Indians at Fort Pierre, 34 Cong. 1 sess., HED 130, serial 859; Meyers, *Ten Years*, 104–5; Hiram Martin Chittenden, *History of Early Steamboat Navigation on the Missouri River: Life and Adventures of Joseph La Barge* (1903; reprint, Minneapolis: Ross & Haines, 1962), 202–3.

38. Proceedings, March 3–5, 1856, pp. 22–39, Harney to sw, March 8, 1856, pp. 1–4, and Davis to President, May 10, 1856, pp. 6–8, all in Council with the Sioux Indians at Fort Pierre, 34 Cong. 1 sess., HED 130, serial 859; William T. Hagan, *Indian Police and Judges: Experiments in Acculturation and Control* (New Haven CT: Yale Univ. Press, 1966), 25, 40–43; Prucha, *Great Father*, 1:600–604.

39. Proceedings, March 5, 1856, p. 39, and Harney to sw, March 8, 1856, pp. 1–4, both in Council with the Sioux Indians at Fort Pierre, 34 Cong. 1 sess., HED 130, serial 859; Pleasonton to Capt. Henry W. Wharton, March 5, 1856, USACC: West, LS, SE, vol. 269; Pleasonton to Hoffman, March 5, 1856, AGO:LR, M567, roll 539; Meyers, *Ten Years*, 105.

40. Minutes of a Council Held at Fort Pierre, April 19, 1856, and Davis to President, May 31, 1856, both in AGO:LR, M567, roll 539; Twiss to Commissioner of Indian Affairs, June 24, 1856, Manypenny to McClelland, June 25, 1856, and McClelland to President, June 26, 1856, all in Council with the Sioux Indians at Fort Pierre, 34 Cong. 1 sess., HED 130, serial 859, pp. 10–12.

41. Harney to sw, May 23, 1856, AGO:LR, M567, roll 539; Harney to Cooper, March 9, June 30, 1856, "Official Correspondence Relating to Fort Pierre," SDHC 1 (1902): 422–24, 428.

42. Cooper to Harney, June 20, 1856, "Official Correspondence Relating to Fort Pierre," SDHC 1 (1902): 426–27; Alfred J. Vaughn to Cumming, February 15, 1856,

AGO:LR, M567, roll 539; James W. Denver to Robinson, November 10, 1858, BIA:LS, M21, roll 60.

---

9. Return to Florida

1. Lt. Loomis L. Langdon to Col. Harvey Brown, February, 25, 1856, Maj. John Munroe to Samuel Cooper, March 12, 1856, Capt. Henry Clay Pratt to Brown, April 6, 1856, Munroe to Cooper, April 6, 1856, and Maj. Lewis G. Arnold to Brown, April 9, 1856, all in AGO:LR, M567, roll 542.

2. John D. Sheldon and seven others to Munroe, April 1, 1856, USACC: Florida, LR, box 25; Munroe to Cooper, April 22, 1856, USACC: Florida, LS, vol. 5; Capt. Simeon L. Sparkman to Munroe, April 30, 1856, USACC: Florida, LR, box 25.

3. Munroe to Cooper, May 18, July 1, 1856, AGO:LR, M567, roll 542; Sparkman to Munroe, May 21, 1856, USACC: Florida, LR, box 25.

4. John E. Turkett to SW, June 2, 1856, and Cooper to Munroe, May 1, 1856, both in USACC: Florida, LR, box 24; Munroe to James E. Broome, June 12, 1856, AGO:LR, M567, roll 542; Davis to Harney, July 10, 1856, AGO:LS, M565, roll 18.

5. Davis to Harney, July 10, 1856, and Cooper to Harney, August 31, 1856, both in AGO:LS, M565, roll 18; Harney to Davis, August 31, 1856, and Davis Endorsement, September 3, 1856, AGO:LR, M567, roll 539; Davis to Broome, September 13, 1856, SW:LS, M6, roll 38; Cooper to Harney, September 25, 1856, AGO:LS, M565, roll 18; Worth to Scott, February 14, 1856, in Sprague, *Origin*, 441–44.

6. ARSW for 1849, and George W. Crawford to Twiggs, August 21, 1849, 31 Cong. 1 sess., SED 1, serial 549, pp. 90–96, 117–18; Jeanne Twiggs Heidler, "The Military Career of David Emanuel Twiggs" (Ph.D. diss., Auburn University, 1988), 150–60.

7. Charles M. Conrad to Thomas Brown, March 21, 1851, 32 Cong. 1 sess., HED 2, serial 634, pp. 157–58; Resolution of the Legislature of Florida, January 12, 1853, 32 Cong. 2 sess., *Senate Misc. Doc.* 51, serial 670, p. 1; George C. Bittle, "Florida Frontier Incidents during the 1850s," FHQ 49 (October 1970): 153–56.

8. Davis to Broome, September 13, 1856, SW:LS, M6, roll 38; ARSW for 1856, 43 Cong. 2 sess., SED 5, serial 876, pp. 3–26; Jesup to Col. Daniel D. Tompkins, October 2, 1856, OQMG:LS, M745, roll 33; Capt. William Maynadier to Harney, September 17, 1856, and Jesup to Harney, November 4, 1856, both in USACC: Florida, LR, box 25.

9. Maynadier to Harney, September 17, 1856, USACC: Florida, LR, box 25; Capt. Stewart Van Vliet to Jesup, October 27, 1856, OQMG: Correspondence, consolidated file, box 377; Davis to Harney, November 4, 1856, SW:LS, M6, roll 38; William H. Garrett to Manypenny, September 8, 1856, 34 Cong. 3 sess., SED 5, serial 875, pp. 695–97; *Laws and Treaties*, 2:756–63.

10. Capt. Justus McKinstry to Page, October 28, 1856, USACC: Florida, LR, box 25; Pleasonton to Commanding Officers at Forts Dallas and Capron, November 12, 1856, and Pleasonton to Capt. John H. Winder, November 12, 1856, both in USACC: Florida, LS, vol. 5; Harney to Thomas, November 23, 25, 1856, AGO:LR, M567, roll 539; Circular, Headquarters, Department of Florida, November 22, 1856, AGO:LR, M567, roll 539.

11. Harney to Broome, November 25, 1856, USACC: Florida, LS, vol. 5; Jesse Carter to Harney, November 26, 1856, USACC: Florida, LR, box 24; Harney to Thomas, November 25, 1856, AGO:LR, M567, roll 539.

12. Harney to Cooper, December 5, 1856, AGO:LR, M567, roll 539; Davis to McClelland, November 3, 22, 1856, AGO:LR, M567, roll 540; Cooper to Harney, December 10, 1856, AGO:LS, M565, roll 18; Pleasonton to Capts. Joseph Roberts, John P. McCown, and John A. Mitchell, and Maj. Sterne H. Fowler, December 29, 1856, USACC: Florida, LS, vol. 5.

13. Memorial of the Citizens of St. Augustine to General Harney, January 5, 1857, Carter to Harney, January 10, 1857, D. Dummett to Harney, January 12, 1857, and Carter to Col. Gustavus Loomis, May 12, 1857, in USACC: Florida, LR, box 27, all Harney to Thomas, January 19, 1857, AGO:LR, M567, roll 558.

14. Special Order no. 6, January 10, 1857, USACC: Florida, General and Special Orders, 1857; Howard, *My Life and Experiences*, 1:74–77; Oliver Otis Howard, *Autobiography* (New York: Baker and Taylor, 1907), 1:76–77.

15. Order no. 2, January 5, 1857, and Order no. 3, January 8, 1857, both in USACC: Florida, General and Special Orders, 1857; Harney to Thomas, January 14, 1857, AGO:LR, M567, roll 558.

16. Harney to Thomas, January 14, 1857, AGO:LR, M567, roll 558; Harney to Thomas, February 21, 1857, AGO:LR, M567, roll 559; Capt. James W. Albert to Col. James Taylor, February 8, 1857, Miscellaneous Manuscripts, box 15, P. K. Younge Library of Florida History, University of Florida; Capt. Gustavus A. DeRussy to Lt. William H. Lewis, February 7, 1857, USACC: Florida, LR, box 27.

17. Pleasonton to Page, January 22, 1857, USACC: Florida, LS, vol. 5; Special Order

no. 14, January 27, 1857, USACC: Florida, General and Special Orders; Col. Justin Dimick to Page, February 6, 1857, USACC: Florida, LR, box 27; Lt. William A. Webb to Capt. Carter L. Stevenson, February 22, 1857, USACC: Florida, LR, box 29; Capt. Abner Doubleday to Dimick, March 10, 1857, USACC: Florida, LR, box 27, Pleasonton to Dimick, February 15, 1857, USACC: Florida, LS, vol. 5; Harney to Thomas, February 21, 1857, AGO:LR, M567, roll 559.

18. Capt. Robert Bullock to Page, February 18, 1857, USACC: Florida, LR, box 27; Carter to Munroe, February 28, 1857, USACC: Florida, LR, box 28; Pleasonton to McKinstry, February 20, 1857, USACC: Florida, LS, vol. 5; Cooper to Harney, January 30, 1857, AGO:LS, M565, roll 28; Harney to Cooper, February, 28, 1857, AGO:LR, M567, roll 559.

19. Harney to Thomas, March 8, 1857, AGO:LR, M567, roll 559; Stevenson to Pleasonton, March 6, 1857, USACC: Florida, LR, box 29; Lt. Oliver O. Howard to Pleasonton, March 4, 1857, USACC: Florida, LR, box 28; Pleasonton to Dimick, March 8, 1857, and Pleasonton to Pratt, McCown, and Capt. John P. Robinson, March 8, 1857, both in USACC: Florida, LS, vol. 5; Harney to Thomas, March 21, 1857, AGO:LR, M567, roll 558.

20. Capt. Abner D. Johnston to Harney, March 18, 1857, USACC: Florida, LR, box 28; Pleasonton to Stevenson, March 21, 1857, USACC: Florida, LS, vol. 5; Harney to Thomas, March 21, April 10, 11, 1857, AGO:LR, M567, roll 558.

21. General Order no. 14, Headquarters of the Army, November 13, 1857, 35 Cong. 1 sess., HED 2, serial 943, p. 52; General Order no. 9, April 8, 1857, and Special Order no. 46, April 9, 1857, both in USACC: Florida, General and Special Orders; Harney to Thomas, April 10, 11, 1857, AGO:LR, M567, roll 558; Contract between Bvt. Brig. Gen. Wm. S. Harney, U. S. Army and Lewis Daugherty, Fort Myers, Florida, April 21, 1857, and Harney to Cooper, April 22, 1857, both in AGO:LR, M567, roll 558; Robert J. Walker to Lewis Cass, June 15, 1857, quoted in *Jefferson Davis, Constitutionalist: His Letters, Papers, and Speeches,* ed. Dunbar Rowland (Jackson: Mississippi Department of Archives and History, 1923), 3:143–44; Harney to Cooper April 23, 1857, AGO:LR, M567, roll 560; General Order no. 13, April 27, 1857, USACC: Florida, General and Special Orders; Special Order no. 62, May 8, 1857, AGO: Orders, SO, vol. 6.

22. Cooper to Loomis, May 6, 1857, Memorandum of the plan of operations proposed to be carried out by General Harney in the Department of Florida during the summer months, and Cooper to Loomis, May 30, September 1, 1857, all in USACC: Florida, LR, box 27; Loomis to Cooper, May 24, 1857, AGO:LR, M567, roll 558.

23. Loomis to Maj. Irvin McDowell, August 30, December 6, 1857, USACC: Florida, LS, vol. 5; ARSW for 1857, 35 Cong. 1 sess. HED 2, serial 943, p. 5.

24. Loomis to McDowell, January 30, 1858, p. 236, Loomis to Cooper, May 8, 1858, pp. 241–42, and Proclamation by Gustavus Loomis, Col. 5th Inf., Commanding the Department of Florida, May 8, 1858, p. 244, all in 35 Cong. 2 sess., SED 1, serial 975; Prucha, *Sword of the Republic*, 305–6.

10. Civil Unrest in Kansas and Utah

1. General Order no. 3, July 15, 1857, USACC: Utah, Orders, vol. 7; Harney to Samuel Cooper, July 24, 1857, AGO:LR, M567, roll 560; Capt. Jesse A. Gove to Maria Gove, July 19, 1857, in *The Utah Expedition, 1857–1858: Letters of Capt. Jesse A. Gove, 10th Inf. U.S.A., of Concord, N.H., to Mrs. Gove, and Special Correspondence of the New York Herald*, ed. Otis G. Hammond, New Hampshire Historical Society Collections, 12 (Concord: New Hampshire Historical Society, 1928), 5–8.

2. Harney to Cooper, April 23, 1857, AGO:LR, M567, roll 560; Special Order no. 62, May 8, 1857, AGO: Orders, vol. 6; Samuel Adams Drake, "Recollections of the Old Army in Kansas," 4–5, Beinecke Rare Book and Manuscript Library, Yale University.

3. Allan Nevins, *Ordeal of the Union: A House Dividing, 1852–1857* (New York: Charles Scribner's Sons, 1947), 113–16, 380–93, 408–11, 437–46, 471–80; Allan Nevins, *The Emergence of Lincoln: Douglas, Buchanan, and Party Chaos, 1857–1859* (New York: Charles Scribner's Sons, 1950), 90–95, 133–99, 231–34, 264–70; James A. Rawley, *Race and Politics: "Bleeding Kansas" and the Coming of the Civil War* (Lincoln: Univ. of Nebraska Press, 1969), 79–99, 158–68, 202–52; Alice Nichols, *Bleeding Kansas* (New York: Oxford Univ. Press, 1954), 9–16, 57–70, 94–95, 105–16, 141–50, 172–85; Kenneth Stampp, *America in 1857: A Nation on the Brink* (New York: Oxford Univ. Press, 1990), 3–18; Robert W. Coakley, *The Role of Federal Military Forces in Domestic Disorders, 1789–1878* (Washington DC: Center of Military History, United States Army, 1988), 145–72.

4. Walker to James K. Buchanan, March 26, 1857, in F. G. Adams, ed., TKSHS, 5:290; KWH, November 28, 1857; Walker to Cass, June 15, 1857, quoted in Rowland, *Davis*, 3:143–44; James P. Shenton, *Robert John Walker, a Politician from Jackson to Lincoln* (New York: Columbia Univ. Press, 1961), 145–49.

5. Governor Walker's Inaugural Address, May 27, 1857, and Walker to Cass, July 15, 1857, both in Adams, TKSHS, 5:328; Shenton, *Walker*, 150–58.

6. Walker to Cass, July 15, 1857, in Adams, TKSHS, 5:343–48; Drake, "Recollections," 4–5; KWH, November 28, 1857, Harney to Cooper, April 23, 1857, AGO:LR, M567, roll 560; General Order no. 2, May 31, 1857, USACC: West, General and Special Orders Issued by the Troops Serving in Kansas, vol. 268; Howard, *My Life and Experiences*, 1:82.

7. Cooper to Harney, May 8, 1857, and Cooper to Smith, April 1, 1857, both in Adams, TKSHS, 5:302; W. Stitt Robinson Jr., "The Role of the Military in Territorial Kansas," in *Territorial Kansas: Studies Commemorating the Centennial* (Lawrence: Univ. of Kansas Publications, Social Science Studies, 1954), 86–92; Coakley, *Role of Federal Military Forces*, 3–23, 148–74.

8. Walker to Harney, May 30, 1857, and Harney to Walker, June 1, 1857, both in Robert James Walker Papers; Walker to Harney, July 6, 1857, 35 Cong. 1 sess., SED 8, serial 918, p. 35; Walker to Cass, July 15, 1857, Walker to Harney, July 14, 1857, Harney to Walker, July 15, 1857, and "To the People of Lawrence. Proclamation," July 15, 1857, all in Adams, TKSHS, 5:341–48, 350, 351, 355–58.

9. Lt. Col. George W. Lay to Harney, May 28, 1857, HQA:LS, M857, roll 5; Elliott, *Scott*, 597–600, 648–50; Skelton, "Commanding General," 117–21; Skelton, *Profession*, 131, 233.

10. Leonard J. Arrington, *Great Basin Kingdom: An Economic History of the Latter-day Saints, 1830–1900* (Cambridge MA: Harvard Univ. Press, 1958), 3–4, 6–22, 31–33, 39–42, 50–51; Norman F. Furniss, *The Mormon Conflict* (New Haven CT: Yale Univ. Press, 1960), 1–20, 45–61; Stampp, *America in 1857*, 196–203; Richard D. Poll, "The Mormon Question Enters National Politics, 1850–1856," *Utah Historical Quarterly* 25 (April 1957): 117–34.

11. David H. Burr to Thomas A. Hendricks, March 28, 1857, 35 Cong. 1 sess., HED 71, serial 956, pp. 118–20; Stampp, *America in 1857*, 197–203.

12. Lay to Harney, May 28, 1857, HQA:LS, M857, roll 5; Harney to John B. Floyd, June 7, 1857, and "Memorandum concerning the force about to March to Utah," June 7, 1857, both in AGO:LR, M567, roll 560.

13. Circular to the Adjutant General, Quartermaster General, Commissary General, Surgeon General, Paymaster General, and Chief of Ordnance, May 18, 1857, 35 Cong. 1 sess., HED 71, serial 956, pp. 4–5; Jesup to Harney, June 5, 1857, OQMG:LS, M745, roll 33; Alexander Majors and William H. Russell to Harney, June 12, 1857, and Harney to Cooper, June 12, 1857, both in AGO:LR, M567, roll 560; Raymond W. Settle and Mary Lund Settle, *War Drums and Wagon Wheels: The*

Story of Russell, Majors and Waddell (Lincoln: Univ. of Nebraska Press, 1966), 49–50; Risch, *Quartermaster Support of the Army*, 323–24.

14. Harney to Cooper, June 12, 13, 1857, Harney to Thomas, June 15, 1857, and Endorsement by Scott, June 22, 1857, on Harney to Cooper, June 12, 1857, all in AGO:LR, M567, roll 560; Lay to Harney, June 26, 1857, HQA:LS, M857, roll 5.

15. June 24, 1857, entry, diary of Capt. John Walcott Phelps, in *The Utah Expedition, 1857–1858: A Documentary Account of the United States Military Movement under Colonel Albert Sidney Johnston, and the Resistance by Brigham Young and the Mormon Nauvoo Legion*, ed. LeRoy R. Hafen and Ann W. Hafen (Glendale CA: Arthur H. Clark, 1958), 91; Almina R. Hancock, *Reminiscences of Winfield Scott Hancock* (New York: Charles R. Webster, 1887), 30–31, 35–37; Richard F. Burton, *The City of the Saints and Across the Rocky Mountains to California*, ed. Fawn F. Brodie (1862; reprint, New York: Alfred A. Knopf, 1963), 651.

16. Lay to Harney, June 26, 29, 1857, HQA:LS, M857, roll 5; General Order no. 12, June 30, 1857, AGO: Orders.

17. Position and Distribution of the Troops in the Department of the West, June 30, 1857, 35 Cong. 1 sess., HED 2, serial 943, pp. 72–73; Lay to Harney, May 28, 1857, HQA:LS, M857, roll 5.

18. Jesse Gove to Maria Gove, June 28, 1857, in Hammond, *Utah Expedition*, 5–8; Special Order no. 25, July 9, 1857, USACC: West, General and Special Orders Issued by the Troops Serving in Kansas, vol. 268; Thomas to Harney, July 1, 1857, 35 Cong. 1 sess., HED 71, serial 956, p. 9; George Walton, *Sentinel of the Plains: Fort Leavenworth and the American West* (Englewood Cliffs NJ: Prentice-Hall, 1973), 87–88.

19. Pleasonton to Buchanan, July 11, 1857, AGO:LR, M567, roll 560; Cooper to Harney, July 15, 1857, AGO:LS, M565, roll 18; Thomas to Harney, July 17, 1857, AGO:LR, M567, roll 553.

20. General Order no. 3, July 15, 1857, USACC: Utah, Orders, vol. 7; War Department to Benjamin McCulloch, July 8, 1857, and McCulloch to Floyd, July 21, 1857, both in AGO:LR, M567, roll 563.

21. Walker to Cass, July 15, 1857, in Adams, *TKSHS*, 5:341–48; Walker to "The President or the Secretary of War," July 16, 1857, AGO:LR, M567, roll 575; Cooper to Harney, July 17, 1857, AGO:LS, M565, roll 18.

22. Harney to Floyd, August 8, 1857, AGO:LR, M567, roll 560; Pleasonton to Capt. Stewart Van Vliet, July 28, 1857, 35 Cong. 1 sess., HED 2, serial 943, pp. 27–28; Har-

ney to Brigham Young, July 28, 1857, in Hafen and Hafen, *Utah Expedition,* 39–40; McCulloch to Floyd, July 21, 1857, AGO:LR, M567, roll 563.

23. Harney to Floyd, August 8, 1857, AGO:LR, M567, roll 560; Walker to Cass, August 8, 1857, in Adams, *TKSHS,* 5:372–74.

24. Harney to Thomas, August 8, 1857, 35 Cong. 1 sess., HED 71, serial 956, p. 17; Sumner to Thomas, August 9, 1857, in LeRoy R. Hafen and Ann W. Hafen, eds., *Relations with the Indians of the Plains, 1857–1861* (Glendale CA: Arthur H. Clark, 1959), 26–28; Sumner to Thomas, September 20, 1857, in Adams, *TKSHS,* 5:300–302; William Y. Chalfant, *Cheyennes and Horse Soldiers: The 1857 Expedition and the Battle of Solomon's Fork* (Norman: Univ. of Oklahoma, 1989), 181–210; Lt. Gaylord Marshall to Cooper, August 2, 1857, 35 Cong. 1 sess., HED 71, serial 956, pp. 17–18; Marshall to Cooper, August 4, 1857, AGO:LR, M567, roll 553.

25. Harney to Thomas, August 8, 1857, 35 Cong. 1 sess., HED 71, serial 956, p. 17; Harney to Floyd, August 8, 1857, AGO:LR, M567, roll 560; Harney to Thomas, August 22, 1857, AGO:LR, M567, roll 553; Sumner to Thomas, August 9, 1857, in Hafen and Hafen, *Relations with the Indians,* 26–28.

26. Scott to Floyd, August 19, 1857, 35 Cong. 1 sess., HED 71, serial 956, pp. 12–13; Lay to Harney, June 29, 1857, HQA:LS, M857, roll 5; Endorsement by Scott, August 18, 1857, on Harney to Thomas, August 8, 1857, AGO:LR, M567, roll 553.

27. Pleasonton to Van Vliet, July 28, 1857, 35 Cong. 1 sess., HED 2, serial 943, pp. 27–28; Pleasonton to Van Vliet, August 16, 1857, USACC: Utah, LS, vol. 1; Brigham Young to John R. Young, September 4, 1857, quoted in Juanita Brooks, *The Mountain Meadows Massacre* (Norman: Univ. of Oklahoma Press, 1962), 22; Journal History of the Church of Jesus Christ of Latter-day Saints, Church Historical Department, Salt Lake City, Utah, August 25, 1857.

28. McDowell to Harney, August 29, 1857, 35 Cong. 1 sess., HED 71, serial 956, p. 13; ARSW for 1857, 35 Cong. 1 sess., HED 2, serial 943, p. 6; Cass to Walker, September 1, 1857, in Adams, *TKSHS,* 5:382; General Order no. 8, September 11, 1857, USACC: Utah, Orders, vol. 7. Charles P. Roland, *Albert Sidney Johnston: Soldier of Three Republics* (Austin: Univ. of Texas Press, 1964), 188–90, maintains, erroneously, that Harney was retained in Kansas partly because he did not want to go to Utah.

29. Walker to Harney, September 1, 1857, and Harney to Floyd, September 3, 1857, both in AGO:LR, M567, roll 560.

30. Walker to Harney, September 21, 1857, Pleasonton to Col. Joseph E. Johnston, September 22, 1857, Pleasonton to Maj. John Sedgwick, September 22, 1857, Walk-

er to Harney, September 26, 1857, Special Order no. 77, September 26, 1857, Special Order no. 78, September 28, 1857, Special Order no. 85, October 3, 1857, and "To the People of Kansas," September 10, 1857, all in Adams, TKSHS, 5:303–12, 391.

31. Harney to Walker, October 9, 10, 1857, in Adams, TKSHS, 5:314; Walker to Cass, October 10, 1857, 35 Cong. 1 sess., SED 8, serial 918, pp. 96–97.

32. Harney to Cooper, October 11, 31, 1857, AGO:LR, M567, roll 554, and Harney to Thomas, November 12, 1857, AGO:LR, M567, roll 560; Special Order no. 111, November 7, 1857, and Special Order no. 136, December 3, 1857, both in USACC: West, General and Special Orders Issued by the Troops Serving in Kansas, vol. 268; Cooper to Floyd, November 27, 1857, 35 Cong. 1 sess., HED 2, serial 943, pp. 58–61.

33. Walker to Cass, December 15, 1857, and "Address to the People of Kansas," December 21, 1857, both in Adams, TKSHS, 5:421–30, 465–68; Cooper to Harney, December 9, 1857, AGO:LS, M565, roll 19; Special Order no. 1, January 1, 1858, USACC: West, General and Special Orders Issued by the Troops Serving in Kansas, vol. 268; Harney to Cooper, January 9, 1858, AGO:LR, M567, roll 580; Rawley, *Race and Politics*, 223–56; Stampp, *America in 1857*, 281–329.

34. James W. Denver to Harney, January 9, 1858, and Harney to Denver, January 12, 1858, both in Adams, TKSHS, 5:473; Special Order no. 12, January 10, 1858, USACC: West, General and Special Orders Issued by the Troops Serving in Kansas, vol. 268; Cooper to Harney, February 19, 1858, AGO:LS, M565, roll 19; "Proceedings of a Board of Officers Convened at Washington Arsenal, D.C.," February 19, 1858, AGO:LR, M567, roll 580.

35. Van Vliet to Pleasonton, September 16, 1857, 35 Cong. 1 sess., HED 71, serial 956, pp. 24–26; General Order no. 8, April 15, 1858, AGO: Orders; Cooper to Harney, April 17, 1858, AGO:LS, M565, roll 19.

36. Col. Edmund B. Alexander to Cooper, October 9, 1857, 34 Cong. 1 sess., HED 2, serial 943, pp. 29–31; "Proclamation by the Governor," September 15, 1857, 35 Cong. 1 sess., HED 71, serial 956, pp. 34–35; Jesse Gove to Maria Gove, September 21, 1857, in Hammond, *Utah Expedition*, 59–61.

37. Alexander to Cooper, October 9, 1857, 35 Cong. 1 sess., HED 2, serial 943, pp. 29–31; "To the People of Utah Territory," November 21, 1857, 35 Cong. 1 sess., HED 71, serial 956, p. 92; Furniss, *Mormon Conflict*, 109–17, 143–44; Roland, *Johnston*, 193–96.

38. ARSW for 1857, 35, Cong. 1 sess., HED 2, serial 943, pp. 3, 6–9; Message from the President of the United States to the Two Houses of Congress, December 8, 1857,

35 Cong. 1 sess., HED 2, serial 943, pp. 23–26; Circular from Headquarters, January 11, 1858, 35 Cong. 1 sess., SED 1, serial 975, pp. 31–32; Risch, *Quartermaster Support of the Army*, 326–29.

39. General Order no. 8, April 15, 1858, AGO: Orders; General Order no. 3, May 17, 1858, USACC: Utah, Orders, vol. 8; Capt. Don Carlos Buell to Col. Francis Lee, May 17, 1858, USACC: Utah, LS, vol. 2; Harney to Floyd, May 19, 1858, AGO:LR, M567, roll 580; Lt. Henry Lee Scott to Harney, May 28, 1858, Harney to Assistant Adjutant General, June 10, 1858, and Endorsement by McDowell, August 2, 1858, all in AGO:LR, M567, roll 574.

40. Harney to Assistant Adjutant General, May 27, 1858, 35 Cong. 1 sess., SED 1, serial 975, pp. 105–6; Buell to Johnston, June 1, 1858, USACC: Utah, LS, vol. 2; Harney to Cooper, June 5, 1858, AGO:LR, M567, roll 595; General Order no. 6, June 7, 1858, USACC: Utah, Orders, vol. 8.

41. *LWT*, June 18, August 20, 1858.

42. Harney to Assistant Adjutant General, June 26, July 15, 1858, USACC: Utah, LS, vol. 2; "Position of the reinforcements in march for Utah, commanded by Brig. Gen. William S. Harney, Headquarters in the Field, June 30, 1858," 35 Cong. 2 sess., SED, serial 975, pp. 782–83; Hiram Martin Chittenden and Alfred Talbot Richardson, eds., *Life, Letters, and Travels of Father Pierre-Jean DeSmet, S.J., 1801–1873* (New York: Francis P. Harper, 1905), 1:69; Buell to DeSmet, June 21, 1858, USACC: Utah, LS, vol. 2; *The Denver Field and Farm*, February 22, 1908.

43. Furniss, *Mormon Conflict*, 173–75, 182–97, 200–202; Lazarus W. Powell and McCulloch to Floyd, June 26, 1858, 35 Cong. 2 sess., SED 1, serial 975, pp. 168–72; Harney to Assistant Adjutant General, July 15, August 3, 1858, 35 Cong. 2 sess., SED 1, serial 975, pp. 130–33.

44. Harney to Cooper, August 7, 1858, AGO:LR, M567, roll 580; Maj. Edward D. Townsend to Harney, August 6, 1858, AGO:LS, M565, roll 19.

45. [A. C. Brown], "The Utah Expedition," *Atlantic Monthly* 3 (March 1859): 365; Scott to Floyd, October 30, 1858, HQA:LS, M857, roll 5.

---

11. The Pacific Northwest

1. Capt. George E. Pickett to Pleasonton, August 3, 1859, and Capt. Geoffrey Phipps Hornby to Pickett, August 3, 1859, 40 Cong. 2 sess., SED 29, serial 1316, pp. 153–54; PD, July 30, 1859; *Daily Alta California*, August 11, 1859; Keith Murray,

The Pig War (Tacoma: Washington State Historical Society, 1968), 38–40; James O. McCabe, *The San Juan Water Boundary Question* (Toronto: Univ. of Toronto Press, 1965), 38–49.

2. General order no. 10, September 13, 1858, AGO: Orders; Townsend to Harney, September 14, 1858, AGO:LS, M565, roll 19.

3. Isaac I. Stevens to Manypenny, December 26, 1853, 33 Cong. 1 sess., SED 34, serial 698, pp. 6–9; "Reports from the Department of the Pacific," 34 Cong. 1 sess., HED 1, pt. 2, serial 841, pp. 77–89; ARSW for 1856, 34 Cong. 3 sess., SED 5, serial 876, pp. 147–216; Robert Ignatius Burns, *The Jesuits and the Indian Wars of the Northwest* (New Haven CT: Yale Univ. Press, 1966), 61–157, 287–356; Kent D. Richards, *Isaac I. Stevens: Young Man in a Hurry* (Provo UT: Brigham Young Univ. Press, 1979), 195–234, 331–33; Carl P. Schlicke, *General George Wright: Guardian of the Pacific Coast* (Norman: Univ. of Oklahoma Press, 1988), 141–96; E. A. Schwartz, *The Rogue River Indian War and Its Aftermath, 1850–1980* (Norman: Univ. of Oklahoma Press, 1997), 93–147.

4. Townsend to Harney, September 14, 1858, AGO:LS, M565, roll 19; Harney to Gibson, September 8, 1858, OQMG: Correspondence, box 377; Harney to Chief of the Engineer Corps, September 13, 1858, AGO:LR, M567, roll 580; Jesup to Lt. Thomas Swords, September 16, 1858, OQMG:LS, M745, roll 34; Harney to Floyd, September 17, 1858, AGO:LR, M567, roll 580; Capt. James B. Ricketts to Surgeon Gen. Thomas Lawson, August 29, 1858, AGO: Surgeons' Papers, Benjamin F. Harney; Pierre-Jean DeSmet to Francis DeSmet, September 19, 1858, Pierre-Jean DeSmet Collection.

5. Chittenden and Richardson, *DeSmet*, 2:732–40, Harney to Floyd, September 17, 1858, and Harney to McDowell, October 19, 1858, both in AGO:LR, M567, roll 580.

6. *Daily Alta California*, October 17, 1858; Harney to McDowell, October 19, 1858, AGO:LR, M567, roll 580; Col. George Wright to Maj. William W. Mackall, September 30, 1858, and Gen. Newman S. Clarke to Thomas, October 29, 1858, both in 35 Cong. 2 sess., SED 1, serial 975, pp. 403–4, 411–13.

7. Chittenden and Richardson, *DeSmet*, 2:740–42; Harney to Assistant Adjutant General, October 24, 1858, AGO:LR, M567, roll 585; PD, October 22, 1858.

8. Pleasonton to Wright, October 24, 1858, USACC: Oregon, LS, vol. 1; Wright to Pleasonton, October 28, 1858, and Harney to Assistant Adjutant General, October 29, 1858, both in AGO:LR, M567, roll 585; ARCIA for 1858, 35 Cong. 2 sess., SED 1, serial 974, pp. 355–56.

9. Pleasonton to DeSmet, October 28, 1858, AGO:LR, M567, roll 585; Special Order no. 4, October 4, 1858, USACC: Oregon, General and Special Orders, vol. 1; Chittenden and Richardson, *DeSmet,* 2:743.

10. General Order no. 3, October 31, 1858, USACC: Oregon, General and Special Orders, vol. 1; Hazard Stevens, *The Life of Isaac Ingalls Stevens* (Boston: Houghton Mifflin, 1900), 2:284; PD, February 18, 1859; *Oregon Statesman,* November 23, 1858; James W. Nesmith to Charles E. Mix, November 19, 1858, OSIA:LS, M560, roll 611.

11. Harney to Assistant Adjutant General, November 4, 5, 1858, AGO:LR, M567, roll 585.

12. Harney to Assistant Adjutant General, November 5, 22, 1858, AGO:LR, M567, roll 585; Samuel Cooper to Harney, February 23, 1859, AGO:LS, M565, roll 19.

13. DeSmet to Pleasonton, November 12, December 9, 1858, February 12, May 25, 1859, and Pleasonton to DeSmet, January 1, 1859, all in USACC: Oregon, LR, box 1; Chittenden and Richardson, *DeSmet,* 2:744–47, 764–66.

14. Wright to Pleasonton, April 12, 1859, and Ami P. Dennison to Wright, April 12, 1859, both in USACC: Oregon, LR, box 3; Pleasonton to Nesmith, April 13, 1859, and Pleasonton to Commanding Officer at Fort Dalles, April 14, 1859, both in USACC: Oregon, LS, vol. 1; Nesmith to Pleasonton, April 15, 1859, USACC: Oregon, LR, box 2; Harney to Assistant Adjutant General, April 19, 1859, AGO:LR, M567, roll 608.

15. Capt. Frederick T. Dent to Pleasonton, May 19, 1859, USACC: Oregon, LR, box 1; DeSmet to Pleasonton, May 25, 1859, AGO:LR, M567, roll 608; Burns, *Jesuits and the Indian Wars,* 249–58, 340–43, 350–51; Pleasonton to Commanding Officer at Fort Walla Walla, May 23, 1859, USACC: Oregon, LS, vol. 1; Harney to Assistant Adjutant General, May 21, 1859, AGO:LR, M567, roll 608, Harney to Kamiakin, May 31, 1859, USACC: Oregon, LS, vol. 1.

16. Harney to Adolphus Red Feather, Harney to Victor Happy Man, and Harney to Spokane Garry, May 31, 1859, all in USACC:Oregon, LS, vol. 1; Harney to Assistant Adjutant General, June 1, 1859, AGO:LR, M567, roll 608; Edward R. Geary to Alfred B. Greenwood, September 1, 1859, 36 Cong. 1 sess., SED 2, serial 1023, p. 758; Chittenden and Richardson, *DeSmet,* 2:767–68.

17. DeSmet to Pleasonton, May 28, 1859, Pleasonton to DeSmet, June 1, 1859, and Harney to Assistant Adjutant General, June 3, 1859, all in AGO:LR, M567, roll 608; Geary to Harney, May, 14, 1860, USACC:Oregon, LR, box 4; Richards, *Stevens,* 193–234, 323.

18. W. Turrentine Jackson, *Wagon Roads West: A Study of Federal Road Surveys and Construction in the Trans-Mississippi West, 1846–1869* (1952; reprint, New Haven CT: Yale Univ. Press, 1965), 84–85, 89–106; Oscar Osburn Winther, "Inland Transportation and Communication in Washington, 1844–1859," *Pacific Northwest Quarterly* 30 (October 1939): 371–80; Capt. Rufus Ingalls to Pleasonton, November 22, 1858, and Harney to Assistant Adjutant General, November 29, 1858, both in AGO:LR, M567, roll 585; Harney to Charles H. Mason, January 4, 1859, USACC:LS, vol. 1.

19. Endorsement by Floyd, March 26, 1859, on Harney to Assistant Adjutant General, November 29, 1859, AGO:LR, M567, roll 585; Special Order no. 40, April 27, 1859, USACC:Oregon, General and Special Orders, vol. 1; Pleasonton to Capt. Henry D. Wallen, April 28, 1859, AGO:LR, M567, roll 608; Capt. George Thom to Pleasonton, April 1, 1859, USACC:Oregon, LR, box 3; Richards, *Stevens,* 99–100, 122–23, 323; Jackson, *Wagon Roads West,* 84–85, 260.

20. Lt. James L. White to Pleasonton, July 31, August 16, 1859, USACC: Oregon, LR, box 3; Lt. John Mullan to Pleasonton, October 1, 1859, USACC: Oregon, LR, box 2; White to Pleasonton, January 8, April 2, 1860, USACC: Oregon, LR, box 5; Mullan to Pleasonton, June 1, 1860, USACC:Oregon, LR, box 4; Jackson, *Wagon Roads West,* 260–78.

21. Capt. Henry D. Wallen to Pleasonton, July 1, December 23, 1859, USACC: Oregon, LR, box 3; Harney to Assistant Adjutant General, September 15, 1860, AGO:LR, M567, roll 609; Harney to Assistant Adjutant General, October 6, 1859, AGO:LR, M567, roll 608; Pleasonton to Capt. Andrew Jackson Smith, March 29, 1860, USACC: Oregon, LS, vol. 2; Special Order no. 37, March 28, 1860, USACC: Oregon, General and Special Orders, vol. 1; Jackson, *Wagon Roads West,* 84–88, 104–6.

22. McCabe, *San Juan Water Boundary Question,* 3–19; Murray, *Pig War,* 7–13, 23–29; Dorothy O. Johansen and Charles M. Gates, *Empire of the Columbia: A History of the Pacific Northwest* (New York: Harper & Brothers, 1957), 184–200, 266–69; William L. Marcy to Stevens, July 14, 1855, and Marcy to John F. Crampton, July 17, 1855, both in 40 Cong. 2 sess., SED 29, serial 1316, pp. 144–45.

23. Murray, *Pig War,* 29–32; Barry M. Gough, *The Royal Navy and the Northwest Coast of North America, 1810–1914: A Study of British Maritime Ascendancy* (Vancouver: Univ. of British Columbia Press, 1971), 154–55; Archibald Campbell to Cass, February 10, 1858, 40 Cong. 2 sess., SED 29, serial 1316, pp. 7–10, and Campbell to Capt. James C. Prevost, May 18, 1859, 40 Cong. 2 sess., SED 29, serial 1316, 107–8; McCabe, *San Juan Water Boundary Question,* 36–37.

24. Affidavit of Lyman Cutler, September 7, 1859, 40 Cong. 2 sess., SED 29, serial 1316, pp. 183–84, and A. G. Dallas to Harney, May 10, 1860, 40 Cong. 2 sess., SED 29, serial 1316, pp. 260–61; Charles John Griffin to James Douglas, June 15, 1859, San Juan Island Correspondence, Envelope 1, British Columbia Provincial Archives.

25. Isaac Foney to Floyd, January 5, 1859, copy in USACC: Oregon, LR, box 2; J. M. Haggaret, Samuel McCauley, J. E. Higgins, and nineteen others to Harney, July 11, 1859, 40 Cong. 2 sess., SED 29, serial 1316, pp. 149–50; Harney to Assistant Adjutant General, July 19, 1859, AGO:LR, M567, roll 608. Murray, in *Pig War*, 35–36, maintains that Harney decided on the spot how he would respond to the residents' request and dictated a petition that would justify that decision. However, evidence does not support a conclusion that Harney chose his course of action on July 9. Murray's sources are Harney's July 19 letter to the assistant adjutant general and an unpublished account written thirty years later by Captain Granville O. Haller, who was not present with Harney on San Juan Island. See also Granville O. Haller, "San Juan and Secession: Possible Relation to the War of the Rebellion–Did General Harney Try to Make Trouble with English to Aid the Conspiracy?–A Careful Review of His Orders and the Circumstances Attending the Disputed Possessions during the Year 1859," reprinted from *Tacoma Sunday Ledger*, January 1896, 1–16 (date, place, and publisher of reprint unlisted).

26. Harney to Assistant Adjutant General, July 19, 1859, AGO:LR, M567, roll 608; Stevens, *Isaac Stevens*, 2:290. Richards, Isaac Stevens's definitive biographer, states that he and Harney did not see each other until sometime in August. See Richards, *Stevens*, 329.

27. Special Order no. 72, July 16, 1859, USACC: Oregon, General and Special Orders, vol. 1; Geographical Memoir, n.d., Pleasonton to Casey, July 18, 1859, and Pleasonton to Pickett, July 18, 1859, both in 40 Cong. 2 sess., SED 29, serial 1316, pp. 137–38, 145–47; Harney to Assistant Adjutant General, July 19, 1859, AGO:LR, M567, roll 608.

28. Order no. 1, July 27, 1859, 40 Cong. 2 sess., SED 29, serial 1316, p. 117; Affidavit of Lyman Cutler, September 7, 1859, both in 40 Cong. 2 sess., SED 29, serial 1316, pp. 183–84; John F. DeCourcy to James Douglas, July 29, 1859, "Correspondence relative to the occupation of the Island of San Juan by United States' troops," August to October 1859, *British Foreign Office Documents*, 66–67.

29. "Protest of Governor Douglas against the Occupation of San Juan Island," August 2, 1859, and "Message of Governor Douglas to the Legislature of Vancouver's Island," August 3, 1859, 40 Cong. 2 sess., SED 29, serial 1316, pp. 117–18;

Walter N. Sage, *Sir James Douglas and British Columbia* (Toronto: Univ. of Toronto Press, 1930), 266–69.

30. Casey to Pickett, July 31, 1859, Pickett to Pleasonton, August 3, 1859, Geoffrey P. Hornby to Pickett, August 3, 1859, and Pickett to Hornby, August 3, 1859, all in 40 Cong. 2 sess., SED 29, serial 1316, pp. 151–57; Hornby to James Douglas, August 4, 1859, "Correspondence relative to the occupation of the Island of San Juan by United States' troops," August to October 1859, *British Foreign Office Documents,* pp. 72–73.

31. Harney to Douglas, August 6, 1859, Pleasonton to Pickett, August 6, 1859, and Harney to Senior Officer of the United States Navy Commanding Squadron on the Pacific Coast, August 7, 1859, all in 40 Cong. 2 sess., SED 29, serial 1316, pp. 157–59.

32. Harney to Cooper, August 7, 1859, and W. R. Drinkard to Harney, September 3, 1859, both in 40 Cong. 2 sess., SED 29, serial 1316, pp. 150–51, 148–49.

33. Campbell to Harney, August 14, 1859, Harney to Campbell, August 16, 1859, and Campbell to Cass, August 18, 1859, all in 40 Cong. 2 sess., SED 29, serial 1316, pp. 120–23.

34. Drinkard to Scott, September 16, 1859, 40 Cong. 2 sess., SED 29, serial 1316, pp. 161–62; Elliott, *Scott,* 665–66; PD, August 12, 1859; *Weekly Oregonian,* August 13, 1859; *Daily Alta California,* July 30, 1859.

35. Reavis, *Harney,* 319, 345; Stevens, *Isaac Stevens,* 2:293–94. Murray, *Pig War,* 20–21, 35, provides the most comprehensive discussion of explanations for Harney's decision and concludes that it is impossible to determine what motivated him. Richards, *Stevens,* 329, agrees. The British and Canadian perspectives are Sage, *Sir James Douglas,* 265; Gough, *Royal Navy,* 157; and McCabe, *San Juan Water Boundary Question,* 39, 57–58. Andrew Fish, "The Last Phase of the Oregon Boundary Question: The Struggle for San Juan Island," *Quarterly of the Oregon Historical Society* 22 (September 1921): 211, ascribes Harney's decision to the prevailing negative view of the Hudson's Bay Company.

36. Harney to Charles H. Mason, January 4, 1859, and Harney to George L. Curry, January 8, 1859, both in USACC: Oregon, LS, vol. 1; Harney to Assistant Adjutant General, July 19, 1859, AGO:LR, M567, roll 608; Watson, "The Uncertain Road to Manifest Destiny," in *Manifest Destiny and Empire,* ed. Haynes and Morris, 68–71, 74–76, 98–102; Skelton, *Profession,* 333–38.

37. Casey to Pleasonton, August 12, 1859, 40 Cong. 2 sess., SED 29, serial 1316, pp.

164–67; McCabe, *San Juan Water Boundary Question*, 43, 51; Wesley J. Gordon, *General George E. Pickett in Life and Legend* (Chapel Hill: Univ. of North Carolina Press, 1998), 59–60.

38. Douglas to Harney, August 13, 1859, Harney to Douglas, August 24, 1859, excerpt from *British Colonist*, August 17, 1859, and Harney to Cooper, August 29, 1859, all in 40 Cong. 2 sess., SED 29, serial 1316, pp. 171–72, 173, 176–77, 177–79.

39. Casey to Pleasonton, August 22, 1859 (two letters), Harney to Assistant Adjutant General, September 14, 1859, Harney Endorsement, September 19, 1859, on Richard D. Gholson to Harney, August 21, 1859, and Harney to Secretary of War, October 10, 1859, all in 40 Cong. 2 sess., SED 29, serial 1316, pp. 180–82, 185–86.

40. Journal History of the Mormon Church, November 14, 1859; *Weekly Oregonian*, October 22, 1859; Thomas to Cooper, October 22, 1859, 40 Cong. 2 sess., SED 29, serial 1316, pp. 188–89, and Scott to Harney, November 15, 1859, 40 Cong. 2 sess., SED 29, serial 1316, p. 203; Harney to Floyd, August 30, 1860, AGO:LR, M567, roll 629; Elliott, *Scott*, 667.

41. Thomas to Cooper, October 22, 1859, Scott to Douglas, October 25, 1859, Douglas to Scott, October 26, 29, 1859, Scott to Douglas, November 2, 1859, and Douglas to Scott, November 3, 1859, all in 40 Cong. 2 sess., SED 29, serial 1316, pp. 188–89, 192–95.

42. Scott to Douglas, November 5, 1859, Special Order by Scott, November 5, 1859, and Thomas to Harney, November 9, 1859, all in 40 Cong. 2 sess., SED 29, serial 1316, pp. 197–99, 202–3.

43. Scott to Harney, November 15, 1859, Special Order by Scott, November 15, 1859, and Harney to Assistant Adjutant General, November 17, 1859, all in 40 Cong. 2 sess., SED 29, serial 1316, pp. 203–4; Harney to Cooper, November 17, 1859, AGO:LR, M567, roll 609.

44. Col. Henry K. Craig to Lt. William T. Welcker, September 15, 1859, USACC: Oregon, LR, box 3; Harney to Cooper, December 26, 1859, USACC: Oregon, LS, vol. 1; Alexander C. Badger to Mrs. Alexander C. Badger, October 8, 1860, Badger Collection.

45. Pleasonton to Commanding Officer of Fort Vancouver, July 23, 1859, Lt. Henry V. DeHart to Pleasonton, July 24, 1859, Pleasonton to Commanding Officer of Fort Vancouver, July 30, 1859, DeHart to Thomas, August 4, 5, 1859, and Charges and Specifications exhibited against First Lieutenant Henry V. DeHart of the 3d Regiment of Artillery, August 5, 1859, all in AGO:LR, M567, roll 609.

46. Lt. Henry C. Hodges to Pleasonton, March 15, 1860, Pleasonton to Commanding Officer of Fort Vancouver, March 21, 1860, Charges and Specifications exhibited against 1st Lt. Henry C. Hodges, Adjutant, 4th Infantry, April 4, 1860, Hodges to Thomas, March 28, 1860, Endorsement by Scott, May 10, 1860, Endorsement by Floyd, August 15, 1860, on Harney to Cooper, June 21, 1860, and Charges and Specifications preferred against Brig. Gen. William S. Harney, U.S. Army, July 30, 1860, all in AGO:LR, M567, roll 629.

47. Mary Harney to Mrs. Daniel M. Frost, February 17, 1860, WSH; Townsend to Harney, May 16, 1860, AGO:LS, M565, roll 19.

48. Baynes to Capt. Lewis C. Hunt, March 20, 1860, Hunt to Pleasonton, March 29, 1860, Scott to Harney, November 15, 1859, and Pleasonton to Pickett, April 10, 1860, all in 40 Cong. 2 sess., SED 29, serial 1316, pp. 203, 210–11; Harney to Floyd, August 30, 1860, AGO:LR, M567, roll 629.

49. Pleasonton to Pickett, April 10, 1860, Special Order no. 41, April 10, 1860, and Pickett to Capt. George Bazalgette, April 30, 1860, all in 40 Cong. 2 sess., SED 29, serial 1316, pp. 210–11, 212, 257.

50. Scott to Floyd, May 14, 1860, Cooper to Harney, June 8, 1860, and Hunt to Maj. Erasmus D. Keyes, April 24, 1860, all in 40 Cong. 2 sess., SED 29, serial 1316, pp. 212–14; Lord Lyons to Cass, June 6, 1860, and Cass to Lyons, June 8, 1860, 40 Cong. 2 sess., SED 29, serial 1316, pp. 256–57, 258–59.

51. General Order no. 6, July 5, 1860, USACC: Oregon, General and Special Orders, vol. 1; Harney to Floyd, August 30, 1860, AGO:LR, M567, roll 629; Correspondence with General Harney, 38 Cong. 1 sess., HED 98, serial 1057, pp. 1–29.

52. Journal History of the Mormon Church, October 12, 1860; Capt. Julius P. Garesché to Harney, October 26, 1860, and Harney to Cooper, October 29, 1860, both in AGO:LR, M567, roll 629; McCabe, *San Juan Water Boundary Question,* 106–34; Thomas McArthur Anderson, "Army Episodes and Anecdotes; or Life at Vancouver Barracks," unpublished manuscript, Beinecke Rare Book and Manuscript Library, Yale University.

---

12. Loyal Soldier

1. *DMSJ,* May 11, 1861; William T. Sherman, *Memoirs of General William T. Sherman* (New York: D. Appleton, 1875), 1:167–74; Ulysses S. Grant, *Personal Memoirs* (New York: Charles L. Webster, 1885), 1:236–38; James W. Covington, "The Camp Jackson Affair: 1861," *MHR* 55 (April 1961): 207–11.

2. Allan Nevins, *The Emergence of Lincoln: Prologue to the Civil War, 1859–1861* (New York: Charles Scribner's Sons, 1950), 318–28; Arthur Roy Kirkpatrick, "Missouri on the Eve of the Civil War," MHR 55 (January 1961): 99–100; Doris Davis Wallace, "The Political Campaign of 1860 in Missouri," MHR 70 (January 1976): 162–67.

3. Albert Castel, *General Sterling Price and the Civil War in the West* (Baton Rouge: Louisiana State Univ. Press, 1968), 7–10; Audrey Louise Olson, "St. Louis Germans, 1850–1920: The Nature of an Immigrant Community and Its Relation to the Assimilation Process" (Ph.D. diss., University of Kansas, 1970), 13–14; William E. Parrish, *Frank Blair: Lincoln's Conservative* (Columbia: Univ. of Missouri Press, 1998), 50–59, 60–64; William F. Lyon, "Claiborne Fox Jackson and the Secession Crisis in Missouri," MHR 58 (July 1964): 422–30; Wallace, "Political Campaign of 1860," 167–82.

4. Judge J. Williams to Buchanan, November 21, 1860, AGO:LR, M567, roll 630; Cooper to Harney, November 21, 1860, AGO:LS, M565, roll 20; Harney to Cooper, December 2, 1860, Lt. David R. Jones to Maj. Henry W. Wessels, November 26, 1860, Wessels to Cooper, December 11, 1860, and Harney to Cooper, December 17, 1860, all in AGO:LR, M567, roll 630; Robert E. Miller, "Daniel Marsh Frost, C.S.A.," MHR 85 (July 1991): 382–85; Jay Monaghan, *The Civil War on the Western Border, 1859–1865* (Boston: Little, Brown, 1955), 100–123; Christopher Phillips, *Damned Yankee: The Life of General Nathaniel Lyon* (Columbia: Univ. of Missouri Press, 1990), xiii–xiv, 14, 104–20, 124–26.

5. Kirkpatrick, "Missouri on the Eve," 101–3; Lyon, "Claiborne Fox Jackson," 422–23.

6. Thomas to Harney, January 26, 1861, and Lt. Col. George W. Lay to Harney, February 13, 1861, both in HQA:LS, M857, roll 5; Harney to Thomas, February 19, 1861, WR, 1:1:654; Heidler, "Twiggs," 209–13.

7. Kirkpatrick, "Missouri on the Eve," 103–6; *Journal and Proceedings of the Missouri State Convention Held at Jefferson City and St. Louis, March, 1861* (St. Louis: George Knapp, 1861), 58, 258, 269; Christopher Phillips, "The Radical Crusade: Blair, Lyon, and the Advent of the Civil War in Missouri," *Gateway Heritage* 10 (spring 1990): 26–31.

8. Francis P. Blair Jr. to Simon Cameron, March 11, 1861, Special Order no. 74, March 13, 1861, and Capt. Seth Williams to Capt. Nathaniel Lyon, March 13, 1861, all in WR, 1:1:656, 658–59.

9. Williams to Capt. Alexander Montgomery, March 19, 1861, AGO:LR, M619, roll

67; Thomas to Harney, March 29, 1861, AGO:LS, M565, roll 20; Townsend to Harney, April 9, 1861, AGO:LR, M619, roll 2; genealogy file, WSH; Ray W. Irwin, "Missouri in Crisis: The Journal of Captain Albert Tracy, 1861," MHR 51 (October 1956): 15–16.

10. Williams to Bvt. Maj. Peter V. Hagner, April 6, 1861, WR, 1:1:661; Harney to Thomas, April 8, 1861, AGO:LR, M619, roll 67; Williams to Hagner, April 9, 10, 1861, and Williams to Maj. Nathaniel Macrae, April 10, 1861, all in WR, 1:1:662–64.

11. "A Proclamation by the President of the United States," April 15, 1861, WR, 3:1:67–68, Cameron to Governors, April 15, 1861, WR, 3:1:68–69, and Claiborne F. Jackson to Cameron, April 17, 1861, WR, 3:1:82–83.

12. Arthur Roy Kirkpatrick, "Missouri in the Early Months of the Civil War," MHR 55 (April 1961): 235–37; DMSJ, April 17, 1861; Jefferson Davis to Jackson, April 23, 1861, WR, 1:1:688.

13. Williams to Lyon, April 18, 1861, WR, 1:1:668; John M. Schofield, *Forty-six Years in the Army* (New York: Century, 1897), 30–33; R. J. Howard to Montgomery Blair, April 16, 1861, AGO:LR, M619, roll 27; Francis P. Blair Jr. to Cameron, April 18, 1861, and Francis P. Blair Jr. to Montgomery Blair, April 20, 1861, both in BFP, box 6; Harney to Townsend, April 16, 1861, WR, 1:1:666–67.

14. Harney to John A. Brownlee, April 22, 1861, WR, 1:1:670; Townsend to Harney, April 19, 1861, AGO: Generals' Papers, William S. Harney; Francis P. Blair Jr. to Cameron, April 18, 1861, BFP, box 6.

15. Lyon to F. J. Dean, April 16, 1861, WR, 1:1:667; Cameron to Richard Yates, April 20, 1861, Cameron to Commander of the Arsenal at St. Louis, April 20, 1861, WR, 1:1:669, Harney to Brownlee, April 22, 1861, WR, 1:1:670, and Harney to Townsend, April 20, 1863, in Reavis, *Harney,* 354.

16. Kirkpatrick, "Missouri in the Early Months," 237–38; Thomas to Harney, April 21, 1861, WR, 1:1:669; Harney to Thomas, April 22, 1861, AGO:LR, M619, roll 27; Phillips, "Radical Crusade," 38–39.

17. MD, April 21, 1861; Powell Conrad to Robert Young Conrad, April 26, 1861, Holmes Conrad Papers; Harney to O'Fallon, May 1, 1861, in Reavis, *Harney,* 388–92.

18. MD, April 27, 1861; Lyon to Cameron, April 30, 1861, and Cameron to Lyon, WR, 1:1:675; Phillips, *Lyon,* 164–68.

19. Jackson to J. W. Tucker, April 28, 1861, James O. Broadhead Papers; Davis to

Jackson, April 23, 1861, WR, 1:1:688; Kirkpatrick, "Missouri in the Early Months," 238–39.

20. Covington, "The Camp Jackson Affair," 201–2; MD, May 7, 1861; Lyon to Thomas, May 11, 1861, WR, 1:3:4–5; James Peckham, *Gen. Nathaniel Lyon, and Missouri in 1861* (New York: American News, 1866), 139–43; William E. Parrish, "General Nathaniel Lyon: A Portrait," MHR 49 (October 1954): 9–11; Phillips, *Lyon*, 179–84.

21. Frost to Lyon, May 10, 1861, WR, 1:3:5–6, and Lyon to Frost, May 10, 1861, WR, 1:3:6–7; Covington, "The Camp Jackson Affair," 205–7; Phillips, *Lyon*, 185–89.

22. MR, May 11, 1861; MD, May 13, 1861; DMSJ, May 11, 1861; Covington, "The Camp Jackson Affair," 207–11; Phillips, *Lyon*, 189–92.

23. Lyon to Thomas, May 11, 1861, WR, 1:3:4–5, and Lyon to Thomas, May 12, 1861, WR, 1:3:9; MD, May 13, 1861; Covington, "The Camp Jackson Affair," 210–12; Peckham, *Lyon*, 162–63.

24. William E. Parrish, *Turbulent Partnership: Missouri for the Union, 1861–1865* (Columbia: Univ. of Missouri Press, 1963), 24–26; Phillips, *Lyon*, 197–98; Kirkpatrick "Missouri in the Early Months," 240–41.

25. General Order no. 10, May 11, 1861, Harney to Townsend, May 13, 1861, and "Proclamation," May 12, 1861, all in WR, 1:3:369–70; John F. Darby to Reavis, March 17, 1878, newspaper clipping in genealogy file, WSH; W. A. Croffut, ed., *Fifty Years in Camp and Field: Diary of Major-General Ethan Allen Hitchcock, U.S.A.* (New York: G. P. Putnam's Sons, 1909), 428–31. Hitchcock, who described his relationship with Harney as "cold," claimed that Harney asked him to join in the meeting with Krum and Darby and that Krum, not Harney, wrote the proclamation. The language and tenor of the piece indicate that Harney wrote it.

26. MR, May 11, 1861; DMSJ, May 10, 13, 1861; MD, May 13, 1861; Lyon to Thomas, May 12, 1861, WR, 1:3:9.

27. Peckham, *Lyon*, 188–89; Harney to Townsend, May 14, 1861, "To the People of the State of Missouri," May 14, 1861, Harney to Cameron, May 15, 1861, and Harney to Townsend, May 17, 1861, all in WR, 1:3:371–72, 374. Hitchcock claimed that he, Krum, and Darby advised Harney about this proclamation, too, and that he, Hitchcock, wrote most of it. However, there is no corroborating evidence for his claim. Like Harney, Hitchcock approved of slavery and opposed secession. But he also opposed the use of force against those states that had already seceded. Thus it seems unlikely that he advocated a position as strong as the one Harney took.

28. MD, May 15, 1861; DMSJ, May 14, 1861; George Caleb Bingham to James S. Rollins, May 16, 1861, in C. B. Rollins, ed., "Letters of George Caleb Bingham to James S. Rollins," MHR 33 (July 1939): 514; Abraham C. Myers to Twiggs, May 16, 1861, WR, 1:4:501.

29. Francis P. Blair Jr. to Montgomery Blair, ca. May 20, 1861, and Franklin A. Dick to Benjamin Farrar, May 16, 1861 (two letters), all in BFP, box 6; Special Order no. 135, May 16, 1861, WR, 1:3:374; Parrish, *Turbulent Partnership*, 27–28.

30. Montgomery Blair to Farrar or Francis P. Blair Jr. in Reavis, *Harney*, 376–77; Dick to Farrar, May 18, 1861, BFP, box 6; Lincoln to Francis P. Blair Jr., May 18, 1861, in Reavis, *Harney*, 382.

31. Capt. Nelson Cole to Lyon, May 16, 1861, WR, 1:3:10–11; James O. Broadhead to Edwin Draper, May 21, 1861, Broadhead Papers; Robert E. Shalhope, *Sterling Price: Portrait of a Southerner* (Columbia: Univ. of Missouri Press, 1971), 158–59.

32. Agreement, May 21, 1861, and "To the People of the State of Missouri," May 21, 1861, WR, 1:3:374–75; Thomas C. Reynolds, "Gen. Sterling Price and the Confederacy," typescript, MOHS, n.d., 21–22; Castel, *Price*, 15–19.

33. MD, May 22, 1861; DMSJ, May 22, 1861; MR, May 21, 1861; LWT, May 21, 1861.

34. Broadhead to Montgomery Blair, May 22, 1861, Broadhead Papers; Thomas T. Gantt to Montgomery Blair, May 21, 1861, BFP, box 6; Francis P. Blair Jr. to Cameron, May 24, 1861, WR, 1:3:375–76.

35. Harney to Gen. Sterling Price, May 24, 1861; Price to Harney, May 27, 1861, and Harney to Townsend, with enclosures, May 30, 1861, all in WR, 1:3:378–79; Francis P. Blair Jr. to Montgomery Blair, ca. May 25, 1861, BFP, box 6.

36. Francis P. Blair Jr. to Montgomery Blair, ca. May 25, 1861, BFP, box 6; Harney to Price, May 27, 1861 (three letters), WR, 1:3:379–80, and Price to Harney, May 28, 29, 1861, WR, 1:3:380–81.

37. Harney to Thomas, May 29, 1861, WR, 1:3:377.

38. Thomas to Harney, May 27, 1861, WR, 1:3:376, and Harney to Thomas, May 31, 1861, WR, 1:3:381, and Francis P. Blair Jr. to Lincoln, May 30, 1861, WR, 1:3:222–25; Peckham, *Lyon*, 221–22.

39. Harney to Thomas, May 31, 1861, WR, 1:3:381; Gantt to Montgomery Blair, May 31, 1861, BFP, box 6.

40. Harney to Thomas, June 5, 1861, WR, 1:3:383; Francis P. Blair Jr. to Montgomery Blair, June 1861, BFP, box 6.

41. *MR*, June 1, 1861; General Order no. 5, May 31, 1861, and Special Order no. 4, June 1, 1861, *WR*, 1:3:381–82; *LWT*, June 7, 1861; Castel, *Price*, 23–24.

42. Thomas L. Snead, *The Fight for Missouri from the Election of Lincoln to the Death of Lyon* (New York: Charles Scribner's Sons, 1866), 196–200; Shalhope, *Price*, 165–66; Castel, *Price*, 24; Phillips, *Lyon*, 211–14.

43. *LWT*, June 21, 1861; Lyon to Lt. Col. Chester Harding Jr., June 18, 1861, *WR*, 1:3:385; Kirkpatrick, "Missouri in the Early Months," 244–46.

44. General Order no. 30, June 6, 1861, *WR*, 1:3:384; Alexander Ramsey to Maj. Gen. Henry W. Halleck, August 26, 1862, *WR*, 1:13:597, and Samuel J. Kirkwood to Edwin M. Stanton, September 8, 1862, *WR*, 1:13:620; Harney to Cameron, November 9, 1861, AGO:LR, M619, roll 30.

45. Skelton, *Profession*, 215–16; Halleck to Stanton, May 20, 1863, AGO:LR, M619, roll 157; General Order no. 220, July 16, 1863, AGO: Orders; General Order no. 178, October 31, 1862, *WR*, 1:11:pt. 3:352; Special Order no. 24, AGO: Personnel, "Proceedings of a Court Martial . . . Hammond . . . 1864," file 4743; Harney to Thomas, July 2, 1862, AGO:LR, M619, roll 105, and Harney to Thomas, June 30, 1866, AGO:LR, M619, roll 481; "John DeLaney's sister" to John DeLaney, July 19, 1861, MFC; Anthony W. Smith to "Father and Mother," July 29, 1861, Anthony W. Smith Papers.

46. Andrew Rolle, *John Charles Frémont: Character as Destiny* (Norman: Univ. of Oklahoma Press, 1991), 190–213; Robert L. Turkoly-Jozik, "Frémont and the Western Department," *MHR* 82 (July 1988): 377–84.

---

13. Our Old Friend

1. "Sand Creek Massacre," 39 Cong. 2 sess., *SED* 26, serial 1277, pp. 1–228; Stan Hoig, *The Sand Creek Massacre* (Norman: Univ. of Oklahoma Press, 1961), 110–22, 145–56.

2. Utley, *Frontiersmen in Blue*, 214–43, 259–86, 297–303; Rodman Wilson Paul, *Mining Frontiers of the Far West, 1848–1880* (New York: Holt, Rinehart and Winston, 1963), 56–58, 68–70, 87–89, 96–97, 109–16, 138–45; Donald J. Berthrong, *The Southern Cheyennes* (Norman: Univ. of Oklahoma Press, 1963), 224–30.

3. Utley, *Frontiersmen in Blue*, 307–30; Donald Chaput, "Generals, Indian Agents, Politicians: The Doolittle Survey of 1865," *Western Historical Quarterly* 3 (July 1972): 269–72; Harry Kelsey, "The Doolittle Report of 1867: Its Preparation and Shortcomings," *Arizona and the West* 8 (summer 1975): 107–12.

4. James Harlan to Edwin M. Stanton, July 31, 1865, AGO:LR, M619, roll 367; "Report of D. N. Cooley, as president of the Southern Treaty Commission," October 30, 1865, and "Official report of the proceedings of the council with the Indians of the west and southwest, held at Fort Smith, Arkansas, in September 1865," 39 Cong. 1 sess., HED 1, serial 1248, pp. 480–96, 496–537.

5. Jesse H. Leavenworth to John R. Doolittle, December 1, 1865, and agreement signed by the chiefs and headmen of the Arapaho, Comanche, and Kiowa tribes of Indians of the Upper Arkansas, and the Arapahos south of the Arkansas River, August 23, 1865, both in BIA:LR, M234, roll 198.

6. "Record of Meetings of Commissioners to Treat with the Cheyennes," BIA: Treaties, T494, roll 7; *Laws and Treaties,* 2:679–85; John B. Sanborn et al. to Harlan, October 23, 1865, BIA:LR, M234, roll 198.

7. Robert M. Utley, *Frontier Regulars: The United States Army and the Indian, 1866–1891* (New York: Macmillan, 1973), 98–107, 113–25; James C. Olson, *Red Cloud and the Sioux Problem* (Lincoln: Univ. of Nebraska Press, 1965), 32–57; George Bird Grinnell, *The Fighting Cheyennes* (1915; reprint, Norman: Univ. of Oklahoma Press, 1956), 230–62; *Congressional Globe,* 40 Cong. 1 sess., pp. 673, 756; "Condition of the Indian Tribes: Report of the Joint Special Committee, Appointed under Joint Resolution of March 3, 1865," 39 Cong. 2 sess., *Senate Report* 156, serial 1279, pp. 3–10.

8. *Statutes at Large,* 14:17–18; ARCIA for 1867, 40 Cong. 2 sess., HED 1, serial 1326, p. 4; *Congressional Globe,* 40 Cong. 1 sess., p. 670; Prucha, *Great Father,* 1:488–90; Arthur P. Mattingly, "The Great Plains Peace Commission of 1867," *Journal of the West* 15 (July 1976): 25–27.

9. Orville H. Browning to Stanton, July 29, 1867, AGO:LR, M619, roll 556; Harney to Thomas, August 8, 1867, AGO:LR, M619, roll 554; William T. Sherman to John Sherman, August 3, 1867, William T. Sherman Papers, vol. 21; ARSW for 1867, 40 Cong. 2 sess., HED 1, vol. 2, pt. 1, serial 1324, pp. 65–68; Robert G. Athearn, *William Tecumseh Sherman and the Settlement of the West* (Norman: Univ. of Oklahoma Press, 1956), 171–73.

10. Douglas C. Jones, *The Treaty of Medicine Lodge: The Story of the Great Treaty Council as Told by Eyewitnesses* (Norman: Univ. of Oklahoma Press, 1966), 15–17; *New York Times,* July 28, 1867; [George William Curtis], "What Shall Be Done with the Indians," *Harper's Weekly* 11 (August 17, 1867): 514–15; *Nebraska City News,* August 9, 1867, quoted in Athearn, *Sherman,* 174; *Montana*

Post, August 10, 1867, quoted in Athearn, *Sherman*, 173–74; UD, February 2, August 31, 1867.

11. PIPC, August 6, 1867, Sherman to Maj. Gen. Winfield S. Hancock, August 7, 1867, Sherman to Bvt. Maj. Gen. Christopher C. Augur, August 7, 1867, Nathaniel B. Taylor to G. P. Beauvais, August 8, 1867, Taylor to Henry M. Mathews, August 8, 1867, and Browning to Taylor, August 8, 1867, all in ID:SCIPC, box 671 A.

12. PIPC, August 12, 13, 16, 24, 31, 1867, ID:SCIPC, box 671 A.

13. PIPC, August 31, September 4, 5, 6, 12, 13, 14, 18, 19, 20, 1867, ID:SCIPC, box 671 A; Athearn, *Sherman*, 174–82.

14. Athearn, *Sherman*, 183; Andrew Johnson to Gen. Ulysses S. Grant, October 4, 1867, roll 892, and Grant to Augur, October 5, 1867, roll 893, both in BIA:LR, Upper Platte Agency, M234.

15. Jones, *Treaty of Medicine Lodge*, 15–29, 66–74, 206–7; Henry M. Stanley, *My Early Travels and Adventures in America* (1895; reprint, Lincoln: Univ. of Nebraska Press, 1982), 49, 225–30.

16. PIPC, October 4, 16, 18, 1867, ID:SCIPC, box 671 A; Stanley, *Travels*, 230–34.

17. PIPC, October 19, 20, 1867, and ID:SCIPC, box 671 A; Stanley, *Travels*, 244–58; *Laws and Treaties*, 2:977–84.

18. PIPC, October 21, 22, 24, 28, 1867, ID:SCIPC, box 671 A; Grinnell, *Fighting Cheyennes*, 250–62; Stanley, *Travels*, 258–62; [Henry M. Stanley], "A British Journalist Reports the Medicine Lodge Peace Councils of 1867," *Kansas Historical Quarterly* 33 (autumn 1967): 305–7.

19. Jones, *Treaty of Medicine Lodge*, 130, 143–44, 179–80; *Laws and Treaties*, 2:984–89; Robert M. Utley, ed., *Life in Custer's Cavalry: Diaries and Letters of Albert and Jennie Barnitz* (New Haven CT: Yale Univ. Press, 1977), 115.

20. A. S. H. White to Browning, November 1, 1867, ID:SCIPC, box 671 A, and PIPC, November 2, 3, 12, 13, 26, 1867, ID:SCIPC, box 671 A; *Laws and Treaties*, 2:1008–11; Stanley, *Travels*, 267–85; Olson, *Red Cloud*, 68–69.

21. PIPC, December 11, 12, 1867, January 7, 10, 1868, ID:SCIPC, box 671 A; Report to the President by the Indian Peace Commission, January 7, 1868, 40 Cong. 3 sess., HED 1, serial 1366, pp. 486–510.

22. Grant to Sherman, March 2, 3, 1868, USACC: Platte, LR, box 7; PIPC, April 1, 2, 4, 13, 28, 19, May 9, 24, 25, 28, July 2, 5, October 8, 1868, ID:SCIPC, box 671 A.

23. PIPC, April 13, 28, May 25, June 15, 19, July 2, 5, 1867, ID:SCIPC, box 671 A; *Laws and Treaties,* 2:998–1007, 1012–24.

24. Harney to Thomas, July 31, 1868, AGO:LR, M619, roll 628; Sherman to Browning, August 3, 1868, ID:SCIPC, box 671 A; ARSW for 1868, 40 Cong. 3 sess., HED 1, vol. 3, serial 1367, pp. 3–9; Athearn, *Sherman,* 213–18; Paul Andrew Hutton, *Phil Sheridan and His Army* (Lincoln: Univ. of Nebraska Press, 1985), 28–30, 39–41; *Statutes at Large,* 14:171–77; General Order no. 4, August 10, 1868, USACC: Missouri, Orders, 1866–1869; Sherman to John M. Schofield, August 9, 1868, AGO:LR, M619, roll 629.

25. Sherman to Townsend, September 5, 1868, BIA:LR, Upper Platte, M234, roll 892; Henderson to Sherman, October 14, 1868, William T. Sherman Papers, vol. 24; Utley, *Frontier Regulars,* 137–56; Hutton, *Sheridan,* 37–114; Stan Hoig, *The Battle of the Washita: The Sheridan-Custer Indian Campaign of 1867–1869* (Lincoln: Univ. of Nebraska Press, 1976), xiii–xv, 51–53, 126–44.

26. ARSW for 1868, 40 Cong. 3 sess., HED 1, vol. 3, serial 1367, pp. 3, 8–9, 33–35; Robert W. Larson, *Red Cloud: Warrior Statesman of the Lakota Sioux* (Norman: Univ. of Oklahoma Press, 1997), 121–25.

27. UD, August 15, September 12, 1868; PIPC, October 8, 1868, ID:SCIPC, box 671 A; Brig. Gen. John B. Sanborn and Harney to Charles E. Mix, June 4, 1868, BIA:LR, Upper Platte Agency, M234, roll 893; Richmond Lee Clow, "The Whetstone Indian Agency, 1868–1872," *South Dakota History* 7 (summer 1977): 291–95; D. C. Poole, *Among the Sioux of Dakota: Eighteen Months' Experience as an Indian Agent, 1869–1870* (1881; reprint, St. Paul: Minnesota Historical Society, 1988), xxi–xxvii; Harney to Clark Chambers, Alexander Chambers and Family Papers; Harney to Sherman, September 27, 1868, William T. Sherman Papers, vol. 24.

28. John B. Henderson to Sherman, October 14, 1868, William T. Sherman Papers, vol. 24; PIPC, October 7, 8, 9, 10, 1868, ID:SCIPC, box 671 A; Sherman to Augur, September 28, 1868, C. C. Augur Papers; Resolutions adopted by the Indian Peace Commission, in Nathaniel G. Taylor to the president, December 11, 1868, 40 Cong. 3 sess., HED 2, serial 1366, pp. 831–32.

29. Harney to Sherman, November 23, 1868, 40 Cong. 3 sess., SED 11, serial 1360, pp. 1–5; Richmond Lee Clow, "The Brulé Indian Agencies, 1869–1878," SDHC 36 (1972): 150–52; Poole, *Among the Sioux,* xxi–xxii; Hyde, *Spotted Tail's Folk,* 130–45; Harney to Taylor, November 2, 1868, BIA:LR, Upper Platte Agency, M234, roll 893; Harney to Chambers, October 21, 1868, Alexander Chambers and Family Papers; Lt. Col. Oliver O. Greene to Bvt. Maj. Gen. David S. Stanley, October 16, 1868, USACC: Dakota, LS, vol. 1.

30. Harney to Sherman, November 23, 1868, 40 Cong. 3 sess., *SED* 11, serial 1360, pp. 1–5; Sherman to Augur, November 23, 1868, C. C. Augur Papers; Sherman to Schofield, December 22, 1868, AGO:LR, M619, roll 644; Sherman to Schofield, January 28, 1869, USACC: Missouri, LS, vol. 41.

31. Sherman to Schofield, December 22, 1868, roll 644, Schofield to Speaker of the House of Representatives and President of the Senate, January 6, 1869, roll 644, Harney to Thomas, December 31, 1868, roll 629, Harney to Schofield, February 2, 1869, roll 706, and Col. William A. Nichols to Schofield, January 23, 1869, roll 644, all in AGO:LR, M619; Sherman to Schofield, January 28, 1868, USACC: Missouri, LS, vol. 41.

32. Speech of Walter A. Burleigh, February 9, 1869, *UD*, February 27, 1869; Report of the Committee on Appropriations on Support of Indians, February 22, 1869, 40 Cong. 3 sess., *House Report* 29, serial 1388, pp. 1–8; *Statutes at Large*, 16:39–40.

33. Ely S. Parker to Jacob D. Cox, February 9, 1870, 41 Cong. 2 sess., *HED* 138, serial 1417, pp. 1–2; *Statutes at Large*, 16:353–54; "Estimate of necessary expenses to be incurred in promoting the civilization of the Indian on the Missouri River," April 13, 1869, Sanborn to Cox, April 15, 1869, and Parker to Cox, April 16, 1869, all in BIA: special files, M574, roll 66; Parker to Harney, May 7, 1869, BIA:LR, M21, roll 90; Extract of Parker to Harney, June 1, 1869, and J. C. O'Connor to Parker, June 7, 1869, both in AGO:LR, M619, roll 710.

34. Harney to John A. Rawlins, May 25, 1869, BIA:LR, Upper Platte Agency, M234, roll 894; Harney to Rawlins, May 28, 1869, BIA: special files, M574, roll 66; Cox to Rawlins, June 9, 1869, endorsement by Rawlins, June 9, 1869, all in Parker to Cox, June 14, 1869, and endorsement by Cox, June 14, 1869, AGO:LR, M629, roll 710.

35. Harney to Rawlins, April 27, 1869, BIA: special files, M574, roll 66; Poole, *Among the Sioux*, xxiv, 15, 29–38; Harney and Sanborn to Browning, May 20, 1868, Secretary of the Interior: Indian Division, LR, box 21; Capt. George M. Randall to Gov. John A. Burbank, July 1, 1869, BIA:LR, Upper Platte Agency, M234, roll 894; Bvt. Maj. James A. Hearn to Parker, September 26, 1869, 41 Cong. 2 sess., *HED* 1, vol. 3, serial 1414, pp. 760–61.

36. Robert M. Utley, "The Celebrated Peace Policy of General Grant," *North Dakota History* 20 (July 1953): 121–27, 131–32; *Statutes at Large*, 16:566; Prucha, *Great Father*, 1:496–533; Prucha, *American Indian Treaties*, 288–92, 301–10.

14. A Time for Reflection

1. Katherine Lindsay François, "Social Customs of Old St. Louis," MHSB 10 (January 1954): 156–57; Ruth K. Field, "Some Misconceptions about Lucas Place," MHSB 20 (July 1964): 119–21.

2. Report of Committee on Invalid Pensions on a bill granting a pension to Mary E. Harney, April 24, 1890, 51 Cong. 1 sess., *House Report* no. 1695, serial 2812, pp. 1–2; Harney to Maj. Thomas Vincent, October 18, 1873, AGO:ACP, file 4205, 1873.

3. G. L. Russell, comp., *A Century Passes but Memory Lingers On: The Centennial History of Sullivan, Missouri* (Union MO: Sullivan Centennial Committee, 1958), 101; *St. Louis Globe Democrat*, May 13, 1889; *St. Louis Post–Dispatch*, August 28, 1928, news clippings file, WSH.

4. Harney to Townsend, January 7, February 28, April 3, 1870, AGO:LR, M666, roll 229; Harney to Mrs. John M. Harney, October 28, 1875, WSH; Harney to Townsend, October 24, 1877, AGO:LR, M666, roll 372.

5. Robert E. Lee to Harney, February 26, 1870, in *Personal Reminiscences, Anecdotes, and Letters of Gen. Robert E. Lee,* ed. William J. Jones (New York: D. Appleton, 1875), 279; Harney to Grant, June 29, 1874, Ulysses S. Grant Papers, LC, series 1B, reel 2; Grant to John F. Long, December 25, 1879, and Harney to Grant, October 24, 1881, both in Ulysses S. Grant Papers, MOHS; Harney to Davis, March 15, 1879, Jefferson Davis Papers; P. G. T. Beauregard to Reavis, January 23, 1882, WSH; Butler to Davis, January 29, 1882, in Rowland, *Davis,* 9:145–46, and Butler to Davis, January 8, 1884, Rowland, *Davis,* 9:274–75; Harney to George Wallace Jones, May 19, 1883, George Wallace Jones Collection, letterbook 14.

6. Harney to Charles Mason, Thomas B. Florence, and six others, January 8, 1868, WSH; Harney to Townsend, April 1872, AGO:ACP, file 2286, 1872; John J. Killoren, *"Come Blackrobe": DeSmet and the Indian Tragedy* (Norman: Univ. of Oklahoma Press, 1948), 360–61; Testimony before House Committee on Indian Affairs, February 4, 1874, in Reavis, *Harney,* 432–37.

7. John M. Harney to Julius S. Welsh, June 1874, NHB; William S. Harney to Mrs. John M. Harney, October 28, 1875, WSH.

8. Harney to Jones, October 26, 1881, George Wallace Jones Collection, letterbook 14; Butler to Davis, January 29, 1882, in Rowland, *Davis,* 9:145–46; miscellaneous clipping, news clippings file, WSH.

9. Harney Genealogy, NHB; miscellaneous clipping, news clippings file, WSH;

Butler to Davis, November 12, 1883, 9:268–69, Butler to Davis, December 14, 1884, 9:315–17, and Butler to Davis, March 7, 1885, 9:350–51, all in Rowland, *Davis;* Copy of Last Will and Testament of Wm. S. Harney, October 24, 1884, WSH.

10. *New York Times,* February 14, 1888; Thomas A. Gonzalez, *The Caloosahatchee* (Estero FL: Koreshan Unity, 1932), 46–47; Lt. Col. Alexander J. Dallas to Adjutant General, May 9, 1889, AGO:ACP, file 2746, 1889, and Capt. Henry G. Litchfield to Adjutant General, May 11, 1889, AGO:ACP, file 2637, 1889; *St. Louis Globe Democrat,* May 13, 1889.

11. Harney to Mason, Florence, and six others, January 8, 1868, WSH.

12. Buker, *Swamp Sailors,* 139–40; Julian J. Ewell and Ira S. Hunt Jr., *Sharpening the Combat Edge: The Use of Analysis to Reinforce Military Judgment* (Washington DC: Department of the Army, 1974), 39, 119, 158, 187.

SELECTED BIBLIOGRAPHY

This is a bibliography of principal sources. It does not include all items cited in the notes or numerous additional materials that contain similar or indirectly related information.

Unpublished Sources

MANUSCRIPTS

Illinois State Historical Library:

    C. C. Augur Papers

    Black Hawk War Papers

Library of Congress:

    Blair Family Papers

    Ulysses S. Grant Papers

    Andrew Jackson Papers

    William T. Sherman Papers

Minnesota Historical Society:

    Alexander Chambers and Family Papers

    Wharncliffe (Edward Wortley) Papers

Missouri Historical Society:

Badger Collection
Nettie H. Beauregard Papers
James O. Broadhead Papers
Mary C. Clemens Collection
Richard Graham Papers
Ulysses S. Grant Papers
William S. Harney Papers
Hitchcock Collection
Stephen Watts Kearny Papers
LaMotte-Coppinger Papers
Mullanphy Family Collection
C. F. Ruff Papers
Anthony W. Smith Papers
George R. Taylor Collection

Southern Historical Collection, University of North Carolina Library:

Austine Papers
Thomas Butler King Papers

Other Repositories:

Anderson Family Collection, Henry E. Huntington Library
Mrs. Mason Barret Collection, Tulane University Library
Holmes Conrad Papers, Virginia Historical Society
Jefferson Davis Papers, Museum of the Confederacy

U.S. GOVERNMENT DOCUMENTS, NATIONAL ARCHIVES
AND RECORDS SERVICE

Record Group 48. Records of the Office of the Secretary of the Interior:

Indian Division: Segregated Correspondence of the Indian Peace Commission, 1867–68.

Record Group 75. Records of the Bureau (Office) of Indian Affairs:

Documents Relating to the Negotiation of Ratified and Unratified Treaties with Various Tribes of Indians, 1804–69.
Letters Sent by the Bureau (Office) of Indian Affairs, 1824–81.
Letters Received by the Bureau (Office) of Indian Affairs, 1824–60: Texas Agency, 1847–59; Upper Platte Agency, 1846–70.

Records of the Oregon Superintendency of Indian Affairs, 1848–73: Letters Sent, 1857–61.

Special Files of the Bureau (Office) of Indian Affairs, 1807–1904.

Record Group 92. Records of the Office of Quartermaster General:

Letters Sent, Main Series, 1818–70.

Record Group 94. Records of the Adjutant General's Office, 1783–1917:

Appointment, Commission, and Personnel Branch Files, 1783–1917.

General Orders of the War Department, 1809–80.

Generals' Papers and Books: Thomas S. Jesup, 1818–38: Letters Sent; Letters Received; Orders Issued from Headquarters, Army of the South; William S. Harney 1861–64.

Letters Received by the Office of the Adjutant General, 1805–21.

Letters Received by the Office of the Adjutant General, Main Series, 1822–60.

Letters Received by the Office of the Adjutant General, 1861–70.

Letters Sent by the Office of the Adjutant General, Main Series, 1800–1900.

Orders, 1797–1939; Orders and Circulars, 1794–1910; General Wool's Orders, 1846–47.

Personal Papers of Surgeons, 1839–1914.

Records Relating to Wars, 1812–1943: Mexican War, 1845–50: Letters Received, 1845–48; Letters Received from Officers; Miscellaneous Papers, Orders, Army of Occupation.

Returns from Regular Army Infantry Regiments, June 1821–December 1916.

Special Orders, War Department, 1811–61.

Record Group 98. Records of the United States Army Commands, 1784–1821:

Division of the South: Letters Sent, 1816–21; Eighth Military Department, 1815–21: Orderly Books of the Adjutant General and General Orders Received.

Orderly Book for the Company of Capt. F. Amelung, 1st Infantry, 1818–19.

Orderly Books for the Company of Capt. William Laval, 1st Infantry, 1818–20.

Record Group 99. Records of the Office of the Paymaster General:

Letters Received, 1833–36.

Letters Sent, 1831–37.

Paymasters' Bonds, 1824–35.

Record Group 107. Records of the Office of the Secretary of War:

Letters Received by the Secretary of War, Main Series, 1801–70.

Letters Sent by the Secretary of War Relating to Military Affairs, 1800–89.

Record Group 108. Records of the Headquarters of the Army:

Letters Sent by the Headquarters of the Army, Main Series, 1828–1903.

Record Group 153. Records of the Judge Advocate General (Army):

Court-Martial Case Files.

Record Group 393. Records of the United States Army Continental Commands, 1821–1920:

Department of Dakota, 1866–1911: Letters Received, 1867–69.

Department of Florida, 1850–58: General and Special Orders, 1857; Letters Received, April 1856–August 1858; Letters Sent, April 1856–August 1858.

Department of Oregon, 1858–61: General and Special Orders Issued, 1858–61; Letters Received, 1858–61; Letters Sent, 1858–61.

Department of the Platte, 1866–91: Letters Received, 1867–69.

Department of Utah, 1857–61: Letters Sent, 1857–61; Orders, 1857–61.

Department of the West, 1853–65: General and Special Orders Issued by the Troops Serving in Kansas, May 1857–May 1858; Letters Sent by the Sioux Expedition, April 1855–July 1856; Special Orders, January 1858–November 1861.

Military Division of the Missouri, 1866–91: General Orders and Circulars, 1866–1869; Letters Sent, 1868–71.

Ninth Military Department, 1838–45: Letters Sent, May 1840–June 1841; Orders and Special Orders Issued and Received from the War Department, May 1838–March 1843; Orders and Special Orders Issued, May 1840–June 1841.

Western Division, 1821–37: Letters Received, 1825–31; Letters Sent, June 1821–July 1836; Orders and Special Orders Issued, 1820–53; Orders and Special Orders Issued by General Henry Atkinson, June 1819–January 1826; Orders and Letters Received by General Henry Atkinson, 1821–27.

Published Sources

U.S. GOVERNMENT PUBLICATIONS

American State Papers: Documents, Legislative and Executive, of the Congress of the United States. 38 vols. Washington DC: Gales and Seaton, 1821–61.

American State Papers: Indian Affairs. 2 vols. Washington DC: Gales and Seaton, 1832–43.

American State Papers: Military Affairs. 7 vols. Washington DC: Gales and Seaton, 1832–61.

American State Papers: State and Public Documents in the United States from the Ascension of George Washington, Exhibiting a Complete View of Foreign Relations since That Time. 12 vols. Boston: T. B. Wirt and Son, 1819.

Annual Reports of the Commissioner of Indian Affairs, 1848–70, in *House and Executive Documents.* Washington DC: U.S. Congress, 1825–70.

Annual Reports of the Secretary of the Interior, 1849–70, in *House and Senate Executive Documents.* Washington DC: U.S. Congress, 1825–70.

Annual Reports of the Secretary of War, 1824–70, in *House and Senate Executive Documents.* Washington DC: U.S. Congress, 1825–70.

Biographical Directory of the American Congress, 1771–1971. Washington DC: GPO, 1971.

Carter, Clarence E., and John Porter Bloom, eds. *The Territorial Papers of the United States.* 28 vols. Washington DC: GPO, 1934–72.

Coakley, Robert W. *The Role of Federal Military Forces in Domestic Disorders, 1789–1878.* Washington DC: Center of Military History, United States Army, 1988.

Congressional Globe. Washington, 1867–71.

Heitman, Francis B., comp. *Historical Register and Dictionary of the United States Army from Its Organization, September 29, 1789 to March 2, 1903.* 2 vols. Washington DC: GPO, 1903.

Kappler, Charles J., comp. *Indian Affairs: Laws and Treaties.* 2 vols. Washington DC: GPO, 1903–4.

Risch, Erna. *Quartermaster Support of the Army: A History of the Corps, 1775–1939.* Washington DC: Quartermaster Historian's Office, Office of the Quartermaster General, 1962.

Skelton, William B. "The Army Officer as Organization Man." In *Soldiers and Civilians: The U.S. Army and the American People*, ed. Garry D. Ryan and Timothy K. Nenninger, 61–70. Washington DC: National Archives and Records Administration, 1987.

Statutes at Large, 1789–1873. 17 vols. Boston: Little, Brown, 1850–73.

Thian, Raphael P. *Notes Illustrating the Military Geography of the United States, 1813–1880.* Washington DC: GPO, 1881.

House of Representatives. *House Executive Documents:*

"Letter from the Secretary of War . . . relating to an engagement between United States troops and the Sioux Indians near Fort Laramie." 33 Cong. 2 sess., February 8, 1885. No. 63. Serial 788.

"Letter of the Secretary of War, communicating correspondence with General Harney." 36 Cong. 1 sess., June 20, 1860. No. 98. Serial 1057.

"Message from the President . . . communicating minutes of a council held at Fort Pierre with the Sioux Indians by General Harney." 34 Cong. 1 sess., July 24, 1856. No. 130. Serial 859.

"Message from the President . . . relative to an invasion . . . by Mexico." 29 Cong. 1 sess., May 11, 1846. No. 196. Serial 485.

"Message from the President to the two houses of Congress." 35 Cong. 1 sess., December 8, 1857. No. 2. Serial 942.

"Message from the President . . . transmitting reports . . . the Utah Expedition." 35 Cong. 1 sess. No. 71. Serial 956.

"President Polk's Message on Mexican War Correspondence," 30 Cong. 1 sess., May 11, 1846. No. 60. Serial 520.

Senate. *Senate Executive Documents:*

"Message of the President . . . communicating correspondence between the executive department and the present governor of Kansas." 35 Cong. 1 sess., December 22, 1857. No. 8. Serial 918.

"Message of the President . . . communicating correspondence of Lieutenant General Scott, in reference to the island of San Juan, and of Brigadier General Harney." 36 Cong. 1 sess., January 30, 1860. No. 10. Serial 1027.

"Message of the President . . . communicating . . . information in relation to the occupation of San Juan, in Puget Sound." 40 Cong. 2 sess., February 22, 1868. No. 29. Serial 1316.

"Sand Creek Massacre." 39 Cong. 2 sess., February 4, 1867. No. 26. Serial 1277.

Senate. *Senate Miscellaneous Documents:*

"Resolution of the Legislature of Florida . . . expelling the Seminole Indians." 32 Cong. 2 sess., January 14, 1853. No. 51. Serial 670.

Senate. *Senate Reports:*

"Condition of the Indian Tribes: Report of the Joint Special Committee, appointed under Joint Resolution of March 3, 1865." 39 Cong. 2 sess. No. 156. Serial 1279.

The War of the Rebellion: A Compilation of the Official Records of the Union and Confederate Armies. 130 vols. Washington DC: GPO, 1880–1901.

NEWSPAPERS

Daily Alta California (San Francisco), 1858–60
Daily Missouri State Journal (St. Louis), 1861
Kansas Weekly Herald (Leavenworth), 1854–57
Liberty Weekly Tribune, 1858–62
Missouri Democrat (St. Louis), 1861
Missouri Republican (St. Louis), 1834–35, 1861, 1884
New York Times, 1888
Niles' Weekly Register, 1831–41
Oregon Statesman (Salem), 1858–60
Pioneer and Democrat (Olympia WA), 1858–60
St. Augustine News, 1838–41
St. Louis Globe Democrat, 1884–89
Tallahassee Floridian, 1839–40
Texas State Gazette (Austin), 1849–54
Union and Dakotaian (Yankton SD), 1867
Weekly Oregonian (Portland), 1858–60

ARTICLES AND BOOKS

Anonymous. "Notes on the Passage across the Everglades." *Tequesta* 20 (1960): 57–65.

Arrington, Leonard J. *Great Basin Kingdom: An Economic History of the Latter-Day Saints, 1830–1900.* Cambridge MA: Harvard University Press, 1958.

Athearn, Robert G. *Forts of the Upper Missouri.* Englewood Cliffs NJ: Prentice-Hall, 1967.

———. *William Tecumseh Sherman and the Settlement of the West.* Norman: University of Oklahoma Press, 1956.

Atkinson, Henry. "General Henry Atkinson's Report of the Yellowstone Expedition of 1825." *Nebraska History* 44 (June 1963): 65–82.

Atkinson, Henry, and Benjamin O'Fallon. "Journal of the Atkinson–O'Fallon Expedition." Edited by Russell Reid and Clell G. Gannon. *North Dakota Historical Quarterly* 4 (October 1929): 5–56.

Bandel, Eugene. *Frontier Life in the Army, 1845–1861.* Edited by Ralph P. Bieber. Glendale CA: Arthur H. Clark, 1932.

Bassett, John Spencer, ed. *The Correspondence of Andrew Jackson.* 7 vols. Washington DC: Carnegie Institution of Washington, 1926–35.

Bauer, K. Jack. *The Mexican War, 1846–1848.* New York: Macmillan, 1974.

———. *Surfboats and Horse Soldiers: U.S. Naval Operations in the Mexican War, 1846–1848.* Annapolis MD: United States Naval Institute, 1969.

———. *Zachary Taylor: Soldier, Planter, Statesman of the Old Southwest.* Baton Rouge: Louisiana State University Press, 1985.

Berthrong, Donald J. *The Southern Cheyennes.* Norman: University of Oklahoma Press, 1963.

Boyd, Mark F. "Asi-Yahola or Osceola." *Florida Historical Quarterly* 33 (January and April 1955): 249–305.

Buker, George E. *Swamp Sailors: Riverine Warfare in the Everglades, 1835–1842.* Gainesville: University Presses of Florida, 1975.

Burns, Robert Ignatius, S.J. *The Jesuits and the Indian Wars of the Northwest.* New Haven CT: Yale University Press, 1966.

Carriker, Robert C. *Father Peter John DeSmet: Jesuit in the West.* Norman: University of Oklahoma Press, 1995.

Castel, Albert. *General Sterling Price and the Civil War in the West.* Baton Rouge: Louisiana State University Press, 1968.

Chittenden, Hiram Martin, and Alfred Talbot Richardson, eds. *Life, Letters, and Travels of Father Pierre-Jean DeSmet, S.J., 1801–1873.* 4 vols. New York: Francis P. Harper, 1905.

Clark, Satterlee. "Early Times at Fort Winnebago, and Black Hawk War Reminiscences." *Collections of the State Historical Society of Wisconsin* 8 (1879): 310–21.

Clarke, Dwight L. *Stephen Watts Kearny: Soldier of the West.* Norman: University of Oklahoma Press, 1961.

Clow, Richmond Lee. "The Brulé Indian Agencies, 1868–1878." *South Dakota Historical Collections* 36 (1972): 143–204.

———. "Mad Bear: William S. Harney and the Sioux Expedition of 1855–1856." *Nebraska History* 61 (summer 1980): 133–51.

———. "The Whetstone Indian Agency, 1868–1872." *South Dakota History* 7 (summer 1977): 291–308.

Coffman, Edward M. *The Old Army: A Portrait of the American Army in Peacetime, 1784–1898.* New York: Oxford University Press, 1986.

Covington, James W. "The Camp Jackson Affair: 1861." *Missouri Historical Review* 55 (April 1961): 197–212.

Coyer, Richard Joseph. "'This Wild Region of the Far West': Lieutenant

Sweeny's Letters from Fort Pierre, 1855–1856." *Nebraska History* 63 (spring 1982): 232–54.

Drum, Richard C. "Reminiscences of the Indian Fight at Ash Hollow." *Collections of the Nebraska State Historical Society* 16 (1911): 143–51.

Elliott, Charles Winslow. *Winfield Scott: The Soldier and the Man.* New York: Macmillan, 1937.

Furniss, Norman F. T*he Mormon Conflict, 1850–1859.* New Haven CT: Yale University Press, 1960.

Gough, Barry M. *The Royal Navy and the Northwest Coast of North America, 1810–1914: A Study of British Maritime Ascendancy.* Vancouver: University of British Columbia Press, 1971.

Hafen, LeRoy R., and Ann W. Hafen, eds., *Relations with the Indians of the Plains, 1857–1861.* Glendale CA: Arthur H. Clark, 1959.

———, eds. *The Utah Expedition, 1857–1858: A Documentary Account of the United States Military Movement under Colonel Albert Sidney Johnston, and the Resistance by Brigham Young and the Mormon Nauvoo Legion.* Glendale CA: Arthur H. Clark, 1958.

Hagan, William T. *Indian Police and Judges: Experiments in Acculturation and Control.* New Haven CT: Yale University Press, 1966.

———. *The Sac and Fox Indians.* Norman: University of Oklahoma Press, 1958.

Hammond, Otis G., ed. *The Utah Expedition, 1857–1858: Letters of Capt. Jesse A. Gove, 10th Inf., U.S.A., of Concord, N.H., to Mrs. Gove, and special correspondence of the New York Herald.* New Hampshire Historical Society Collections. vol. 12. Concord: New Hampshire Historical Society, 1928.

Hancock, Almina R. *Reminiscences of Winfield Scott Hancock.* New York: Charles R. Webster, 1887.

Harmon, George D. "The United States Indian Policy in Texas, 1845–1860," *Mississippi Valley Historical Review* 17 (December 1930): 377–403.

———. *Sixty Years of Indian Affairs: Political, Economic, and Diplomatic, 1789–1850.* Chapel Hill: University of North Carolina Press, 1941.

Hietala, Thomas R. *Manifest Design: Anxious Aggrandizement in Late Jacksonian America.* Ithaca NY: Cornell University Press, 1985.

Hoig, Stan. *The Peace Chiefs of the Cheyennes.* Norman: University of Oklahoma Press, 1980.

———. *The Sand Creek Massacre.* Norman: University of Oklahoma Press, 1961.

Hoopes, Alban W. "Thomas S. Twiss, Indian Agent on the Upper Platte, 1855–1861." *Mississippi Valley Historical Review* 20 (December 1933): 353–64.

Howard, Oliver Otis. *Autobiography.* 2 vols. New York: Baker and Taylor, 1907.

————. *My Life and Experiences among Our Hostile Indians: A Record of Personal Observations, Adventures, and Campaigns among the Indians of the Great West.* Hartford CT: A. D. Worthington, 1907.

Hoyt, William D., Jr., ed. "A Soldier's View of the Seminole War: Three Letters of James B. Dallam." *Florida Historical Quarterly* 25 (April 1946): 356–62.

Hyde, George E. *Red Cloud's Folk: A History of the Oglala Sioux Indians.* Norman: University of Oklahoma Press, 1937.

————. *Spotted Tail's Folk: A History of the Brulé Sioux.* Norman: University of Oklahoma Press, 1961.

Irwin, Ray W. "Missouri in Crisis: The Journal of Captain Albert Tracy, 1861." *Missouri Historical Review* 51 (October 1956): 8–21.

Jackson, Donald, ed. *Ma-Ka-Tai-Me-She-Kia-Kiak: Black Hawk, an Autobiography.* Urbana: University of Illinois Press, 1955.

Jackson, W. Turrentine. *Wagon Roads West: A Study of Federal Road Surveys and Construction in the Trans-Mississippi West, 1846–1869.* 1952. Reprint, New Haven CT: Yale University Press, 1965.

Jarvis, Nathan S. "An Army Surgeon's Notes on Frontier Service, 1833–1848." *Journal of the Military Service Institution of the United States* (July 1906): 3–8; (September and October 1906): 275–86.

Jones, Douglas C. *The Treaty of Medicine Lodge: The Story of the Great Treaty Council as Told by Eyewitnesses.* Norman: University of Oklahoma Press, 1966.

Kinzie, Mrs. John H. *Wau–Bun: The "Early Day" in the North-West.* New York: Derby and Jackson, 1856.

Kirkpatrick, Arthur Roy. "Missouri in the Early Months of the Civil War." *Missouri Historical Review* 55 (April 1961): 235–66.

————. "Missouri on the Eve of the Civil War." *Missouri Historical Review* 55 (January 1961): 99–108.

Lyon, William H. "Claiborne Fox Jackson and the Secession Crisis in Missouri." *Missouri Historical Review* 58 (July 1964): 422–41.

Mahon, John K. *History of the Second Seminole War, 1835–1842.* Gainesville: University of Florida Press, 1967.

Mattes, Merrill J. *The Great Platte River Road: The Covered Wagon Mainline via Fort Kearny to Fort Laramie.* Lincoln: University of Nebraska Press, 1969.

Mattingly, Arthur H. "The Great Plains Peace Commission of 1867." *Journal of the West* 15 (July 1976): 23–37.

Mattison, Ray H., ed. "The Harney Expedition against the Sioux: The Journal of Capt. John B. S. Todd." *Nebraska History* 43 (June 1962): 89–130.

McCabe, James O. *The San Juan Water Boundary Question*. Toronto: University of Toronto Press, 1965.

McCann, Lloyd E. "The Grattan Massacre." *Nebraska History* 37 (March 1956): 1–25.

McReynolds, Edwin C. *Missouri: A History of the Crossroads State*. Norman: University of Oklahoma Press, 1962.

———. *The Seminoles*. Norman: University of Oklahoma Press, 1957.

Meyers, Augustus. *Ten Years in the Ranks of the U.S. Army*. New York: Stirling Press, 1914.

Miller, Robert E. "Daniel Marsh Frost, C.S.A." *Missouri Historical Review* 85 (July 1991): 381–401.

Motte, Jacob Rhett. *Journey into Wilderness: An Army Surgeon's Account of Life in Camp and Field during the Creek and Seminole Wars, 1836–1838*. Edited by James F. Sunderman. Gainesville: University of Florida Press, 1953.

Murray, Keith. *The Pig War*. Tacoma: Washington State Historical Society, 1968.

Nevins, Allan. *The Emergence of Lincoln: Douglas, Buchanan, and Party Chaos, 1857–1859*. New York: Charles Scribner's Sons, 1950.

———. *The Emergence of Lincoln: Prologue to Civil War, 1859–1861*. New York: Charles Scribner's Sons, 1950.

———. *Ordeal of the Union: A House Dividing, 1852–1857*. New York. Charles Scribner's Sons, 1947.

Nichols, Alice. *Bleeding Kansas*. New York: Oxford University Press, 1954.

Nichols, Roger L. *Black Hawk and the Warrior's Path*. Arlington Heights IL: Harlan Davidson, 1972.

———. *General Henry Atkinson: A Western Military Career*. Norman: University of Oklahoma Press, 1965.

Olson, James C. *Red Cloud and the Sioux Problem*. Lincoln: University of Nebraska Press, 1965.

Parrish, William E. *Frank Blair: Lincoln's Conservative*. Columbia: University of Missouri Press, 1998.

———. "General Nathaniel Lyon: A Portrait." *Missouri Historical Review* 49 (October 1954): 1–18.

———. *Turbulent Partnership: Missouri for the Union, 1861–1865*. Columbia: University of Missouri Press, 1963.

———, ed. *A History of Missouri*. 5 vols. Columbia: University of Missouri Press, 1971–.

Paul, R. Eli, ed. "Battle of Ash Hollow: The 1909–1910 Recollections of General N. A. M. Dudley." *Nebraska History* 62 (fall 1981): 373–99.

Peckham, James. *Gen. Nathaniel Lyon, and Missouri in 1861.* New York: American News, 1866.

Phillips, Christopher. *Damned Yankee: The Life of General Nathaniel Lyon.* Columbia: University of Missouri Press, 1990.

Poll, Richard D. "The Mormon Question Enters National Politics, 1850–1856." *Utah Historical Quarterly* 25 (April 1957): 117–34.

Poole, D. C. *Among the Sioux of Dakota: Eighteen Months' Experience as an Indian Agent, 1869–1870.* 1881. Reprint, St. Paul: Minnesota Historical Society, 1988.

Price, Catherine. *The Oglala People, 1841–1879: A Political History.* Lincoln: University of Nebraska Press, 1996.

Prucha, Francis Paul. *American Indian Policy in the Formative Years: The Indian Trade and Intercourse Acts, 1790–1834.* Cambridge MA: Harvard University Press, 1962.

———. *American Indian Treaties: The History of a Political Anomaly.* Berkeley: University of California Press, 1994.

———. *Broadax and Bayonet: The Role of the United States Army in the Development of the Northwest, 1815–1860.* Madison: State Historical Society of Wisconsin, 1953.

———. *The Great Father: The United States Government and the American Indians.* 2 vols. Lincoln: University of Nebraska Press, 1984.

———. *A Guide to the Military Posts of the United States, 1789–1895.* Madison: State Historical Society of Wisconsin, 1964.

———. *The Sword of the Republic: The United States Army on the Frontier, 1783–1846.* New York: Macmillan, 1968.

Rawley, James A. *Race and Politics: "Bleeding Kansas" and the Coming of the Civil War.* Lincoln: University of Nebraska Press, 1969.

Reavis, Logan U. *The Life and Military Services of General William Selby Harney.* St. Louis: Bryan, Brand, 1878.

Remini, Robert V. *Andrew Jackson and the Course of American Empire, 1767–1821.* New York: Harper & Row, 1977.

Richards, Kent D. *Isaac I. Stevens: Young Man in a Hurry.* Provo UT: Brigham Young University Press, 1979.

Rippy, J. Fred. "Border Troubles along the Rio Grande, 1848–1860." *Southwestern Historical Quarterly* 23 (October 1919): 91–111.

Rodenbough, Theophilus. *From Everglade to Cañon with the Second Dragoons.* New York: D. Van Nostrand, 1875.

Roland, Charles P. *Albert Sidney Johnston: Soldier of Three Republics*. Austin: University of Texas Press, 1964.

Rowland, Dunbar, ed. *Jefferson Davis, Constitutionalist: His Letters, Papers, and Speeches*. 10 vols. Jackson: Mississippi Department of Archives and History, 1923.

Ruby, Robert H., and John A. Brown. *Indians of the Pacific Northwest: A History*. Norman: University of Oklahoma Press, 1981.

Sage, Walter N. *Sir James Douglas and British Columbia*. Toronto: University of Toronto Press, 1930.

Sellers, Charles G. *James K. Polk, Continentalist, 1843–1846*. Princeton NJ: Princeton University Press, 1966.

Shalhope, Robert E. *Sterling Price: Portrait of a Southerner*. Columbia: University of Missouri Press, 1971.

Shearer, Ernest C. "The Carvajal Disturbances." *Southwestern Historical Quarterly* 55 (October 1951): 201–30.

Shenton, James P. *Robert John Walker, a Politician from Jackson to Lincoln*. New York: Columbia University Press, 1961.

Skelton, William B. *An American Profession of Arms: The Army Officer Corps, 1784–1861*. Lawrence: University Press of Kansas, 1992.

——. "Army Officers' Attitudes toward Indians, 1830–1860." *Pacific Northwest Quarterly* 67 (July 1976): 113–24.

——. "The Commanding General and the Problem of Command in the United States Army, 1821–1841." *Military Affairs* 34 (December 1970): 111–22.

——. "Officers and Politicians: The Origins of Army Politics in the United States before the Civil War." *Armed Forces and Society* 6 (fall 1979): 22–48.

——. "Professionalization in the U.S. Army Officer Corps during the Age of Jackson." *Armed Forces and Society* 1 (August 1974): 443–71.

Sherman, William T. *Memoirs of General William T. Sherman*. 2 vols. New York: D. Appleton, 1875.

Smith Justin H. *The War with Mexico*. 2 vols. 1919. Reprint, Gloucester MA: Peter Smith, 1963.

Smith, Sherry L. "Beyond Princess and Squaw: Army Officers' Perceptions of Indian Women." In *The Women's West*, ed. Susan Armitage and Elizabeth Jameson, 63–75. Norman: University of Oklahoma Press, 1987.

——. *The View from Officers' Row: Army Perceptions of Western Indians*. Tucson: University of Arizona Press, 1990.

Sprague, John T. *The Origin, Progress, and Conclusion of the Florida War*. 1848. Reprint, Gainesville: University of Florida Press, 1964.

Stampp, Kenneth. *America in 1857: A Nation on the Brink.* New York: Oxford University Press, 1990.

Stanley, Henry M. *My Early Travels and Adventures in America.* 1895. Reprint, Lincoln: University of Nebraska Press, 1982.

Stevens, Hazard. *The Life of Isaac Ingalls Stevens.* 2 vols. Boston: Houghton Mifflin, 1900.

Sturtevant, William C. "Chakaika and the 'Spanish Indians': Documentary Sources Compared with Seminole Tradition." *Tequesta* 13 (1953): 35–73.

Tate, Michael L. *The Frontier Army in the Settlement of the West.* Norman: University of Oklahoma Press, 1999.

Taylor, Emerson Gifford. *Gouverneur Kemble Warren: The Life and Letters of an American Soldier, 1830–1882.* Boston: Houghton Mifflin, 1932.

Unruh, John D., Jr. *The Plains Across: The Overland Emigrants and the Trans-Mississippi West, 1840–1860.* Urbana: University of Illinois Press, 1979.

Utley, Robert M. *Frontier Regulars: The United States Army and the Indian, 1866–1891.* New York: Macmillan, 1973.

———. *Frontiersmen in Blue: The United States Army and the Indian, 1848–1865.* New York: Macmillan, 1967.

———. *The Indian Frontier of the American West, 1846–1890.* Albuquerque: University of New Mexico Press, 1984.

Vielé, Teresa Griffin. *Following the Drum: A Glimpse of Frontier Life.* 1858. Reprint, Austin TX: Steck-Vaughn, 1968.

Wallace, Anthony F. C. "Prelude to Disaster: The Course of Indian-White Relations Which Led to the Black Hawk War of 1832." *Wisconsin Magazine of History* 65 (summer 1982): 247–88.

Wallace, Doris Davis. "The Political Campaign of 1860 in Missouri." *Missouri Historical Review* 70 (January 1976): 162–83.

Watson, Samuel J. "The Uncertain Road to Manifest Destiny: Army Officers and the Course of American Territorial Expansion, 1815-1846." In *Manifest Destiny and Empire: American Antebellum Expansionism,* ed. Sam W. Haynes and Christopher Morris, 68–114. College Station: Texas A&M University Press, 1997.

Weigley, Russell F. *Towards an American Army: Military Thought from Washington to Marshall.* New York: Columbia University Press, 1962.

Whitney, Ellen M., ed. *The Black Hawk War, 1831–1832.* 3 vols. Springfield: Illinois State Historical Library, 1970–75.

Winders, Richard Bruce. *Mr. Polk's Army: The American Military Experience in the Mexican War.* College Station: Texas A&M University Press, 1997.

Winfrey, Dorman H., and James M. Day, eds. *The Indian Papers of Texas and the Southwest, 1825–1916*. 5 vols. 1959. Reprint, Austin TX: Pemberton Press, 1966.

Winther, Oscar Osburn. "Inland Transportation and Communication in Washington, 1844–1859," *Pacific Northwest Quarterly* 30 (October 1939): 371–86.

Abercrombie, John J., 6

Abraham (African-American Seminole), 60

Adams, John Quincy, 8, 12

Agua Nueva, Mex., 93

Albert (slave), 46

Aleck Scott, 105–6, 111

Alexander, Edmund B., 176–77

Alexandria LA, 12

Amelung, Ferdinand K., 10–11

American Fur Company, 28, 125

Antigua, Mex., 97

Anton Lizardo, Mex., 96

Anzeiger des Western (St. Louis), 231

Apaches, 124, 153, 245, 247, 257–58, 260

Arapahos, 122, 123, 128, 144, 242–43, 245, 246, 247, 250, 257, 259–60

Arbuckle, Matthew, 51, 84

Arikaras, 17–18, 19, 24, 29

Arkansas, 45, 51, 57, 79, 84, 90, 92, 96, 228, 236, 237, 246

Arkansas River, 12, 51, 250, 251, 253, 254, 265

Armistead, Lewis, 167

Armistead, Walker K., 64, 75–77

Armstrong, William, 26, 27

army: brevets in, 67; as constabulary, xiv, 9, 11, 22, 24, 42, 107, 159–60, 163, 165, 168, 175–76, 180, 280–81, 284; contentious officers in, xvi, 20, 83, 183, 211; courts-martial in, 12; detached service in, 13, 15, 74; and dueling by officers, 1–2, 11, 51–52; as expansibile, xiv, 15, 45, 67, 87, 91; and health of soldiers in, 14, 21, 56, 103, 125, 139; and Indian leadership patterns, 38, 57, 63, 143; and knowledge of Florida topography, 62, 74; and lack of training in Indian fighting tactics, xvi, 15, 57–58, 74, 281; Mexican War casualties of, 103; officer advancement in, 11, 54, 284; officer training in, 9, 13; and officers' relationships with Indian women, 35; officers' disdain for volunteers in, 67; and officers' views of Bureau of Indian Affairs, 107, 124, 127; and officers' views of Indians, xvi, 30, 58, army (*cont.*)

73, 283; organization of, 74, 163–64, 169, 178; professionalization of, 56; recruiting for, 13–14, 57, 87, 169; reductions in strength of, xiv, 15, 82, 107; and roving columns, 110, 113, 124, 282; Second Seminole War casualties of, 56, 57; and total war, xvi, 124, 133, 145, 186, 265, 283. *See also under* Harney, William S., military career of; *and individual departments and units*

Arpiukci (Seminole), 62, 67, 68, 69, 70, 73, 77, 78, 150, 154, 155

Ash Hollow, 129–33. *See also under* battles

Ashley, William H., 17, 30

Assiniboins, 30

Astoria OR, 193

Atchafalaya Bay, 10

Atchinson KS, 174

Atkinson, Henry, 18,19, 21, 23, 24, 32, 34, 63, 126, 141; on Atkinson-O'Fallon expedition, 25–31; and Black Hawk War, 39–42

Atkinson-O'Fallon expedition, 24–31

Atlantic Monthly, 181

Augur, Christopher C., 257, 259, 262, 268; appointed to Indian Peace Commission, 256

Austin TX, 111, 112, 114, 117, 276

Australia, 126

Bad Axe River, 52. *See also under* battles

Bad Lands, 135

Bad River, 125

Bankhead, James, 67

Bank of the United States, 48, 52

Bannocks, 262

Barataria Bay, 10

Barnes, Ellis, 196

Barnes, Joseph K., 212

Barnitz, Albert, 260

Barry, William, 218

Bates, Edward, 234

Baton Rouge Barracks, 7, 8, 14, 82, 186, 276–77

Baton Rouge LA, 7, 10, 11, 13, 14, 16, 18, 229

battles: Ash Hollow, 129–33, 134, 137, 140, 141, 142, 172, 253, 255, 263; Bad Axe, 41–42; Buena Vista, 95; Bull Run, 241; Caloosahatchee, 71–72, 73, 77, 141; Cerro Gordo, xv, 98, 99–101, 284; Chapultepec, 102–3; Churubusco, 101–2, 103; Horseshoe Bend, 6; Lake Okeechobee, 65, 66; Lockahatchee, 65–66; New Orleans, 6, 277

Baynes, R. Lambert, 205–6, 211–12

Bazalgette, George, 211–12

Bazin, Charles, E., 179–80

Beall, Benjamin L., 82

Bean, Sylvanus, 80, 84

Bear Rib (Hunkpapa Sioux), 141

Bear's Tooth (Crow), 261

Beauregard, Nettie H., 274, 279

Beauregard, P. G. T., 98, 226, 229, 277

Bell, John, 5

Bent, William, 247

Benton, Jesse, 1–2

Benton, Thomas Hart, 1–2, 24, 241

Biddle, Ann, 44, 47, 49, 52, 84, 87

Biddle, Nicholas, 52

Biddle, Thomas, 44, 52

Big Blue River, 128

Big Cypress Swamp, 78, 146, 147, 149, 151, 153–56

Bigelow (army sergeant), 71, 72

Big Horn (Miniconjou Sioux), 255

Big Horn Mountains, 250

Big Sandy River, 177

Big Sioux River, 139

Bingham, George Caleb, 233

Black Bear (Oglala Sioux), 265

Blackfeet, 18, 30, 141, 262, 267

Black Hawk (Sac), 37–42, 63

Black Hawk War, xv, 24, 37–42, 43, 47, 280; causes of, 37–39; conclusion of, 42

Black Hills, 135

Black Kettle (Cheyenne), 243, 247, 259, 265

Blair, Francis P., Jr., 217, 221, 224, 226, 227–28, 230, 232, 233, 235–37, 239, 241; urges removal of Harney in Missouri, 225, 234; transmits Harney removal order, 238

Blair, Montgomery, 222, 228, 241; drafts Lincoln's order to remove Harney in Missouri, 234

Blount, William, 2

Blue Water Creek, 128–33, 134, 140, 142. *See also* Ash Hollow; battles, Ash Hollow

Board of Indian Commissioners, 270

Bonneville, Benjamin L. E., 124, 222

Boonville MO, 239

Bordeaux, James, 121

Boston, 13

Bowlegs, Billy. *See* Emathla

Bozeman Trail, 250, 255, 261, 262, 265

Brave Bear (Brulé Sioux), 121

Brazos River, 108, 113, 114

Brazos TX, 93, 94, 95

Brent, Robert C., 17

British Colonist (Victoria BC), 206

British Columbia, 182, 186, 194, 195, 198, 201, 206; gold discoveries in, 186; Indian raids emanating from, 195, 198; Winfield Scott in, 208. *See also* U.S.-Canada boundary dispute

Broadhead, James O., 236

Brooke, George M., 108, 110–12; disagrees with Harney over frontier defense in Texas, 110; death of, 112

Brooks, Preston, 161

Broome, James E., 149, 151, 152

Brown, Jacob, 32–33

Brown, John, 161

Browning, Orville H., 252, 254

Brownsville TX, 116

Brulé Sioux, 120–21, 128–34, 136, 137–38, 243, 250, 255, 260, 262–63, 265, 267

Buchanan, James, 162, 163, 166, 168, 170, 173, 174, 176, 177, 180; assigns Harney to Kansas, 162; authorizes Utah expedition, 165; and San Juan Island crisis, 201–2, 207, 212. *See also* Utah expedition

Buell, Don Carlos, 179

Buena Vista. *See under* battles

buffalo, 30; disappearance of, 108, 256, 258

Buffalo Hump (Comanche), 111

Bull Run. *See under* battles

Bureau of Indian Affairs, 122, 124, 127, 128, 137, 138, 144, 145, 183, 184, 188, 190, 192, 246, 247, 250; creation of, 107; investigation of, 246; and place in federal bureaucracy, 107, 251, 261, 266, 267, 270, 272, 278

Burleigh, Walter A., 269

Burlington KS, 174

Burr, David H., 165

Butler, A. P., 161

Butler, Edward George Washington, 5, 6, 277, 279

Caddos, 11, 113, 114

Cady, Albemarle, 131

Calhoun, John C., xiv, 15, 18

Call, Richard K., 59

Callava, José, 16

Calling Forth Act of 1795, 163

Caloosahatchee River, 70, 71–72, 73, 77, 153, 155. *See also under* battles

Camargo, Mex., 115

Cameron, Simon, 222–23, 225–26, 228, 234, 238

Camp Armistead TN, 49

Campbell, Archibald, 195, 201–2, 205, 207

Camp Gibson FL, 147

Camp Jackson MO, 215–16, 229–32, 234, 239, 240

Canada, xv, 6, 15, 38, 56, 69, 82, 122, 184. *See also* U.S.-Canada boundary dispute

Cantonment Barbour IA, 31

Cantonment Montpelier AL, 15, 16

Cape May NJ, 106

Cape Sable FL, 154, 155

Carlisle Barracks, 106

Carr, Paddy (Creek), 62

Carrington, Henry B., 250

Carroll, William, 1–2

Carson, Kit, 247

Carter, Jesse, 151

Carvajal, José Maria, 115–16

Cascade Mountains, 184, 185

Casey, Silas, 198, 200, 205–6, 207, 209

Cass, Lewis, 32, 59, 170, 173, 174, 202, 212

Cerro Gordo. *See under* battles

Chakaika (Spanish Seminole), 75, 76, 204; attacks Harney's command, 71–72; hanged by Harney, 77

Chambers, Clark, 266

Chambers, Talbot, 18

Chapultepec. *See under* battles

Charleston SC, 57, 150, 222, 223

Charlotte Harbor FL, 66, 70, 153

Cherokees, 246

Cherry Creek, 244, 245

Chew, Beverly, 10

Cheyenne agency, 267

Cheyenne River, 127

Cheyennes, 29, 123, 124, 128, 144, 145, 172, 180, 242–43, 245, 246, 247, 250, 251, 257–60

Chicago, 266

Chickasaws, 82, 246–47

Chippewas, 31

Chisolm, Jesse, 247

Chitto Tustenuggee (Seminole), 69, 70, 73, 78

Chivington, John M., 242–43, 252, 261

Choctaws, 82, 246–47

Chokoloskee FL, 155

cholera, 105–6, 125

Chouteau, Pierre, 121, 139

Christian, William, 7, 12

Churchill, Samuel B., 222

Churubusco. *See under* battles

Cincinnati, 85

Cimarron River, 258

Civil War, xiv, xv, 56, 143, 175, 216, 239, 244, 245, 252, 275, 280, 283, 286. *See also* Missouri

Clallams, 198

Clark, Satterlee, 34–35, 36

Clark, William, 26

Clarke, Newman S., 185, 187, 191, 213

Clemens, James, 48, 49

Clinch, Duncan L., 59

Coacoochee (Seminole), 57, 62, 63, 64

Cody, William "Buffalo Bill," 265

Coeur d'Alenes, 187, 188, 189, 191

Coffee, John, 1

Coi Hadjo (Seminole), 62, 64

Coleman, Richard M., 20–21

Colt, Samuel, 67. *See also under* Harney, William S., military career of

Columbia River, 187–88, 194

Colville WA, 185, 188, 189

Comanches, 86, 112, 114, 124, 244, 247, 257, 258–60
Compromise of 1820, 160
Compromise of 1850, 160, 165
Confederate Indians, agreements with, 247
Confederate States of America, 221, 227, 246
Congress, xiv, 26, 45, 53, 111, 144, 150, 154, 155, 161, 162, 174, 175, 177, 180, 183, 191, 192, 244, 250, 251, 261, 263, 264, 269, 270; appropriates funds for military road building, 192; appropriates funds for Second Seminole War, 59; approves annexation of Texas, 86; approves funds for Indian police, 143; approves funds for Indian Peace Commission treaties, 269; approves remounting Second Dragoons, 86; authorizes Atkinson-O'Fallon expedition, 24; blamed by Harney for inadequate resources, 126; creates Board of Indian Commissioners, 270; creates Department of the Interior, 107; creates Department of Utah, 165; creates Mounted Rifle Regiment, 122; and creation of Indian Peace Commission, 251–52, 253; and declaration of war against Mexico, 86, 284; dismounts Second Dragoons, 82; ends treaty system, 272; expands army for war against Mexico, 87; Harney confident of support from, 269; Harney testifies before, 278; orders study of condition of Indians, 245–46; passes deficiency appropriation for Utah expedition, 178; passes first army officer retirement law, 240; passes Indian Removal Act, 58; passes Kansas-Nebraska

Act, 122; reduces size of army, xiv, 7, 15, 82
Connor, Patrick E., 124
Conrad, Charles M., 113
Cooke, Philip St. George, 163, 173; in battle of Ash Hollow, 131–32
Cooley, Dennis N., 246–47
Coomb, Robert L., 7, 11
Cooper, Samuel, 156, 206, 209, 212
Corpus Christi TX, 86, 111, 276
Council Bluffs IA, 18, 24, 25–26, 27, 28, 30, 31, 139
Council Grove KS, 174, 247
Courtine, Marie, 103–4
Cox, Jacob D., 270
Craighead, Thomas B., 5
Crampton, John F., 195, 206, 213
Creeks, 2, 59, 62, 150, 155, 157, 246
Crockett, Davy, 6
Croghan, George, 83
Crook, George F., 153, 272
Crosbie, Henry R., 199
Crow Feather (Sans Arc Sioux), 141
Crows, 29, 261
Cumberland College, 5, 6
Cumberland River, 2, 3
Cumming, Alfred, 168, 173–74, 176
Curry, George L., 204
Custer, George Armstrong, 265
Cutler, Lyman, 197, 198, 201, 204, 207

Dade, Francis K., 59
Daily Alta California (San Francisco), 187, 203
Daily Missouri State Journal (St. Louis), 223, 232, 233, 236
Dallam, James B., 71, 72
Dallas, A. G., 197
Darby, John F., 232, 339 n.25 n.27
Daugherty, Lewis, 156
Davis, Jefferson, 9, 25, 37, 277, 281; de-

Davis, Jefferson (*cont.*)
 scribes Harney, 8; as president of
 Confederate States, 221, 223, 228, 229,
 231; as secretary of war, 119, 121, 124,
 125, 126, 127, 129, 132, 137, 144, 145,
 147, 149–51, 155, 156
Davy. *See* Holartochee
DeCourcy, John F., 199, 200
DeHart, Henry V., 210
Delawares, 88, 108, 127–28
Dennison, Ami P., 190
Denver, 242, 243, 263, 264
Denver, James W., 175
Department of California, 238
Department of Dakota, 252
Department of Florida, 147, 148, 156
Department of Missouri, 251, 263
Department of Oregon, xv, 183, 188,
 189, 209, 212, 238; Harney as com-
 mander of, 183–212; Indian-white
 relations in, 183–92; road building
 in, 192–93; San Juan crises in, 182,
 194–214
Department of the Pacific, 183, 209, 238
Department of the Platte, 256
Department of the West, xv, 122, 163,
 178, 180, 209, 216, 225, 234, 237, 240,
 241, 245
Department of Utah, 168, 171, 178, 179
DeSmet, Pierre-Jean, 254, 262, 263, 265,
 277–78; meets Harney first time,
 105–6; as chaplain on Utah expedi-
 tion, 179; in Department of Oregon,
 186–91, 213; death and funeral of, 277
DeSoto MO, 235
Dick, Franklin A., 234
Division of Missouri, 251
Dixon, Joseph, 193
Dixon's Ferry IL, 39, 40, 41
Dodge, Grenville M., 245, 246
Donelson, Andrew Jackson, 6

Doolittle, John R., 246
Doolittle Committee, 246, 250
Douglas, James, 195, 197, 199, 200–201,
 203, 206, 208–9, 212
Douglas, Stephen A., 162
Drinkard, W. R., 201, 207
dueling, 1–2, 11, 51–52

East Florida, 1, 6, 8, 12, 14–16, 58, 204
Easton KS, 174
Eaton, John Henry, 6
Eighth Military Department, 10, 14,
 107, 108, 112, 113, 117
Emathla (Seminole), 55–56, 57, 60, 64
Emporia KS, 174
Eola, Lake, 280
Eustis, Abraham, 64–65, 66
Evans, John, 242, 245
Everglades, 34, 64, 66, 67, 68, 73, 74,
 76–78, 103, 151, 153–56, 241
Ewing, Charles, 215–16
Ewing, Thomas, 111

Fanning, Alexander C. W., 55–56, 57, 60
Fashion, 152
Fayetteville TN, 2
federal Indian policy. *See* U.S. Indian
 policy; *and individual legislative
 acts*
Fetterman, William J., 250
Fetterman disaster, 250–51
Fifth Infantry Regiment, 149, 154, 155,
 159, 165, 166
Fillmore, Millard, 115, 165
Fire Heart (Blackfoot), 141
First Artillery Regiment, 17, 100, 149
First Dragoon Regiment, 82, 83; organ-
 ization of, 45
First Infantry Regiment, 7, 8, 13, 17, 18,
 19, 21, 23–24, 25, 27, 30, 31, 32, 34, 38,
 43, 64

Fleming, Hugh, B., 120–21

Florida, xvi, 16, 26, 42, 81, 82, 88, 126, 141, 160, 166, 204, 220, 227, 267, 281, 282, 283, 286; and Second Seminole War, 55–79; and Third Seminole War, 146–58. *See also* East Florida; Everglades; Florida Keys

Florida Keys, 146, 154. *See also* Key Biscayne; Key Largo; Key West

Florissant Valley, 81, 219

Floyd, John B., 156, 165, 170, 171, 176, 177, 180–81, 182, 183–84, 186, 189, 193, 201, 213–14. *See also* San Juan Island; Utah expedition

Ford, John S. "Rip," 115

Fort Armstrong IL, 38–39

Fort Atkinson NE, 18, 21, 23, 25, 30, 123. *See also under* treaties with Indians

Fort Bassinger FL, 153

Fort Belle Fontaine MO, 18, 22, 23, 25, 31, 79, 126

Fort Bellingham WA, 195, 197, 198

Fort Benton MT, 192, 193

Fort Bridger WY, 177, 262, 276

Fort Brooke FL, 60, 63, 147, 151, 152, 153, 154

Fort Buford ND, 265

Fort C. F. Smith MT, 250, 251, 261, 262, 265

Fort Chadbourne TX, 113

Fort Claiborne LA, 11, 12

Fort Coffee OK, 45

Fort Crawford WI, 31, 32, 38, 42

Fort Dade FL, 60, 62

Fort Dallas FL, 67, 68, 76, 78

Fort Dalles OR, 192, 193

Fort Dearborn IL, 31

Fort Denaud FL, 153

Fort Gates TX, 111

Fort Gibson OK, 45, 46, 51, 52. *See also under* treaties with Indians

Fort Graham TX, 108

Fort Grattan NE, 133

Fort Harker KS, 256

Fort Howard WI, 43

Fort Jesup LA, 32

Fort Kearny NE, 122, 125, 126, 128–29, 133, 159, 166, 172, 173, 179, 180

Fort King FL, 69–70, 72, 75

Fort Kiowa SD (American Fur Company), 28

Fort Laramie WY, 120–21, 122, 123, 125, 127, 128–29, 133–34, 136, 138, 159, 165, 166, 179, 250; peace councils at, 254, 255, 261, 262–63, 265. *See also under* treaties with Indians

Fort Larned KS, 256

Fort Lauderdale FL, 67, 73, 76

Fort Leavenworth KS, 46, 82, 111, 125, 126, 127, 128, 145, 147, 156, 159, 192, 218, 223, 254, 256; description of, 169; as Harney's headquarters, 160, 162–63, 166–68, 170–71, 173, 176, 178–80

Fort Lyon CO, 242

Fort Martin Scott TX, 112

Fort Mason TX, 112

Fort McKavett TX, 113

Fort Meade FL, 146

Fort Mellon FL, 60, 62–63, 65, 70, 75, 77, 78

Fort Mims AL, 2

Fort Myers FL, 152, 153, 154, 155, 160

Fort Phantom Hill TX, 113

Fort Phil Kearny WY, 250, 251, 261, 262, 265

Fort Pierre SD, 125, 126, 127, 129, 135, 138, 139, 189, 255, 262, 263, 267, 283; Harney conducts peace council at, 136, 140–44; miserable conditions at, 135–36, 138–39

Fort Randall SD, 144, 265

Fort Reno WY, 265

Fort Rice ND, 262

Fort Riley KS, 122, 167, 174, 218, 223

Fort Scott KS, 218

Fort Scott WY, 177

Fort Selden LA, 13

Fort Shackleford FL, 149

Fort Simcoe WA, 190

Fort Smith AR, 45, 46, 84, 246

Fort Steilacoom WA, 197, 198, 207

Fort Sullivan ME, 17

Fort Sully SD, 250, 254, 267

Fort Sumter SC, 222, 223

Fort Townsend WA, 195, 198, 208

Fort Towson OK, 51

Fort Van Buren FL, 70, 71–72

Fort Vancouver WA, 187, 189, 190–91, 192, 197, 208

Fort Walla Walla WA, 190, 192–93

Fort Washita OK, 80, 82, 83

Fort Winnebago WI, 34–37, 277

Fourth Artillery Regiment, 57, 125, 126, 149, 155, 159, 165, 166, 169

Fox River, 32, 34, 37

Fraser River, 186, 195

Fredericksburg TX, 113

Frémont, John C., 91, 241

Frost, Daniel M., 219, 220, 233; and Camp Jackson, 229–31

Gaines, Edmund Pendleton, 17, 32–33, 38, 84

Galveston Island, 10

Gamble, Hamilton R., 234

Gantt, Thomas T., 236, 238

Garesché, Julius P., 213

Garey's Ferry FL, 69

Garnett, Robert S., 187

Geary, John W., 161, 163

Gibbon, John, 116

Graham, Catherine, 44

Graham, Eliza, 219

Graham, Richard, 44

Grand River agency, 267

Grant, Ulysses S., 215, 230, 241, 246, 266, 270, 277; Harney on rail tour with, 263; Indian peace policy of, 272

Grattan, John L., 120–21. See also Grattan Massacre

Grattan Massacre, 120–21, 124, 129, 131, 132, 142, 145, 282

Gray, Alexander, 7

Great Britain, xv, 1–2, 3, 17, 31, 183, 194. See also San Juan Island; U.S.–Canada boundary dispute

Green Bay WI, 32, 34

Green River, 177

Grey Head (Cheyenne), 257

Griffin, Charles John, 194, 195, 197

Grignou, Julia, 35

Grundy, Felix, 6, 86

Gwynne, Thomas P., 19, 21

Hagner, Peter V., 221, 222

Hall, Calvin, 76

Halleck Hadjo (Seminole), 66

Haller, Granville O., 200, 203, 333 n.25

Hamilton, Alexander, 15

Hancock, Winfield Scott, 179, 251, 254, 259, 261

Hannah (household servant), 47, 48, 50, 51, 53

Hannibal MO, 237

Happy Man, Victor (Flathead), 191

Hardee, William J., 97, 111, 112, 113

Harlan, James, 246–47

Harney, Ann Biddle, 52, 117–18, 279

Harney, Benjamin F., 5, 7, 13, 14, 17, 31, 82, 105–6, 126; in Second Seminole War, 75; in Mexican War, 103; illness of 128; death of, 186

Harney, Eliza, 13

Harney, Elizabeth Brown, 69, 117–18, 280

Harney, Hannah Mills, 3

Harney, James, 5, 12

Harney, John Milton, 5

Harney, John Mullanphy, 82, 117, 280

Harney, Lake (FL), 63

Harney, Lake (OR), 193

Harney, Margaret, 3, 46

Harney, Mary Caroline, 35–36, 44, 283

Harney, Mary Mullanphy, 46–49, 50, 52, 53, 81, 106, 117, 211, 241, 279; physical description of, 44; marries Harney, 43–44; education of, 44; illness of, 48–49; urges husband to resign from army, 87; lives in France, 118–19, 211; death of, 213

Harney, Mary St. Cyr, 276, 277, 279–80; marries Harney, 279

Harney, Selby (uncle), 3

Harney, Thomas (brother), 117

Harney, Thomas (father), 2–4

Harney, Thomas (grandfather), 3

Harney, William S.,

life of: parents, 3–4, 46; birth, 3; frontier influences, 3, 4, 5, 40; youth, 4–7; siblings, 3, 5, 12, 13, 117; brother Benjamin, 5, 7, 17, 31, 75, 82, 103, 105–6, 126, 128, 186; education, 5; homesickness, 12–13; death of sister Eliza, 13; illnesses, 14, 17, 20, 47, 51, 75, 79, 81; dines with Indians, 29, 141, 274; races with Indians, 29–30, 37; children, 35–36, 44, 52, 69, 82, 106, 117–18, 211, 278, 279–80, 283; weddings, 43, 279; owns slaves, 46, 81, 218; indebtedness, 46, 47, 49, 51, 53, 117, 279; murders household servant, 47; flees prosecution, 47–48; criminal trial, 50, 51; issues challenge to duel, 51; and first wife's

money; 52, 53, 54, 107, 117, 210; travels to Cuba, 75, 81; residences, 81, 117, 210, 222, 241, 274, 275, 277, 279, 280; assists Ann Biddle, 84–85; strained family life, 44–45, 53, 87, 107, 117–19, 147, 211, 278–79; at Cape May, 106; declines to participate in politics, 118; travels to France, 118–19, 121; use of alcohol, 135, 256; death of first wife, 213; retirement years, 240–41, 274–80; revises will, 279–80; death and burial, 280

military career of: significance, xiv–xvii, 24, 31, 45, 57–58, 77, 78–79, 119, 124, 133, 135, 144, 145, 148, 157, 160, 176, 180–81, 183, 192, 193, 213, 216, 239–40, 244, 272–73, 280–86; influence of Andrew Jackson, 6, 15–16, 25–26, 30, 45, 49, 53, 204, 241, 271, 277, 281, 285; enters army, 7–8; informal training, 9, 12, 13, 22, 31, 34, 39, 42, 46, 281; and Lafitte pirates, 10–11; promoted to first lieutenant, 11; in northwestern Louisiana, 11–13; sits on courts-martial, 12, 111, 241; as recruiting officer, 13–14; leaves of absence, 14, 17, 32–33, 43, 64, 75, 79, 81, 82, 87, 118–19, 211, 214; commands ceremonial guard in Pensacola, 16; at Fort Belle Fontaine, 18–22, 24; courts-martial, 20, 21, 84–85, 94–95, 101; on Atkinson-O'Fallon expedition, 24–31; proposes to explore Pacific Northwest, 25–26; disregards channels of communication, 25, 33, 170, 186, 201; heroic view of officership, 26, 74; first experience with Indian treaties, 28; views regarding Indians, xvi, 30, 36, 42, 62–63, 73, 113, 114, 126, 141, 142, 143, 189, 191, 263, 265, 271, 278, 283; promoted to captain,

Harney, William S. (*cont.*)

31; on garrison duty in New Orleans, 31; travels to Washington DC, 32, 45, 47, 57, 82, 106, 147, 150, 176, 186, 212, 226–28, 241, 261, 269, 278; helps build Fort Winnebago, 34–35; punishes enlisted men 36, 80–81; in Black Hawk War, 39–42; boldness in combat situations, 41, 42, 56, 64, 65, 68, 75, 96, 100–101; uses political influence for advancement, 45, 53, 82; promoted to major, 45; as paymaster, 45–53, 126; promoted to lieutenant-colonel, 53; in Second Seminole War, 55–79; reputation as Indian fighter, 57, 75, 77, 79, 110, 111, 113, 133, 145, 187, 246, 247, 252, 253, 264; riverine tactics, 57, 74, 75–77, 78, 147–48, 154, 156, 281; explores upper St. John's River, 62, 63; in Battle of Lockahatchee, 66; considers Seminole removal impractical, 66, 148; disdain for volunteers, 67; and Colt weapons, 67, 68, 72, 76, 148, 150, 154, 176; penetrates Everglades, 68, 75–77, 78; attacked on Caloosahatchee River, 71–72, 75, 77; seeks revenge on Florida Indians, 72–73, 75–77; suggests army reforms; 73–74; dresses troops as Indians, 75, 76; hangs Indians, 76, 77, 188; breveted colonel, 79; receives sword from Florida legislature, 79; in Texas prior to Mexican War, 80, 82–85, 88, 90–91; seeks command of Fort Leavenworth, 82; leads unauthorized invasion of Mexico, 88, 90–91; in Mexican War, 88–104; and Indians as scouts, 88, 127–28; ability to command questioned, 91, 93; promoted to colonel, 91; commands

Second Dragoons, 91, 95, 106, 112, 115; campaigns with Wool in Chihuahua, 92–93; commands Scott's cavalry, 96–103; wins acclaim in Battle of Cerro Gordo, 98, 100–101; breveted brigadier general, 101; hangs deserters, 102–3; in Mexico City, 103–4; censured by Polk, 104; inspects military posts and equipment, 106, 176; in New York City, 106, 118, 150, 186; in Texas following Mexican War, 106–18; as interim commander of Eighth Military Department, 107, 108, 112, 114, 117; and innovative equipment, 108, 117; considers infantry useless against mounted Indians, 110, 113–14, 137, 278; blames traders for Indian difficulties, 112, 127, 134, 141, 278; pursues Mexican revolutionaries, 115–16; recommends tariff on Mexican goods, 116; commands expedition against Sioux, 119, 121, 124–45; commands in brevet brigadier general rank, 125; determined to crush Sioux, 126, 127, 129, 132; prefers field duty over administration, 126–27, 160, 171, 183; blames Bureau of Indian Affairs for Sioux difficulties, 128; crushes Sioux at Ash Hollow, 129–33; reveals no remorse over noncombatant deaths, 132, 140; known as Mad Bear and Great White Chief, 134; leads winter march, 135; suspends Indian agent, 138; subject of soldiers' doggerel, 139; recommends Indians farm, 141, 142, 189, 278; dictates treaty with Sioux, 141–43; approves selection of Sioux chiefs, 143; advocates Indian police, 143, 268, 283; commands Department of Florida in Third Seminole War, 148–58; orders cease-fire in Florida, 150–51; conducts relentless campaign in Florida, 153–55; commands troops in Kansas, 156, 162–80; commands Utah expedition, 159, 165–73, 178–80, 327 n.28; provides posses comitatus, 163, 174–75; threatens to hang Brigham Young, 168; orders training at Fort Leavenworth, 175; promoted to brigadier general, 179; *New York Times* on, 179, 280; *Atlantic Monthly* on, 181; commands Department of Oregon, 183–212; and Indian affairs in Pacific Northwest, 183–92; ordered to wage total war against Indians, 186; lifts ban on settlement in Washington Territory, 188; endorses proposal to concentrate Indians, 191; encourages road building in Pacific Northwest, 192–93; and occupation of San Juan Island, 198–212, 333 n.25 n.26, 334, n.35; rejects joint U.S.-British occupation of San Juan Island, 200; as expansionist, 204–5; refuses to leave Department of Oregon voluntarily, 209; relieved of command in Oregon, 212; commands Department of the West, 216; pursues Kansas border ruffians, 218–19; and defense of St. Louis arsenal, 221–26; refuses to swear in home guards in Missouri, 224; loyalty to Union, 224–25, 226–28, 233, 238, 240; fears impact of Civil War on Missouri, 224–25, 237; relieved of command of Department of the West, 226; captured by Confederate troops, 226; returned to command of Department of the West, 229; Missouri proclamations, 232–33, 339 n.25 n.27; pulls down secessionist flag, 233; and Price-Harney agreement, 235–38; considers requesting reassignment from Missouri, 237; relieved of command of Department of the West second time, 238; mistakes made in Missouri, 239–40; retired, 240; sits out Civil War, 241; breveted major general, 244; on Southern Treaty Commission, 246; reputation among Indians, 246, 252, 254, 255, 257, 259, 261, 262, 264, 268; on Peace Commission of 1865, 247; on Indian Peace Commission, 252–67; commands Indian Peace Commission escort, 256–57; at Medicine Lodge peace council, 256–60; at Fort Laramie peace council, 262–63; on railroad tour, 263; heads Sioux reservation, 264–70; overspends on Sioux reservation, 266–71; recommends moving Bureau of Indian Affairs to War Department, 270, 278; relieved as head of Sioux reservation, 270; testifies before Congress, 278

personal traits of, xvi, 24, 54, 276, 281, 286; ambitious, 25, 45, 53, 88; brave, 41, 56, 66, 75, 96, 101; contentious, 19, 33, 83, 92–93, 94–95, 210; cursing, 80, 83, 84, 92, 128, 140, 152, 179, 208, 284; disdain for teamsters, 128, 139–40, 179; generous, 62, 85, 106, 113, 117, 275; hunter, 5, 36, 71; impulsive, 13, 24, 36, 65, 88, 91, 204; innovative, 57, 67, 73–74, 75 108, 117, 143, 148; outdoor skills, 24, 31, 34–35; physical description, 8, 134, 162, 256, 279; religiosity, 5, 21, 44, 83, 118, 179; stubborn, 20, 33, 83, 205, 212; violent, xvi,

Harney, William S. (*cont.*)

13, 36, 47, 48, 51, 53, 57, 80, 82, 115, 140, 152–53, 179–80, 276, 284

and relationships with military and public figures: Francis P. Blair Jr., 224–26, 232–37; Benjamin L. E. Bonneville, 222; George M. Brooke, 108, 110–12; Jefferson Davis, 8, 25, 37, 119, 121, 125, 126–27, 129, 132, 137, 144, 147–48, 149, 150–51, 155, 277; Pierre-Jean DeSmet, 105–6, 179, 186, 188–92, 213, 254, 262, 278–79; John B. Floyd, 166, 171, 178, 180–81, 183–84, 186, 189, 193, 201, 213–14; Edmund Pendleton Gaines, 32–33, 38, 84; Ulysses S. Grant, 263, 270, 277; John B. Henderson, 252, 255, 259; Oliver Otis Howard, 133, 152; Andrew Jackson, 14–16, 25–26, 30, 45, 48, 49, 53, 95, 277, 281, 285; Thomas S. Jesup, 57, 60, 62–67, 126, 149–50, 167, 168; Stephen Watts Kearny, 19–20, 23, 25, 26, 45, 79, 84, 281; Abraham Lincoln, xv, 25, 40, 234–35, 285; Little Thunder, 131–33, 141–43; Nathaniel Lyon, 218–19, 222–25; Osceola, 62, 77, 283; Ely S. Parker, 246, 270; James K. Polk, 85, 95, 104; Sterling Price, 235–38; Logan Uriah Reavis, xvii, 203; Satanta, 256, 257; John M. Schofield, 224, 269; Winfield Scott, 25, 32–33, 84–85, 88, 91, 93–95, 96, 101, 103, 110, 129, 132, 163, 164, 165, 168, 170, 171–72, 178, 181, 189, 207–8, 209, 210–11, 212, 213, 221, 224–25, 226, 228–29, 234, 238, 285, 286; William T. Sherman, 253, 263, 264, 266–70; Persifor F. Smith, 113–14, 116; Spotted Tail, 131–34, 138, 255, 261, 265; Edwin V. Sumner, 93, 95, 97, 172; Zachary Taylor, 25, 39, 40, 43, 71, 72; David E.

Twiggs, 19, 34, 35, 53, 66, 91, 98, 100–101; Thomas S. Twiss, 137–38, 140, 144, 190; Robert K. Walker, 156, 162–63, 167, 168, 170, 171, 173–75, 180; John E. Wool, 90–93. *See also individual listings for these persons*

Harney City SD, 265

Harneywold, 81

Haro Strait, 194, 203, 214

Harper's Ferry [VA] WV, 226, 253

Harper's Weekly, 253

Hartsuff, George K., 149

Havana, Cuba, 16, 75, 81

Hays, Robert, 2

Hays, Stockley, 1

Haysborough, 2, 4, 5

Hazelwood, 219

Hazen, William B., 264

Hell Gate River, 193

Henderson, J. Pinckney, 88

Henderson, John B., 254, 255, 257, 259–60, 261, 262, 264, 281; appointed to Indian Peace Commission, 252

Henry (slave), 81

Hickok, James "Wild Bill," 265

High Forehead (Miniconjou Sioux), 120–21

Hitchcock, Ethan Allen, 232, 339 n.25 n.27

HMS *Ganges*, 205

HMS *Plumper*, 199

HMS *Pylades*, 206

HMS *Satellite*, 199, 208

HMS *Tribune*, 199

Hodges, Henry C., 210–11

Hoffman, William, 135, 138

Holartochee (Seminole), 60

Holato Mico (Seminole), 71, 72, 75, 77, 78, 149, 155, 156, 157

Holmes, Rueben, 25

Hornby, Geoffrey P., 200, 203, 205–6

Horseshoe Bend. *See under* battles

Houston, Sam, 6, 26

Howard, Oliver Otis, 152, 272; on Harney as Indian fighter, 133, 280

Howe, Marshall S., 83

Hubbs, Paul K., Sr., 197, 198, 207

Hudson, Margaret. *See* Harney, Margaret Hudson

Hudson's Bay Company, 182, 194, 195, 197, 198, 203, 334 n.35

Hunkpapa Sioux, 29, 135, 141, 250, 262, 267

Hunt, Lewis C., 211, 212

Hunter, John, 215–16

Hyattville KS, 174

Illinois, 24, 31, 47, 49, 90, 225–26, 281. *See also* Black Hawk War

Indian Key, 75, 77

Indian Peace Commission, 251–63, 266–67, 272, 273, 277, 278, 283, 286; creation of, 251–52; members of, 252, 256; recommendations of, 261, 266–67. *See also* treaties with Indians, at Fort Laramie in 1868; ——, at Fort Rice; ——, at Medicine Lodge Creek

Indian police, 143, 268, 283

Indian Removal Act, 58

Indian River, 149

Indian Territory, 82, 108, 114, 157, 247, 260, 265

Indians. *See individual tribes*

Ingalls, Rufus, 192

Interior Department, 107, 144, 185, 243, 261, 266, 267

Iron Shell (Brulé), 131, 263

Istokpoga, Lake, 151, 153, 154

Jackson, Andrew, 2–3, 5, 7, 9, 40, 59, 95; shot, 1; in War of 1812, 1–2, 6; and

East Florida, 1, 6, 8, 14–16; influence on Harney of, 3, 6, 15–16, 22, 25–26, 30, 45, 49, 53, 204, 241, 271, 277, 281, 285

Jackson, Claiborne Fox, 218, 220, 223, 228, 229, 231, 239, 240; rejects call for Union volunteers, 223; forms Missouri state guard, 231–32

Jackson, Rachel, 1, 2, 15

Jacksonville FL, 69

Jalapa, Mex., 97, 100

J. C. Swon, 229

Jefferson Barracks MO, 31, 32, 33, 42, 45–47, 64, 125, 169, 221, 223

Jefferson City MO, 220, 221, 239

Jennison, Charles, 219

Jesup, Thomas S., 57, 62–68, 74, 179, 281; strategy in Second Seminole War of, 60, 62, 64; considers Seminole removal impractical; 63, asks to be relieved in Florida, 66, as quartermaster general, 125, 149, 167

John (guide for Harney in Everglades), 75–76

John L. Stephens, 187

Johnson, Andrew, 246, 251, 256, 262, 267; appoints Indian Peace Commission, 252

Johnston, Abraham, 83–84

Johnston, Albert Sidney, 173, 176–78, 179. *See also* Utah expedition

Johnston, Joseph E., 98, 179, 226

Jones, Roger, 110

Jones, Sam. *See* Arpiucki

Juan de Fuca Straits, 194

Julesburg CO, 245

Jumper. *See* Otee-Ematular

Jupiter Inlet, 65, 67

Kamiakin (Yakima), 184, 186, 188, 189–91

Kane, Elias K., 49

Kansas, xv, 124, 181, 217, 219, 236, 247, 283, 286; activities of Indian Peace Commission in, 256–60; Harney pursues border ruffians in, 218–19; Harney selected to command troops in, 156, 160; struggle over slavery in, 160–63, 173–76. *See also* Utah expedition

Kansas City MO, 233, 237

Kansas-Nebraska Act, 122, 160

Kansas Pacific Railroad, 263

Kansas River, 167

Kaskaskia IL, 49

Kearny, Philip, 102

Kearny, Stephen Watts, 19, 23, 24, 45, 84, 91, 102; clashes with Harney, 19–20; on Atkinson-O'Fallon expedition, 25–31; on Harney as Indian fighter, 79, 281

keelboats, 4, 23, 25–27, 30, 39

Keokuk (Sac), 38

Ke-sho-ko (Winnebago), 44; has child with Harney, 35–36

Key Biscayne, 70, 71, 72, 73, 75, 77

Key Largo, 68

Key West, 150

Kickais, 113

Kickapoo KS, 174

Kickapoo River, 42

Kickapoos, 39, 108

Kicking Bird (Kiowa), 258

Kingsbury, James W., 25

Kinzie, John H., 35

Kinzie, Juliette, 35

Kiowas, 122, 244, 247, 256, 257, 258–60

Kissimmee River, 64, 65, 153

Kittitas, 186

Klamath River, 184

Klamaths, 143

Knife River, 29

Krum, John R., 232, 339 n.25 n.27

Lafitte, Jean, 8, 10–11

Langdon, Loomis L., 146

Laredo TX, 110, 276

Lawless, L. E., 50

Lawrence KS, 161, 163, 170, 174

Lay, George, 207, 208

Leavenworth, Henry, 17–18, 24, 25

Leavenworth, Jesse H., 247, 254, 258

Leavenworth KS 174

Lebanon MO, 236

Lecompton KS, 162, 175

Lee, Francis, 178

Lee, Robert E., 98, 226, 277

Letcher, Robert, 226

Lewis, Meriwether, 26

Lewis and Clark expedition, 26, 28

Liberty MO, 226, 228

Liberty (MO) *Weekly Tribune,* 179, 236

Lincoln, Abraham, xv, 25, 217, 221, 222, 233, 238, 240, 241, 285; in Black Hawk War, 40; calls for Union volunteers, 223, 238; and removal of Harney in Missouri, 234–35

Linn, Lewis F., 53, 82

Lipans, 112, 114

Little Arkansas River, 247, 259. *See also under* treaties with Indians

Little Cheyenne River, 267

Little Rock AR, 51

Little Thunder (Brulé), 128, 134, at Grattan Massacre, 121; at battle of Ash Hollow, 129–33; at Fort Pierre council, 141–43

Llano River, 112

Lobos Island, 95

Lockahatchee River, 65. *See also under* battles

Long, Stephen H., 26

Long Chin (Brulé), 137

Long Mandan, (Two Kettle Sioux), 141, 255

Long Soldier (Hunkpapa Sioux), 262

Loomis, Gustavus, 154, 156–57; ordered to follow Harney's strategy in Florida, 156

Loring, William W., 100

Louisiana, 4, 5, 14, 17, 34, 107; as location of Harney's initial service, 7–13; Second Dragoons with Harney in, 82

Lucas Place, 277, 279, 280

Lyon, Nathaniel, 218, 220, 223, 225–26, 240, 241; foils Harney on Kansas border, 219; transferred to St. Louis arsenal, 222; questions Harney's loyalty to Union, 224; enlists home guards in Missouri, 226, 228; and Camp Jackson, 229–31; proclaims war in Missouri, 239

Macomb, Alexander, 34, 38, 41; in Second Seminole War, 69–72

Majors, Alexander, 167, 176

Majors and Russell, 167, 169

Maldonado, Juan, 112

Man Afraid of His Horse (Oglala), 121, 134, 263

Manatee River, 146

Mandans, 29, 30

Manypenny, George, 128, 144

Marcy, William L., 87, 88, 95, 195, 206, 213

Marmaduke, John B., 239

Marsh, John, 31

Marshall, Thomas, 226

Mason, Charles H., 192, 204

Matamoros, Mex., 86, 88, 90, 92, 116

McClellan, George B., 98, 203

McClelland, Robert, 144, 151

McCulloch, Ben, 170, 171, 180

McLaughlin, John T., 55, 78, 103

Medellín, Mex., 96–97

Medicine Lodge Creek, 256, 257; treaty councils at, 258–60, 261. *See also under* treaties with Indians

Mellon, Charles, 55

Memphis, 45, 46, 50, 106

Menominees, 32, 38–39

Mexican War, xiv, 85–103, 108, 117, 122, 167, 210, 219, 226, 277, 280, 281, 284; American casualties in, 103; battle of Cerro Gordo, xv, 98, 99–101, 284; battle of Churubusco, 101–2, 103; battle of Chapultepec, 102–3; causes of, 85–86; conclusion of, 103; reaction of American citizens to, 87; U.S. strategy in, 87

Mexico, 106, 204; and border unrest following Mexican War, 108, 112, 114–16. *See also* Mexican War

Mexico City, xv, 82, 93, 98, 101, 103–4, 284

Miami River, 67, 76

Micanopy (Seminole), 60, 63, 64

Miles, Nelson A., 153, 272

Mills, Hannah. *See* Harney, Hannah Mills

Miniconjou Sioux, 120, 128, 134, 136, 250, 255, 262, 276

Minitarees, 29

Mississippi, 2, 4, 37, 106, 220, 277

Mississippi River, xv, 4, 32, 37, 38, 39, 43, 49, 122, 148, 167, 216; Harney among troops moving on, 12, 18, 32; Harney travels on, 49, 51, 105–6, 111; as line beyond which to remove Indians, 58, 245; Sac and Foxes flee across, 41–42

Missouri, xvii, 24, 43, 47, 52, 53, 64, 81, 160, 179, 252, 276, 277, 281, 284, 286; Civil War comes to, 239; on eve of the Civil War, 216–18; secession

Missouri (*cont.*)
  crisis in, xv, 218–40; slaveholding
  in, 217–18. *See also under* Harney,
  William S., military career of; St.
  Louis MO
Missouri Democrat (St. Louis), 228,
  229, 231, 232, 233, 236
Missouri Fur Company, 18
Missouri Republican (St. Louis), 232,
  236, 239
Missouri River, xv, 17, 26, 39, 43, 81,
  192, 217, 239, 244, 245, 250, 253, 255,
  264, 265, 267, 283; and activities of
  Indian Peace Commission, 254–55;
  Atkinson-O'Fallon expedition on,
  25–31; Indian-white conflict on
  upper portion of, 18–19, 23–24, 31,
  245, 274; and location of Fort Leav-
  enworth, 46, 169; and Sioux expedi-
  tion, 125–26, 135, 136, 138, 139, 144
Mix, Charles E., 246
Mobile AL, 2, 6, 15
Monclova, Mex., 88, 92, 93
Monroe, James, 14, 18, 24
Monroe, Lake, 55, 60, 62, 65
Montana Post (Virginia City), 253
Monterey, Mex., 87, 92, 93, 94
Montgomery, James, 218–19, 220
Montgomery AL, 220, 223, 233
Mormons, 120, 160, 164–66, 173, 176, 177,
  179, 180
Mott, Christopher, 190
Moultrie Creek. *See under* treaties
  with Indians
Mounted Rifle Regiment, 100, 122
Mullan, John, 193
Mullan Road, 193
Mullanphy, Ann. *See* Biddle, Ann
Mullanphy, Bryan, 49
Mullanphy, Catherine. *See* Graham,
  Catherine

Mullanphy, John, 44, 52, 53, 81
Mullanphy, Mary. *See* Harney, Mary
  Mullanphy
Munroe, John, 146, 147
Murphy, Thomas, 247, 254, 257
Muskrat, 23, 25, 26, 30
Myers, Abraham C., 233

Nashville, 1–2, 5–6, 14, 15, 26, 49, 53, 86,
  277; during Harney's youth, 4
Natchez Trace, 4
Natchitoches LA, 11, 12, 13
Native Americans. *See individual
  tribes*
Nauvoo IL, 164
Navajos, 143, 245, 262
navy, 10, 197; in Second Seminole War,
  74, 78
Neapope (Sac), 38
Nebraska, 27, 119, 121, 125, 158, 176, 190,
  222, 225, 265, 281. *See also* Indian
  Peace Commission; Sioux expedi-
  tion
Nebraska City News, 253
Neighbors, Robert S., 111
Nesmith, James W., 185, 188, 190
New Iberia LA, 10–11
New Orleans, 4, 6, 10, 16, 19, 31, 97, 104,
  106, 160, 276. *See also under* battles
New River, 67
New Smyrna FL, 152
New York City, 5, 57, 106, 118, 150, 164,
  168, 178, 209, 210, 211
New York Times, 179, 253, 280
Nez Perces, 187–88, 190, 191
Ninth Infantry Regiment, 198
Niobrara River, 129, 135
North Dakota, 17, 19. *See also* Atkin-
  son-O'Fallon expedition
Northern, 207, 209
North Platte NE, 255

North Platte River, 120, 122, 128, 129, 131, 159, 255, 260, 261, 265

Noue, Ludovic de, 118

Nueces River, 86, 111, 116

O'Brien, J. H., 80, 84

O'Fallon, Benjamin, 24, 141; on Atkinson-O'Fallon expedition, 25–31; pistol-whips Crow chiefs, 29, 261

O'Fallon, John, 227

Oglala Sioux, 29, 121, 128–34, 136, 137–38, 140, 243, 255, 261–63, 265, 267

Okeechobee, Lake, 64, 65, 153, 154, 155. *See also under* battles

Olympia WA, 198

Omaha NE, 254, 255, 262

Omahas, 31

One Horn (Miniconjou Sioux), 262

Oregon, 122, 216, 220, 245, 281; Indian-white conflict in, 183–92; military road building in, 192–93. *See also* Department of Oregon

Oregon Statesman (Salem), 188

Oregon Trail, 189, 193. *See also* overland emigration

Orlando FL, 280

Osages, 246

Osceola (Seminole), 59, 62, 63, 64, 77, 283; shares tent with Harney, 62; dies in prison, 64

Otee-Ematula (Seminole), 60, 151, 157

Otoes, 31

overland emigration, xv, 120, 121–22, 125, 127, 144, 145, 189, 193, 244–45, 282

Owen, John, 190

Paiutes, 190

Palatka FL, 147

Palmyra NY, 164

Palouses, 187

Panama, 186, 205

Parker, Ely S., 246, 270

Pass Christian MS, 277, 280

Patterson, Robert, 96

Pawnees, 31, 142, 143, 144

Pay Department, xv, 45–46, 52; Harney as paymaster in, 45–53

Payne's Landing. *See under* treaties with Indians

Pease Creek, 70, 153

Pensacola FL, 6, 14–16

Permanent Indian Frontier, 107, 122

Perrine, Henry, 75

Peter (slave), 46

Pettis, Spencer D., 52

Philadelphia, 84, 106, 114, 117

Phillip. *See* Emathla

Phillips, Asher, 46, 47

Pickett, George E., 182, 199, 200, 201, 203, 204, 207, 208; ordered to San Juan Island by Harney, 198; ordered off San Juan Island by Scott, 209; ordered back to San Juan Island by Harney, 212, 213

Pierce, Franklin, 118, 121, 129, 137, 144, 195

Pillow, Gideon, 98, 100

Pioneer and Democrat (Olympia WA), 187, 188, 202

Platte River, 26, 121, 122, 129, 134, 159, 250, 251, 253, 265

Pleasonton, Alfred, 150, 152, 162, 179, 186, 210, 212

Poinsett, Joel R., 63, 66, 67, 69, 72, 77

Point Isabel TX, 86, 88

Polk, James K., 85, 86, 87, 93, 95, 162, 194; supports Harney against Scott, 95; censures Harney, 104

Ponca Island, 139

Poncas, 27–28

Pontchartrain, Lake, 16

Poole, DeWitt C., 271

Poor Bear (Apache), 258
Pope, John, 240
Porter, David M., 6
Portland OR, 207
Port Lavaca TX, 91
Potawatomis, 38, 39, 40
Potosi MO, 235
Pottawatomie Creek KS, 161
Powder River, 246, 250, 261, 262, 263
Powell. See Osceola
Powell, Lazarus W., 180
Prairie du Chien WI, 31
Presidio de Rio Grande, 88, 90, 91, 92
Prevost, James C., 195
Price, Sterling, 221, 231, 236, 237, 238,
    239, 284; appointed commander of
    state guard in Missouri, 235. See
    also Price-Harney agreement
Price-Harney agreement, 235–36, 238,
    239, 240
Prophet (Winnebago), 38, 39
Puebla, Mex., 101
Puget Sound, 185, 192, 195, 198

Qualchin (Yakima), 186, 187
Quapaws, 246
Quartermaster Department, 97, 167,
    177

Rankin, James, 76
Rawlins, John A., 270
Reavis, Logan Uriah, xvii, 203
Reconstruction, 246, 251
Rector, Elias, 157
Rector, Wharton, 53
Red Cloud (Oglala): at Grattan Mas-
    sacre, 121; refuses to attend Fort
    Laramie council, 261; burns aban-
    doned military posts, 265
Red Eagle Plume (Oglala), 255
Red Feather, Adolphus (Flathead), 191

Red Leaf (Brulé), 137, 263
Red River, 11, 12
Reid, John, 6
Reynolds, John, 39, 40
Reynolds, Thomas C., 218, 221
Reynosa, Mex., 116
Riley, Bennet, 100
Ringgold Barracks TX, 115
Rio del Plan, 98
Rio Grande, 86, 88, 90, 91, 92, 108, 110,
    114, 115–16, 205
Ripley, Eleazer W., 10, 13
Robinson, Benjamin F., 128
Robinson, Charles, 161
Rock River, 37–38, 39, 41
Rocky Mountains, xv, 30, 122, 164, 191,
    216, 276, 279
Rogers, John, 78
Rogue River, 183, 184
Rollins, John H., 111–12
Rosario Strait, 194
Ruff, Charles F., 118
Running Antelope (Hunkpapa Sioux),
    262

Sabine River, 12, 13
Sac and Foxes, 31, 32, 37–40, 127. See
    also Black Hawk War
Safety Committee, 222; approves as-
    sault on Camp Jackson, 230
Salem OR, 193
Salt Lake City, 159, 171, 172, 173, 180, 181,
    192
Salt Lake Valley, 164, 166, 167, 168, 176,
    177, 180
San Antonio, 86, 88, 90–91, 111, 112, 114,
    276
Sanborn, John B., 247, 254, 257, 258,
    262, 263, 265, 270, 271; appointed to
    Indian Peace Commission, 252
Sand Creek Massacre, 242–43, 244, 246,

247, 250, 251, 252, 265; investigations stemming from, 245–46, 251

Sandy (interpreter for Harney), 72

San Francisco, 187, 192, 193, 200

Sanibel Island, 71

San Juan de Ulúa, 96

San Juan Island, 182, 284, 286; description of, 198; Harney creates military crisis over, 198–212; Harney rejects joint occupation of, 200; Harney re-opens military crisis over, 212; international boundary dispute around, 182, 194–95, 197–98; res-olution of boundary dispute over, 214; resolution of military crisis over, 212; role of Winfield Scott in resolving military crisis over, 202, 207–9, 211, 212. *See also under* Harney, William S., military career of

San Luis Potosí, Mex., 87

San Patricios, 102–3

San Saba River, 113

Sans Arc Sioux, 136, 141, 250, 262, 267

Santa Anna, Antonio López de, 93, 95, 98, 100, 102

Santa Fe Trail, 122

Santee Sioux, 245, 254, 262

Saone Sioux, 29

Sarasota Bay, 146

Satanta (Kiowa), 256, 257, 258, 259–60

Satillo, Mex., 87, 93

Savannah Georgian, 5

Schofield, John M., 224, 268, 269, 281

Scott, Walter, 87

Scott, Winfield, xv, 9, 25, 80–81, 82, 87, 88, 129, 132, 163, 165, 167, 170, 179, 189, 199, 201, 207, 211, 212, 224, 226, 228, 234, 238, 286; clashes with Harney, 32–33, 84, 85, 91, 93–95, 170, 171–72, 178, 181, 207–8, 210–11, 212, 213, 285; and failure of tactics in Second

Seminole War, 59; in Mexican War, 93–103; commands invasion of Vera-cruz, 93, 95–97; praises Harney, 101, 132; rejects Harney's defense plan for Texas, 110; makes recommenda-tions for Sioux expedition, 124–25; and presidential campaign, 118, 164; moves headquarters to New York City, 164; rejects Harney's sugges-tions for Utah expedition, 168; and boundary dispute in Oregon, 202, 207–9, 211–12; accepts joint occupa-tion of San Juan Island, 208; sug-gests Harney resign command of Department of Oregon, 209; rec-ommends relieving Harney in Ore-gon, 212; orders Harney to strengthen defense of St. Louis arsenal, 221; reinstates Harney in Missouri, 229

Seattle, 193

Second Artillery Regiment, 149

Second Dragoons Regiment, 64, 65, 76, 82, 92, 108, 166, 170, 173, 280; as-signed to Sioux expedition, 125; as-signed to Utah expedition, 165; com-pared to European hussars, 115; dismounted, 82; Harney as com-mander of, 91, 95, 106, 112, 115; or-ganized, 53, 57; remounted, 86; sent to Florida, 57, 73; sent to Oklahoma, 69; sent to Texas, 106; Sumner as commander of, 93, 95, 170; Twiggs as commander of, 53, 65

Second Infantry Regiment, 125, 127, 136, 178

Second Seminole War, xv, 55–79, 81, 95, 105, 147, 148, 153, 267, 281–82, 284; army casualties in, 56, 57; battle of Caloosahatchee, 71–72; battle of Lake Okeechobee, 65, 66; battle of

Second Seminole War (*cont.*)
 Lockahatchee, 65, 66; Caloosahat-
 chee attack destroys truce in, 73;
 causes of, 58–59; conclusion of, 79;
 cost of, 57, 267. *See also under* Har-
 ney, William S., military career of
Semiahmoo wa, 197
Seminoles, 55–79, 146–58, 204, 227, 246,
 267, 282. *See also* Second Seminole
 War; Seminole War of 1818; Third
 Seminole War
Seminole War of 1818, 58
Senecas, 246
Seventh Infantry Regiment, 18, 100
Shannon, Richard, 81, 84
Shannon, Wilson, 161, 163
Shark River, 77
Shawnee Mission ks, 161, 174
Shawnees, 246
Sheridan, Philip, 244, 263, 264–65, 266
Sherman, William T., 241, 244, 252, 254,
 255–56, 260, 261, 262, 264–66, 269, 281;
 present at riots after surrender of
 Camp Jackson, 215–16, 230; com-
 mands Division of Missouri, 251;
 appointed to Indian Peace Commis-
 sion, 252; Harney on rail tour with,
 263; appoints Harney to head Sioux
 reservation, 264, 265; and Harney's
 overspending on Sioux reservation,
 268–70
Sherman, Willie, 215–16, 230
Shields, James, 100
Shoshones, 124
Sibley, Henry H., 112
Sioux, xv, xvi, 18, 32, 38, 120, 122, 123,
 124, 127, 128, 129, 132, 134, 136, 140–45,
 166, 186, 240, 246, 250, 251, 265, 270,
 271, 272, 280, 283. *See also* Brulé
 Sioux; Hunkpapa Sioux; Miniconjou Sioux; Oglala Sioux; Sans Arc

Sioux; Santee Sioux; Saone Sioux;
 Sioux expedition; Sisseton Sioux;
 Teton Sioux; Two Kettle Sioux;
 Yankton Sioux; Yantonnai Sioux
Sioux City ia, 270, 271
Sioux expedition, xv, xvi, 119, 124–45,
 162, 165, 169, 171, 179, 281, 283, 284;
 battle of Ash Hollow during, 129–33,
 134, 140, 141; and Fort Pierre peace
 council, 136–37, 141–44; prepara-
 tions for, 124–28; reasons for, 120–
 24; winter march during, 135–36. *See
 also under* Harney, William S., mili-
 tary career of
Sisseton Sioux, 262
Sixth Infantry Regiment, 23, 25, 30, 125,
 126, 129, 131, 133, 166, 179
Skloom (Yakima), 188, 189
Slidell, John, 86
Smith, Anthony W., 241
Smith, Caleb, 234
Smith, Joseph, 164
Smith, Persifor F., 113, 163, 282; dis-
 agrees with Harney over frontier
 defense in Texas, 113–14, 116; and
 Utah expedition, 178; death of, 178
Smoky Hill River, 251, 264
Snakes, 262
Snake Warrior. *See* Chitto Tustenuggee
Soakrum Settlement fl, 146
Solomon River, 172
South Dakota, 17, 29, 123, 135, 138, 139,
 250, 264; Harney heads Sioux reser-
 vation in, 264–70. *See also* Atkinson-
 O'Fallon expedition; Fort Pierre sd;
 Sioux expedition
Southern Treaty Commission, 246–47
South Platte River, 180
Spanish Indians, 71
Spokane Garry (Spokane), 191
Spokanes, 187

Spotted Tail, 255, 265; at Grattan Massacre, 121; at battle of Ash Hollow, 129–32; submits to arrest, 137–38; meets with Indian peace commissioners, 261

Springfield MO, 237, 275

Stanley, Henry M.: describes Harney, 256; on Harney's knowledge of Indians, 257

Stanton, Frederick P., 162, 175, 256

Star of the West, 186, 202

State of Deseret, 165

St. Augustine FL, 57, 62, 64, 152; Harney lauded by citizens of, 77, 79

St. Augustine News (Florida), 70, 73, 75, 77

St. Cyr, Mary. *See* Harney, Mary St. Cyr

Steele, James, 247

Steilacoom WA, 192

Stem, Jesse, 112

Stephens, James, 146

Steptoe, Edward J., 186, 190

Stevens, Hazard, 198, 203

Stevens, Issac I., 184, 195, 203; and Indian affairs in Department of Oregon, 188, 191; and road-building in Pacific Northwest, 192–93; and alleged conversation with Harney about San Juan, 198, 333 n.26

Stevenson, Carter L., 155

Stewart, Robert M., 218, 220

Stillman, Isaiah, 39–40

St. John, 254

St. John's River, 55, 57, 60, 62, 63, 64, 65, 69

St. Joseph MO, 236, 237

St. Louis arsenal, 126, 284; Camp Jackson debacle evolves from contention over, 228–32; disagreement over defense of, 222–26; strategic importance of, 220–21, 224

St. Louis MO, xvi, xvii, 17, 18, 19, 23, 25, 26, 32, 45, 46, 48, 49–50, 52, 53, 57, 111, 125, 135, 139, 174, 180, 191, 209, 260, 270, 274–75; in the early 1830s, 43–44; on the eve of the Civil War, 217, 221–26, 229–30, 232–34; as Harney's principal place of residence, 47, 64, 69, 84, 87, 104, 106, 111, 127, 150, 216, 222, 274; and riots following surrender of Camp Jackson, 215–16, 231–32; as site of first meeting of Indian Peace Commission, 252, 254. *See also* St. Louis arsenal

St. Louis Times, 278

St. Louis University, 277

Stockton, Robert F., 91

Sullivan MO, 275–76

Sully, Alfred, 251

Sumner, Charles, 161

Sumner, Edwin V., 170; commands Second Dragoons, 93, 95, 145, 170; with Harney in Mexican War, 97; Harney compared with, 110, 124, 145; and posses comitatus in Kansas, 163, 176; Harney blames loss of cattle herd on, 172

Superior, Lake, 18

Sycamore Creek, 40

Tallahassee Floridian, 70

Tall Bull (Cheyenne), 257, 259

Tampa Bay, 60, 62, 63, 65, 66, 71, 150, 151

Tampa FL, 146, 147

Tampico, Mex., 93, 95, 97

Tappan, Samuel F., 257, 262, 267; appointed to Indian Peace Commission, 252

Tawakonis, 113

Taylor, Daniel, 232

Taylor, Edward B., 250

Taylor, Nathaniel G., 254, 261, 266–67;

Taylor, Nathaniel G. (*cont.*)
    appointed to Indian Peace Commis-
    sion, 252; elected president of peace
    commission, 254
Taylor, Zachary, 25, 39–40, 43, 81, 90,
    164; in Second Seminole War, 64–66,
    69, 71–73, 75; refuses Harney's re-
    quest for guard detail, 71–72; and
    start of Mexican War, 86–87; and
    Army of Occupation in Mexican
    War, 88, 92–93, 95; questions Har-
    ney's ability to command, 91
Teason, Joseph, 131
Ten Bear (Comanche), 258
Teninos, 190
Tennessee, 1–6, 14, 17, 43, 46, 49, 53, 228
Tenth Infantry Regiment, 159, 165, 166,
    173
Terry, Alfred H., 252–53, 257, 262; ap-
    pointed to Indian Peace Commission,
    252
Teton River, 28
Teton Sioux, 28
Texas, xv, 11, 12, 82, 86, 88, 103, 122, 127,
    134, 204, 216, 220, 221, 264, 281, 282,
    284; annexation of, 86; federal assets
    surrendered to Confederates in, 221;
    gains independence, 86; Harney in
    after Mexican War, 107–18; Harney in
    prior to Mexican War, 80–81, 82–84,
    86–88, 90–92; Indian-white relations
    in, 107–18
Texas Rangers, 86, 111, 115
Texas State Gazette (Austin), 110, 111
Third Artillery Regiment, 75–76
Third Infantry Regiment, 100
Third Seminole War, 146–58, 281; causes
    of, 148–49; conclusion of, 157; and in-
    ducements to Seminoles to emigrate,
    149, 150, 157. *See also under* Harney,
    William S., military career of

Thomas, Lorenzo, 234, 238
Thompson, Wiley, 59
Thury, Louis de, 118
Todd, John, 129
Topeka ks, 161
Topographical Corps, 74, 192, 193
Towson, Nathan, 46–47, 49–53, 276
Tracy, Albert, 222
Trade and Intercourse Act of 1834, 122
Treasury Department, 53
treaties with Indians: by Atkinson-
    O'Fallon with upper Missouri
    tribes, 27–29, 31; at Fort Atkinson,
    123; at Fort Bridger, 262; at Fort Gib-
    son, 59; at Fort Laramie in 1851, 123,
    261, 263; at Fort Laramie in 1868,
    262, 265; at Fort Rice, 262; Indians'
    construing of, 28, 123, 143; at Little
    Arkansas River, 247, 250, 259; at
    Medicine Lodge Creek, 260, 261, 264,
    267; at Moultrie Creek, 58; at
    Payne's Landing, 59
Treaty of Guadalupe-Hidalgo, 107
Treaty of Washington of 1846, 183, 194,
    197
Treaty of Washington of 1871, 214
Trinity River, 108
Turkett, John E., 147
Tuskegee (Seminole), 66
Twiggs, David, 35
Twiggs, David E., 19, 34, 35, 65, 66, 69,
    73, 91, 96, 98, 100, 149, 179, 281;
    fathers child with mixed-blood
    Winnebago woman, 35; as first
    commander of Second Dragoons,
    53; on Harney as combat leader, 101;
    surrenders federal assets to Confed-
    erates in Texas, 221
Twiss, Thomas S., 128, 134, 190; at-
    tempts to obstruct Harney, 137–38,
    140, 144; suspended by Harney, 138

Twist, Nicholas, 102
Two Bears (Yantonnai), 143
Two Kettle Sioux, 141, 250, 255, 262, 267
Two Thousand Mile Creek, 30

Umatillas, 191
Union and Dakotaian (Yankton), 253
Union MO, 50, 51
Union Pacific Railroad, 262
Union Springs AR, 237
U.S.-Canada boundary dispute, 182; causes of, 183, 194–95; military crises over, 198–212; resolution of, 214. *See also under* Harney, William S., military career of; San Juan Island
U.S. Constitution, 163
U.S. Indian policy: of acculturation, 255, 260, 261, 268, 271, 272; of concentration, xv, 251, 260, 261, 271, 273, 281; of end of treaty system, 272; Indian Removal Act, 58; of licensing trade, 28; peace policy of Ulysses S. Grant, 272; Permanent Indian Frontier, 107, 122; of removal, 37, 58–59, 148, 157, 245, 281, 282; Trade and Intercourse Act of 1834, 122. *See also* Bureau of Indian Affairs; Indian Peace Commission
U.S. Military Academy, xvi, 6, 7, 9, 11, 16, 45, 56, 83, 115, 120, 152, 219, 285
USS *Massachusetts,* 198, 209; Harney's authority over, 197; lands U.S. troops on San Juan Island, 198, 200, 201; Winfield Scott establishes temporary headquarters on, 208
USS *Shubrick,* 205–6
Utah, xv; as military department, 168; Mormon defense of, 177; Mormon theocracy in, 165; polygamy in, 165; settled by Mormons, 164. *See also* Utah expedition

Utah expedition, xv, 159, 165–73, 176–80, 204, 257, 283, 286; beginnings of, 159, 171; conclusion of, 180; delay recommended by Harney of, 168; Harney's command of, 159, 165–73, 178–80; Albert Sidney Johnston as commander of, 173, 176–78; as largest military operation since Mexican War, 167; and problems with supplies, 167–68; reasons for, 165; Winfield Scott's orders to Harney regarding, 165–66. *See also under* Harney, William S., military career of

Vancouver Island, 182, 194
Vancouver WA, 187
Van Dorn, Earl, 124
Van Vliet, Stewart, 171, 172–73, 176
Vaughn, Alfred J., 145
Veracruz, Mex., 82, 93, 94, 104; invasion of, 95–97
Vermillion Bay, 10
Victoria BC, 197, 199, 208
Vielé, Theresa, 115, 140
Villeré, Jacques, 8
Volusia FL, 55, 57, 60

Wacos, 86, 113
Walker, Robert J., 167, 168, 171, 173–75; appointed governor of Kansas Territory, 156, 162; insists on having Harney in Kansas, 156, 162, 170; on Kansas statehood, 162; calls for posses comitatus, 163, 174, 175; thanks Harney, 174
Walla Wallas, 187
Walla Walla WA, 192
Wallen, Henry D., 193
War between the States. *See* Civil War
War Department, 2, 17, 19, 25, 34, 43, 45,

War Department (*cont.*)

59, 66, 69, 73, 74, 75, 79, 85, 90, 91, 106, 111, 112, 113, 124, 125, 126, 127, 136, 139, 141, 143, 144, 150, 154, 156, 157, 168, 176, 177, 193, 200, 206, 212, 213, 216, 219, 223, 224, 225, 226, 232, 233, 234, 237, 238, 240, 241, 276, 277, 284; assembles forces for Third Seminole War, 149; assigns Harney to command Department of the West, 216; assigns Albert Sidney Johnston to command Utah expedition, 173; assigns Nathaniel Lyon to bolster St. Louis arsenal defenses, 222; assigns Persifor F. Smith to lead Utah expedition, 178; and debate over roving columns, 110, 113; designates John Mullan to build road, 193; grants Harney discretion for movement of Utah expedition troops, 168; ignores Harney's recommendations on Mexican border problems, 112; and lack of formal orders for Utah expedition, 165; orders Harney to disperse Kansas border ruffians, 218; and placement of Bureau of Indian Affairs, 251, 261, 266, 267, 270, 272, 278; and prohibition of dueling, 51; refuses to build more forts in Department of Oregon, 189; reorganizes western commands, 122; retires Harney, 240; rewards Harney for service in Second Seminole War, 79; Winfield Scott's dissatisfaction with organizational structure of, 164; sends Second Dragoons to Florida, 57; and total war, 133; uniform administrative procedures of, 9

War of 1812, 1, 6, 8, 17, 55, 56, 277

War of the Rebellion. *See* Civil War

Warren, Gouverneur K., 129; observations at Ash Hollow, 132

Washington: Indian-white conflict in, 183–92; military road building in, 192–93. *See also* San Juan Island; U.S.-Canada boundary dispute

Washington, George, 15

Washington College, 277

Washington DC, 2, 32, 40, 45, 47, 49, 57, 70, 87, 93, 103, 106, 120, 121, 128, 149, 161, 164, 168, 173, 176, 180, 182, 183, 192, 200, 201, 216, 222, 234, 256, 260, 261, 267, 277; Harney buried in, 280; Harney travels to, 32, 45, 47, 57, 82, 106, 147, 150, 176, 186, 212, 226–28, 241, 261, 269

Washington Globe, 70

Washington University, 224

Washita River, 82

Weekly Oregonian (Portland), 202

Wessels, Henry, 218

Western Department, 17, 18, 32

Western Division, 84

West Florida, 12

West Point. *See* U.S. Military Academy

Whartenby, Richard, 7, 10

Whatcom WA, 193

Whetstone agency, 267–68, 271

Whetstone Creek, 265, 266

Whidbey Island, 195

Whistler, William, 32

White, Edward Douglass, 5

White Antelope (Cheyenne), 243

White Paint Creek, 27

White River, 41, 127, 135

Whiteside, Samuel, 39, 40

Wide Awake clubs, 217, 222

Wild Cat. *See* Coacoochee

William Gaston, 75

Williamson, D. G., 80, 84

Winnebagos, 31, 32, 34, 39, 42

Wisconsin, xvi, 24, 31, 32, 246, 281, 283.
    See also Black Hawk War; Fort Win-
    nebago
Wisconsin River, 31, 32, 34, 41
Withlacoochee River, 59–60, 69
Woodson, Daniel, 161
Wool, John E., 179, 184–85, 195, 225, 241,
    281; and Harney's march into Mex-
    ico, 91; in Mexican War, 90–93
wooling, 81, 83
Worth, William J., 96, 108; announces
    end of Second Seminole War, 79;
    and role in Harney's court-martial,
    94; death of, 108
Wortley, Edward, 106
Wright, George, 187, 190, 212
Wright, Thomas, 50
Wyandots, 246
Wynkoop, Edward, 257

Yaholoochee (Seminole), 60
Yakimas, 187, 188, 191
Yankton Sioux, 28, 254
Yantonnai Sioux, 28, 143, 250, 262, 267
Yates, Richard, 225, 228
Yavapais, 244
Yazoo, 96
Yeatman, James E., 234
Yellowstone River, 18, 24, 30, 265
Young, Brigham, xv, 165, 166, 171, 173,
    176; appointed governor of Utah,
    165; resists federal authority, 165;
    Harney threatens to hang, 168;
    characterizes Harney as blood-
    thirsty, 176; declares martial law,
    176; accepts federal authority, 180